DAILY
IN THE
WORD

A NEW TESTAMENT READING GUIDE

DAILY
IN THE
WORD

DAN BETZER

Compiled and Edited by
Janet R. McNish

Thomas Nelson Publishers
Nashville • Camden • New York

Published in Nashville, Tennessee, by Thomas Nelson, Inc. and distributed in Canada by Lawson Falle, Ltd., Cambridge, Ontario.

Printed in the United States of America.

Scripture quotations in this publication are from The New King James Version. Copyright © 1979, 1980, 1982, Thomas Nelson, Inc., Publishers.

Library of Congress Cataloging in Publication Data

Betzer, Dan.
  Daily in the Word.

  1. Bible. N.T.—Criticism, interpretation, etc.
2. Devotional calendars.   I. Title.
BS2361.2.B47 1983   225.6   83-17464
ISBN 0-8407-5864-2

Preface

Daily in the Word is a New Testament reading guide. It is designed to help and encourage you to read through the New Testament in a year. There are several ways this guide will assist you in doing this.

First, this book provides a workable plan for reading through the New Testament. That plan divides the New Testament into 365 daily segments, each of which takes only a few minutes of reading time. If you read the passage specified every day, you will easily get through the New Testament by the end of the year.

Second, this book gives brief bits of information and insight that will add to your understanding and appreciation of the biblical text. These will enhance your reading of the Bible while requiring only a small investment of time.

Third, the comments on each portion of a day's reading are followed by a series of simple questions designed to fix in your mind some of the basic content of the biblical passage. These questions may at first seem simplistic, but their purpose, while simple, is important. Their function is to encourage you to look again at the biblical passage and notice some of the facts in it: Who said or did what? When? Where? What was the reaction? Why? We usually forget very quickly what we have read; these questions will help you to review and remember the content of each passage.

Fourth, at the end of each series of questions is a question designed to help you think through and apply the biblical passage you have just read. Reading the Bible ought to change our lives as we take its lessons to heart, and these application questions will help you make the New Testament a vital, practical part of your life.

Before you begin to use this book, you should also understand what it is not. Most importantly, it is not a substitute for the New Testament itself. You should never read this book by itself, but only *after* reading the day's designated biblical passage. If on a given day you have time to read only one thing, it should be God's Word itself.

Also, this book is not a study guide. It is not designed to help you do in-depth exploration of the Bible. There are many other books to help you in that area. The purpose of this book, as stated above, is to help you and encourage you simply to read through the New Testament in a year, in the process remembering its contents and beginning to apply some of its teaching.

As you read your New Testament and use this book each day, commit your time and your mind to the Lord and allow Him to speak to you through His Word. And as you allow His Word to "dwell in you richly" (Col. 3:16), your life will enjoy consistent, spiritual growth, true joy, and wonderful fellowship with our loving heavenly Father.

DAN BETZER

1. Abraham
2. 42

MATTHEW

JANUARY 1
Matthew 1:1–17

Introduction

The Gospel of Matthew has often been called "The Portrait of the King." Matthew wrote primarily for a Jewish audience, as opposed to Luke, who wrote for the Greek and Roman world. Matthew is the publican, the despised tax collector. His station was Capernaum, where much of Jesus' ministry was based.

The Genealogy of Jesus Christ (1:1–17)

Matthew, writing from a Jewish perspective, was attempting to show the complete Jewishness of Jesus and His royal lineage. The first seventeen verses are the genealogy of the King.

The characters in this genealogy are a "who's who" of Israel's history. Christ's story physically begins with Abraham, the marvelous man of faith who, at age ninety-nine years, received the promise that through his seed the whole world would be blessed. His aging wife Sarah would conceive and bear a son.

Verse 5 mentions Rahab, a prostitute. When Joshua sent out two spies into Canaan (one of whom is believed to have been Salmon), Rahab saved their lives by allowing them to hide on the roof.

Later Rahab and Salmon married. Their firstborn child was Boaz, who later married Ruth, the Moabitess. Boaz and Ruth had a child named Obed, who had a son named Jesse. And Jesse had a number of sons, one of whom was David. So Rahab was the great-great-grandmother of King David! Who would have ever guessed that a woman like Rahab would be in the genealogy of the Lord Jesus Christ?

Parallel passage: Luke 3:23–38.

1. With whom does Matthew begin Jesus' genealogy? (1:2) *Abraham*
2. How many generations are traced through this genealogy? (1:17) *42*
3. Perhaps there are people in your life whom you have "written off." How can you relate this passage to those feelings?

JANUARY 2
Matthew 1:18—2:12

Christ Born of Mary (1:18—25)

If you take away the virgin birth of our Lord from the gospel, you might as well write *finis* to the whole book. What happened to Mary physically is what happens to a person spiritually who is born again: the very life of Jesus Christ is born within that person and begins to grow and function.

Now when Joseph learned that Mary was pregnant, he could have accused her before the judges, and she would have been punished for adultery. Instead he decided to acquire a quiet and discreet divorce, until an angel of the Lord appeared to convince him otherwise.

1. What did Joseph plan to do? (1:19)
2. Who appeared to Joseph? (1:20)
3. Which prophet is quoted to Joseph? (1:23)*
4. Has God ever asked something of you that went against society's mores? What was your response?

Wise Men from the East (2:1—12)

Jesus' birthplace fulfilled the Old Testament prophecy of Micah 5:2. Joseph and Mary apparently decided to live in Bethlehem until Jesus was somewhat older, for a few years probably passed before the wise men from the East came to Jerusalem.

In our Christmas pageants we sing, "We three kings of orient are," and we have named them—Caspar, Melchior, and Balthasar. The truth of the matter is, we don't know how many there were, we don't know their names, and we don't even know where they came from. We do know they were "magi," or very wise men, who were probably astronomers, not astrologers. These men had seen an extraordinary star and had done some digging to learn that the Hebrews believed the Messiah's birth would be marked by such a celestial display. So they came in search of Him.

1. Where did the wise men first search for Jesus? (2:1) *Jerusalem*
2. Whom did Herod consult? (2:4) *priests + scribes*
3. What did Herod wish the wise men to do? (2:8) *Find the Christ*
4. What did the wise men bring the child Jesus? (2:11) *Gold, my* *frankincense*
5. How did the wise men return to their homeland? (2:12) *alternate ro*
6. These apparently pagan wise men were obedient to God's warning and did not report back to Herod. How obedient are you as God's child to His instructions?

---

*You will need a concordance or a reference Bible.

8

1. Angel of the Lord to warn that Herod planned to kill Jesus.
2. Until the death of Herod
3. Killed all children under age 2
4. Rachel's children were killed
5. Russia, Ireland

JANUARY 3
Matthew 2:13–23

The Flight into Egypt and the Massacre of the Innocents (2:13–18)

Verses 13–15 fulfill the Old Testament prophecy found in Hosea 11:1. The Sinai peninsula was considered part of Egypt, thus "Egypt" wasn't as far away as it sounds to us.

Herod was a madman. Josephus gives us some insight into the psyche of this tyrant, and it is not a pretty picture. Virtually anything could throw Herod into a killing rage, as his family knew well. When the magi did not return as he had instructed them, the king was "exceedingly angry." As the history books tell us, Herod's virulent temper usually resulted in someone's death, and that is what happened in this case. The total of those children killed would have been about twenty or twenty-five, according to historians.

1. Who appeared to Joseph and why? (2:13)
2. How long did the holy family stay in Egypt? (2:15)
3. Herod issued what decree? (2:16)
4. What prophecy did Herod's decree fulfill? (2:17–18)
5. Where in our world today are people being killed because of the killers' rejection of Christ?

The Home in Nazareth (2:19–23)

Joseph made the decision not to return to Judea or to the Jerusalem/Bethlehem area because Herod's son, Archelaus, was now on the throne. For all Joseph knew, this young man might be as crazy as his father. And God warned him in a dream that it was not safe for Jesus there. So the holy family went north into Galilee to the city of Nazareth, and thus fulfilled that which was spoken by the prophets.

Nazareth is located at the extreme north end of the occupied West Bank, so it is now primarily Arab-occupied. In Christ's time people asked, "Can anything good come from Nazareth?" You can really understand that question if you have ever been in the town. It is a very dirty, congested place. This is the place where Jesus grew up. You will later read that even here Jesus was not accepted. In Capernaum, just a few miles away, Jesus had great acceptance, but not in the town where He was raised.

1. How did Joseph know when to return home? (2:19–20)
2. What prophecy did the family's new home fulfill? (2:23)
3. At what time, if any, in your life have you listened to God's call to go to a new place?

1. When Herod died

9

John the Baptist Prepares the Way (3:1–12)

There are two things about John the Baptist that will occupy much of our time in this study: (1) He was the "herald of the king," and (2) he was a preacher who understood the meaning of the word *repentance*.

John's message was repentance, and one can only imagine the strength of his presentation. Yet the only people he was really hard on were the professing "saints" who in reality possessed nothing. Look at verse 7.

Today, *repentance* has become a nearly forgotten word in evangelism. Preachers try to do by psychology what only the Holy Spirit can do in the inner person. Others try to manipulate the audience into some kind of response that might have a temporary effect, but only the Holy Spirit can truly bring a person to Christ. The Bible says the Spirit will reprove one of sin. So a real case of conversion is *always* attended by repentance. John preached it, Jesus preached it, Paul preached it, and woe to those of us who don't preach it.

Parallel passages: Mark 1:1–8; Luke 3:1–18; John 1:19–28.

1. What was John's message? (3:2) *Repent*
2. What prophet did John quote? (3:3) *Isaiah* — *locusts*
3. How was John dressed and what did he eat? (3:4) *Camel's hair*
4. What did John call the Pharisees and Sadducees? (3:7)
5. Of what behavior and attitudes have you repented since your conversion?

4. brood of vipers

John Baptizes Jesus (3:13–17)

Jesus' baptism took place at Bethabara, which is near the Allenby Bridge that now connects Israel and Jordan. The highly fortified site is an exceedingly dangerous place. The bridge is nothing more than a tiny, wooden, one-lane crossing over the very narrow, very dirty, and very disappointing Jordan. You have probably heard the old song "I Walked Today Where Jesus Walked" in which there is the line, "I saw the mighty Jordan roll." Well, that is not a very accurate portrayal. Yet it is a most sacred place, since Jesus was baptized there.

Parallel passages: Mark 1:9–11, Luke 3:21–22.

1. How did John react to Jesus' request to be baptized? (3:14)
2. What happened immediately following Jesus' baptism? (3:16)
3. What did the voice say? (3:17)
4. How important do you consider baptism to be in your life?

1. He wanted to be baptized by Jesus
2. He went up. Heavens were opened. Saw the spirit of God.
3. This is my beloved Son, in whom I am well pleased.

Matthew 4:1–22

Satan Tempts Jesus (4:1–11)

It is a near certainty that, after your highest moments in the Lord, temptation will come with deep fury. Jesus experienced this immediately after His baptism, as He sought His Father's will in the carrying out of the divine revelation. Some commentators feel that the three forms of temptation were symbolic of the three Jewish religious parties—the Sadducees, the Pharisees, and the Herodians—which were to bait Jesus constantly and in the end bring about His death.

Parallel passages: Mark 1:12–13; Luke 4:1–13.

1. How long did Jesus fast? (4:2) *40 days 40 nights*
2. What were the temptations? (4:3, 5–6, 8–9)
3. What did Jesus say to Satan in each case? (4:4, 7, 10)
4. Who helped Jesus? (4:11) *angels*
5. In making life choices, which one of these areas of temptation has been most difficult for you to overcome?

Jesus Begins His Galilean Ministry

Jesus left the Judean foothills and wilderness and began His trek toward Galilee, where He spent most of His earthly ministry. He apparently spent a few days in Nazareth, perhaps with His mother, and then went to Capernaum—beautiful Capernaum by the sea with its palm trees, blue skies, and warm waters.

There Jesus began His preaching ministry. Notice that His first sermon (see v. 17) is reminiscent of John the Baptist's.

Then Jesus began to duplicate His vision in the lives of a chosen few. First, He called two brothers who were fishermen. Have you ever wondered what Jesus saw in those two fishermen? It must have been something quite unusual, for He reached out to them, and they immediately left their nets and followed Him.

When Jesus comes into your life, He brings value and purpose for living. Without Him it is very difficult to find that purpose. It isn't just knowing Jesus, it's following Him; it is becoming a true disciple, through obedience to His Word.

Parallel passages: Mark 1:14–20; Luke 4:14–15.

1. What prophecy did Jesus fulfill in this passage? (4:14–16)
2. What was Jesus' first sermon? (4:17)
3. Which two disciples did Jesus choose first? (4:18)
4. Are you a true disciple? How has Christ's entering your life changed the way you live?

JANUARY 6
Matthew 4:23–5:12

Jesus Heals a Great Multitude (4:23–25)

The territory Jesus covered was not a big area. Today, by car, one can travel between the two most distant parts of that area in a couple of hours. Jesus concentrated on a target area—Galilee—and His renown spread. His ministry was basically quite simple in approach. He preached, inspiring men and women to new dimensions of living. He taught, showing them the reality of His kingdom. And He healed them.

Parallel passage: Luke 6:17–19.

1. How far did the news of Jesus spread? (4:24–25)
2. How can we use Jesus' ministry as a model for our own?

The Beatitudes (5:1–12)

Christ's Sermon on the Mount, as recorded in Matthew 5–7, may well be the most important document ever given to mankind. It is the revelation of the character God expects from His children.

The frontispiece of this moral code is called the Beatitudes, the eight traits that distinguish those who have entered the kingdom by way of repentance. They are not easy. Outside of Christ they cannot be achieved.

Parallel passage: Luke 6:20–23.

1. According to verses 3–10, what are those characteristics that allow one to inherit God's kingdom?
2. On a sheet of paper list each of those characteristics. Now, take a good look at yourself and see if you can name one way in which your life embodies each characteristic. How many could you list?

JANUARY 7
Matthew 5:13–48

Teachings on Marriage and Adultery (5:13–32)

After the Beatitudes comes the Sermon on the Mount itself. Jesus taught in the first segment that we as believers are special to God, that we give the earth its flavor.

Parallel passages for verses 13–26 are Mark 9:50 and Luke 14:34–35.

Some highly practical teachings hit us squarely between the eyes as we read verses 21–32. Even our innermost feelings and emotions can cause us to commit such acts as murder or adultery in our hearts. Thus, attitudes are of utmost importance.

Jesus imparted vital teachings concerning marriage in verses 31–32. The Lord said nothing about incompatibility, mental cruelty, or any of the other convenient arrangements we accept today. Only adultery.

Parallel passages: Matthew 19:9; Mark 10:11–12; Luke 16:18.

1. To what two things does Jesus compare believers? (5:13–14)
2. Why did Jesus come? (5:17)
3. What did Jesus say about righteousness? (5:20)
4. What is Jesus' teaching concerning anger? (5:22–26)
5. What does Jesus call adultery in the heart? (5:28)
6. Think of an area in your life where your outward actions may not be in tune with your inner thoughts. Apply these teachings to that area.

Go the Second Mile (5:33–48)

Jesus taught here that our word is our bond. He warned against profanity and unfaithfulness to promises. Our word is to be good. We need to learn all over again (if, indeed, we ever did know) the meaning of words. What are we actually saying?

What a teaching in verses 38–42! The believer doesn't just do the absolutely necessary or whatever it takes to get by. He goes beyond that. Whether it is a relationship at home, with his employer, at church, or anywhere else, the believer goes the second mile. After all, Jesus did that, didn't He?

Parallel passages: Luke 6:29–30; 6:27–28; 6:32–36.

1. What does Jesus say about swearing? (5:34–37)
2. "An eye for an eye, and a tooth for a tooth"—what is Jesus' teaching concerning this saying? (5:39–42)
3. What behavior are we to aim for? (5:48)
4. What has been your reaction to someone who has hurt you badly?

13

JANUARY 8
Matthew 6:1–18

Do Good to Please God (6:1–4)

This chapter continues the Sermon on the Mount in which our Lord carefully taught us the standards God expects from His servants. Let us bear in mind that these teachings are not idealistic hopes expressed by the Master but very down-to-earth goals for which we must strive.

Our hope and belief that goodness will be rewarded was never negated by Jesus, as we learn in this passage. But the rewards are not material ones. They are spiritual. Don't be hoodwinked by all the materialistic teaching going on today. The Bible is a book that deals with spiritual principles; our rewards will be spiritual.

1. How should charitable deeds be done? (6:1–4)
2. What is the motivation for your charitable deeds?

Prayer and Fasting (6:5–18)

Jesus did not direct His words here to the prayerless Christian; that comes elsewhere. His words in this segment were directed to the zealous prayer warrior with warnings to be careful, lest his or her prayers be in vain. Prayer can become a formalized ritual almost without our noticing it. True prayer is conversation with and supplication to God. It need not be relegated to a ritual by anyone who properly understands it.

Is it possible that we ask amiss in our prayers? Yes, I believe it is. We have been given incorrect values for so many years that we have come to believe God is a great welfare agency in the sky, waiting to dole out whatever we ask. Such is not the case at all, and for every added blessing we have, we would do well to be very grateful.

Parallel passage: Luke 11:2–4.

Jesus' teaching about fasting is similar to His teaching in verses 1–4. We are not to tell about our fasting in order to impress people with our spirituality. The only One who needs to know that we are fasting is our Heavenly Father.

1. Where should we pray? (6:6)
2. What does Jesus say about forgiveness? (6:15)
3. How should we fast? (6:16–18)
4. How do your prayers measure up to Jesus' model prayer?

Lay Up Treasures in Heaven (6:19–23)

In the previous lesson, we read Jesus' words about rewards. I indicated to you that these rewards are not material, but rather spiritual. Verses 19–21 teach the reality of that application. "Do not lay up for yourselves treasures on earth" (v.19).

Anything that can deteriorate is not worth your soul. My wife and I owned a beautiful convertible shortly after we were married. Now, twenty-five years later, that car is without doubt part of a junk pile somewhere. But the spiritual treasures my wife and I have received over the years keep on enriching our lives.

Parallel passage: Luke 12:33–36.

1. Define "earthly treasures." (6:19)
2. What is the lamp of the body? (6:22)
3. What kinds of things do you expose your eyes to? Do they contribute to your body's being full of darkness or light?

God and Mammon (6:24–34)

Jesus made the statement in verse 24 to show us that we cannot serve God and the world system at the same time. This world system is under God's judgment of death; it will be destroyed. If you are serving it, you are wasting your life, and you are neglecting God.

There is a big difference between being shiftless and worrying chronically. God has no time for those who will not work and care for their families. However, neither does He want us to be chronic worriers about the future.

Should the believer be prudent? Should the believer save, if he can? Of course! Jesus was talking about the kind of anxiety that overrides everything else. That kind of tension will never prolong life—but it can shorten it. If all our hopes and plans are for the distant future, and we die tomorrow, then we have wasted our lives. But we have today to live. Plan to live life to its fullest!

Parallel passages: Luke 16:13; Luke 12:22–32.

1. What should we not worry about? (6:25)
2. What does Jesus say about the birds of the air? (6:26)
3. What Old Testament king does Jesus mention? (6:29)
4. What kind of people worry about material things? (6:32)
5. For what should we seek first? (6:33)
6. Keep track of your thoughts today. How much of your time is spent in nonproductive anxiety?

JANUARY 10
Matthew 7:1–12

Do Not Judge (7:1–6)

Was Jesus saying in this passage that we should not form opinions or that we should not come out against the evil that plagues our world? No, not at all. He simply was saying that we should not form judgments against people. One of the rules that the Jewish elders taught the children of Jesus' day was to "think kindly of other people."

What *right* do we have to judge another? Are we perfect? Are we the example for all humanity? You and I don't even know all the facts about each other, so how can we make fair judgments?

In addition, we cannot be impartial in our judgments. We are prejudiced. Come on; admit it! All of us are. I fight certain prejudices all the time; so do you. So with that kind of irrational thinking, how can I judge someone else?

Parallel passages: Luke 6:37–38, 41–42.

1. What will your judgment be if you judge others? (7:2)
2. What should you do instead of judging others? (7:5)
3. What people in your personal life or what larger groups of people are you standing in judgment of?

Keep Asking, Seeking, Knocking (7:7–12)

The relationship we have with God is a parent-child relationship. God loves us as His children. So when we pray we remember that relationship and pray on that basis.

We come to God in prayer because we believe God is concerned with our lives. When we ask according to our spiritual and eternal good (and, yes, often our temporal good), God either fulfills or changes the desires of our hearts.

Verse 12 is a general rule for good behavior. Note that this rule, known of course as the Golden Rule, is written in the positive, not in the negative Jewish form: "Do not do unto others what is hateful to you."

Parallel passage: Luke 11:9–13.

1. Whose prayers will be answered? (7:8)
2. What is the Golden Rule? (7:12)
3. Analyze your prayers. Which requests have to do with your spiritual and eternal good?

16

JANUARY 11
Matthew 7:13–29

The Narrow Way (7:13–14)

There is a hard way and an easy way of doing things. The hard way leads to sacrifice now and abundance later. The easy way leads to temporal success and eventual poverty. The crowd is going to opt for the easy way. We live in a nation where the majority rules, but that does not mean the minority ought not to have the right to express itself and live according to the dictates of conscience.

This passage says we each are responsible for our actions. No one else, no other person on this earth but you will answer to God concerning your life.

Parallel passage: Luke 13:24.

1. Describe the way that leads to destruction. (7:13)
2. How many choose the narrower path? (7:14)
3. What issues are you addressing as a Christian?

You Will Know Them by Their Fruits (7:15–20)

Those who speak in the name of the Lord have a tremendous obligation to truth and biblical veracity. Using God's Word and work for selfish motives is an age-old problem.

One test of a false prophet is this: Is that person working for his own self-gain? Another sign is that false prophets teach their own words or try to make God's Word conform to their words.

Parallel passage: Luke 6:43–44.

1. How will false prophets come? (7:15)
2. How do you recognize a true prophet? (7:16)
3. What are some of the characteristics of false prophets today?

I Never Knew You (7:21–29)

How sad to think that a person can be deceived about his or her spiritual status by putting faith in good works. Christ within us is the only hope of glory, and God blesses the word of Christ alone. So all our works can truly be the filthy rags Isaiah talked about unless we are living Christ's life by faith and have been truly born again by the Spirit.

Parallel passages: Luke 13:25–27; 6:47–49.

1. Who will enter the kingdom of heaven? (7:21)
2. What did the wise man do? (7:24)
3. What did the foolish man do? (7:26)
4. What areas of your life are still built on sand?

JANUARY 12
Matthew 8:1–22

Jesus Heals (8:1–17)

When Jesus had completed His sermon, He must have been physically exhausted. But when a leper approached Him as He came down the mountain, He healed him.

Now Jesus could have healed that leper from long distance, but He touched the man physically—something no one else would have dared to do. It had doubtless been years since anyone had touched that man. There is a great lesson in this for the church. It isn't enough to build our great buildings, erect our large signs, and expect hurting people to come to us; we must reach out to them and touch them right where they are.

When Jesus entered Capernaum, a Roman centurion met Him just inside the gate. We may think of centurions as animals in armor who cared only about fighting and bloodshed. That is not true. Centurions exemplified the highest quality Rome could offer. They were hard-working, well-educated men who upheld the dignity and honor of Rome in all that they did. This centurion was so compassionate that his servant's illness was bothering him terribly—so much so that he came to Jesus and asked for help.

What a day Jesus had had! He had given the greatest sermon of all time, healed a leper and then a centurion's servant. Needing rest, Jesus went to Peter's house in Capernaum where again He was met with human need.

Parallel passages: Mark 1:40–45; Luke 5:12–16; Luke 7:1–10; Mark 1:29–34; Luke 4:38–44.

1. What did the leper say to Jesus? (8:2)
2. How did the centurion feel about himself? (8:8)
3. What does Jesus say about the place of non-Jews in the kingdom? (8:11)
4. What does Jesus' healing of the centurion's servant say about the breadth of our ministry?

The Cost of Discipleship (8:18–22)

These five brief verses on the subject of discipleship are among the most vital in the New Testament. If you are a true disciple, you will never belong to yourself. Your first priority will be doing God's will.

Parallel passage: Luke 9:57–62.

1. What did Jesus tell the would-be followers? (8:20–22)
2. What are the priorities in your life?

JANUARY 13
Matthew 8:23–9:8

Winds and Waves Obey Jesus (8:23–27)

Jesus often wanted solitude after long and difficult public ministry. We read here that Jesus, wanting to leave the multitudes for a time, got into a boat and departed with His disciples. As is common on the Sea of Galilee, a sudden storm arose. The disciples panicked and then were awed by Jesus' power to calm the sea.

The lesson we learn is this: As long as we are with Jesus, we are all right. It's when we get in storms away from Him that we have real problems.

Parallel passages: Mark 4:35–41; Luke 8:22–25.

1. What was Jesus doing when the storm hit? (8:24)
2. What did Jesus say to His disciples? (8:26)
3. How did the disciples react? (8:27)
4. How well do you trust God when you face life's difficulties?

Jesus Heals Two Demon-possessed Men and a Paralytic (8:28–9:8)

Jesus and His followers crossed from Capernaum to the eastern side of the Galilee, which is the area we now call the Golan Heights.

Demons are fallen angels—those beings who followed Lucifer in rebellion against God. Demons have great knowledge and strength, though in no way approaching the knowledge and strength of God. Make no mistake about it; demons are real.

Jesus knew that, of course; and so did the people of His day.

But what was the reaction of the people? The area citizens apparently were more concerned about pigs than about the tormented men.

When Jesus had returned to Capernaum, some men brought Him a paralyzed man. There was nothing about that paralytic that was beyond the help of Jesus, neither his sin nor his illness. There is nothing in your life either that cannot be reached by God. Oh, if we could only understand how deeply God loves us, how much He longs to deliver us from our oppressions and illnesses!

Parallel passages: Mark 2:1–12; 5:1–20; Luke 5:17–26; 8:26–39.

1. Where did Jesus meet the demon-possessed men? (8:28)
2. How did the demons react to Jesus? (8:29–31)
3. How did the scribes react to Jesus' forgiveness of the paralytic? (9:3)
4. Do you believe Jesus has the authority to forgive sin? How do you apply that truth?

19

Matthew, the Tax Collector (9:9—17)

In this segment Jesus transcends even His healings by calling a despised tax collector to Himself and placing him in the ministry. Matthew had worked for the Roman government, and since he was a Jew, as the townspeople were, he was considered not only a crook but a traitor to his own people.

Verses 12 and 13 contain a principle that we must keep ever before us. What an easy trap for us to allow church activities to become exclusive—a country club for the saints. We become uneasy around unbelievers, but the work we are called to involves reaching the lost and teaching the saints. That is our mandate; nothing else.

Parallel passages: Mark 2:13–22; Luke 5:27–39.

1. What did the Pharisees think of the company Jesus kept? (9:11)
2. What are Jesus' well-known words to the Pharisees? (9:12–13)
3. What did the disciples of John ask Jesus? (9:14)
4. What kinds of people are part of your congregation?

Jesus Raises the Dead, Heals the Afflicted (9:18—31)

This passage is amazing because the ruler who came to Jesus, requesting His help, was the director of the synagogue, and, as such, was a part of that segment of the Jewish people who wanted Jesus dead. But Jesus didn't show any resentment as we might have.

The flute was used in most funeral observances (see v. 23)—even among the Romans. In fact, Seneca records that they played so loudly at Emperor Claudius' funeral that Claudius had to have heard them even in death. The richer a man was, the more mourners and flute players he had.

Parallel passages: Mark 5:21–43; Luke 8:40–56.

1. What did the ruler of the synagogue ask of Jesus? (9:18)
2. Who touched Jesus and why? (9:20–21)
3. Whom did Jesus meet as He left the ruler's house? (9:27)
4. What was Jesus called? (9:27)
5. How are you helping to spread the gospel?

JANUARY 15
Matthew 9:32–10:15

The Compassion of Jesus (9:32–38)

To remain neutral about Jesus Christ is impossible. The old song asks, "What will you do with Jesus? Neutral you cannot be." That's true. And it is shown clearly in verses 32–34.

In the meantime, despite the furor He created, Jesus went about His work.

Verse 36 has to motivate us. All of our contests and drives are fine, but they will not sustain our motivation for long. We will get weary in well-doing. We must be compelled ("constrained," as Paul put it, by the love of Jesus and His compassion for those around us.

1. Who met Jesus on the way? (9:32)
2. What did the Pharisees say? (9:34)
3. How did Jesus feel about the people? (9:36)
4. What situations have aroused your compassion recently?

The Twelve Apostles (10:1–15)

One of the first things Jesus did in His earthly ministry was put together a staff of workers. Any successful minister will do the same. Without those twelve men, the work would have perished when Jesus ascended to the Father.

One of the disciples, Simon the Canaanite, was a zealot. Zealots were a sort of underground political party of Jews committed to the overthrow of Rome and absolute liberty for Israel. Under ordinary circumstances, Simon would have killed Matthew the tax collector on sight. Now here they were, working together for the Lord.

Jesus spent some three years with these men—teaching them, training them, helping them, and loving them. With that kind of background and upon their infilling with the Holy Spirit at Pentecost, those men (except for Judas, of course) embarked upon a mission that spanned the globe.

Parallel passages: Mark 3:13–19; Mark 6:7–13; Luke 6:12–16; Luke 9:1–6.

1. What authority was given the Twelve? (10:1)
2. Who were the disciples? (10:2–3)
3. What places were the Twelve to avoid? (10:5)
4. What were the disciples not to carry? (10:9–10)
5. In trying to spread the Word, how can we spend our time more profitably?

JANUARY 16
Matthew 10:16–42

Persecutions Are Coming (10:16–26)

When Jesus commissioned the twelve apostles, He never promised them an easy task. Quite the opposite. He told them how really tough it was going to be.

Look at Jesus' words in verse 16. The world system will never be a part of God's kingdom. The two are as far apart as east from west. To be a Christian in this hostile world environment is difficult because the world's values can easily sidetrack us.

Parallel passages: Mark 13:9–13; Luke 21:12–17.

1. What attributes must the disciples have? (10:16)
2. How were the disciples to defend themselves? (10:19–20)
3. Whom should a disciple try to emulate? (10:25)
4. What specific forces in your life tend to sidetrack you from becoming a stable Christian?

Jesus Teaches the Fear of God (10:27–31)

Jesus was teaching a healthy fear or respect that results from understanding God's attributes—justice, honor, wrath, and holiness.

Parallel passage: Luke 12:2–7.

1. Whom should we not fear? (10:28)
2. How well does God know us? (10:30)
3. How much does God value us? (10:31)
4. Do you fear the Lord? Why don't present-day Christians show greater reverence for God?

Christ Brings Division (10:32–42)

Verses 38 and 39 are very important. So much of today's shallow theology contradicts their clear teaching. Paul preached the crucified life over and over again—we are crucified with Christ.

Parallel passages: Luke 12:8–9; 51–53; Luke 14:26–27.

1. What must we do before others? (10:32)
2. Why did Christ come? (10:34–35)
3. Who is worthy of Christ? (10:37–39)
4. Even what small token of acceptance will be recognized? (10:42)
5. Are you prepared to stand for the Lord even if it produces division in your family?

22

JANUARY 17
Matthew 11:1–24

John the Baptist Sends Messengers to Jesus (11:1–19)

This is one of the most gripping, compelling dramas in all the Bible. It is the continuing story of John the Baptist. The last time Matthew gave us a glimpse of this giant for God, he was standing waist-deep in the Jordan, preaching the eternal message: "Repent!"

John was a fearless figure, preaching with such fervor that word of his ministry reached as far away as Jerusalem. He drew huge crowds. Now that might not sound like much to you until you stop to think that those coming from Jerusalem had to travel about twenty miles each way—by horse, camel, or foot—down one of the more treacherous roads in all the world.

Jesus said that John was the prophet foretold in Malachi 3:1 (see v. 10) and the greatest prophet ever born. That's some build-up. Yet, even John got discouraged. Let's face it. We all occasionally grow discouraged. Satan might not be able to fell you with overt sin; but perhaps he can throw you off course through discouragement.

Parallel passage: Luke 7:18–35.

1. What question did John's disciples ask Jesus? (11:3)
2. How did Jesus answer John's question? (11:4–6)
3. Who was John, according to Jesus? (11:9)
4. To what does Jesus compare His generation? (11:16–17)
5. Think of a time in your life when you discarded a person or passed up an opportunity because that person or opportunity did not live up to your expectation.

Woe to the Impenitent Cities (11:20–24)

Chorazin and Bethsaida were near Capernaum. Today these cities are only ancient ruins. What could these cities have been had they responded to Jesus?

What about our nation? No nation has ever had the light that the United States has received and done less with it.

Parallel passage: Luke 10:13–15.

1. How would the people in Tyre and Sidon have responded? (11:21)
2. What was Capernaum's unique position? (11:23)
3. In what ways is the United States failing to respond to the gospel's demands?

JANUARY 18
Matthew 11:25–12:14

Jesus Gives True Rest (11:25–30)

In this blessed segment of Scripture, Jesus gives His first general invitation to come to Him; up to this point, the invitation had been to the beginning disciples. Now He reaches out to us all with a marvelous invitation.

Jesus gave this invitation in the hearing of people who literally "bent themselves out of shape" trying to achieve spiritual happiness. They tried to approach God by impossible human achievements, by rituals, by denying bodily necessities; and as a result, they were driven to weariness and despair.

The term *yoke* (v. 29) involves submission. There is no rest until we learn to submit ourselves to Him. You may protest that the Christian life is too tough, but it isn't. Jesus said that His yoke was easy. In comparison to the yoke of Satan, to the cruel bondage he imposes, Christ's yoke is easy and it brings the rest we so desperately seek.

Parallel passage: Luke 10:21–22.

1. How do we come to know God? (11:27)
2. What invitation does Jesus give? (11:28–29)
3. How can you achieve inner peace in your life?

Lord of the Sabbath (12:1–14)

The disciples here were not stealing. The law (see Deut. 23:25) expressed clearly that a hungry traveler could do exactly what these men were doing, provided they used their hands to take the grain and not a sickle. Jesus answered the Pharisees as He always answered—from His deep knowledge of the Word of God. He reminded them of what King David did when he and his traveling band of followers became hungry.

In this chapter we read that the enemies of Christ made their final decision regarding Him. They not only rejected Him but sought to eliminate Him.

Parallel passages: Mark 2:23–3:6; Luke 6:1–11.

1. What were the disciples doing? (12:1)
2. What did David's men do when they were hungry? (12:4)
3. What does Jesus say that the Scriptures are really saying? (12:6–7)
4. Whom did Jesus heal on the Sabbath? (12:10–13)
5. In what areas do our churches tend to put the welfare of the people on the back burner?

JANUARY 19
Matthew 12:15–32

Behold My Servant (12:15–21)

When Jesus realized that His previous confrontation with the Pharisees signaled His approaching death, He withdrew from Capernaum. Jesus still needed to teach His disciples many things. It was not time for Him to die.

Jesus understood the principle of timing. Charles Blair, pastor of Calvary Temple in Denver, once said, "It is not enough for God to tell you to do a certain thing; you must wait until He tells you *how* to do it and *when* to do it. Unless you have all three instructions—*what* to do, *how* to do it, and *when* to do it—you are heading for difficulty."

Only Jesus can ever truly give this world justice. We claim "liberty and justice for all" in our pledge of allegiance to the flag, but justice does not exist in our nation or world. Justice has become a situational ethic. In any society where God is pushed aside, where He is not considered the beginning and conclusion of all matters, justice becomes nothing more than an interpretation of the courts, bent around the mold of circumstances. But Christ will not have that kind of never-never-land jurisprudence. When He comes to establish His kingdom, there will be justice that meets the standards of a holy God.

1. What order did Jesus give the crowds? (12:16)
2. What will God's servant announce? (12:18)
3. What will this servant not do? (12:19)
4. What will be some of this servant's characteristics? (12:20)
5. Name one situation—either present-day or in our history—when God's justice and human justice seem to be at odds.

The Unpardonable Sin (12:22–32)

Verses 31 and 32 are chilling verses concerning the unpardonable sin—the state in which a person has gone beyond all forgiveness, because he has gone beyond all repentance. Only the Holy Spirit can bring a person to God; that is clearly stated in the Word. If a person rejects the work of the Holy Spirit, repentance becomes impossible, and without repentance there is no forgiveness of sins.

Parallel passages: Mark 3:20–30; Luke 11:14–23.

1. Whom did Jesus heal? (12:22) Why did his healing stir up controversy? (12:23)
2. With what did the Pharisees charge Jesus? (12:24)
3. How did Jesus answer His accusers? (12:25–28)
4. In what ways have our divided loyalties caused us to be a house divided against itself?

25

JANUARY 20
Matthew 12:33–50

A Tree Is Known by Its Fruits (12:33–42)

The theme found in verses 33–37 runs throughout the Gospels—a tree is good only if it produces fruit; thus, a person is good only if his life produces works that bear out his faith.

In verses 38–42 the Pharisees and scribes continue their harassment of Jesus. In the past several days, the Pharisees had heard the greatest sermon ever preached, they had seen a leper instantly healed, and they had seen incurably sick people marvelously delivered.

It is a characteristic of the spiritually immature that they want to see miracle piled upon miracle. They go wherever they think the action is. But if there's any work that requires their initiative—some labor, some thinking, some dedication—they take off like a roadrunner.

Jesus sharply rebuked these miracle-hoppers.

Parallel passages: Mark 8:11–12; Luke 6:43–45; 11:29–32.

1. What did Jesus call the Pharisees? (12:34)
2. What kind of words did Jesus denounce? (12:36)
3. What did the Pharisees want? (12:38)
4. What was likened to the sign of Jonah? (12:40)
5. Who did Jesus proclaim was among them? (12:42)
6. What steps do you take to make certain your words reflect Jesus' teachings?

Jesus' Family Sends for Him (12:43–50)

Verses 46–50 contain a curious story. At this time Jesus' brothers were not His followers. They did not believe in Him. Those with whom He had grown up did not accept Him as the Great Teacher and Messiah. Even Jesus' friends tried to restrain Him from His work. So His disciples were men He probably had not known until He called them. And the common bond was formed among them as they ministered side by side.

It takes more than common ancestry to be close to another person. Real friendship is based on a common goal or principle or a common experience. For that reason, many of us feel closer to our family in God than we do to many of our family members.

Parallel passages: Mark 3:31–35; Luke 8:19–21; 11:24–26.

1. What happens when an unclean spirit leaves a person and then returns? (12:45)
2. What did Jesus ask concerning His family? (12:48)
3. Whom did Jesus consider His family? (12:50)
4. What are you doing to fill your life with positive spiritual values?

JANUARY 21
Matthew 13:1–23

The Parable of the Sower (13:1–9)

Up to this point, Jesus had taught primarily in synagogues or other public gathering places. But now, facing the expressed opposition and hatred of the Pharisees, Jesus left those ordained places of speaking and taught solely in the out-of-doors. Chapter 13 opens a long series of marvelous parables that Jesus gave us. The meaning of the word *parable* is very complex, but for our purpose it means simply "an earthly story with a heavenly meaning."

Parallel passages: Mark 4:1–9; Luke 8:4–8.

1. Where did the seed fall? (13:4–8)
2. What happened to the seeds as they fell? (13:4–8)
3. How did Jesus end His parable? (13:9)
4. How do we prepare ourselves so that we can be like the person in verse 9?

The Purpose of the Parables (13:10–23)

Jesus' answer to the disciples' question was very frank: Not everyone had an ear for spiritual truths in those days (and goodness knows what He would say today), but those to whom it was given to know the mysteries of the kingdom would understand His purposes. Then He explained the parable. The seed is, of course, the Word of God.

Now some of the seed fell by the wayside. This type of hearer receives the Word, but no spiritual difference ever emerges.

Some of the seed fell on stony ground. This is the hearer who listens with his emotion, not the heart and mind. No spiritual roots take hold.

Then some seed fell among thorns. Such listeners are so preoccupied with the things of this world that the seed doesn't have a chance to grow.

Finally, in some places the spiritual seed took hold. The Word was received.

Parallel passages: Mark 4:10–20; Luke 8:9–15.

1. What did the disciples ask Jesus? (13:10)
2. What prophet does Jesus quote? (13:14)
3. Why can't people understand the parables? (13:15)
4. How do you receive the seed?

Parables of the Kingdom (13:24–32)

Here begins a series of parables that begin "The kingdom of heaven is like...." The parable in verses 24–30 is much like the Parable of the Sower but with an important difference. In the first parable only good seed was sown—the Word of God. But in this parable, an enemy comes in and adds bad seeds.

Farmers in those days were constantly on guard against enemies who would come into their fields at night and sow tares.

The parable in verses 31 and 32 should be encouraging to small churches. Out of small things great things can grow.

Parallel passages: Mark 4:30–32; Luke 13:18–21.

1. What happened while the sower slept? (13:25)
2. What was the sower's solution? (13:30)
3. What is the least of all seeds? (13:31–32)
4. In what ways do we plant good seed and/or weeds in our hearts?

Leaven, Hidden Treasure, and the Pearl of Great Price (13:33–46)

In the two brief parables at the end of this passage, Jesus makes an important point well worth remembering: the kingdom of heaven is of such great worth that we should be willing to give up everything in order to gain it.

The parables in verses 44–46 teach the same lesson. The kingdom of heaven is priceless.

Parallel passage: Luke 13:20–21.

1. What did the woman do with the leaven? (13:33)
2. Who sowed the good seed? (13:37) the bad seed? (13:39)
3. What did the man do when he found a treasure in a field? (13:44) and the pearl? (13:46)
4. How valuable do we consider the kingdom of heaven in our lives?

JANUARY 23
Matthew 13:47–14:12

The Parable of the Dragnet (13:47–52)

This parable is sometimes called the Parable of the Good and Bad Fish. In it, Jesus describes the work of the angels in separating the wicked from the just at the end of the age. The end of time is when grace ends, when time ends, and when the ultimate judgment takes place. This is the seventh and last parable in this sequence of parables.

Verse 52 describes Matthew's ideal of the Christian teacher. He combines the newness of Jesus' teachings with the richness of the ancient Jewish teachings.

1. What happened when the net was pulled to shore? (13:48)
2. What should every scribe be like? (13:52)
3. How are you living your life in preparation for the time depicted in this parable?

Jesus Rejected; John the Baptist Beheaded (13:53–14:12)

Jesus headed south again and came to the town where He grew up. The rejection He suffered there must have hurt Him deeply.

The players in this next drama are well known (see 14:1–12): Herod, the king; Herodias, his promiscuous wife; the daughter of Herodias, who was, according to historians, Salome, although the Scriptures do not name her; and John the Baptist. Herod the Tetrarch, "the ruler of a fourth part," was only a puppet king, a vassal of Rome, ruling a divided part of Palestine.

Herod's troubles began when he seduced Herodias, his brother's wife, in Rome. When the story was finished, it contained a beheaded John the Baptist, a dead (and also beheaded) Salome—although you must go to the history books for that story—and a lost kingdom, for Emperor Caligula stripped Herod of his provincial throne and banished him to Europe for the remainder of his days. Sin is contagious. Once it gets a foothold in your life, it will begin to spread like a wind-swept fire in a dry brush field.

Parallel passages: Mark 6:1–6; 6:14–29; Luke 4:16–30; 9:7–9.

1. Who did the people recognize Jesus as? (13:55–56)
2. What was Jesus' response to their unbelief? (13:58)
3. Who did Herod think Jesus was? (14:2)
4. Why had Herod jailed, but then protected, John the Baptist? (14:3, 5)
5. What did John's disciples do? (14:12)
6. What are your convictions costing you?

JANUARY 24
Matthew 14:13–36

Feeding the Five Thousand (14:13–21)

Jesus has just been told that John the Baptist had been beheaded. What tremendous sorrow He must have felt. The man who had heralded His coming was gone. And perhaps Jesus saw a hint of His own destiny.

Verse 14 tells us that He was "moved with compassion." Did you ever stop to think how inconvenient it is to have compassion? Compassion will mean a constant infringement upon your time, your privacy, your own comfort. Compassion is inconvenient. But it is involved in the whole servant principle. Christians are servants—not only of God, but of people around them.

Parallel passages: Mark 6:30–44; Luke 9:10–17; John 6:1–14.

1. What did Jesus do when He heard of the death of John the Baptist? (14:13)
2. What did the disciples want to do with the crowd? (14:15)
3. How much food was left? (14:20)
4. How many people ate that evening? (14:21)
5. When was the last time you were moved with compassion?

Jesus Walks on the Sea (14:22–36)

The Sea of Galilee is prone to quick storms, and Jesus could see that the disciples who were crossing the sea in a little boat were in distress. The Sea of Galilee is not very big—about seven miles wide and thirteen miles long—and from the vantage point of the Golan Heights or the Mount of Beatitudes you can see virtually every boat on the water. Jesus decided to go to the disciples to assure them of their safety. It was about three in the morning.

One of the most interesting facets of this story is that when Jesus approached the fear-stricken disciples, they did not recognize Him. They were so preoccupied with their situation that they did not recognize that divine help was on the way to them.

Parallel passages: Mark 6:45–56; John 6:15–21.

1. What did the disciples think when they saw Jesus approaching them? (14:26)
2. What did Peter want to do? (14:28)
3. What happened to Peter? (14:30–31)
4. What was the disciples' reaction when Jesus got into the boat? (14:33)
5. When did you last recognize the hand of God in your life?

JANUARY 25

Matthew 15:1–28

Defilement Is from Within (15:1–20)

The trip from Jerusalem to Galilee, only a two-hour drive today, was a journey of several days for the scribes and Pharisees who came to Jesus. Thus, it was obviously an important trip for them. They had a question prepared for Him, a question not based on the Old Testament law but on tradition. That tradition was as important to them as the law itself.

Parallel passage: Mark 7:1–23.

1. What question did the scribes and Pharisees ask Jesus? (15:2)
2. How did Jesus answer? (15:3–6)
3. What really defiles a person, according to Jesus? (15:11)
4. Are you ever guilty of what Jesus spoke of in 15:8–9?

A Gentile Shows Her Faith (15:21–28)

This passage is an account of the only trip recorded in the Bible that Jesus made outside Israel during His adult life. Tyre and Sidon (presently Lebanon) were to the northwest of Galilee. As Jesus and His disciples traveled, a Canaanite woman of that region, a heathen who nonetheless had great faith in Jesus, came out to them and asked Jesus to heal her daughter. Notice the verbal test to which Jesus put her faith.

Parallel passage: Mark 7:24–30.

1. What was wrong with the Canaanite woman's daughter? (15:22)
2. What was the disciples' reaction to the woman's request? (15:23)
3. To whom was Jesus sent? (15:24)
4. In what ways does God test our faith today?

Jesus Heals Multitudes and Feeds Four Thousand (15:29–39)

From the area of Tyre and Sidon, Jesus and the disciples traveled to the region east of the Sea of Galilee known as Decapolis.

Next Jesus miraculously fed a large crowd of people from just a few loaves of bread and fish.

The village of Magdala to which Jesus crossed over the sea at the end of this passage is now just a few piles of rock located just south of Capernaum.

Parallel passage: Mark 8:1–10.

1. What kinds of physical problems did Jesus heal? (15:30–31)
2. Who was glorified by Jesus' healings? (15:31)
3. Why did Jesus want to feed the multitude? (15:32)
4. How much food did Jesus begin with? (15:34) How much was left over? (15:37) How many people were fed? (15:38)
5. What does this passage say about God's ability to meet our physical needs?

The Pharisees and Sadducees Seek a Sign (16:1–4)

Here we see the Pharisees and Sadducees who opposed each other on many issues, united in their hatred of Jesus.

Parallel passage: Mark 8:11–12.

1. What did the Pharisees and Sadducees ask of Jesus? (16:1)
2. What did Jesus call them? (16:3)
3. What did Jesus say they would be given? (16:4)
4. Is it more important to be looking for signs of the times or Jesus? Why?

Leaven of the Pharisees and Sadducees (16:5–12)

Throughout the Bible, leaven often has the connotation of "an evil influence." Jesus warned repeatedly against false doctrines that lead people to spiritual death.

Parallel passage: Mark 8:13–21.

1. What circumstances prompted Jesus' warning about leaven? (16:5)
2. What events did Jesus remind the disciples of to show He was not talking about physical bread? (16:8–10)
3. What are some ways in which we can learn correct doctrine so as to be able to recognize and reject false doctrine?

JANUARY 27
Matthew 16:13–28

Peter Confesses Jesus as the Christ (16:13–20)

Near the end of His ministry, Jesus was alone with His disciples at a place called Caesarea Philippi in northern Galilee. Jesus asked His disciples two important questions, the second of which was critical. From the answer to that question, Jesus would be able to determine whether or not the disciples understood His earthly presence.

Parallel passages: Mark 8:27–30; Luke 9:18–21.

1. What two questions did Jesus ask His disciples? (16:13, 15)
2. What did His disciples answer to the first? (16:14) To the second? (16:16)
3. Why did Jesus call Peter "blessed"? (16:17)
4. What was Jesus' final warning to His disciples? (16:20)
5. Jesus said He would build His church on the truth that He is the Christ. On what other grounds do we sometimes try to build the church today?

Jesus Predicts His Death and Resurrection (16:21–23)

At this point in His ministry, Jesus tried to prepare His disciples for what was ahead—the journey to Jerusalem and His crucifixion and resurrection. His disciples, however, were not ready to accept the idea that Jesus would not set up God's physical kingdom on earth at that time.

Parallel passage: Mark 8:31–33

1. What was Jesus attempting to tell His disciples? (16:21)
2. What was Jesus' response to Peter's rebuke? (16:23)
3. The disciples misunderstood the true nature of God's kingdom. What are some modern misunderstandings about that kingdom?

Take Up the Cross and Follow Him (16:24–28)

In this passage, Jesus stressed that to follow Him, a person must follow a set of values not normally recognized by the world. He talks of a life of commitment, a life that would not necessarily be one of prosperity measured by today's standards.

Parallel passage: Mark 8:34–9:1

1. What does Jesus say a person must do to follow Him? (16:24)
2. What promise does Jesus make to His followers? (16:27)
3. What does "deny himself, take up his cross, and follow Me" mean in your life?

33

JANUARY 28
Matthew 17:1–21

Jesus Transfigured on the Mount (17:1–13)

We do not really know which mountain was the scene of the Transfiguration. Some say Mount Tabor in Galilee; others say Mount Hermon in southern Lebanon. What is important is not *where* the Transfiguration took place but *that* it took place.

It is important to remember that Jesus knew what was about to happen to Him. Although He was God, He was God incarnate, that is, God clothed in human flesh. He suffered pain, anguish, and humiliation just as do other human beings. His was to be a physical pain and an anguish of soul as He took on the sin of the world. God sent Moses and Elijah to comfort and strengthen Jesus.

The description of Jesus' transfiguration is much like John's description of the risen Christ in Revelation: "and His countenance was like the sun shining in its strength" (Rev. 1:16).

Parallel passages: Mark 9:2–13; Luke 9:28–36

1. Which disciples witnessed the Transfiguration? (17:1)
2. What did Peter want to do? (17:4)
3. How did God's message come; what did He say? (17:5)
4. What mistake did Peter make that we are tempted to make today?

A Boy Is Healed (17:14–21)

As Jesus and the three disciples descended to the plain, they were met by a man who asked Jesus to heal his son. Jesus in this passage describes what even the smallest amount of faith can accomplish.

Parallel passages: Mark 9:14–29; Luke 9:37–43.

1. What was wrong with the man's son? (17:15)
2. Why was Jesus upset with His disciples? (17:16–17, 20)
3. How much faith does a person need to begin to make a difference? (17:20)
4. What does this passage have to say to those whose faith is new?

Jesus Again Predicts His Death and Resurrection (17:22–23)

While journeying through Galilee on His way to Jerusalem, Jesus predicted His fate. This was His second prediction concerning His future. Compare the prediction with the first one in Matthew 16:21–23.
Parallel passages: Mark 9:30–32; Luke 9:43–45.

1. What did Jesus predict about His future? (17:22–23)
2. How does this prediction differ from His first prediction? (17:23)
3. How did the disciples react? (17:23)
4. In what ways do we try to force God to do things as we think best?

Peter and His Master Pay Their Taxes (17:24–27)

It took a great deal of money to operate the temple in Jerusalem. Exodus 30:13 ordered every male Jew over twenty years old to pay an annual temple tax of one-half shekel, which equaled about two days' pay, to support the temple.

There may have been an ulterior motive behind the tax collectors' question, for the authorities seemed determined to find something with which they could charge Jesus. Jesus' answer, which reflected the conditions of His time, referred to the fact that a conquering nation, such as Rome, imposed taxes on the conquered nation, not on its own people. Jesus then carried that further to imply that since the temple was the house of God, God would not tax His own people. By His action in this passage, Jesus was saying that while we might be legally free to do what we wish, we are not free to set bad examples for other people.
Parallel passage: Mark 11:22–23.

1. In what town did the tax collector approach Peter? (17:24)
2. Where was Peter to find the money to pay the tax? (17:27)
3. How can you apply this teaching to your feelings about taxation today?

JANUARY 30
Matthew 18:1–14

Who Is the Greatest? (18:1–5)

It is difficult to understand how Jesus' disciples could have even asked the question in this passage after having heard Jesus teach throughout His ministry. Their question indicates that, even this near the end of Jesus' earthly ministry, the disciples still did not understand the true nature of the kingdom of God.

Parallel passages: Mark 9;33–37; Luke 9:46–48.

1. What question did the disciples ask Jesus? (18:1)
2. What kind of person did Jesus say would enter the kingdom of heaven? (18:2–3)
3. What influences or values in today's world get in the way of our becoming like the people about whom Jesus spoke?

Jesus Warns of Offenses (18:6–9)

These verses constitute a serious warning to anyone whose responsibility it is to train children in the faith. That warning extends beyond parents; it includes all members of the community of faith as they relate to those who are young in their faith, regardless of chronological age.

Parallel passages: Mark 9:41–50; Luke 17:1–2.

1. What fate would be better than that of causing a person young in the faith to sin? (18:6)
2. According to this passage, what should you do if your hand, foot, or eye causes you to sin? (18:8–9)
3. How can we apply this drastic teaching to our lives today?

The Parable of the Lost Sheep (18:10–14)

The lesson from this classic parable is very simple. No one is insignificant enough, unworthy enough for God not to care what happens to him. In teaching, Jesus used situations and characters with whom the people of His day could identify to make His point.

Parallel passage: Luke 15:3–7.

1. Why has the Son of Man come? (18:11)
2. What did the shepherd do when he found the lost sheep? (18:13)
3. What is God's will concerning "one of these little ones"? (18:14)
4. How might this parable be applied to the educational programs of our churches?

JANUARY 31
Matthew 18:15–35

Dealing with a Sinning Brother (18:15–20)

Knowing that His earthly ministry was coming to an end, Jesus took every possible moment to teach His disciples.

Jesus considered disputes among His followers to be a serious matter. In this passage, Jesus instructed them to handle conflicts in an honest, loving manner.

Verses 18 and 19 should not be taken out of context to mean that a believer can ask for anything he wants on earth in a "binding" prayer and it will be granted. This passage deals strictly with those who refuse to come under the church's discipline.

Parallel passage: Luke 17:3.

1. What does Jesus say to do if one Christian has a dispute with another? (18:15)
2. What is the reason for taking two or three witnesses with you? (18:16)
3. What does Jesus say about when "two or three are gathered in [His] name"? (18:20)
4. How might this passage be applied to today's very large congregations (or even smaller ones), where disputes are bound to occur?

The Parable of the Unforgiving Servant (18:21–35)

Here, Jesus and His disciples continue to deal with the same general theme of disputes. Since Jewish rabbis taught that a person should forgive up to three times, Peter was probably astonished to find that his own generous estimate of how many times a person should forgive was far from enough.

Parallel passage: Luke 17:4.

1. Jesus said that a person should forgive how many times? (18:22)
2. How did the king treat the servant who owed him a large sum? (18:27)
3. What happened to that same servant when he refused to forgive a debt owed him? (18:34)
4. How does this passage apply to the very human tendency we have to hold grudges?

Marriage, Divorce, and Celibacy (19:1–12)

As He reached the borders of Judea on His way to Jerusalem, Jesus again encountered the Pharisees. These religious officials were still trying to trick Jesus with some difficult questions. This time the subject was divorce, and Jesus' answer left little room for interpretation.

Jesus also touched upon celibacy—the absence of all sexual relationships. He implies that this is a special grace given to those who will accept it.

Parallel passage: Mark 10: 1–12.

1. What question did the Pharisees ask Jesus? (19:3)
2. What was Jesus' first answer? (19:6)
3. What argument did the Pharisees use against Jesus' answer? (19:7)
4. What was Jesus' final answer? (19:9)
5. Is celibacy an acceptable lifestyle? (19:11–12)
6. With divorce rates rapidly rising, how does Jesus' teaching apply today?

Jesus Blesses Little Children (19:13–15)

Again in this passage, as in Matthew 18:1–5, Jesus affirmed the simple unquestioning faith of a child.

1. Why were the children brought to Jesus? (19:13)
2. What was Jesus' reaction? (19:14–15)
3. How does this passage help us understand the proper nature of our own faith?

Jesus Counsels the Rich Young Ruler (19:16–22)

Jesus again encountered the insatiable desire we humans have to earn our own salvation. The answer Jesus gave the young man simply reiterates what He had been teaching all along—that faith required more than an external show. It required an attitude that affected one's whole lifestyle.

Parallel passages: Mark 10:17–22; Luke 18:18–23.

1. What question did the rich young ruler ask of Jesus? (19:16)
2. What was Jesus' answer? (19:17–19)
3. Did the young man lack anything? (19:21)
4. What was the young man's response? (19:22)
5. How far are we willing to go to further God's kingdom?

FEBRUARY 2
Matthew 19:23–30

With God All Things Are Possible (19:23–30)

To understand the first verses of this passage, one must know something about the cities of Jesus' day. The walls of these ancient cities had great gates through which traffic passed during the day. But in many cities these great gates were closed at night. The only access to the city after dark was through a very small gate called "the eye of the needle." A camel could get through the gate only with great and painful difficulty. In the first verse Jesus is talking about persons with worldly priorities. Remember the attitude of the rich young ruler in the passage immediately preceding this one?

Throughout this passage, Jesus was talking about motivations—as He did throughout His ministry. Many religious men and women are motivated by something other than the furthering of God's kingdom. Thus, those who appear to be first—or, in other terms, "pillars of the church"—may be last in line when it comes to entering heaven.

Parallel passages: Mark 10:23–31; Luke 18:24–30.

1. To what did Jesus compare a rich person's ability to enter the kingdom of heaven? (19:24)
2. What was Jesus' answer to His amazed disciples' question, "Who then can be saved?" (19:25–26)
3. What did Peter ask Jesus? (19:27)
4. What will be the disciples' reward? (19:28)
5. What is the reward for those who have given up something for Jesus' sake? (19:29)
6. What is our motivation for being active Christians? How does it compare with Jesus' idea of motivation?

FEBRUARY 3
Matthew 20:1–19

The Parable of the Workers in the Vineyard (20:1–16)

This parable is related to the preceding passages—the one about the rich young ruler and the other about who shall be first in the kingdom of heaven. The truth of this parable is that the rich young ruler might have ended up being first in the kingdom had he repented even later in life—that is, if his motivation for wanting to enter the kingdom had changed.

Through this parable again runs the theme of motivation. We do not serve the Lord for rewards alone. We know that there will be rewards, but the fact is that if we become dedicated to Christ, rewards do not matter. The joy comes in following Christ throughout this life. Heaven, crowns, diadems, mansions—all of these are just frosting on the cake.

1. What did the landowner agree to pay the workers in his vineyard? (20:2)
2. How many hours later did the landowner hire other workers? (20:3, 5–6)
3. How much did all of the workers receive for their work? (20:9–10)
4. Again, Jesus said, "So the last will be first and the first last." (20:16) What did He mean by this?
5. What rewards are we seeking in our lives today?

Jesus Again Predicts His Death and Resurrection (20:17–19)

In this passage, Jesus predicts for the third time His death and resurrection. His other predictions came in Matthew 16:21–23 and Matthew 17:22–23. Although Jesus has tried to prepare His disciples for what will happen in Jerusalem, His disciples are still taken by surprise by the events of the last week.

Parallel passages: Mark 10:32–34; Luke 18:31–34.

1. What did Jesus predict would happen to Him in Jerusalem? (20:18–19)
2. What groups of people would be involved in Jesus' fate? (20:18–19)
3. If you had been looking for the traditional Jewish Messiah who would put an end to Roman rule and would bring in God's kingdom in Judea, what would have been your reaction to Jesus' prediction of His death?

FEBRUARY 4
Matthew 20:20–34

Salome Asks a Favor (20:20–28)

Salome, the mother of James and John, asked Jesus for a favor for her two sons. Jesus knew what was ahead of Him, but He also knew the dangers James and John would face if they too were willing to suffer *this* kind of "exaltation." Jesus knew that James, who would be killed by the sword, would become the first martyr among the disciples. He also knew that John would live to be nearly one hundred years old but would suffer terrible treatment in captivity on the island of Patmos. James and John represent two kinds of Christian suffering— one requiring an early death; the other requiring a day by day living of the life Christ requires of us.

Parallel passages: Mark 10:35–45; Luke 22:24–27.

1. What did the mother of James and John ask Jesus? (20:21)
2. Who did Jesus say had the power to grant Salome's wish? (20:23)
3. How did the other disciples react to Salome's request? (20:24)
4. How does one become great? (20:26–28)
5. Who do we call great today? Is that person a servant?

Two Blind Men Receive Their Sight (20:29–34)

Jesus and His disciples have now traveled all the way down the Jordan Valley to Jericho.

Parallel passages: Mark 10:46–52; Luke 18:35–43.

1. What did the two blind men call Jesus? (20:30)
2. What did Jesus ask the blind men? (20:32)
3. How did Jesus heal the blind men? (20:34)
4. When was the last time you thanked Jesus for something for which you had asked?

FEBRUARY 5
Matthew 21:1–17

The Triumphal Entry (21:1–11)

After Jesus healed the two blind men, He began the steep trek upward from Jericho to Jerusalem. (Jericho is about one thousand feet below sea level and Jerusalem nearly twenty-six hundred feet above sea level but the two cities are only about fifteen miles apart.) There must have been a good deal of traffic on the road, for hundreds of thousands of pilgrims traveled to Jerusalem yearly for Passover.

Matthew 21:5 refers to the Old Testament prophecy in Zechariah 9:9 concerning the Messiah.

The Jewish people had long awaited a messiah to overturn the Roman government and restore Judah to its former glory. Only Jesus knew that His "Triumphal Entry" was really the beginning of a series of events that would lead to humiliation and death.

Parallel passages: Mark 11:1–10; Luke 19:28–38.

1. Where did the disciples find the donkey and the colt? (21:1–2)
2. What Old Testament prophecy is Jesus fulfilling in this passage? (21:5)
3. What did the disciples lay on the donkey? (21:7)
4. Does Matthew report that palm branches were spread in Jesus' path? (21:8)
5. Think of an instance when we have valued the wrong things in our leaders.

Jesus Cleanses the Temple (21:12–17)

Jesus was anything but meek and mild in this passage. He rid the temple—and not too gently—of one of its greatest nuisances. Because pilgrims came from many miles away, they were unable to bring sacrificial animals with them. They could purchase the animals in the temple; but in order to do so, the pilgrims had to have the proper temple currency. In exchanging currency, the temple moneychangers charged outrageous exchange rates and thus made a tremendous profit. In verse 13, Jesus refers to Isaiah 56:7 and Jeremiah 7:11.

Parallel passages: Mark 11:1–11; Luke 19:45–48; John 2:13–22.

1. What was Jesus' first act after He entered Jerusalem? (21:12)
2. Whom did Jesus heal? (21:14)
3. What was the reaction of the scribes and Pharisees? (21:15)
4. Where did Jesus spend the night? (21:17)
5. Are there any "moneychangers" in our "temples"? Name some instances where large profits are made in the name of God.

FEBRUARY 6
Matthew 21:18–27

The Fig Tree Withered (21:18–22)

Jesus' first act on the second day of Holy Week was a strange one. The lesson here is that if something is not doing its job it is worthless.

Mark 11:13 tells us that it was not the right season for figs. However, immature figs would have been on the tree if it had not been barren. The rabbis of the Jews believed that a curse was effective, particularly if the curse came from a righteous person—as was the case here.

Perhaps Jesus' action alluded to the commitment of His own followers and whether that commitment would bring forth fruit.

Parallel passage: Mark 11:12–14.

1. What happened to the fig tree? (21:19)
2. What illustration did Jesus use to make His point? (21:21)
3. What connection did Jesus make between belief and prayer? (21:22)
4. What does this passage say to those of us who bear Christ's name but who bear very little fruit?

Jesus' Authority Questioned (21:23–27)

In this showdown in the temple Jesus was clearly the winner. Jesus appeared not to answer the chief priests and elders, but in reality He did answer them by countering with a question. The answer to that question was the same as the answer to the question the chief priests and elders posed.

Parallel passages: Mark 11:27–33; Luke 20:1–8.

1. What question did the chief priests and elders ask Jesus? (21:23)
2. What question did Jesus ask the authorities? (21:25)
3. Why did the authorities have trouble answering Jesus' question? (21:25–27)
4. Name some priorities today that pose a threat to Jesus' authority.

FEBRUARY 7
Matthew 21:28–46

The Parable of the Two Sons

This parable of Jesus addresses the issue of hypocrisy. Although the temple authorities claimed to be followers of God, they did not, in fact, follow God. On the other hand, the common person claimed to find little or no favor with God. But those common people were the ones who were seeking and following Jesus. Who, then, was in reality following God's will?

1. What did the man ask of his two sons? (21:28, 30)
2. What did each of the two sons answer and subsequently do? (21:29–30)
3. To whom did Jesus compare the two sons? (21:31)
4. Who showed the people the right way? (21:32)
5. Try to rephrase the parable using the Sunday churchgoer who immediately shoves his religion to the lowest priority as he walks out the doors of the church.

The Parable of the Wicked Vinedressers (21:33–46)

This parable is similar to the one immediately preceding it because it is directed toward the religious authorities. God had left religious matters in the hands of these authorities, and they had failed. In this passage, Jesus hints that He is Israel's long-awaited Messiah.

Jesus prophesies concerning those who would reject Him. History tells us that about forty years later, Jerusalem was indeed laid waste, utterly destroyed, by the Romans.

In verse 42, Jesus refers to Psalm 118:22–23.

Parallel passages: Mark 12:1–12; Luke 20:9–19.

1. To whom did the landowner entrust the vineyard? (21:33)
2. What happened when it came time to harvest the grapes? (21:35–36)
3. Whom did the landowner finally send and how was he treated? (21:37–39)
4. What did Jesus say would happen to those who rejected Him? (21:43)
5. Jesus can be rejected even in the name of Christianity. Name some incidents in history that reflect that rejection. Are there times in your personal life when you have rejected Jesus even though you remained a "Christian" to the outside world?

FEBRUARY 8
Matthew 22:1–22

The Parable of the Wedding Feast (22:1–14)

Jesus had been teaching in the temple courtyard when He was approached by priests and elders. In the conversation that followed, Jesus told several powerful parables that dealt with the rejection of the Messiah by those leaders and the ensuing results of that rejection.

In this first parable the guests were the nation of Israel, and the servants were the prophets.

Parallel passage: Luke 14:15–24.

1. To what occasion did the king invite guests? (22:2)
2. What was the guests' response? (22:3–6)
3. Who finally came to the feast? (22:9–10)
4. What happened to the one guest not wearing wedding clothes? (22:13)
5. Name some times when you have been like the guest without wedding clothes. Outwardly you have gone to church, taken communion, done all the proper things, but your inner self has not been in tune with God's will.

The Pharisees Ask about Paying Taxes (22:15–22)

By this time Jesus had so angered the religious leaders that they felt they had no alternative but to kill Him.

There was a difference of opinion among the Jewish leaders concerning paying taxes to Rome. The very conservative Jews (the Pharisees) were against paying such taxes, saying they went to support a heathen state. The more liberal Jews (the Herodians) felt that, as long as the Jews were ruled by Rome, there was no problem with paying taxes. In this passage, the two groups joined forces to trap Jesus, for it seemed that no matter how He answered their question, He would anger one side or the other.

Parallel passages: Mark 12:13–17; Luke 20:20–26.

1. What question did the Pharisees and Herodians ask Jesus? (22:17)
2. What did Jesus answer? (22:21)
3. How did the questioners react? (22:22)
4. Does our government always proceed from the starting point that the prime mover is God? At what point does it become morally impossible to be a believer and continue to support a government that does not operate from that starting point?

The Sadducees Ask about the Resurrection (22:23–33)

In this passage we read about another group of Jews, the Sadducees, who took a crack at trapping Jesus. Although they were not great in number, the Sadducees were very powerful because they were the wealthy aristocrats. Their question deals with one of their basic tenets: They did not believe in the resurrection.

The question referred to a Jewish custom. If a man died without fathering children, it was his brother's obligation to marry the widow and father children for his brother. The children, then, would be legally regarded as his brother's children. The living brother, however, could refuse to marry the widow. In that case, the two were required to go before the elders of the city. The woman would loosen the shoe of her brother-in-law, spit in his face, and curse him. The custom was seldom carried out.

With His answer, Jesus told the Sadducees that their belief about the resurrection was completely in error.

Parallel passages: Mark 12:18–27; Luke 20:27–40.

1. What question did the Sadducees ask Jesus? (22:24–28)
2. What will the dead be like, according to Jesus' answer? (22:30)
3. What did Jesus say about the resurrection of the dead? (22:32)
4. How does Jesus' answer bolster your belief in a life after death?

The Scribes Ask about the First Commandment (22:34–40)

This time, the Pharisees tried to trap Jesus. They asked a loaded question. If Jesus would not answer in the legalistic fashion the Pharisees favored, they would have Him. But Jesus' answer was correct. In adding the second commandment, Jesus summed up our faith.

Parallel passages: Mark 12:28–34; Luke 10:25–28.

1. What did the Pharisees ask Jesus? (22:36)
2. What was Jesus' answer? (22:37–40)
3. What does this passage say about the manner in which we witness to others?

FEBRUARY 10
Matthew 22:41–23:26

Jesus Asks a Question (22:41–46)

In this passage Jesus asked the Pharisees a question and used Psalm 110 to show that the answer He received was not an adequate one.

Parallel passages: Mark 12:35–37; Luke 20:41–44.

1. What did Jesus ask the Pharisees? (22:42)
2. What did the Pharisees answer? (22:42)
3. What did David call the Messiah? (22:43)
4. Name some areas in your life where you have not given Jesus full allegiance.

Woe to the Scribes and Pharisees (23:1–26)

In this passage, we read that Jesus finally attacked those who had been attacking Him—the religious leaders of the day. He comes down very hard on those religious professionals whose hearts were worldly and often wicked.

It is sometimes difficult for us to understand why the Jews of Jesus' day relegated so much authority to these religious leaders. The Jews believed the authority of these leaders came in a direct line from Moses. This continuity of authority was considered extremely important.

In verse 5, Jesus was referring to little leather boxes called phylacteries. Filled with verses of Scripture, these phylacteries were (and still are by Orthodox Jews) worn on wrists and foreheads. Evidently, some religious leaders were wearing very large boxes to show others how very religious they were.

The next verses contain a series of "woes." The word *woe* in Scripture means both wrath and sorrow.

Parallel passages: Mark 12:37–40; Luke 11:46; 20:45–47.

1. What did Jesus say about imitating the actions of the scribes and Pharisees? (23:3)
2. What are the really important teachings of the law? (23:23)
3. What does Jesus say about outward pretense? (23:25–26)
4. Look at each of the "woes" and try to name one practice of current churchgoers that would be similar to each one.

FEBRUARY 11
Matthew 23:27–24:2

Continued Woes upon the Pharisees (23:27–36)

Just prior to Passover, the Jews customarily whitewashed all the roadside tombs, which were built into hillsides, so that the pilgrims on their way to Jerusalem could see them clearly and not inadvertently touch them. Touching a tomb made a person ceremonially unclean and therefore unfit to enter the temple.

Jesus mentioned Abel and Zechariah. Abel was in the first book, Genesis, and Zechariah the last book historically, 2 Chronicles. The Jews had literally destroyed God's spokesmen from beginning to end.

Parallel passages: Mark 17:37–40; Luke 20:45–47.

1. What did Jesus say the scribes and Pharisees were like? (23:27)
2. What were the religious leaders like on the outside? On the inside? (23:28)
3. Name some instances in which we, like the Pharisees, are different on the inside than what we appear to be on the outside.

Jesus Weeps over Jerusalem (23:37–39)

Forty years later the great city of Jerusalem was reduced to rubble when Roman legions under Titus swept down from Mount Scopus. People were slaughtered in the streets.

Parallel passage: Luke 13:34–35.

1. What simile did Jesus use to describe His feelings about Jerusalem? (23:37)
2. What would happen to the temple? (23:38)
3. When will Jerusalem see Jesus again? (23:39)
4. Are there prophetic voices being ignored today? Name some reasons why Jesus may be lamenting over the United States just as he lamented over Jerusalem.

Jesus Predicts the Temple's Destruction (24:1–2)

The view of the temple through the majestic Kidron Valley was magnificent. It was enough to give the Jews the sense that their institutions, their traditions, and their value systems would last forever.

Parallel passages: Mark 13:1–2; Luke 21:5–6.

1. What did Jesus' disciples do in this passage? (24:1)
2. What was Jesus' response? (24:2)
3. What are some things in which we invest our hope? Are they eternal?

48

FEBRUARY 12
Matthew 24:3–28

Troubles and Persecutions (24:3–14)

Matthew 24 is known as the Olivet discourse. In it, Jesus spoke of future happenings. He gave instructions and warnings to His disciples, who seemed to realize—finally—that Jesus had never intended to accept an earthly throne and that, in fact, before the week was out, He would be killed.

Parallel passages: Mark 13:3–13; Luke 21:7–19.

1. Whom does Jesus warn His disciples against? (24:5)
2. To what does Jesus liken the first signs of trouble? (24:8)
3. What will happen to the disciples? (24:9)
4. Who will be saved? (24:13)
5. When will the end come? (24:14)
6. Name some happenings in today's world that point to the prediction that "the love of many will grow cold." (24:12)

The Great Tribulation (24:15–28)

It is to the Jews that Jesus directed the remarks recorded in this passage. The abomination of desolation, described in Daniel 11 and 12, is the time when the Antichrist will reveal his true colors to Israel. He will set up his despicable reign in the newly constructed temple in Jerusalem. The Israelites will then flee Jerusalem. Many believe they will flee to Petra, the ancient rose-red city southeast of the Dead Sea in the Hashemite kingdom of Jordan.

Parallel passages: Mark 13:14–23; Luke 21:20–24.

1. What will the Great Tribulation be like? (24:21)
2. Who will appear on the scene during this time? (24:24)
3. How will the Son of Man appear? (24:27)
4. Make a list of events occurring in our day that may signal that Christ will return soon.

FEBRUARY 13
Matthew 24:29–44

The Coming of the Son of Man (24:29–31)

The sign of the Son of Man has been interpreted in various ways—as a star similar to the one that proclaimed Christ's birth, as the cross of Christ, and as Christ Himself. Imagery in nature always accompanies apocalyptic—that is, "end time"—passages. No matter how one chooses to interpret this passage, its core truth is simply that, in the end, God's will for history will triumph.

Parallel passages: Mark 13:24–27; Luke 21:25–28.

1. What changes in nature will take place after the Tribulation? (24:29)
2. How will the Son of Man appear? (24:30)
3. How is the trumpet used? (24:31)
4. What message does this passage hold for us today?

The Parable of the Fig Tree (24:32–35)

The fig tree was the most common tree in Palestine, and people could tell the season by looking at it. In like manner, by looking for the signs of Christ's coming, we can tell we are close to that event.

Parallel passages: Mark 13:28–31; Luke 21:29–33.

1. What was the lesson of the fig tree? (24:32–33)
2. What did Christ say about His teachings? (24:35)
3. How do we Christians live our lives to show that we really believe Christ will return?

No One Knows the Day or Hour (24:36–44)

No one knows the time or day; but many of the signs that are often overlooked—that is, the less dramatic signs—are happening now. Isaiah predicted that the desert would blossom like a rose, and Ezekiel 47 tells of the connecting of the Dead Sea and the Mediterranean Sea by a great waterway. That is being done, and soon the Negev Desert will indeed blossom.

Parallel passage: Mark 13:32–37.

1. Who alone knows the day or hour of the end time? (24:36)
2. To what Old Testament time does Jesus compare the coming of the Son of Man? (24:37–39)
3. What advice does Jesus give concerning the end time? (24:44)
4. What does this passage say to those who are tempted to set dates for the world's end?

FEBRUARY 14
Matthew 24:45–25:13

The Faithful Servant and the Bad Servant (24:45–51)

Next comes a series of parables dealing with being prepared for the Second Coming. This first parable stresses the need to continue to carry out one's duties even though it may seem that Christ has disappeared. Christians fulfill their appointed tasks even though it seems that Christ is not part of the world.

Parallel passage: Luke 12:41–48.

1. Who is a faithful servant? (24:45–46)
2. Who is a bad servant? (24:48–49)
3. What will be the fate of the bad servant? (24:51)
4. In what areas of our lives are we good servants? In what areas of our lives are we bad servants? Can we achieve continuity so that we can more often be good servants?

The Wise and Foolish Virgins (25:1–13)

This parable is one of the most difficult passages in the New Testament. All ten virgins were willingly awaiting the bridegroom, but five were wise and five were foolish. What made each one wise or foolish was her state of readiness. This is an important point.

The parable deals with stewardship—stewardship of every facet of life, here symbolized by the oil in the virgins' lamps.

1. Why did the ten virgins go out? (25:1)
2. What was the difference between the five wise virgins and the five foolish virgins? (25:3–4)
3. What happened when the bridegroom arrived late? (25:8–10)
4. Were the five foolish virgins allowed the enter the wedding feast late? (25:11–12)
5. What did Jesus admonish? (25:13)
6. What is the motivation for our own discipleship?

The Parable of the Talents (25:14–30)

This is another parable dealing with readiness for the end time. This segment stresses that a believer must be involved in works; faith without works is not enough. We not only *wait* for the Lord to return; we *work* until He comes.

In this parable, the master, of course, is Christ; and His holdings are the kingdom of God. A talent was a sum of money, roughly equal to about one thousand dollars in our currency. It is obvious in this parable that the master wasn't interested in saving his possessions; he wanted the greatest possible good accomplished with them.

It is important to remember that each person is given talents according to his ability, his experience, and his capacity. As our capacity increases, so do our talents. We need to pray for such faithfulness in our assignments that our capacity increases accordingly.

Parallel passage: Luke 19:11–27.

1. What did the master give his servants? (25:15)
2. What did the first servant do with his master's property? (25:16) the second servant? (25:17) the third servant? (25:18)
3. What was the master's response to the investment of the first two servants? (25:21, 23)
4. What was the third servant's excuse for handling his master's money in the manner he did? (25:24–25)
5. What was the master's response? (25:26–28) What happened to the servant? (25:30)
6. What has God given you to use to build the kingdom? Which servant do you most resemble?

FEBRUARY 16
Matthew 25:31–46

The Son of Man Will Judge the Nations (25:31–46)

This parable deals with the judgment of the nations. This judgment will take place at the Second Coming, when Christ returns to rule the earth for a thousand years.

Sheep represent innocence and usefulness, while goats represent riotous and quarrelsome living.

This passage forces us, even now, before the time of trials and tribulations, to take a hard look at our social positions. Some Christians preach against what is often called "the social gospel." It is true that simply doing good works will not save a person; however, every born-again child of God takes on a very strong social conscience, just as Jesus did. He always stopped to help the needy around Him. Today, many are needy. According to this parable, we will be judged by how we have responded to the needs of people around us.

1. When will the judgment take place? (25:31)
2. Who will be judged? (25:32)
3. Why did Jesus judge favorably those on His right? (25:35–36, 40)
4. What was the punishment for those on His left? (25:41)
5. Why did Jesus send those on His left away? (25:45)
6. What does this parable say to the large churches with splendid facilities? What does it say to each individual Christian?

FEBRUARY 17
Matthew 26:1–16

The Plot to Kill Jesus (26:1–5)

Jesus knew His time on earth was limited and His time with His disciples, drawing to a close. Those plotting against Jesus knew they had to avoid any hint of riot, for the Romans would not tolerate civil unrest and disobedience.

Parallel passages: Mark 14:1–2; Luke 22:1–2; John 11:45–53.

1. What did Jesus predict? (26:2)
2. Who was the high priest? (26:3)
3. According to the chief priests and elders, when was the wrong time to capture Jesus? (26:5)
4. Such clandestine plotting still goes on today. Name some of the world's trouble spots where this kind of plotting is evident.

The Anointing at Bethany (26:6–16)

Jesus had returned to Bethany, one of the places He loved best. Bethany was situated high atop the Mount of Olives, overlooking Jerusalem. It was here that Jesus was anointed. The woman was probably Mary of Bethany.

This apparently was the final straw for Judas. He was the pursekeeper among the disciples. He was the one who administered whatever they might give to the poor.

The thirty pieces of silver were equal to about twenty dollars in our currency.

Parallel passages: Mark 14:3–11; John 12:1–8; Luke 22:3–6.

1. At whose home did Jesus stay while He was in Bethany? (26:6)
2. With what was Jesus anointed? (26:7)
3. How did the disciples react? (26:8–9)
4. How did Jesus respond? (26:10–13)
5. What did Judas Iscariot do? (26:16)
6. What are some ways you use your resources to show your love for Christ?

FEBRUARY 18
Matthew 26:17–35

Jesus Celebrates Passover (26:17–30)

Visitors to Jerusalem today can go to the place of the Last Supper. The upper room through which one is taken dates back only to the time of the Crusades (A.D. 1100–1300), but it is believed to have been built on the site of the original upper room.

This Last Supper instituted what we call the Lord's Supper, or Holy Communion.

Parallel passages: Mark 14:12–26; Luke 22:7–23; John 13:21–30.

1. How did the disciples locate the upper room? (26:17–19)
2. What announcement did Jesus make as He and the twelve disciples sat down to eat? (26:21)
3. How did the disciples react? (26:22)
4. When did Jesus say He would again drink from the cup with His disciples? (26:29)
5. How did the Last Supper end? (26:30)
6. Holy Communion is often minimized in our churches. Why do you partake of the Lord's Supper?

Jesus Predicts Peter's Denial (26:31–35)

The walk from atop Mount Zion eastward toward the slopes of the Mount of Olives is a beautiful one. Leaving Mount Zion, you make your way into the Kidron Valley and walk over the Ophel, David's ancient city. Passing the tomb of David's beloved son Absalom, you pass through the Kidron. Looking up to the left you can see the massive eastern walls of Jerusalem. Then there is a right turn in the path, and you begin a strenuous climb that culminates at a grove of olive trees several hundred yards away—the Garden of Gethsemane.

Parallel passages: Mark 14:27–31; Luke 22:31–34; John 13:36–38.

1. What did Jesus predict? (26:31)
2. What did Jesus promise? (26:32)
3. What did Jesus say of Peter? (26:34)
4. How did Peter and the other disciples respond? (26:35)
5. Peter and the other disciples overestimated both their righteousness and their courage. Try to think of a time when you have been guilty of the same thing.

FEBRUARY 19
Matthew 26:36–56

The Prayer in the Garden (26:36–46)

This passage again shows that there was indeed an inner circle among the disciples, for it was the same three disciples who had accompanied Jesus during the Transfiguration that accompanied Him to His place of prayer in the garden.

This passage is a revelation of Christ's nature. Even Jesus needed people around Him in a time of crisis. Jesus asked God that the cup of suffering be removed from Him, but He ended His prayer with a sentence that could sum up prayer for all humanity.

Parallel passages: Mark 14:32–42; Luke 22:39–46.

1. Whom did Jesus take with Him into the garden? (26:37)
2. What request did He make of the three disciples? (26:38)
3. What was Jesus' prayer? (26:39)
4. What did the disciples do while Jesus prayed? (26:40,43,45)
5. As He anguishes over the human condition, what might Christ ask of the church today?

Betrayal and Arrest in Gethsemane (26:47–56)

While still speaking to Peter, Jesus probably could see the light from torches moving up from the Kidron Valley. The crowd that came to arrest Jesus was probably made up of the high priest's servants or the temple guard. We are not certain why it was necessary for Judas to give the captors a sign of Jesus' identity, since Jesus had been a very public figure. Perhaps the soldiers' headgear and the darkness made Jesus difficult to pick out from the others.

The question in verse 50 is found only in Matthew. It may have been intended as a rebuke, since Jesus obviously knew why Judas was there.

Jesus' reaction to Peter's hasty action against the high priest's servant was a reminder that all He had to do was speak the word and He could be free, but He knew that was not God's will.

Parallel passages: Mark 14:43–50; Luke 22:47–53; John 18:3–12.

1. What was the sign that identified Jesus? (26:48)
2. What did Peter do? (26:51)
3. What was Jesus' response and why was that His response? (26:52–54)
4. What did the disciples do? (26:56)
5. It isn't difficult to worship Christ in our Western society. What if we really faced persecution? How would we react?

Jesus Faces the Sanhedrin (26:57–68)

Jesus' trial before the Sanhedrin was the greatest mockery in mankind's history. Jesus Christ, the flawless, anointed Son of God, stood before corrupt mortals who dared to judge Him.

The trial itself was highly questionable. It is unlikely that the full Sanhedrin would have met on Passover night. In addition, the Sanhedrin heard capital cases in the daytime only, and the verdict also had to be reached in the daytime. In capital cases, however, the conviction could not be reached until the following day. Therefore, such a trial could not be held on the eve of a Sabbath or of a religious festival.

Witnesses had to be cross-examined separately, according to the law of the Pharisees, but this law was also ignored at Jesus' trial (see vv. 60–61).

It is possible that the "trial" was a mere gathering of Caiaphas and his friends in an attempt to obtain some evidence to take to the Roman governor. If Jesus could be trapped into making some claim to messiahship that could be interpreted as a move toward the Jewish throne, then Caiaphas and his friends would have charges to bring before Pilate.

Tradition puts the house of Caiaphas south of Zion Gate, near the southwest corner of the Old City and outside the present walls.

Parallel passages: Mark 14:53–65; Luke 22:54–55, 63–71; John 18:13–14, 19–24.

1. Where was Jesus taken? (26:57)
2. Who followed Jesus and His captors? (26:58)
3. What was the first charge against Jesus? (26:61)
4. What was the second charge against Jesus? (26:63)
5. How did Jesus answer the charges? (26:64)
6. What did the high priest label Jesus' answer? (26:65)
7. What could a member of the Sanhedrin have done to prevent Jesus' unfair trial? What can you do to help protect people from miscarriages of justice?

FEBRUARY 21
Matthew 26:69—27:10

Peter Denies Jesus (26:69—75)

We learn in this passage that the prophecy Jesus made on His way to the Garden of Gethsemane came true. Peter failed in his first test of courage, but he did not always fail. He spread the gospel message for about thirty years following Jesus' resurrection and ascension. He was convicted to die by crucifixion under the Emperor Nero. Peter, however, felt he was not worthy to die in the same manner as his Lord and therefore requested to be crucified upside down.

Parallel passages: Mark 14:66–72; Luke 22:56–62; John 18:15–18, 25–27.

1. Who approached Peter the first time and how did he answer? (26:69–70)
2. What reminded Peter of Jesus' prophecy? How did he react when he remembered? (26:74b–75)
3. Sometimes our actions deny Jesus just the same as Peter's direct denial. Think of one time your actions denied that you were one of Christ's followers.

Jesus Delivered to Pilate (27:1—2)

Pontius Pilate was the Roman procurator, or governor, over Judea. He was stationed at Caesarea, but because of the Passover and the possibility of Jewish unrest during that time, he was in Jerusalem.

Parallel passages: Mark 15:1; Luke 23:1–2; John 18:28–32.

1. What happened early in the morning? (27:1)
2. How was Jesus handed over to Pilate? (27:2)
3. Jesus was arrested on false charges. If you should have a similar experience, what would you do?

Judas Hangs Himself (27:3—10)

Judas Iscariot apparently spent a restless night also. When he betrayed Jesus, he may have thought Jesus would never be condemned.

Judas' disposal of the thirty pieces of silver refers to the prophecy in Zechariah 11:13. Verse 9 also refers to Zechariah 11:13.

1. What did Judas attempt to do? (27:3)
2. How did the chief priests and elders react? (27:4)
3. What did Judas then do? (27:5)
4. What did the chief priests and elders do with the silver? (27:6–7)
5. What lesson does Judas' belated repentance hold for us? (27:3–10)

Matthew 27:11–14

Jesus Faces Pilate (27:11–14)

Pilate worked his way up to the position of governor of Judea through various military commands and administrative posts. In A.D. 26 he became procurator of Judea—a post he held for about ten years until Rome recalled him.

Judea had never been a popular assignment among the Romans, but Pilate created problems for himself. He had no sympathy for the Jews and made no attempt to understand the most important facet of their lives—their religion. For example, he knew of the Jewish hatred of graven images. His predecessors, understanding the teaching based upon the Ten Commandments, had removed all eagles and other images from the Roman standards when they came into office. Pilate, however, insisted upon their display—an act that brought about a major riot in which many were killed. Pilate had to back down. His reaction against an assembly in Samaria resulted in another wholesale slaughter. This time he was recalled to Rome. Tradition has it that Pilate committed suicide.

Parallel passages: Mark 15:2–5; Luke 23:3–5; John 18:33–38.

1. What did Pilate ask Jesus and how did Jesus answer? (27:11)
2. How did Jesus answer the accusations of the chief priests and elders? (27:12)
3. What was Pilate's reaction? (27:14)
4. Had you been the Roman governor, would you have been puzzled by the charges? Knowing you had to answer to Caesar, how would you have handled the situation?

Taking Barabbas' Place (27:15–26)

Pilate seems to be caught in the middle here. The Roman emperor Tiberius, to whom Pilate was accountable, did not look kindly on governors who treated their subjects harshly (and it was for this very reason that Pilate was later recalled, as you read earlier). At the same time Tiberius showed no mercy to anyone suspected of plotting insurrection. It is quite likely that Pilate wanted to release Jesus. In giving the crowd a choice between Jesus and Barabbas, he probably thought he had found a way out of his dilemma. But the crowd refused to cooperate.

Parallel passages: Mark 15:6–15; Luke 23:17–25.

1. What was the Roman governor's custom at every Passover festival? (27:15)
2. What message did Pilate receive from his wife? (27:19)
3. Who stirred up the crowd? (27:20)
4. What was Pilate's reaction to the crowd's "Crucify Him!"? (27:24)
5. What did the crowd answer? (27:25)
6. Name some instances in which we at least symbolically choose Barabbas over Jesus.

Soldiers Mock Jesus (27:27–31)

The praetorium was the government house when the Roman procurator was in Judea. Two sites for its location have been proposed: the Castle of Antonia, which was located at the northwest corner of the temple area, and the palace of Herod. The latter was located at the western wall of the Old City at what is now called the Citadel. According to the Jewish historian Josephus, later procurators lived there.

The scarlet robe was probably a cloak, called a sagum, belonging to one of the Roman soldiers. The reed probably symbolized a scepter.

Parallel passages: Mark 15:16–20; John 19:2–3.

1. Where did the soldiers take Jesus? (27:27)
2. How did the soldiers mock Jesus? (27:28–30)
3. Often our own actions or those of our nation or our churches mock Jesus. Name an example of such mocking.

The King on a Cross (27:32–44)

The Romans used crucifixion as a punishment for those they considered the lowest class of criminal, among them rebels and slaves. In the glory of the Resurrection, we often overlook the horrible form of death that crucifixion is. Crucifixion was a torturous, slow death. The convicted man was beaten, then forced to carry the crossbeam to the site of the crucifixion. The victim was usually stripped, but in deference to the Jews' abhorrence of nudity, the soldiers draped a loincloth around Jesus' waist. The victim's hands were nailed or tied to the crossbeam. His body rested on a block, and his legs were spread out in an unnatural position. His feet were nailed to the upright portion of the cross just above the ground. Sometimes death took an extraordinarily long time. Thirst, the cutting off of circulation, and exposure added to the pain.

The traditional stations of the Cross begin in the Via Dolorosa, which is one of the main east-west streets of the Old City.

Golgotha, from the Aramaic word *galgalta*, means "skull," or "head." It has been assumed that Golgotha was a rounded hill outside of the city that looked like a skull or head.

The drink offered Jesus was prophesied in Psalm 69:21, and the casting of lots for His garments may be a fulfillment of the prophecy in Psalm 22:18.

The Roman custom was to put a *titulus* around the neck of the criminal so that all might know the crime. In this case, the crime was high treason. The Jews helped instigate Jesus' capture, but the manner of execution and the crime for which he was condemned were most certainly Roman.

Parallel passages: Mark 15:21–32; Luke 23:26–43; John 19:17–27.

1. Who helped Jesus carry His cross? (27:32)
2. Where was Jesus crucified? (27:33)
3. What did the soldiers offer Jesus? (27:34)
4. What was written above Jesus' head? (27:37)
5. Three kinds of people insulted Jesus. Who were they? (27:39, 41, 44)
6. How would you react to the execution of such a seemingly righteous man today?

Jesus Dies on the Cross (27:45–56)

Jesus did not take as long to die as did some men. For some, death came only after several days. For Jesus, death came after a few hours. The sixth hour is noon; the ninth hour, 3:00 P.M.

Jesus' cry to God is a quote from Psalm 22:1. It may be that the drink offered Jesus at this time was *posca*, a drink made of water, sour wine, and egg. If so, this may have been an act of mercy on the part of the soldiers. Some, however, have seen it as one more cruelty and thus a fulfillment of Psalm 69:21.

Parallel passages: Mark 15:33–41; Luke 23:44–49; John 19:28–30.

1. What happened at the sixth hour? (27:45)
2. What were Jesus' words from the cross? (27:46)
3. Whom did some of the people think Jesus was calling? (27:47)
4. What three things happened when Jesus died? (27:51–52)
5. Who were watching from a distance? (27:55–56)
6. What does the renting of the veil mean to you?

Jesus Is Buried (27:57–61)

There are two possible sites of Christ's burial. The Holy Sepulchre is located within the current city walls and is enshrined by a large church. Then there is Gordon's Calvary and the attendant garden tomb, well outside the walls and adjacent to the historical execution site.

Parallel passages: Mark 15:42–47; Luke 23:50–56; John 19:38–42.

1. Who asked for the body of Jesus? (27:57)
2. How was the tomb sealed? (27:60)
3. Who else was at the tomb? (27:61)
4. Why don't we know the exact location of Jesus' tomb? Is it important? Why? Why not?

Pilate Sets a Guard (27:62–66)

Since Pilate granted the wish of the Jewish religious leaders for a guard at the tomb, the guard was probably Roman. This passage appears only in Matthew.

1. Why did the religious leaders want a guard? (27:63–64)
2. How was the tomb left? (27:66)
3. In what way do you feel the power of the Resurrection in the world today?

FEBRUARY 26
Matthew 28:1–20

He Is Risen (28:1–20)

Often great detail is given to the Crucifixion, while far less is given to the Resurrection. But the rest of the New Testament presupposed the Resurrection, and it is, indeed, the cornerstone of the Christian faith. As Paul wrote in 1 Corinthians 15:12–13: "Now if Christ is preached that He has been raised from the dead, how do some among you say that there is no resurrection of the dead? But if there is no resurrection of the dead, then Christ is not risen. And if Christ is not risen, then our preaching is vain and your faith is also vain."

Verses 11–15 counteract the story making the rounds at the time Matthew's gospel was written—that is, that Jesus' body was stolen by the disciples to make Jesus' resurrection predictions appear to be true. According to Justin Martyr in his *Dialogue With Trypho*, the story was still told with some credence as late as the second century A.D. The story does not hold together, for it is unlikely that the disciples would have died the martyrs' deaths they did for a belief in a false resurrection.

Jesus' parting words in this gospel of Matthew have helped to give the church the vision of its worldwide mission.

The Resurrection appearances differ in each of the Gospels, but some of the parallel passages are Mark 16:1–10, 14–18; Luke 24:1–12, 36–49; John 20:1–10, 19–23; and Acts 1:6–8.

1. Who went to look at the tomb? (28:1)
2. What happened? (28:2–4)
3. What did the angel tell the women to do? (28:7)
4. What is the first Resurrection appearance reported in Matthew? (28:9–10)
5. What deal was made between the guards and the religious officials? (28:11–15)
6. What charge did Jesus give His disciples? (28:19–20)
7. How are you living out the Great Commission (vv. 19–20) in your life?

MARK

FEBRUARY 27
Mark 1:1–20

Preparing the Way (1:1–8)

John the Baptist needed no fancy buildings, no spotlights, not even a public address system. He had a calling and a message, and his message was received.

John's garment of camel's hair would have been much rougher than the soft garments worn by the wealthy. The Arabs still eat wild locust when food is scarce. Wild honey was probably the honey of wild bees, although it may have been the gum that dripped off the trees.

Parallel passages: Matthew 3:1–12; Luke 3:1–18; John 1:19–28.

1. What was John's mission? (1:4)
2. Where did John baptize the people? (1:5)
3. What did John wear? (1:6)
4. What was John's message? (1:7–8)
5. How would you respond to such a humble messenger today?

John Baptizes Jesus (1:9–11)

John must have been surprised when Jesus insisted upon being baptized. This passage describes one of the instances when Jesus received divine confirmation of His ministry.

Parallel passages: Matthew 3:13–17; Luke 3:21–22.

1. What symbolized the Holy Spirit? (1:10)
2. What did the voice say? (1:11)
3. What does baptism mean to you?

The Beginning of Ministry (1:12–20)

Jesus began His actual ministry in Galilee after a period of temptation in the wilderness. Both Matthew and Luke give fuller details.

Parallel passages: Matthew 4:1–22; Luke 4:1–15; 5:1–11.

1. Where did Jesus go? (1:12)
2. Who tempted Jesus and who helped Him? (1:13)
3. What message did Jesus preach? (1:14–15)
4. How does the world often make it difficult to be obedient?

FEBRUARY 28
Mark 1:21–45

Jesus Casts Out an Unclean Spirit (1:21–28)

Jesus and His disciples traveled to Capernaum, where they went to the synagogue on the Sabbath. There they encountered a demon-possessed man.

In all likelihood, demons are some of the fallen angels who took part in Satan's rebellion against God. They have intellect, feelings, and incredible power. But they do not have nearly enough power to challenge Christ or a Spirit-filled believer. Any believer on the front line of ministry will, at times, be aware of demonic oppression, but he can never be demon possessed.

Parallel passage: Luke 4:31–37.

1. Why did Jesus go to the synagogue? (1:21)
2. What was the reaction to Jesus' teaching? Why? (1:22)
3. What was the result of Jesus' casting out the demon? (1:27–28)
4. What is the difference between demon oppression and demon possession?

Peter's Mother-in-law Healed (1:29–34)

Jesus and the disciples went from the synagogue to Peter's home, which was a short walk away on the edge of the Sea of Galilee. There they found Peter's mother-in-law, who was sick with a fever. Jesus acted out His role as a servant who ministers to the needs of others.

Parallel passages: Matthew 8:14–17; Luke 4:38–44.

1. What did Jesus do when told the woman was sick? (1:31)
2. How quickly was the woman healed? (1:31)
3. How did Jesus spend the evening? (1:32–34)
4. What do we learn about our own ministry from this passage?

Preaching and Healing in Galilee (1:35–45)

Jesus and the disciples next traveled throughout Galilee, teaching, casting out demons, and healing the sick.

Parallel passages: Matthew 8:1–4; Luke 4:42–44; 5:12–16.

1. Why did Jesus say He had come into the world? (1:38)
2. What was the leper's statement of faith? (1:40)
3. What was the result of the healing and the man's telling about it? (1:45)
4. What does this passage say to those who feel that some people do not deserve to be ministered to?

MARCH 1
Mark 2:1—3:6

Jesus Forgives and Heals a Paralytic (2:1–12)

The action of the four men who lowered their paralyzed friend through the roof was not as drastic as it sounds to us, because back then roofs were typically earthen and could be repaired fairly easily.

Parallel passages: Matthew 9:1–8; Luke 5:17–26.

1. Why did the paralytic's friends have to find an unusual way to get their friend to Jesus? (2:3–4)
2. What did Jesus say to the paralytic? (2:5, 11)
3. What did the paralytic do in response to Jesus? (2:12)
4. In Jesus' day sick people were judged sinful. How would Jesus look at this belief today? What does that say to us?

Matthew and the Question of Fasting (2:13–22)

Jesus called Matthew, a tax collector, to be one of His disciples. Tax collectors were generally unpopular, because they often extracted more money from people than was required. Jesus was also asked why His disciples did not fast twice a week.

Parallel passages: Matthew 9:9–17; Luke 5:27–39.

1. What did the scribes and Pharisees say when they saw with whom Jesus was eating? (2:16)
2. What was Jesus' response? (2:17)
3. Have some of our practices become ritual rather than expressions of inner faith? Name one that has lost meaning for you.

Jesus Is Lord of the Sabbath (2:23—3:6)

Jewish ritual about the Sabbath had reached a point where it no longer served its original purpose, that of benefiting our relationship with God. Instead, obedience to the ritual was elevated above obedience to God's higher law of love.

Parallel passages: Matthew 12:1–14; Luke 6:1–11.

1. What specifically did Jesus' disciples do to raise the Pharisees' first question? (2:23–24)
2. What Old Testament precedent did Jesus cite for His disciples' action? (2:25–26)
3. What general principle did Jesus cite in His disciples' defense? (2:27–28)
4. How does our observance of Sunday, the Christian holy day, benefit mankind? Do we use this as a criterion for our observance?

MARCH 2
Mark 3:7–27

A Great Multitude Follows Jesus (3:7–12)
In the last two lessons, critics of Jesus have begun to emerge. These critics were those religious leaders for whom the law itself had become more important than the intention behind the law. These critics would grow in number as Jesus continued His ministry. In this passage, Jesus needed some time to Himself.

Parallel passages: Matthew 12:15–21; Luke 6:17–19.

1. Where did Jesus and His disciples go? (3:7)
2. From where did the crowd come? (3:7–8)
3. What did Jesus do to get away from the crowd? (3:9)
4. What order did Jesus give to the evil spirits? (3:12)
5. Why is time alone with God important?

The Twelve Apostles (3:13–19)
For three years Jesus pumped into the disciples everything of Himself that He could. This moment was truly the beginning of the church with its apostolic mission, although Mark probably had in mind the mission more closely associated with Jesus—to preach and to cast out demons.

Parallel passages: Matthew 10:1–4; Luke 6:12–16.

1. Why did Jesus choose the twelve apostles? (3:14–15)
2. Who were the first three disciples chosen? (3:16–17)
3. Who were the other disciples? (3:18–19)
4. Jesus made disciples. What are you doing to make disciples?

A House Divided Cannot Stand (3:20–27)
This passage describes what must have been a heartbreaking situation for Jesus. Even His family did not understand His mission.

Parallel passages: Matthew 12:22–30; Luke 11:14–23.

1. Because of the multitudes, what was it that Jesus and His disciples could not do? (3:20)
2. What did Jesus' family intend to do about the situation and why? (3:21)
3. What did the religious leaders charge? (3:22)
4. Summarize Jesus' rebuttal of His critics. (3:23–29)
5. How do you respond to criticism by those who don't understand your obedience to God?

MARCH 3
Mark 3:28–4:9

The Unpardonable Sin (3:28–30)

These are three of the most difficult verses in all the Bible. The verses must be seen in the context of the preceding verses, that is, verses 20–27. Blasphemy against the Holy Spirit is beyond redemption.

Parallel passages: Matthew 12:25–37; Luke 11:17–23.

1. What is the unpardonable sin? (3:29)
2. Why did Jesus address this issue? (3:30)
3. In what ways is it possible to blaspheme the Holy Spirit?

Jesus' Mother and Brothers Send for Him (3:31–35)

Again, Jesus' family comes for Him. For Jesus, obedience to the will of God was far more important than even the most precious earthly relationships. Jesus' response to their visit must be seen in this context. It is not meant to deny the importance of commitment in earthly relationships.

Parallel passages: Matthew 12:46–50; Luke 8:19–21.

1. What did Jesus answer His mother and brothers? (3:33–34)
2. Who is Jesus' family? (3:35)
3. How do we reconcile our earthly commitments with our obedience to God's will?

The Parable of the Sower (4:1–9)

The *parable* has been called an earthly story with a heavenly meaning. It is the ultimate illustration.

Notice the difference in the yield, even though the soil was good. Like the soil, not all people have the same capabilities.

Parallel passages: Matthew 13:1–9; Luke 8:4–8.

1. Why did Jesus teach from a boat? (4:1)
2. The seed landed in four places. Where were they and how did the seed fare? (4:4–8)
3. How did Jesus end the parable? (4:9)
4. What does this parable say to us about spreading the Word of God?

MARCH 4
Mark 4:10–29

The Purpose of Parables (4:10–20)

"Those around Him with the twelve" indicates that Jesus was preparing others as disciples, as well as the Twelve we are so familiar with. Some theorize that Jesus taught in parables in order to keep the truth of the secret of the kingdom of God from those on the outside. But most agree that Jesus taught in parables as an aid to understanding. The images He used were images of His day—images that the people could understand.

Parallel passages: Matthew 13:10–23; Luke 8:9–15.

1. What does the sower sow? (4:14)
2. What do the soils represent? (4:15–16, 18, 20)
3. Jesus taught in parables so that people could understand. How can we apply Jesus' teaching techniques to our own?

Light Under a Basket and the Parable of the Growing Seed (4:21–29)

What a simple parable! We are the light of the world. We have to be in a place where our light can be seen without difficulty.

This second parable deals with the secrecy and mystery of the growing process. Both Matthew and Luke omit this parable. Matthew instead has the parable of the tares (see Matt. 13:24–30).

Parallel passage: Luke 8:16–18.

1. What will happen to those things kept secret? (4:22)
2. What happens to those who hear? (4:24)
3. To what is the kingdom of God compared in the second parable? (4:26–27)
4. How does the seed grow? (4:28)
5. What does the parable of the growing seed tell us about the work of the Holy Spirit in people's lives?

MARCH 5
Mark 4:30–5:20

The Parable of the Mustard Seed (4:30–34)

This parable forms a pair with the preceding parable. Its lesson is that great results can come out of small beginnings. Again Mark adds an explanation of Jesus' use of parables.

Parallel passages: Matthew 13:31–32, 34; Luke 13:18–19.

1. To what did Jesus compare the kingdom of God? (4:31)
2. How much did Jesus teach the people? (4:33)
3. What happened when Jesus was alone with His disciples? (4:34)
4. What does this parable say to those of us with feelings of inadequacy and inferiority?

Wind and Waves Obey Jesus (4:35–41)

The Sea of Galilee is known for its sudden ferocious storms. One moment it can be sunny and calm; the next, stormy and wild.

Parallel passages: Matthew 8:23–27; Luke 8:22–25.

1. Where was Jesus when the storm began? (4:38)
2. What did the disciples ask Jesus? (4:38)
3. How did Jesus still the storm? (4:39)
4. What did Jesus ask His disciples? (4:40)
5. What was the disciples' reaction? (4:41)
6. We all have storms of another nature in our lives. What does this passage say about Jesus' role during those times in our lives?

A Demon-possessed Man Healed (5:1–20)

Here, Jesus is in pagan territory. The country of the Gadarenes (or Gerasenes) lay near Lake Tiberias. In ancient tales, tombs were a favorite hiding place for demons and madmen.

Jesus' command to the demoniac whom He had healed is particularly significant, for it is a command to spread the word.

Parallel passages: Matthew 8:28–34; Luke 8:26–39.

1. Describe the condition of the man whom Jesus met. (5:2–5)
2. Who was actually speaking to Jesus? (5:7)
3. What was the name given? (5:9)
4. Where did Jesus send the demons? (5:13)
5. What command did Jesus give the man whom He had healed? (5:19)
6. How are we like the people of Gadara, who asked Christ to leave?

MARCH 6
Mark 5:21–43

A Girl Restored to Life and a Woman Healed (5:21–43)

These two stories deal with people at different ends of the social spectrum. Jairus was a ruler of the synagogue. The woman, whose name we do not even know, was suffering from a disease for which there apparently was no help and which caused her great anguish and embarrassment. In the moment of their need, the ruler and the unknown woman became equals. Both were helpless, and each one had to depend upon Jesus' mercy.

Notice that the inner circle of disciples appears again in this passage. Jesus chose the three to accompany Him to Jairus' house.

Both healings were healings by touch.

Parallel passages: Matthew 9:18–26; Luke 8:40–56.

1. What did Jairus ask of Jesus? (5:23)
2. From what did the woman suffer? (5:25)
3. How was the woman healed? (5:28)
4. What did Jesus tell the woman? (5:34)
5. Who accompanied Jesus to Jairus' house? (5:37)
6. What did Jesus do to the people around the child? (5:40)
7. What was Jesus' final order? (5:43)
8. Jesus healed two very different kinds of people. What does this say about the inclusiveness of our own mission?

MARCH 7
Mark 6:1–29

Jesus Rejected at Nazareth (6:1–6)

Capernaum is about twenty-five miles from Jesus' hometown of Nazareth. At Capernaum Jesus stilled the sea, healed a woman with an incurable disease, and raised a child from the dead. Yet in His nearby hometown the people reacted with disbelief.

Parallel passages: Matthew 13:53–58; Luke 4:16–30.

1. What did Jesus do on the Sabbath? (6:2)
2. How did the people react? (6:2–3)
3. What was Jesus' explanation for this reaction? (6:4)
4. Was He able to perform miracles there? (6:5)
5. How effective is our ministry with the people who know us best?

Sending Out the Twelve (6:7–13)

Jesus knew His time was growing ever shorter, so He gave His men some "on-the-spot" training. Jesus taught His disciples to be content with what they had and with that which was necessary to carry out their ministry.

Parallel passages: Matthew 10:5–15; Luke 9:1–6.

1. How did Jesus send out the disciples? (6:7)
2. What instructions did Jesus give about their lifestyle? (6:8–11)
3. What were the results of the disciples' first attempts? (6:13)
4. How do Jesus' lifestyle instructions apply to us in our ministry?

John the Baptist Beheaded (6:14–29)

This is quite a story of palace intrigue—of a courageous prophet of God, of a pathetically immoral and cowardly king, of an equally immoral queen whose enchanting ways brought kingdoms to ruin, and of a daughter who sold her soul to her mother.

Parallel passages: Matthew 14:1–12; Luke 9:7–9.

1. Who did Herod think Jesus was? (6:16)
2. Why did Herod put John in prison? (6:17–18)
3. Who wanted to kill John? What was Herod's intent? (6:19–20)
4. What did the princess demand? (6:25)
5. Herod and his friends were in a drunken stupor. His actions, which led to his downfall, might not have been the same had he been sober. How can we apply this passage to the popularity of alcoholic beverages in today's society?

MARCH 8
Mark 6:30—44

Feeding the Five Thousand (6:30—44)

The feeding of the five thousand is such an important miracle that it is recorded in all four Gospels. It clearly shows Jesus' lordship over every aspect of nature.

Jesus evidently felt a need to get away from the crowds that followed Him everywhere He went. He and His disciples had departed by boat to a deserted place near the northwest edge of the Sea of Galilee. It is beautiful there with great trees and sloping verdant hills that disappear into the blue of the lake. But the multitudes found Jesus.

The two hundred pennyworth, or denarii, was about $40 with the purchasing power in the first century of about $140—an impossible sum for the disciples to come by.

The loaves were probably small round ones made of barley meal and would have been slightly larger than our baker's buns.

Note that in this account there is no mention of the boy who offered his food. It reads as if the five loaves and two fishes were food the disciples had brought with them for their short retreat from the ever-present crowds.

The twelve baskets of leftovers, like the wine at Cana (see John 2:6), symbolize that abundance is characteristic of God's good will. The lesson here is that Christ is more than sufficient for our needs.

Parallel passages: Matthew 14:13—21; Luke 9:10—17; John 6:1—14.

1. What did the disciples report to Jesus? (6:30)
2. How did Jesus feel when He saw that the crowds had arrived ahead of Him? (6:34)
3. What did the disciples want to do about feeding the people? (6:36)
4. How did Jesus respond? (6:37)
5. How were the people grouped? (6:40)
6. How much food was left? (6:43)
7. When trying to satisfy our needs, how do we incorporate the teaching in this passage—that Christ is sufficient to meet all our needs?

MARCH 9
Mark 6:45–56

Jesus Walks on the Sea (6:45–52)

If you look deeply into these verses of Scripture, it becomes apparent that the disciples still did not realize the true power and identity of their Master. They had seen incredible things and had even been imbued with tremendous power from Jesus, but they still did not realize that Jesus was the long-awaited Messiah, the Son of God.

The real miracle in this story is not Christ's walking on water; it is rather the dawning—and underline *dawning* for it indeed was a bare beginning—in the hearts of the disciples about who Christ really was.

Parallel passage: Matthew 14:22–33.

1. What did Jesus see as He looked out over the sea? (6:48)
2. Who did the disciples think He was? (6:49)
3. What happened when Jesus got into the boat? (6:51)
4. If we could understand Christ in His full authority, beauty, and love, how would our personal lives be different? How would the world be different?

Many Touch Him and Are Made Well (6:53–56)

Gennesaret was probably the fertile plain south of Capernaum. This is another of Mark's summaries to show the end of a section. The border of His garment refers to the fringe or tassel that every Israelite man wore at the corners of his mantle.

Parallel passages: Matthew 14:34–36; John 6: 15–21.

1. What happened as Jesus and His disciples left the boat? (6:54)
2. What happened everywhere Jesus went? (6:56)
3. Perhaps our church services emphasize features that keep the true Christ from reaching the people. Can you name any of these?

Defilement Is from Within (7:1–23)

This segment deals with ceremonial defilement and the improper emphasis on traditions. William Barclay in his commentary gives us some insight into the particular controversy we read about here. According to Barclay, the hands had to be washed in a certain way before each meal and between each of the courses. The water itself had to be kept in special large stone jars so that it was ceremonially clean, and would not be used for any other purpose. The first step was to hold the hands with fingers pointing upward. The water poured over them had to run down at least to the wrist. The minimum amount of water used was to equal one and a half eggshells full. Each hand was then cleaned with the fist of the other hand; but since the water was now unclean, the hands had to be turned downward and ceremonially clean water poured from the wrist down to the fingertips. After all this, the hands were considered ceremonially clean.

This rather complicated explanation shows just how intricate Jewish legalism had become in Jesus' day. This was the kind of legalism that Jesus was addressing—the kind that was so wrapped up in itself that it lost the original intent of the law.

Parallel passage: Matthew 15:1–20.

1. What did the religious leaders notice? (7:2)
2. What rules did the Pharisees follow? (7:3–4)
3. What prophet did Jesus quote in His answer? (7:6)
4. How does the teaching of the Pharisees cancel out the Word of God? (7:9–13)
5. What makes a person unclean? (7:15)
6. What did Jesus say about unclean foods? (7:19)
7. What specifically makes a person unclean? (7:20–23)
8. We can probably take Jesus' list and be more explicit about what makes us unclean. Looking at the list in verses 21 and 22, look at your life and name some specific practices or attitudes that make you "unclean."

MARCH 11

Mark 7:24–37

A Gentile Shows Her Faith (7:24–30)

Jesus had been ministering in northern Galilee around Bethsaida and Capernaum. In this passage we read of His journey to Tyre and Sidon, which today is southern Lebanon. The woman who followed Jesus was a Gentile, not one of the chosen of Israel to whom the Messiah had come. Jesus tested her faith first, and her faith proved great—greater than that of many of His own people.

Parallel passage: Matthew 15:21–28.

1. What did the Gentile woman ask of Jesus? (7:26)
2. How did Jesus test the woman's faith? (7:27)
3. How did the woman pass the test? (7:28)
4. What should be our attitude when our prayers seem not to be answered?

Jesus Heals a Deaf-mute (7:31–37)

In this passage, Jesus has left Tyre and Sidon and moves to the region of the Decapolis along the southeast coast of the Sea of Galilee—a distance of about forty miles.

Jesus' method of healing changed again and again. His principles never varied, but His methods changed constantly.

There is no actual parallel passage. Matthew abridges the story and uses it in an account of many healings (see Matt. 15:29–31).

1. How did Jesus heal the deaf-mute? (7:33–34)
2. What order did Jesus give the people? (7:36)
3. How did the people respond? (7:37)
4. Sometimes methods of reaching others need to be changed to fit the needs of the times. Name some newer methods of teaching people about Christ.

Feeding the Four Thousand (8:1–10)

This account of a second miraculous feeding is similar to the account of feeding the five thousand. Again, as in Matthew's account, compare the numbers—of people, of loaves, of fish, of food remaining. One difference is the length of time the people had been with Jesus. The location of Dalmanutha is unknown; it may have been Magdala.

Parallel passage: Matthew 15:32–39.

1. How long had the people been with Jesus? (8:2)
2. How many loaves of bread were there? (8:5) How many fish? (8:7)
3. How much was left over? (8:9)
4. These people had been with Jesus a long time. Why do you suppose our churches cannot keep people more than an hour?

The Pharisees Seek a Sign (8:11–12)

Again, the religious leaders try to argue with Jesus—and after all that Jesus had just done!

Parallel passage: Matthew 16:1–4.

1. What did the Pharisees ask of Jesus? (8:11)
2. How did Jesus react? (8:12)
3. Name some times when you have not been content with your faith in Christ alone and have asked for something more.

Beware of the Leaven of the Pharisees and Herod (8:13–21)

Still upset because the Pharisees had asked for yet another sign, Jesus took the stillness and privacy of those moments to warn the disciples about the insincerity and doctrines (the leaven) of small-minded people.

Parallel passage: Matthew 16:5–12.

1. Did the disciples understand what Jesus was trying to teach them? (8:17–21)
2. In what ways have our churches lost the main purpose of their existence—trying to tell people about Christ?

MARCH 13
Mark 8:22–30

A Blind Man Healed at Bethsaida (8:22–26)

Again, Jesus used two methods of healing—the direct command and the use of spittle. This healing is unique in that it required two treatments.

There are no parallel accounts, unless Matthew includes it in his summary of healings (see Matt. 15:29–31).

1. How did the blind man get to Jesus? (8:22)
2. What did Jesus do before healing the man? (8:23)
3. What could the man see at first? (8:24)
4. What was Jesus' final admonition? (8:26)
5. Recall a time when your first venture in faith did not turn out perfectly. Did you persevere, as the blind man of Bethsaida did?

Peter Confesses Jesus as the Christ (8:27–30)

This passage marks a turning point in Jesus' ministry. Up to now, He had ministered primarily in the area of Capernaum. Now He seems to enter a time of solitude in which He is content to be alone with the disciples, instructing them in the ways of the kingdom.

Peter's confession was the first step on the road to salvation for all of us. "If you confess with your mouth the Lord Jesus and believe in your heart that God has raised Him from the dead, you will be saved" (Rom. 10:9).

Parallel passages: Matthew 16:13–20; Luke 9:18–21.

1. What did Jesus first ask His disciples? (8:27)
2. What was their answer? (8:28)
3. What was Jesus' second question? (8:29)
4. What did Peter answer? (8:29)
5. Who do you say Christ is?

MARCH 14
Mark 8:31—9:1

Jesus Predicts His Suffering and Death (8:31–9:1)

This is the first of Jesus' three announcements concerning His fate. It may be difficult to understand the disciples' reactions to this and to the other predictions. Throughout Holy Week they act as if they had never heard, let alone understood, these predictions. We have to remember that the Jewish people were looking for a military Messiah—one who would free Judah from Rome's bondage. They were ill-prepared for the true nature of the Messiah—that of the suffering servant.

In rebuking Peter, Jesus was saying that Peter's words had taken on Satan's tone, tempting Jesus to forsake the cross and ultimate atonement.

Jesus also warned His disciples that those who follow Him will suffer the same treatment. This is as true today as it was when Jesus uttered the words. Our suffering is not likely to take the form of outright persecution—at least, not in this nation—but there will be trials and suffering if we follow Jesus' way fully.

Parallel passages: Matthew 16:21–28; Luke 9:22–27.

1. What prediction did Jesus make concerning His future? (8:31)
2. What did Peter do? (8:32)
3. How did Jesus react to Peter? (8:33)
4. What, according to Jesus, is the cost of discipleship? (8:34–37)
5. What does Jesus say will happen to those who are easily swayed from the gospel? (8:38)
6. Name a time, if any, when you feel your faithfulness to the gospel has caused you some form of suffering or derision. If you have not experienced such trials, do you think you have a full understanding of the gospel's radical nature?

MARCH 15
Mark 9:2–13

Jesus Transfigured on the Mount (9:2–13)

Now Mark brings us to the mountaintop known as the Mount of Transfiguration, where the inner circle of disciples received a brief glimpse of glory. Such a glimpse is a rare experience. The apostle Paul wrote about being carried away into the third heaven. Both Isaiah and John (in Revelation) had a glimpse of glory. Here Jesus, who was preparing for the Cross, was given a time of spiritual rejuvenation. This time was important too for the disciples, who would have to carry on Christ's ministry.

Moses represented the Law, Elijah, the Prophets, and Christ, the fulfillment of salvation. What the Law and Prophets could not do, Christ could and did. Jesus was referring to John the Baptist when He told His disciples that Elijah had indeed already come.

Parallel passages: Matthew 17:1–13; Luke 9:28–36.

1. Who went up on the mount with Jesus? (9:2)
2. What change came over Jesus? (9:3)
3. What did the disciples see? (9:4)
4. What did Peter want to do? (9:5)
5. What symbolized God, and what did the voice say? (9:7)
6. How can we spend less time trying to explain God and the Son of God and more time trying to understand and carry out God's will?

MARCH 16
Mark 9:14–32

A Boy Is Healed (9:14–29)

Jesus and the three disciples came down from the mountaintop and were immediately confronted by human need. The child had every symptom of what we know today as epilepsy. The other nine disciples had tried to heal the child, but they were not spiritually prepared.

Parallel passages: Matthew 17:14–21; Luke 9:37–43.

1. What was happening when Jesus came down from the mountaintop? (9:14–18)
2. How did Jesus react? (9:19)
3. How did Jesus answer the father's plea for help? (9:23)
4. How did the father respond? (9:24)
5. What did the disciples ask Jesus and what was His answer? (9:28–29)
6. What do our churches need to do to be more spiritually ready to confront the world? (see v. 29)

Jesus Again Predicts His Death and Resurrection (9:30–32)

This is the second of three predictions that Jesus made about His fate. Still, the disciples did not grasp what He was saying.

Jesus and His disciples were in Caesarea Philippi enroute to Galilee. Jesus appears to have been staying off the main roads because He wanted to avoid the crowds. He needed time to train His disciples before His death.

Parallel passages: Matthew 17:22–23; Luke 9:43–45.

1. What did Jesus predict? (9:31)
2. What feelings were the disciples having? (9:32)
3. Jesus predicted both the Cross and the Resurrection. What should be the trademark of our gospel?

MARCH 17
Mark 9:33–50

Who Is the Greatest? (9:33–37)

This passage shows that the disciples still hadn't learned that serving Christ involved being a servant—that real discipleship involves humility—being willing and ready to stoop to do the tasks of a servant.

The child represents those with little influence.

Parallel passages: Matthew 18:1–5; Luke 9:46–48.

1. What were the disciples arguing about? (9:34)
2. How did Jesus answer the argument? (9:35)
3. Whom did Jesus use to teach His disciples humility? (9:36–37)
4. How often do we find ourselves trying to be greater than someone else or trying to curry the favor of influential people?

Jesus Forbids Sectarianism (9:38–40)

In this passage, Jesus affirms that the common denominator of all our efforts is our love for Christ. Thus squabbling among our present-day denominations is contrary to the gospel.

Parallel passage: Luke 9:49–50.

1. What had the disciples seen that caused them concern? (9:38)
2. What did Jesus say to calm His disciples? (9:39–40)
3. What are some evidences of sectarianism, or denominationalism, in your own community? Is your church guilty of any of these?

Jesus Warns of Offenses (9:41–50)

In this passage, Jesus warned against offending those who are not as strong in the faith as we might happen to be. Judging others can be a devastating thing, and it is so easy to do. We have not walked where our brother or sister has walked. We do not have the same life experiences as they have had. Yet so often we presume to judge. Our judgmental attitude may cause those new in the faith to stumble. Woe to us if that be the case.

Parallel passages: Matthew 18:6–9; Luke 17:1–2.

1. What was Jesus' warning concerning the little ones? (9:42)
2. How does Jesus illustrate His warning? (9:43–47)
3. What was Jesus' final piece of advice in this passage? (9:50)
4. Apply this passage to your attitude toward others who are different from you.

MARCH 18
Mark 10:1–16

Marriage and Divorce (10:1–12)

In this passage, Mark dealt with the sanctity of marriage. The Pharisees brought the question of divorce to Jesus—in an attempt to trick Him into saying something contrary to the law of Moses.

In America these days, over one million children become the victims of divorce every year. An act that has been solemnized in the courts of heaven is not invalidated by decree of the courts of the land. There is a higher law than the law of our land.

Parallel passages: Matthew 19:1–12; Luke 16:18.

1. What did the Pharisees ask Jesus? (10:2)
2. With what question did Jesus counter? (10:3)
3. What was Moses' solution? (10:4)
4. Why, according to Jesus, did Moses write such a law? (10:5)
5. What was Jesus' final answer to the Pharisees? (10:9)
6. What constitutes adultery? (10:12)
7. Why have we come to accept divorce so readily? What can our churches do to counteract such acceptance?

Jesus Blesses Little Children (10:13–16)

In this passage Jesus affirmed certain qualities of children—their innocence and trust—qualities needed to be part of God's kingdom.

Parallel passages: Matthew 19:13–15; Luke 18:15–17.

1. What did the disciples do when people tried to bring children to Jesus? (10:13)
2. What was Jesus' response? (10:14)
3. What does this passage say about the place of children in our churches?

MARCH 19
Mark 10:17–31

Jesus Counsels the Rich Young Ruler (10:17–22)

In this passage, Christ was testing the rich young ruler to see which he treasured more—his earthly possessions or eternal life.

Riches in and of themselves are not sinful, but when they become the prime motivation in a person's life, they do become sinful, because they have replaced God as the priority.

Parallel passages: Matthew 19:16–22; Luke 18:18–23.

1. What question did the rich young ruler ask Jesus? (10:17)
2. What did Jesus answer first? (10:18–19)
3. What was the one thing the young ruler lacked? (10:21)
4. When we put possessions before God, which of the Ten Commandments are we breaking?

With God All Things Are Possible (10:23–31)

To His amazed disciples Jesus then explained that sometimes earthly riches can pose a real problem to a person. (For an explanation of verse 25, see the explanation for the February 2 entry.)

You don't enter God's kingdom with pomp and circumstance just because you have a few dollars. In the house of God, one person is as good as another, regardless of material background.

Parallel passages: Matthew 19:23–30; Luke 18:24–30.

1. What was the disciples' reaction to Jesus' words? (10:24)
2. What did the disciples ask Jesus? (10:26)
3. What point did Peter make and what was Jesus' response? (10:28–31)
4. What have we given up for the gospel?

MARCH 20
Mark 10:32–45

A Third Prediction of Death and Resurrection (10:32–34)

Jesus had left Galilee enroute to Jerusalem. Twice before He had told the disciples exactly what was going to happen to Him, but they could not—or would not—grasp it. Now a third time Jesus tells them what to expect.

Parallel passages: Matthew 20:17–19; Luke 18:31–34.

1. What was going to happen to Jesus? (10:33–34)
2. How did the disciples feel? (10:32)
3. The disciples expected the Messiah to lead a revolution. They *knew* how God would work. Do you ever limit God by your expectations?

Greatness in Serving (10:35–45)

As happened before when Jesus warned of His impending death, the disciples immediately revealed that they had no grasp of eternity. Two of the inner circle of disciples approached Jesus to ask a favor of Him. In His answer, Jesus did not admonish the two for what they had asked. He simply told them that to have that kind of eternal recognition they would have to pay a steep price.

Jesus teaches His disciples that to follow Him one must be a servant. He as the Messiah took on the suffering servant role. His disciples would have to do the same.

Parallel passages: Matthew 18:1–5; Luke 9:46–48.

1. Which two disciples approached Jesus? (10:35)
2. What did the two ask of Him? (10:37)
3. What was Jesus' answer? (10:38)
4. What makes a person great? (10:43–44)
5. Why did the Son of Man come? (10:45)
6. In what ways do we carry out the role of a servant in our lives?

MARCH 21
Mark 10:46–11:11

Jesus Heals Blind Bartimaeus (10:46–52)

Jesus and the disciples were making their way from Galilee down through the Jordan Valley to Jericho and then up to Jerusalem. This was basically the same route that Joseph and Mary had taken on their way to Bethlehem some thirty-three years before. Jericho is a beautiful place with colorful flowers, abundant springs, and the green plain of Gilgal.

Bartimaeus means "son of Timaeus."

Parallel passages: Matthew 20:29–34; Luke 18:35–43.

1. What did Bartimaeus call Jesus? (10:47–48)
2. What was Bartimaeus' request? (10:51)
3. What healed Bartimaeus? (10:52)
4. When has the cry of human need made us "stand still"? (10:49)

The Triumphal Entry (11:1–11)

The Mount of Olives is not really a peak; rather it is a high, sprawling ridge to the east of Jerusalem. There were several villages on or near its crest. Two of them were Bethany and Bethphage, but they were so close in proximity that they are virtually the same settlement.

Try to imagine the vast throngs of people crying out "Hosanna" and waving branches. The procession made its way down the western slopes of the Mount of Olives into the recesses of the Kidron Valley and past the Garden of Gethsemane, then up the steep banks toward the Temple Mount, through the gates, and toward the great temple itself.

Parallel passages: Matthew 21:1–9; Luke 19:28–38.

1. How did the disciples find the colt Jesus was to ride? (11:2–6)
2. What did the disciples throw over the colt? (11:7)
3. What did the people shout? (11:9–10)
4. People are fickle. On Sunday they praised Jesus. On Friday they sought His death. If you had been part of Sunday's crowd, what role do you think you would have played in Friday's mob?

MARCH 22
Mark 11:12–26

The Fig Tree Withered (11:12–14)

This strange story mirrors Israel at that time. Christ came to this nation, hungry for a relationship that had long since been broken by sin. God had always reached for this people like a heartbroken shepherd reaching for the last of the wolf-torn flock. The leaves were out in Israel. John the Baptist had heralded the Messiah's coming. The time was right. But no spiritual fruit grew in Israel at that time.

Parallel passage: Matthew 21:18–22.

1. What did Jesus see in the distance? (11:13)
2. What did Jesus say to the tree? (11:14)
3. How do we bear the fruit of the gospel in our own lives?

Jesus Cleanses the Temple (11:15–19)

The fraudulent money exchange system in the temple infuriated Jesus (see the reading for February 5). Jesus' actions show that righteous indignation has its place. Perhaps as much as any one thing, this action so infuriated the scribes and priests that Jesus' death became inevitable. Just as today, when you cut off the money supply, you really get reactions.

Parallel passages: Matthew 21:12–17; Luke 19:45–48; John 2:13–22.

1. What did Jesus do when He arrived at the temple? (11:15)
2. What Old Testament prophet did Jesus quote? (11:17)
3. How did the religious leaders react? (11:18)
4. Where would our church stand if it found that its money supply depended upon questionable practices?

The Lesson of the Withered Fig Tree (11:20–26)

Without faith it is impossible to please God, but faith without works is dead. George Bernard Shaw said "There are those who see things as they are and ask 'why?' Others see things as they could be and ask 'Why not?'" Thank God for men and women of faith and action.

Parallel passage: Matthew 21:18–22.

1. What happened to the fig tree? (11:21)
2. What is the relationship between prayer and faith? (11:24)
3. What is the relationship between prayer and forgiveness? (11:25)
4. What role do faith and forgiveness have in your prayers?

MARCH 23
Mark 11:27–12:12

Jesus' Authority Questioned (11:27–33)

This passage relates another attempt by the religious leaders to trap Jesus with a particularly dangerous question. If Jesus answered that God had authorized Him (which was true) He would be accused of blasphemy. But if He did not claim God as His authority, then He would lose all validity.

Jesus responded with a question of His own, one which the temple authorities were afraid to answer.

Parallel passages: Matthew 21:23–27; Luke 20:1–8.

1. What was the question asked by the leaders? (11:28)
2. What was the question Jesus asked in reply? (11:29–30)
3. What reasoning led to their answer? (11:31–32)
4. Are we guilty of questioning God's authority?

The Parable of the Wicked Vinedressers (12:1–12)

This may well be Jesus' most poignant parable. His message to the temple authorities who sought to kill Him was: "God sent you prophets, and you killed them. Now God's own Son stands before you, and you seek to kill Him."

Lest we limit Jesus' parable to the Jews only, let us remember that non-Jews were involved in the plot to kill Jesus, and that other Jews wanted to save Jesus. Just what stand would we have taken?

Parallel passages: Matthew 21:33–46; Luke 20:9–19.

1. With whom did the planter leave the care of his vineyard? (12:1)
2. What happened to the servants who came to harvest the vineyard? (12:2–5)
3. Whom did the vinedresser finally send? (12:6) What happened to him? (12:8)
4. What Old Testament Scripture does Jesus quote? (12:10–11)
5. How did the religious leaders react? (12:12)
6. How would we receive God's Son today?

The Pharisees Ask About Taxes (12:13–17)

Once again the religious leaders join forces in an attempt to trick Jesus into incriminating Himself. Jesus' answer to their question of governmental loyalty indicates that the Christian is not one who causes a government consternation by being a tax-evader or cheater. He does his fair share as a citizen of the nation and votes conscientiously within what he believes to be God's will. The difficulty, of course, lies in determining whether the government is carrying out God's will in the midst of complex issues.

Parallel passages: Matthew 22:15–22; Luke 20:20–26.

1. What question did the leaders ask Jesus? (12:14)
2. What was Jesus' answer? (12:17)
3. Name a time when you might have questioned God's place in your government's actions.

Questions on the Resurrection and the First Commandment (12:18–34)

Now it's the Sadducees' turn to try to trap Jesus. This priestly party believed in virtually nothing but perhaps money. Jesus recognized the Sadducees' question as preposterous and turned the tables on them.

Next a scribe approaches Jesus with a pertinent question—one that constituted great debate among the Jews.

If we could apply Jesus' answers to every problem in our world today, there would be no seemingly unsolvable problem. Being the fallible humans that we are, we, of course, cannot perfectly apply His teaching.

Parallel passages: Matthew 22:23–40; Luke 20:27–40; 10:25–28.

1. What predicament did the Sadducees present to Jesus? (12:18–23)
2. Why did Jesus say the Sadducees were wrong? (12:24–27)
3. What was the second question asked of Jesus? (12:28)
4. What did Jesus answer? (12:29–31)
5. How did the scribe respond to Jesus' answer? (12:32–33)
6. What did Jesus say to the scribe? (12:34)
7. Name a situation in which you have attempted to apply the two great commandments.

Jesus Asks a Question (12:35—40)

The three sets of questions found in Mark 12 were attempts to discredit Jesus; none was successful. The first question related to political and civic duties; the second had to do with morals; and the third, with ethics. Now Jesus asks His own question, quoting Psalm 110:1 and giving a warning.

Parallel passages: Matthew 22:41—23:36; Luke 20:41—47.

1. What question did Jesus ask? (12:35)
2. What did David call the Messiah? (12:37)
3. Whom did Jesus warn the people against? (12:38—40)
4. How might this apply to some of the clergy—and even some of the foremost lay people—today?

The Widow's Two Mites (12:41—44)

This passage deals with the motivation for giving. Why do we give what we give? If we love God more than anyone or anything else, we will give to Him. If our heart is in some other arena of life, we will spend our money there, too.

The widow's two mites were probably two *perutas*, the smallest Jewish coins, equal to about half a cent.

Parallel passage: Luke 21:1—4.

1. What was Jesus watching? (12:41)
2. What part of the widow's living was represented by her gift? (12:42)
3. What motivates us to give?

MARCH 26
Mark 13:1–23

Signs of the Times and End of the Age (13:1–23)

The thirteenth chapter of Mark is called "The Little Apocalypse." *Apocalypse* refers to the end times.

Jesus and His disciples were leaving the temple area after a long day. Virtually every kind of authority and critic in Jerusalem had taken a verbal potshot at Jesus. All had missed, but Jesus must have been weary. Now He and the Twelve were headed back toward the Mount of Olives, perhaps to have dinner in Bethany.

One of the disciples commented on the magnificent view of the temple. Jesus, however, was seemingly unimpressed and proceeded to prophesy about the temple. Naturally His disciples asked Him when the prophecy would come about. Jesus' answer was a lesson in eschatology—the study of future happenings. He used the law of double reference, for while much of what He told them had to do directly with the Roman invasion coming in forty years, it also had much to do with the Antichrist and the end of the age as we know it.

Indeed, most of Jesus' closest followers died terrible, violent deaths. It is altogether possible that today's church in the Western World will experience the same thing many of the Christians in the Eastern world are experiencing now.

Beginning in verse 14 Jesus speaks of the Tribulation, particularly the abomination of desolation spoken of by the prophet Daniel.

Parallel passages: Matthew 24:1–28; Luke 21:5–24.

1. What did Jesus prophesy concerning the temple? (13:2)
2. What four disciples came to Jesus privately? (13:3)
3. What did Jesus warn against? (13:5–6)
4. What did Jesus prophesy for the four disciples? (13:9, 11–13)
5. What must happen before the end comes? (13:10)
6. Who will appear during the abomination of desolation? (13:21–22)
7. What signs seem to indicate we are in the end times?

The Coming of the Son of Man (13:24–27)

In this passage Jesus describes in detail His return to this earth at the close of the period of Tribulation, when His feet will once again touch the Mount of Olives, just as the angels prophesied in the first chapter of Acts.

The world will be bracing itself for the Battle of Armageddon when Christ comes back, flanked by all His saints, as clearly pictured by John in Revelation 19. At this time Jesus will institute His thousand-year reign, known as the Millennium.

Parallel passages: Matthew 24:29–31; Luke 21:25–28.

1. What signs of nature will be forerunners of the Parousia (the Second Coming)? (13:24–25)
2. Where will the Son of Man send His angels? (13:27)
3. Are you one of God's elect?

The Parable of the Fig Tree (13:28–29)

This parable compares all the signs of the end time to the coming of summer, specifically the leafing of the fig tree. When all the prophetic signs merge, the return is near.

Parallel passages: Matthew 24:32–33; Luke 21:29–31.

1. When will these things happen? (13:29)
2. Though heaven and earth pass away, what will remain? (13:31)
3. What comfort does that fact bring to you?

No One Knows the Day or Hour (13:32–37)

Although we don't know the day or hour, we can be alert to the times. If there were ever a time to step up our world ministries and world vision, it is now. This is the time to be about God's business.

Parallel passage: Matthew 25:14–15b.

1. What is Jesus' advice? (13:33, 35, 37)
2. How often do our prayers intercede for the world, for humanity?

MARCH 28
Mark 14:1–26

The Plot To Kill Jesus (14:1–11)

While the plot to kill Jesus was being finalized, He was enjoying a dinner at the house of Simon the leper.

It was here that Jesus was honored with costly ointment, worth three hundred pence, or denarii. The equivalent of about sixty dollars in our money, its purchasing power was about four times that in the first century. Mark says some of the disciples were upset; John specifically names Judas Iscariot as the one who was upset.

The statement about the poor always being present is not an excuse for poverty. It is simply used in contrast here—Jesus would not always be with them.

Parallel passages: Matthew 26:1–16; Luke 22:1–6; John 12:1–8.

1. Why did the chief priests determine that during the feast was not a good time to arrest Jesus? (14:2)
2. How was Jesus honored at Simon's house? (14:3)
3. How did the people suggest that the money could have been used? (14:5)
4. What did Jesus answer? (14:6–9)
5. In what ways can we honor Jesus today?

Jesus Celebrates Passover with His Disciples (14:12–25)

Jerusalem is a city of lovely hills, among them, the Mount of Olives, Mount Scopus, and Mount Zion. On the southernmost summit, Mount Zion, is the traditional tomb of David, the house of Caiaphas, and the site of the original Upper Room.

This evening takes on added urgency when we remember that it was Passover time in Jerusalem—the commemoration of the time in Egypt when the angel of death passed over those houses where lamb's blood was sprinkled upon the doorposts. Now we have Jesus, the Lamb whose blood is about to be shed for the sins of all, to save us from eternal death. Thus, we have the parallel.

Parallel passages: Matthew 26:17–29; Luke 22:7–20; John 13:21–30.

1. How did the disciples find the upper room? (14:13–14)
2. How did they end the Passover meal? (14:22–25)
3. How often does your church observe Holy Communion?

MARCH 29
Mark 14:27–52

Prayer in the Garden (14:27–42)

The walk from the upper room to the Mount of Olives was a fifteen-or-twenty-minute one. While on this short walk, Jesus made His prediction about Peter.

Not only was Jesus aware of the tremendous agony that lay ahead of Him; He became more than ever aware of sin. Scholars have often asked which caused Christ the most intense pain—Calvary or Gethsemane's all-night prayer vigil? During this night Jesus was confronted with the sin of the world. What agony that must have caused Him.

Parallel passages: Matthew 26:30–46; Luke 22:31–34, 39–46.

1. Who accompanied Jesus into the garden? (14:33)
2. What did Jesus pray? (14:36)
3. In what state did Jesus find the disciples, three times? (14:37, 40, 41)
4. Jesus is in agony over the sinful world today. How does He find us symbolically sleeping?

Betrayal and Arrest in Gethsemane (14:43–52)

Judas never truly understood who Christ was. He betrayed Jesus for thirty pieces of silver (about twenty dollars), what Jeremiah told us was the price of a gored slave.

Only Mark mentions the anonymous young man in verses 51–52. Most scholars feel the young man was Mark himself.

Parallel passages: Matthew 26:47–56; Luke 22:47–53; John 18:3–12.

1. Who arrived with Judas? (14:43)
2. How did Judas greet Jesus? (14:45)
3. How did Jesus rebuke Judas and the crowd? (14:48)
4. What did the disciples do? (14:50)
5. What did the young man standing at the crowd's edge do? (14:51–52)
6. Name a time when you or your church has in a sense betrayed Jesus with a seeming act of kindness.

MARCH 30
Mark 14:53–65

Jesus' Trial (14:53–65)

As was stated in the introduction to Matthew 26:57–68, the Jewish "trial" was a mockery. Among the fourteen contradictions to the procedure set forth in the appropriate section of the Mishnah, or oral law, are: time of trial (at night *and* during a festival), the lack of a full quorum, the summary condemnation and execution (also during a festival), absence of defense witnesses, prosecution witnesses' not being examined separately, and invalid charge since the claim to messiahship was not true blasphemy.

The trial was held sometime between three and four in the morning. The law required that at least twenty-three of the seventy-one members of the Sanhedrin be present for a capital case.

Christ could have appealed the verdict, since the whole hearing was a farce, but He made no such appeal. Ahead of Him was further humiliation.

Parallel passages: Matthew 26:57–68; Luke 22:54–55, 63–71; John 18:13–14, 19–24.

1. Where was Peter during the trial? (14:54)
2. What problem existed with the witnesses? (14:56–59)
3. What did Jesus do? (14:61)
4. How did Jesus finally answer? (14:62)
5. Jesus was the Suffering Servant, not the earthly King-Messiah. How does the Suffering Servant application fit here?

MARCH 31
Mark 14:66–15:5

Peter Denies Jesus (14:66–72)

As in the Matthew passage, Peter is accused of being one of Jesus' followers. Contrast Matthew and Luke where two *different* servant girls approach Peter.

What a meaningful passage for all of us who have failed in our Christian commitment. The big burly fisherman lost his courage.

Note the difference in the Gospel accounts in the number of times the rooster crowed.

Parallel passages: Matthew 26:69–75; Luke 22:56–62; John 18: 15–18, 25–27.

1. Who first approached Peter? (14:66)
2. Who was the second person to approach Peter? (14:70)
3. How many times did the rooster crow? (14:72)
4. How did Peter react when he realized he had fulfilled Jesus' prediction? (14:72)
5. What has been your reaction when you have failed Christ?

Jesus Faces Pilate (15:1–5)

Consider for a moment the type of people who were in charge of Jesus' trial. Pilate ruled with an iron hand, and was understandably paranoid about being answerable to the seventy-year-old Tiberius, who had been Roman emperor for fourteen years. Tiberius despised his mother, Livia, one of history's most evil women, and once he ascended to the world's mightiest throne, he never again looked upon her. Behind his back Romans called Tiberius "The Mask" because he never showed any emotion.

Those who worked for Tiberius feared him greatly. He wielded his absolute authority through his governors. Palestine was a frontier province, meaning that it was not considered secure.

Jesus stood before Pontius Pilate at about 6:00 A.M., saying nothing in His own defense.

Parallel passages: Matthew 27:1–2, 11–14; Luke 23:1–5; John 18:28–38.

1. What did Pilate ask Jesus? (15:2)
2. What was Jesus' answer? (15:2)
3. How would we answer in the face of such authority?

APRIL 1
Mark 15:6–20

Taking the Place of Barabbas (15:6–15)

Pilate pretty much had the picture: Jesus was an innocent man—in the wrong place at the wrong time. Pilate hated the leaders of the temple; and, if he could thwart them in any way, he would do it. This Jesus was obviously guilty of nothing. He certainly was not going to execute Him and maybe not even scourge Him. Circumventing these Jewish leaders was the challenge, and Pilate thought he had the answer. But in the end, he forsook right for expediency.

Parallel passages: Matthew 27:15–26; Luke 23:13–25; John 18:39—19:16.

1. What was the custom at every Passover festival? (15:6)
2. Whom did the crowd ask for instead of Jesus? (15:11)
3. Did Pilate believe Jesus to be guilty of a crime? (15:14)
4. Think of a time in your life when you forsook right for expediency.

The Soldiers Mock Jesus (15:16–20)

The whip used to scourge Jesus was not an ordinary whip. The *flagellum* was a whip with pieces of razor-sharp stone embedded in the leather straps. A soldier could indeed slice his victim into raw meat.

The thorns in Israel, from which Jesus' crown was fashioned, are long and sharp, and each thorn is coated with a substance that causes terrible infection unless quickly treated.

Parallel passages: Matthew 27:27–31; John 19:1–3.

1. How did the soldiers dress Jesus? (15:17)
2. How did the soldiers salute Him? (15:18)
3. Name some examples of ways we bow before the Lord in mock worship, just as the soldiers did.

The King on a Cross (15:21–32)

The traditional place of execution was Golgotha, the place of the skull. This site was alongside the main road leading to the Damascus Gate. In all probability, Christ was executed at the foot of Calvary, not at its summit.

Prior to fixing the nails in human flesh, the soldiers gave their victim the option of a potion, a myrrh mixture, that would somewhat deaden the pain. But Jesus would not drink it. He endured the pain for the world.

Verse 24 is a fulfillment of Psalm 22:18.

Parallel passages: Matthew 27:32–44; Luke 23:26–43; John 19:17–27.

1. Who helped Jesus carry His cross? (15:21)
2. What did Golgotha mean? (15:22)
3. What did the soldiers do with Jesus' robe? (15:24)
4. What did the passersby and chief priests say? (15:29–32)
5. In our shallow understanding of who Jesus is, what have we asked of Him?

Jesus Dies on the Cross (15:33–41)

Jesus died quickly on the cross. That was partly because Jesus willingly gave His life; no man could take it.

Parallel passages: Matthew 27:45–56; Luke 23:44–49; John 19:28–30.

1. What happened from noon until 3:00 P.M.? (15:33)
2. What did Jesus cry from the cross? (15:34)
3. What happened when Jesus died? (15:38)
4. Who were watching from a distance? (15:40–41)
5. The veil of the temple was rent at Jesus' crucifixion, forever ending the separation between people and God. When was the last time you took advantage of your access to God?

APRIL 3
Mark 15:42—16:8

Jesus Buried in Joseph's Tomb (15:42—47)

Joseph of Arimathea was rather like many of Christ's followers today. He was a quiet follower—not willing to risk anything—that is, until Christ died. Then suddenly he took the ultimate risk. He was quiet at Jesus' trial, then asked for an audience with the Roman governor!

Parallel passages: Matthew 27:57–61; Luke 23:50–56; John 19:38–42.

1. What was Joseph's position in society? (15:43)
2. What was Pilate's first reaction? (15:44)
3. How was Jesus buried? (15:46)
4. Who watched the burial? (15:47)
5. When have we been quiet Christians, perhaps missing the opportunity to speak up?

Christ Is Risen (16:1—8)

It is interesting that the men who should have been there that Sunday morning—the disciples—were not there. Christ had told them repeatedly what was going to happen, but they didn't believe. Is there anything in all of human history that should have been such a breathtaking spectacle as Jesus' resurrection? And the disciples didn't even show up for it!

Parallel passages: Matthew 28:1–10; Luke 24:1–12; John 20:1–10.

1. Which women went to the tomb and why? (16:1)
2. What were they concerned about on the way to the tomb? (16:3)
3. What did they find when they reached and entered the tomb? (16:4–5)
4. What message were the women to take to the disciples and which disciple in particular? (16:7)
5. Name some times when you, like the disciples, have missed resurrection or renewal experiences in your life.

Jesus Appears to Mary Magdalene and Two Disciples (16:9–13)

Evidently Christ could no longer be recognized in the flesh—only in the spirit. Incredible, isn't it? Mary did as Christ commanded her and got a cold reception.

Parallel passages: Matthew 28:1–10; Luke 24:13–35; John 20:11–18.

1. What did Mary Magdalene do? (16:10)
2. What were the disciples doing? (16:10)
3. How did they react to Mary's news? (16:11)
4. How did the others receive the news of the two disciples? (16:13)
5. How would we have received the news?

The Great Commission and the Ascension (16:14–20)

When Christ finally appeared to all eleven disciples, He gave them the Great Commandment, or the Great Commission.

After the Great Commission, the Lord ascended back to God from the Mount of Olives—the place where we believe He will one day reappear.

Parallel passages: Matthew 28:16–20; Luke 24:50–53.

1. What is the Great Commission? (16:15)
2. After the Ascension, what did the disciples do? (16:20)
3. In our daily lives, how do we live out the Great Commission?

LUKE

APRIL 5
Luke 1:1–25

Introduction (1:1–4)

Many Bible scholars believe that the Book of Luke is the greatest account of Christ's life ever given to humanity.

Luke was a physician, a man of culture. And yet at the end of Paul's life, Luke was with Paul in a stinking dungeon beneath Nero's palace, for Paul wrote, "Only Luke is with me" (2 Tim. 4:11).

The Gospel of Luke was written to an unknown person, probably a high-ranking government official. Luke addresses the Book of Acts to this same man. Although Paul wrote more books in the New Testament, Luke wrote the most copy.

1. To whom did Luke address his gospel? (1:3)
2. What was Luke's intent? (1:4)
3. Have you been instructed in the life and ministry of Jesus Christ? Are you convinced of the "certainty of those things"?

The Birth of John Foretold (1:5–25)

In New Testament times, barrenness was a shameful condition. The rabbis began their list of seven kinds of people who were excommunicated from God with "a Jew who has no wife, or a Jew who has a wife and who has no child."

One of the priest's jobs was to prepare both the morning and evening incense in the temple. On the particular day Luke records, it was Zacharias's turn to burn incense in the innermost court of the temple, the Court of the Priests. The waiting people had no idea that he was having a conversation with an angel!

1. What were the names of the childless man and wife? (1:5)
2. What did the angel announce to Zacharias? (1:13–17)
3. Who was the angel? (1:19)
4. What happened to Zacharias? (1:20)
5. How would we receive a message from God?

APRIL 6
Luke 1:26–38

The Birth of Jesus is Announced (1:26–38)

Bear in mind that this story is given us by divine revelation of the Holy Spirit through the pen of a trained physician. If Amos, the shepherd, had written it, or Peter, a fisherman, you might be skeptical. But a doctor wrote this.

The annunciation takes place in Nazareth. The derisive rhetorical question, "Can anything good come out of Nazareth?" (John 1:46) is not without justification. Nazareth is a squalid city, usually filled with noise, tensions, and unrest. But it was there that the greatest news story in history broke.

It is important to understand the significance of Mary's engagement to Joseph. In those days engagement, or betrothal, was as binding as marriage and could be broken only by a divorce. So when Mary found herself pregnant, never having been to bed with a man, both she and Joseph, her fiance, were faced with a difficult situation.

Doesn't it intrigue you that Jesus was born to Mary, an unknown young woman, who lived in Nazareth—a town Josephus the prolific historian of the day never even mentioned in his list of 204 towns and villages in Galilee? But God does not do things the way we would. Paul told the Corinthians that God used the foolish things of life to confound the wise.

1. Who visited Mary? (1:26–27)
2. From whom was Joseph descended? (1:27)
3. What was Mary's reaction to the salutation? (1:29)
4. How did the pregnancy occur? (1:35)
5. What are some opportunities to find God in some of the ordinary places of life?

APRIL 7
Luke 1:39–80

Mary Visits Elizabeth (1:39–56)

In all probability, Mary's journey carried her through the Jordan Valley, up the back slopes of the Mount of Olives and into Jerusalem by way of a garden called Gethsemane.

Verses 46–55 are called the Magnificat. It is the first New Testament hymn and probably the most beautiful.

Elizabeth and Mary are good examples of Christian kinship and friendship. They brought out the best in each other. They inspired each other to worship, praise, and serve the Lord.

1. What happened when Elizabeth heard Mary's greeting? (1:41)
2. How does Mary's great song begin? (1:46)
3. What will people call Mary? (1:48)
4. What has God done in this one act? (1:51–55)
5. How does our work magnify the Lord?

The Birth of John (1:57–80)

The name of Elizabeth and Zacharias's baby meant "Jehovah's gift" or "God's present."

The Scriptures tell us nothing about what kind of parents Elizabeth and Zacharias were, but they must have been good ones. Their son never hesitated to stand up against society if he felt it was wrong. He had the spirituality that allowed him to recognize the Messiah before anyone else.

Pay particular attention to verse 80. In these days when there are temptations to a child, it is difficult for one to grow spiritually without help.

Verse 76 refers to Malachi 3:1, and verse 79 to Isaiah 9:2.

1. What were the friends and neighbors going to name the baby? (1:59)
2. How did Zacharias signal his son's name? (1:63)
3. What happened at that point? (1:64)
4. How did the neighbors react? (1:65–66)
5. How do we help our children grow spiritually?

APRIL 8
Luke 2:1–20

The Birth of Christ (2:1–17)

Why should Jesus be born in Bethlehem? Eight hundred years before, Micah had made a marvelous prophecy that the Messiah would be born there (see Mic. 5:2).

Caesar Augustus stepped in to cause Christ's birth to take place in Bethlehem. Columnist Jim Bishop wrote about it beautifully:

> In Rome, Caesar Augustus learned that many of his subjects were dishonest. He ruled the known world, but the amount of taxes was not commensurate with the number of subjects. He held a council in Rome, and his advisors told Caesar that he could not levy an equitable tax until he had an accurate idea of the populations of the several provinces.
>
> Caesar issued an imperial rescript ordering all subjects, in the winter solstice, to return to the cities of their fathers and there be counted. This, of course, would work hardship on millions of people, and in a two-week period of migration it would upset the economic balance as men left their work to travel to distant cities. But it had to be done. The census would be taken in many tongues and in places along the Rhine River, the Danube, in North Africa, Portugal, Syria, Belgium, Egypt, Palestine and all along the north Mediterranean shore.

Parallel passage: Matthew 1:25—2:1.

1. When did the census take place? (2:2)
2. Why did Joseph go to Bethlehem? (2:5)
3. Name some times in our own lives when there has been no room for Him in the inn.

The Angels' Revelation to the Shepherds (2:8–20)

It is fascinating that the shepherds were the first to hear the greatest story ever told. If there is one thing the gospel does it is this: It hits snobbishness very hard. Shepherds were lowly wanderers who lived in caverns beneath the soil. Few sought their company because the smell of sheep never left them.

1. How did the shepherds feel when the angels appeared? (2:9)
2. What news did the angels bring? (2:11–12, 14)
3. How did the shepherds react? (2:15)
4. How would you react to such news today?

APRIL 9
Luke 2:21–24

Jesus Is Named and Presented in the Temple (2:21–24)

It was traditional that male children born to Jewish families were taken to the local rabbi for circumcision. We often assume that the circumcision and the appearance of the holy family at the temple in Jerusalem take place on the same day. But those events could not have happened at the same time, because by Jewish law, Mary was ceremonially unclean for forty days following Jesus' birth. During this time, she could not have entered the temple or have been involved in any religious ceremony.

The name of the child is *Jeshua* the Hebrew form of the Greek *Jesus*. It means "God is Savior" or "God saves."

Christ is not a surname. It is the Greek version of the Hebrew *Meshiah*, or *Messiah*. Jesus was Jeshua, the Meshiah, or Jesus, the Christ, during His ministry.

When Mary and Joseph brought Jesus to the temple, they were following the law in Leviticus 12:6–8. Mary obviously could not afford a sacrificial lamb, so she brought the religious sacrifice of the poor. It is helpful for us to remember in these days of crass materialism in religious circles that Jesus was born into a home where there were no luxuries.

1. What ceremony were Joseph and Mary performing? (2:22)
2. What sacrifice did Mary and Joseph offer? (2:24)
3. How do your church's monetary values fit in with the picture presented by the holy family?

Simeon and Anna (2:25–40)

Simeon apparently was one of the few Israelites who truly understood the nature of the coming Messiah. Many of that day, who were known as zealots, believed the Messiah would come as a great military man who would bring Rome to her knees and establish Israel as the champion of the world. It would be, they thought, a modern reconstruction of the golden days of King David.

But there were some men in the land who realized that the Messiah would be quite different from that. These men were not only scholars, but they were men who spent time with God and were taught of the Spirit. These men were known as "the quiet in the land." They did not dream of violence, bloodshed, and conquest. They lived in a state of constant prayer and waiting for God to reveal Himself to men.

Less space is spent on Anna, but one thing we know—she had never given up hope. The sorrow in her life had not made her bitter. Her heart was ready for the Christ, and she recognized Him immediately.

1. What had the Holy Spirit promised Simeon? (2:26)
2. How did Simeon describe Jesus? (2:32)
3. How did Anna show her belief? (2:37)
4. How did Jesus grow? (2:40)
5. How can we apply Anna's faithfulness to our own lives?

APRIL 11
Luke 2:41—3:22

The Boy Jesus in the Temple (2:41–52)

By Jewish law, when a boy reached twelve he was considered a man and was required to attend the Passover in Jerusalem.

Luke's emphasis is on Jesus' early interest in religion. Jesus' life changed after this incident in the temple, as He became increasingly aware of His true identity and unique reason for existence in this world.

1. What happened when Mary and Joseph started back home? (2:43)
2. Where did Jesus' parents find Him? (2:46)
3. How did Jesus explain His actions to His parents? (2:49)
4. At what time, if ever, have you become aware of a specific purpose in your life?

The Preaching of John the Baptist (3:1–22)

Luke clearly pinpoints the time of the beginning of John's public ministry. The Roman emperor Tiberius Caesar was in the fifteenth year of his twenty-three year reign.

John's message was fiery to the point of being brutal to Israel. The Jews truly believed that they were God's favored nation and that fact alone was enough for their salvation. "Not so," John said. We have no record that John had any formal training. He had walked in the wilderness alone with his Creator. He trained long years for a ministry of a few months.

The winnowing fork John spoke of was used to toss grain into the air. Naturally, the heavy grain (the good grain) fell to the ground while the chaff was blown away.

Parallel passages: Matthew 3:1–17; Mark 1:1–11; John 1:19–28.

1. Where did John preach? (3:3)
2. Which Old Testament prophet did John quote? (3:4)
3. What did John say about those who bragged that they were Abraham's descendants? (3:8)
4. When was the last time we, like John, spoke out against an established power?

APRIL 12
Luke 3:23—4:13

Genealogy of Jesus (3:23–38)

We do not know why Jesus waited until age thirty to begin His ministry. Some have surmised that Joseph died at a relatively young age and that Jesus, as the eldest child, needed to support His family.

There is a bigger problem in this chapter. The genealogy that Luke gives us is quite different from the one recorded by Matthew. Matthew began his book with genealogy in the first chapter. He was, of course, writing to Jewish people and wanted to establish immediately that Christ was the Messiah. Luke gives his genealogy in the third chapter in order to write an end to the story of John the Baptist before he begins his story of Christ.

Matthew wrote his genealogy from the viewpoint of descent—in other words, he started with Abraham. Luke, on the other hand, began with Jesus and worked backwards to Adam.

The names given from Abraham to David correspond in Matthew and Luke. But the names from David to Jesus differ. Remember, however, that Matthew traced Jesus' genealogy from David's royal lineage. Luke didn't ponder on the royal figures alone, but gave us the actual descent.

Parallel passage: Matthew 1:1–17.

1. How old was Jesus when He began His ministry? (3:23)
2. Take a look at your beliefs about Christ. Do you truly see Him as Savior of the whole world?

Temptation of Jesus (4:1–13)

Try to picture the brutal, wilderness area of Judea, away from civilization and water. There is a rocky area with something of a central spine running north and south through it. Between that spine and the Dead Sea was a terrible wilderness that one writer called "The Devastation."

Natural appetite, earthly ambition, miracles for miracles' sake—those were Satan's temptations of Jesus.

Parallel passages: Matthew 4:1–11; Mark 1:12–13.

1. How long was Jesus in the wilderness? (4:2)
2. What was the first temptation? (4:3) the second? (4:5–7) the third? (4:9–11)
3. Try to name one time when Jesus used miracles for miracles' sake.

Jesus Begins His Galilean Ministry (4:14–30)

The next six chapters of Luke are dedicated to Jesus' first period of ministry, known as His Galilean ministry.

The word *Galilee* means "a circle" and comes from the Hebrew word *Galil*. The country was so named because it was completely encircled by non-Jewish nations. For Jesus' day it had a very large population. The Jewish historian Josephus recorded that there were 204 villages and towns, none with a population of fewer than 15,000.

Worship in a synagogue consisted of reciting the Shema, a prayer, a set reading from the Law, a chosen reading from the Prophets, an explanation and application of the Scriptural passages, and priest's blessing or a layman's prayer.

Parallel passages: Matthew 4:12–17; 13:53–58; Mark 1:14–15; 6:1–6.

1. From what Old Testament prophet did Jesus read? (4:17)
2. What did Jesus announce after He read the Scripture? (4:21)
3. To whom did Jesus compare His own ministry? (4:23–27)
4. How did the people react? (4:28–29)
5. How did Jesus escape? (4:30)
6. How would we react to such an announcement from a person whom we had known all of our lives?

APRIL 14
Luke 4:31–44

A Demon in the Synagogue (4:31–37)

In this passage, Jesus has moved on to Capernaum, located on the north end of the Sea of Galilee. The distance between the two towns is about twenty miles. Nazareth is still a bustling city while Capernaum is in ruins—an archaeologist's dream.

Parallel passage: Mark 1:21–28.

1. Why were the people in Capernaum amazed? (4:32)
2. What did the evil spirit call Jesus? (4:34)
3. What was the result of the miraculous healing? (4:37)
4. What protects Christians from demon possession?

Jesus Heals and Preaches (4:38–44)

Capernaum was Peter's hometown, and his house was within walking distance of the synagogue where Jesus had healed a demon-possessed man.

Luke 4:39 depicts a true healing of body, mind, and spirit. When Jesus touches our lives, it enables us to serve Him more effectively.

Sunset over the Sea of Galilee is a breathtaking sight. On the eastern side of the lake are the Golan Heights, bluffs that turn pink and purple in the light of the setting sun.

Note that even Jesus needed a time of spiritual refreshing (see v. 42).

Parallel passages: Matthew 8:14–17; Mark 1:29–39.

1. What was wrong with Peter's mother-in-law? (4:38)
2. What did Peter's mother-in-law do after she was healed? (4:39)
3. What did Jesus say that He needed to do? (4:43)
4. What routine have you developed for refreshing yourself spiritually?

APRIL 15
Luke 5:1–26

Fishermen Called As the First Three Disciples (5:1–11)

When Jesus first began ministering in Galilee His miracles and teachings attracted huge crowds. Everywhere He went, there was excitement, but Jesus knew that in order for His work to have lasting value, it needed to be consolidated. So He began enlisting outstanding men whom He could teach and commit to carry on His work.

Jesus personally taught men. He duplicated His vision in those men. In turn these men instilled the same concept in others. They in turn propelled the gospel to all the corners of the world.

The Sea of Galilee was a highly productive area for fishing. Even today, commercial fishing is a good business at Tiberias on the lake.

This passage teaches that the Lord sees the *potential* of the raw material; most of us see only the raw material. So when Christ calls us to a task, we need to remember that He sees our potential.

Parallel passages: Matthew 4:18–22; Mark 1:16–20.

1. What did Jesus order Simon to do? (5:4)
2. What was Peter's response? (5:5)
3. What were the results? (5:6)
4. What did Simon say to Jesus then (5:8) and how did Jesus respond? (5:10)
5. Name some areas in your life where you might not be considering your potential for God's work.

Jesus Heals a Leper and a Paralytic (5:12–26)

In an article about lepers, Dr. A. B. MacDonald says: "For some reason there is an attitude to leprosy different from the attitude toward any other disfiguring disease. It is associated with shame and horror, and carries in some mysterious way a sense of guilt, though innocently acquired." Shunned and despised, the man probably hated himself as much as others hated him. But Jesus touched the untouchable.

Parallel passages: Matthew 8:1–4; Mark 1:40—2:1–12.

1. What did the leper say to Jesus? (5:12)
2. What did Jesus order the man to do? (5:14)
3. How did the man's friends get him to Jesus? (5:19)
4. Whom did Jesus anger? (5:21)
5. What authority did Jesus claim for Himself? (5:24)
6. In what ways do we demonstrate a willingness to respond to others' needs?

The Call of Matthew (5:27-32)

Most of this lesson takes place in the area of Capernaum at the north end of the Sea of Galilee. It begins with the calling of another disciple from a secular job to a holy one—Levi (Matthew) was an "IRS" man, a tax collector for the Romans that ruled Palestine.

We don't know what Matthew's personal record was; it might have been spotless. But tax collectors, for the most part, were considered very unscrupulous men. Think of it—Jesus chose one of that crowd to be His disciple.

How quickly we write people off. What we are saying is really directed at Jesus: "Here's a person You cannot do anything for. Not even Your power can change this life." The truth of the matter is that Christ can change *any* life.

Note that Jesus again raises the ire of the religious leaders.
Parallel passages: Matthew 9:9-13; Mark 2:13-17.

1. How did Levi react to Jesus' call? (5:28)
2. Why did the scribes and Pharisees complain? (5:30)
3. How did Jesus answer those leaders? (5:31-32)
4. Apply Jesus' answer to our churches. How much of our ministry is aimed at those inside rather than those outside?

The Question About Fasting (5:33-39)

In this passage Jesus tells us that any religious custom carried out simply for its own sake is useless. Jesus also warns that His new teachings are not compatible with the old Jewish ceremonies. Note two things: Jesus hinted at His own death, and yet another clash with the Pharisees.
Parallel passages: Matthew 9:14-17; Mark 2:18-22.

1. What was the issue posed to Jesus? (5:33)
2. How did Jesus refer to His fate? (5:33)
3. To what two things does Jesus compare His new teachings? (5:36-37)
4. In applying Jesus' message today, how necessary is it to be aware of current world conditions?

APRIL 17
Luke 6:1–19

Questions Concerning the Sabbath (6:1–11)

In chapter 6, the opposition to Jesus is growing louder and more open. The showbread of which Jesus speaks was baked of very special flour and was reserved for priests. It stayed on the sacred table in the tabernacle and was symbolic of the presence of God.

In the second confrontation, Jesus established a basic law—that it is right to help people on any day. Jesus may be going one step further and saying that *not* to do good is to do evil, or to sin (see Jas. 4:17).

According to Exodus 31:14 and 35:2, the penalty for violating the Sabbath law was death. However, this doesn't seem to have been enforced under Roman rule. At any rate, no such formal charge was ever made against Jesus.

Parallel passages: Matthew 12:1–14; Mark 2:23–3:6.

1. What did the disciples do on the Sabbath? (6:1)
2. Which king of Israel did Jesus cite as an example? (6:3)
3. Whom did Jesus heal on the Sabbath? (6:6, 10)
4. How did the scribes and Pharisees react? (6:11)
5. How does our holy day observance stack up against Jesus' idea of proper observance?

Jesus Chooses the Twelve Apostles, Heals Many (6:12–19)

The first six men chosen by Jesus had been influenced to some degree by John the Baptist. The disciples had twelve very different and very ordinary personalities. Ordinary, but *available* to be used.

Parallel passages: Matthew 4:23–25; 10:1–4; Mark 3:13–19.

1. What did Jesus do before He chose the twelve? (6:12)
2. Which four are listed first? (6:14) Which one last? (6:16)
3. What role does prayer play in our making important decisions?

APRIL 18
Luke 6:20–46

Blessings and Woes (6:20–26)

This section is often called Luke's "Sermon on the Plain" as opposed to Matthew's "Sermon of the Mount." Luke lists only four Beatitudes as opposed to Matthew's eight. Here, as in Matthew, Jesus is talking about spiritual virtues.

Parallel passage: Matthew 5:1–12.

1. What four Beatitudes does Luke list? (6:20–22)
2. In today's world, are these characteristics viewed as natural or unnatural behavior? What makes such behavior an achievable goal for us in our society today?

Love for Enemies and Judging Others (6:27–46)

These are extremely hard verses for the human mind to comprehend. Of course we are to love our friends—those who do good to us. But Jesus said we are to love our enemies as well. And He lived that teaching to its fullest on Calvary when He prayed for those who nailed Him to the tree.

You see, the standard Christ lived and espoused is that of the extra margin, the second mile, the other cheek, the undeserved love. We are not measured by the lives of other people. We are measured by the standard God has set.

In verse 38 Jesus gave us the principle of giving—not just money, but of ourselves. He taught us to be generous people, saying that the result of such living is that others are generous toward us. Getting, however, should not be our motive in giving of ourselves, but the *result.*

Verses 41 and 42 give us an insight into the humor of our Lord. Can you picture a fellow who has a rather large board sticking out of his eye trying diligently to remove a speck out of another person's eye?

In this segment Jesus condemned judgmental attitudes. Often Jesus uses the symbolism of a plant's bearing fruit.

Parallel passages: Matthew 5:39–48; 7:1–5, 14, 16–21; 12:33–35.

1. How should we treat our enemies? (6:27–28)
2. What is the Golden Rule? (6:31)
3. What does Jesus say about lending? (6:34–35)
4. What will happen to the blind leading the blind? (6:39)
5. What is the relationship between the heart and mouth? (6:45)
6. By what standards do we in reality judge others?

APRIL 19
Luke 6:47—7:10

The Two House Builders (6:47–49)

Compare this passage with Matthew's version, which gives a more accurate description of the topography of Palestine. There is a similar parable in rabbinical tradition: "To whom can we compare a man who has studied diligently in the Law and has many good works? To a man who has laid a foundation of stones and built upon them with unbaked bricks. Even if great floods come awash against them, the stones will not be dislodged. And to whom can we compare a man who has studied the Law but has no good works? To a man who has built first with bricks and then with stones. Even a little water will cause the stones to crumble at once" (Aboth R. Nathan 24).

The lesson of this parable is simple. If we want the stability that Christ can give to our lives, then we must simply do what He commands from the beginning.

Parallel passage: Matthew 7:24–27.

1. Where did the first man lay his foundation? (6:48)
2. Where did the second man lay his foundation? (6:49)
3. Think of some times in your life when you have been like the second man.

The Centurion's Servant (7:1–10)

Centurions were remarkable men, commanders of a hundred soldiers in the Roman army. Nowhere in the New Testament are they spoken of negatively. Polybius wrote of these men: "They must not be seekers after danger as men who can command, steady in action and reliable."

What is more remarkable about this particular centurion is his attitude toward his servant—since a Roman's servant or slave was no more than chattel to be disposed of when of no longer use.

There was something else quite unusual about this Roman. He was humble. Jesus can do something for the person who has faith and who shows real humility.

Parallel passage: Matthew 8:5–13.

1. How did the centurion feel about his servant? (7:2)
2. What had the centurion done for the Jewish people? (7:4–5)
3. How did Jesus react to the centurion's attitude? (7:9)
4. What does this healing tell us about our tendency to limit our ministry to certain kinds of people?

APRIL 20
Luke 7:11–35

Jesus Raises a Widow's Son (7:11–17)

This healing is found only in Luke. The scene shifts southwest from Capernaum to the little town of Nain (the current village of Nein in the Jezreel Valley, about six miles south of Nazareth).

1. What did Jesus encounter as He reached the gates of Nain? (7:12)
2. What did Jesus feel? (7:13)
3. What did the people say? (7:16)
4. Are you spreading the message that "God has visited His people"?

The Messengers from John the Baptist (7:18–35)

Now comes a most poignant part of sacred Scripture. It would have been nice to have remembered John the Baptist waist-deep in the Jordan, thundering his great message of repentance in the face of the adulterous Herod. But now he is in prison, in the desert palace of King Herod at Machaerus. Perhaps the darkness of the dungeon got to the prophet.

John was going through a time that we all experience, when he needed reassurance, encouragement, and lifting. Jesus did something that was rare for Him: He gave a brief recital of all the things that He was doing.

"John," Jesus was saying, "despite all the darkness, all the imprisonment, the delay, and the mystery, trust Me."

Maybe John somehow expected something different. If Christ were the Messiah, then where were the armies? Why was He not destroying Rome? But Jesus didn't come to bring revenge, killing, and destruction. He came to bring mercy, healing, life, and love. And apparently Jesus' answer was sufficient for John, for we have no record of his ever asking for Christ's credentials again.

After John the Baptist's disciples had gone away satisfied, Jesus paid tribute to His forerunner. In doing so, He quotes Malachi 3:1.

Parallel passage: Matthew 11:2–19.

1. What question did John's disciples ask of Jesus? (7:20)
2. How did Jesus answer? (7:22–23)
3. Who did Jesus say John was? (7:27)
4. To whom did Jesus compare the people of His time? (7:32)
5. What can we do when, like John, we find ourselves discouraged?

116

Jesus and Simon the Pharisee (7:36–50)

Houses of the wealthier classes were rather uniquely constructed around a courtyard. When the weather permitted, dinner was served in that open area. People in the surrounding neighborhoods were welcome to meet special guests. In that way the uninvited, possibly unwelcome, woman was able to mingle among the guests.

Guests did not sit on chairs such as we Westerners know; rather they reclined on couches by the dinner table. So the woman happened to be at Jesus' feet. Evidently this woman had not won any "outstanding woman of the year" awards. In all likelihood she was a prostitute, an outcast from Simon's society. And she recognized in Jesus the chance to leave her sinful past and start all over.

It was not unusual for a Jewish woman of that day to carry about her neck a small alabaster vial of perfume. Perhaps she wished to anoint Him with her only real possession.

Simon's reaction was what we might have expected—self-righteous indignation. It showed the great difference in his attitude and that of the woman. Simon was proud and arrogant; the woman was broken and contrite.

Jesus then told a beautiful story. Five hundred pence is almost a year's pay; fifty pence is about one month's pay.

Jesus' standard of forgiveness is difficult for us to attain. We have difficulty accepting it for ourselves as well as granting it to others.

1. What did the unnamed woman do to Jesus? (7:38)
2. What did Simon the Pharisee think about Jesus? (7:39)
3. How had the woman treated Jesus better than Simon had? (7:44–46)
4. Why were the woman's sins forgiven? (7:47)
5. What are your standards of forgiveness?

APRIL 22
Luke 8:1–15

Women Minister to Jesus (8:1–3)

In chapter 8, Jesus does the work of a traveling evangelist, going from place to place, doing good. It is a characteristic of Luke's Gospel that the ministries, feelings, and witness of women are carefully recorded. Only Luke among the four gospel writers told us those poignant moments in the lives of Elizabeth (the mother of John the Baptist), Mary, and Anna. Only Luke told us of the sorrow of the widow of Nain, whose son Jesus restored to life. Later in this Gospel, he tells us of the domestic life in the home of Mary and Martha in Bethany. And only Luke tells us of the sorrowing women who lined the streets to Calvary.

It is a mistake to label the Mary in this passage as the woman in the preceding chapter who came to Jesus and whose previous life had been immoral and promiscuous. All we are told about her previous life is that she was possessed by demons and Jesus had liberated her from them. We do not know what the spirits that tormented her were. We know that some in that day who suffered from epilepsy were said to be possessed. Mary of Magdala served her Lord; she is mentioned fourteen times in the New Testament.

1. What three women helped Jesus after being healed? (8:2–3)
2. How would Jesus view woman's role in the church today?

The Parable of the Sower (8:4–15)

At this point in Luke's narrative, we are introduced to the parable of the sower. Jesus used a lot of parables during His ministry. He didn't invent this style of teaching, but He certainly employed it enthusiastically. In his Gospel, Matthew told us that at times it was about the only way Christ used to convey His message (see 13:34).

Jesus then gave the disciples the meaning of His parable. The gist of it is this: The truth, or the seed of God's Word, can be planted in your heart over and over again. But if you are not prepared to take that Word in, the strongest seed in the world cannot grow there.

Parallel passages: Matthew 13:1–23; Mark 4:1–20.

1. On what kinds of ground did the seed fall and what happened to the seed? (8:5–8)
2. What was the purpose of teaching in parables? (8:10)
3. Are the things you are living for worth Christ's dying for?

APRIL 23
Luke 8:16–21

The Parable of the Unhidden Light (8:16–18)

Christ stressed on several occasions that a Christian is to be conspicuous. In His Sermon on the Mount, He said that we were to be the light of the world and the salt of the earth. Both of those things—light and salt—are conspicuous, both by their presence and by their absence.

Verse 17 teaches us that it is impossible to live in secret for very long. Your sins will find you out, and your righteousness will be revealed. The great principle in verse 18 is: You cannot stand still in life; you are either going forward or going backward; you are not the same Christian you were last week; you are either a better one or a worse one.

Parallel passage: Mark 4:21–25.

1. What does one do with a lamp? (8:16)
2. What will happen to those who have and have not? (8:18)
3. What kind of Christian are you this week as compared to last week?

Jesus' Mother and Brothers (8:19–21)

Throughout the Gospels, it appears that Jesus had very little support for His ministry among His relatives. Even though His mother knew Him to be the Messiah, Mary appeared confused by His methods.

Parallel passages: Matthew 12:46–50; Mark 3:31–35.

1. What did Jesus' mother and brothers want? (8:20)
2. Who did Jesus say His family was? (8:21)
3. In what ways do you meet the qualifications for being part of Jesus' family?

APRIL 24
Luke 8:22–39

Jesus Calms the Storm (Luke 8:22–25)

It is important to note that despite the fact that the disciples were in the work of the Lord and were, in fact, within a few feet from the physical presence of the Lord, they encountered a terrific storm. The fact that you are a Christian, that you are the work of the Lord, does not mean that you will never have sorrow, grief, tragedy, disappointment, and depression—all of these things are common to people. The important thing is this: Christ may not save you *from* the storm, but He will save you *in* the storm.

Parallel passages: Matthew 8:18, 23–27; Mark 4:35–41.

1. Where were Jesus and His disciples going? (8:22)
2. What did Jesus do? (8:23)
3. What did Jesus ask His disciples? (8:25)
4. How did the disciples react? (8:25)
5. Think of the last time you felt caught up in one of life's "storms." What role did you let Jesus play?

A Demon-possessed Man Healed (8:26–39)

Whether or not this man was the victim of severe mental illness, we cannot know. There are people today who can no longer control their destinies because they have let sin take over their lives. Jesus' command to the demoniac after the healing is the ultimate witness.

Note that both Mark and Luke refer to the country of the Gadarenes. Matthew speaks of the country of the Gergesenes.

Parallel passages: Matthew 8:28–34; Mark 5:1–20.

1. How had the possessed man lived? (8:27)
2. How did the demoniac react when he saw Jesus? (8:28)
3. What was the demoniac's name? (8:30)
4. Where did Jesus send the evil spirits? (8:32–33)
5. What did the man want to do after Jesus had healed him? (8:38)
6. What did Jesus command? (8:39)
7. What does this passage tell us about different roles in ministry?

A Woman Healed and A Girl Restored to Life (8:40—56)

Like Mark, Luke interweaves these stories and thus heightens their drama, for Jairus was a high-ranking official, while the woman with the hemorrhage apparently had no social standing.

Both Matthew and Luke are more explicit than Mark and record that the woman touched the *hem* or *border* of Jesus' garment. This would have been the fringe, or sacred tassel, tied by a blue thread to each corner of the outer garment, or cloak. The cloak's loose end would have hung over Jesus' left shoulder. The tassel hanging from it could have easily been touched by a person behind Jesus.

Parallel passages: Matthew 9:18–26; Mark 5:21–43.

1. Who was Jairus? (8:41)
2. How did Jesus know that someone had touched Him? (8:46)
3. What happened while Jesus was healing the woman? (8:49)
4. How did Jesus heal the child? (8:54)
5. These stories are accounts of great faith on the part of two very different people. Try to relate your own faith to their kind of faith.

Jesus Sends out the Twelve; John the Baptist Beheaded (9:1–9)

Jesus began expanding His ministry. Writers in most commentaries say that the power was for a special time and dispensation. I don't believe that, for the gifts of the Spirit are still in operation today.

Luke gives a short account of John the Baptist's death.

Parallel passages: Matthew 10:5–15; 14:1–12; Mark 6:7–29.

1. What authority did Jesus give the twelve disciples? (9:1)
2. What were Jesus' special instructions? (9:3–5)
3. Why was Herod confused? (9:7–8)
4. What did Herod want to do? (9:9)
5. What does this passage say about our concern for material things?

The Feeding of the Five Thousand (9:10–17)

The feeding of the five thousand is the only miracle recorded in all four Gospels. It marks the highlight of Jesus' ministry in Galilee. The people would have gladly made Jesus king when He performed this outstanding display of divine multiplication; however, Jesus was not seeing crowns, but a cross, ahead of Him.

Bethsaida is a lovely subtropical spot on the northeast shore of the Sea of Galilee. Just down the road there is a kibbutz, Nof Gonosaur. Since about 1920, the people on that kibbutz have worked hard to develop an extremely productive communal farm. They produce three banana crops a year there, and their fields are spread out for miles. This is the place that Jesus fed the five thousand in such a miraculous manner.

The simple message in this miracle is that with God's incalculable power, we can do more than we think.

Parallel passages: Matthew 14:13–21; Mark 6:30–44; John 6:1–14.

1. What did Jesus do with the crowd? (9:11)
2. What did the disciples want to do about food? (9:12)
3. How did the disciples react to Jesus' command to feed the multitude? (9:13)
4. How did Jesus serve the meal? (9:16)
5. Some believe the gospel addresses spiritual needs only. What does this passage say about ministering to a person's physical needs?

Peter Confesses Jesus as the Christ (9:18–21)

This was a key moment in Jesus' life. He was ending His Galilean ministry and heading for Jerusalem, where He would be crucified. He may have wondered if, after all the miracles and excitement, anyone had really heard what He had to say . . . if anyone truly knew who He was. It must have thrilled His heart to hear Peter's response.

I think the key phrase in this segment is the verse, "But who do you say that I am?" (Luke 9:20). It is not enough to know *what* others say about Christ or even to know about Him historically and academically. Paul said, "I know whom [not *what*] I have believed (2 Tim. 1:12).

Parallel passages: Matthew 16:13–19; Mark 8:27–29.

1. What was Jesus' first question? (9:18)
2. How did the disciples answer Jesus? (9:19)
3. What was Jesus' second question? (9:20)
4. Who answered and how? (9:20)
5. Who is Jesus to you personally?

Jesus Foretells His Death (9:22–27)

Jesus has just done miracle after miracle. Now He teaches of His coming death and resurrection, of the principles of the kingdom, and of the life priorities He expects from His followers.

These verses are not overly popular in our day. We don't hear a lot of discussion, especially in the media, about taking up our crosses and following the Lord.

Jesus said that we must be ready to endure anything for His sake. A cross was not a pleasant thing; yet, today, we have made the cross something beautiful—a golden ornament on a carefully crafted necklace. But let's face it: The cross was a rugged tool of torture and death.

Parallel passages: Matthew 16:24–28; Mark 8:30—9:1.

1. What did Jesus predict about His future? (9:22)
2. What are the demands upon those who wish to follow Jesus? (9:23)
3. What will happen to the person who is ashamed of Jesus and His words? (9:26)
4. In verse 25, Jesus speaks of priorities. What are the priorities in your life?

The Transfiguration and a Child's Healing (9:28—43)

We do not know just which mountain was the site of this event. Some believe that it was Mount Tabor, located a few miles to the east of Nazareth. It is a funny-looking mountain, rounded at the top. Though it doesn't look it, it is very steep and rugged. Others believe the site to be Mount Hermon, located in southern Lebanon, north of the Sea of Galilee. A majestic peak, it is well over nine thousand feet high. The location is not nearly as important as the happening itself.

Coming down from the mountain, Jesus and the three disciples were immediately confronted by human need. Jesus probably is not limiting His comments in verse 41 to His disciples.

Parallel passages: Matthew 17:1–8; 14–19; Mark 9:2–8; 14–28.

1. What three disciples accompanied Jesus? (9:28)
2. How did Jesus' appearance change? (9:29)
3. Who appeared with Jesus? What did the three talk about? (9:30–31)
4. What did Peter want to do? (9:33)
5. From where did the voice come and what did it say? (9:35)
6. While Jesus was on the mountain, what had the other disciples attempted? (9:38—40)
7. What was Jesus' reaction? (9:41)
8. How the Transfiguration happened is a mystery. What should its central message be for us today?

APRIL 29
Luke 9:44—48

Jesus Again Predicts His Death
and Settles a Dispute Among His Disciples (9:44—48)

Jesus is now coming to the end of His Galilean ministry and He is preparing the disciples for His death in Jerusalem, an event they are not ready to accept.

They did not want to hear this second prediction. Where were the crowds? Where were the miracles? Where was the excitement? Barclay put it like this: "... in that very moment when they were ready to acclaim Him, Jesus told them He was on the way to die. It would have been so easy to take the way of popular success; it was because of Jesus' greatness that He rejected it and chose the Cross. He would not Himself shirk that Cross to which He called others."

While Christ was calling the disciples to this commitment with Him, they were arguing among themselves about their future when Christ would overturn mighty Rome and establish Himself on the throne. They had totally missed the whole perspective of Jesus' ministry.

This argument might have started when the nine disciples who didn't get to go to the Mount of Transfiguration began harping about it. "Why did Jesus take you fellows and not take us? We are as good as you are." The rejoinder: "Well, if you were so hot, why didn't He take you? We are the ones who are going to be in charge when Christ takes over the world."

And on and on the argument went. Of course, you and I are more sophisticated than that, aren't we? We surely wouldn't get involved in anything like that—nothing so childish or trivial.

Jesus knew the thoughts of the disciples and He ended the discussion with a marvelous object lesson in which He deals with motivation.

Parallel passages: Matthew 17:22—23; 18:1—5; Mark 9:30—37.

1. What did Jesus tell His disciples? (9:44)
2. How did the disciples receive Jesus' words? (9:45)
3. What were the disciples arguing about? (9:46)
4. What example did Jesus give His disciples? (9:47—48)
5. What motivates you to serve the Lord?

125

APRIL 30
Luke 9:49–62

Whoever Is Not Against You Is for You and a Samaritan Village Refuses to Receive Jesus (9:49–56)

Racial and religious intolerance rear their heads in these two passages.

In the first two verses, the disciples felt the intruding fellow was not of their "church" or "denomination," so obviously he could not be used of God.

The next six verses focus on the hard feelings between Jews and Samaritans, which had lasted centuries. Samaritans did everything they could to intimidate travelers going through their area—one of the reasons the story of the good Samaritan is so remarkable. That fellow stopped to help a Jericho citizen even though the two nationalities were supposed to hate each other.

"Another village" (v. 56) may refer to another Samaritan village or it may mean that Jesus and His disciples returned to the Galilean route.

Parallel passage: Mark 9:38–40.

1. Whom did the disciples see? (9:49)
2. What did Jesus tell His disciples? (9:50)
3. Where did Jesus decide to go? (9:51)
4. Why did the people in Samaria refuse to receive Jesus? (9:53)
5. What did the disciples want to do? (9:54)
6. Can you think of a time when a squabble in your church or denomination has kept that church or denomination from making an effective witness?

Cost of Discipleship (9:57–62)

This passage tells us that there is no room for looking backward in the Christian walk. It is impossible to maintain a lukewarm attitude toward the demands of God's kingdom. You are either gung ho in it, or you are out of it. Serving Christ with all your heart, with all your mind, and with all your strength is life's ultimate joy. "The dead" (v. 60) refers to the spiritually dead.

Parallel passage: Matthew 8:19–22.

1. What condition did Jesus give to the first man who wanted to follow Him? (9:58)
2. What did the second man want to do? (9:59) the third man? (9:61)
3. What is your attitude toward the work of God's kingdom?

MAY 1
Luke 10:1–24

The Mission of the Seventy (10:1–12)

There are a number of incidents in Jesus' life that only Luke records. As we mentioned before, Luke gave us more details of the women whom Jesus touched than any other gospel writer. He also gives us more description of Jesus' sojourn to Jerusalem, where He was killed and offered for the sins of man. This is another of those special Lukan passages.

Jesus' warning the cities of their doom if they reject His message leaves nothing to the imagination. Sodom was utterly destroyed. It is a solemn thing to be trivial about the call of God upon your life.

Parallel passage: Matthew 9:37.

1. How and where did Jesus send the men? (10:1)
2. To what does Jesus compare His missionaries? (10:3)
3. How should the missionaries greet people? (10:5)
4. What should the missionaries do in a town where they are not welcome? (10:10–11)
5. What unnecessary things encumber your ministry?

The Unbelieving Towns and the Return of the Seventy (10:13–24)

Something dreadful must have happened at Chorazin, but the Gospels contain no record of it. We have only a portion of what Jesus did during His ministry (see John 21:25). Again, Jesus strikes at those who should have accepted Him as opposed to those who would not have been prepared for Him, yet would probably have been more receptive.

Jesus rejoiced at the return of the seventy, but He cautions them (see v. 20). Jesus made quite a claim in the last two verses. In effect, He was saying "I am the pivot of all history. I am the One to whom all the prophets and the saints and the kings looked forward and for whom they longed."

Parallel passages: Matthew 11:20–27; 13:16–17.

1. What would have happened if the miracles had been performed in Tyre and Sidon? (10:13)
2. To whom will God show more mercy? (10:14)
3. What did Jesus see upon the return of the seventy? (10:18)
4. What warning did Jesus give the seventy? (10:20)
5. For what did Jesus thank God? (10:21)
6. Is Christ your zenith? How much could you lose of your material substance and still keep your faith?

MAY 2
Luke 10:25–37

The Good Samaritan (10:25–37)

This parable itself is found only in Luke, but the question it is meant to answer is found in both Matthew (18:18–30) and Mark (10:17–31).

There are two kinds of parables. One teaches by analogy; the other teaches by direct example. The latter says, "This is what you should imitate (or avoid)." Only Luke preserves these example parables, of which the Good Samaritan is one. Others are the parables of the rich fool, the rich man and Lazarus, and the Pharisee and the tax collector.

What a road the Jericho road is! Jerusalem is situated atop a mountain at above twenty-three hundred feet above sea level, while Jericho is nearly thirteen hundred feet below sea level. So in the almost eighteen miles between Jerusalem and Jericho the road drops thirty-six hundred feet. The old road was one of many curves and bends. Josephus in the first century described the road as "desolate and rocky." And even in the late fourth century Jerome called it "The Bloody Way" because of the thieves and cutthroats who picked off unwary travelers.

A denarius (about twenty cents in silver) was considered a full day's wage, according to Matthew 20:2. Thus, two denarii would probably have been considered several days' compensation.

1. What question did the lawyer ask Jesus? (10:25)
2. What question did Jesus' answer prompt? (10:29)
3. Who passed by the traveler? (10:31–32)
4. What did Jesus command? (10:37)
5. In our own lives, who is really our neighbor, according to our own actions?

MAY 3
Luke 10:38—11:13

Mary and Martha (10:38—42)

This is another of those passages that appear only in Luke, who gives us a delightful character study of Mary and Martha.

Martha has often been given a hard time because of this passage, but Jesus' message was gentle. Martha was a hard worker, and that was commendable. But on that night, Martha had her priorities confused. How much more important it was to hear Jesus' words than to serve Him a full-course meal.

1. Who welcomed Jesus to her home? (10:38)
2. Why was this woman upset? (10:40)
3. What did Jesus answer? (10:41—42)
4. How do we temper the busyness of our service with the time we need for spiritual renewal—for sitting at Jesus' feet and listening to His words?

Jesus' Teaching on Prayer (11:1—13)

Often referred to as the Good Example, Jesus set an example for us in the area of prayer. His prayer, not meant to be the only prayer we ever pray, covers our needs, though not necessarily our desires. Matthew includes this prayer in his Sermon on the Mount.

Jesus follows His example prayer with a parable. It is important to remember that a parable is intended to convey only one truth. This parable teaches us that persistence in prayer is important. Note that verses 11—13 are the grounds for Jesus' assurance that prayers will be answered. Jesus does not here explore what a proper prayer is, but in His example He emphasizes God's will as opposed to a petitioner's will.

Parallel passages: Matthew 6:9—13; 7:7—11.

1. What did one of the disciples request of Jesus? (11:1)
2. What answer did Jesus give? (11:2—4)
3. What did the friend ask for in the parable? (11:5)
4. Why was his request finally answered? (11:8)
5. Why does Jesus say prayers will be answered? (11:13)
6. Prayer takes our unfinished business to God. What have you taken to God this day?

MAY 4
Luke 11:14–26

A House Divided Cannot Stand (11:14–23)

There were quite a few people in Palestine who reportedly could cast out demons. The historian Josephus reports that Solomon was particularly known for his ability to do so, and his methods of exorcism were commonly accepted even in Jesus' day (note v. 19). Jesus shrewdly turned the question about His ability to cast out demons back to His questioners. He then followed this logic with an unanswerable argument.

Parallel passages: Matthew 12:22–30; Mark 3:20–27.

1. What miracle did Jesus perform to cause some to test Him? (11:14)
2. What did some charge Him with? (11:15)
3. What often quoted verse sums up Jesus' answer? (11:17)
4. With what warning does Jesus close? (11:23)
5. What are some things that cause divisions in our own houses (our souls, our churches)?

Return of the Unclean Spirit (11:24–26)

This is one of Jesus' most chilling teachings. You rarely read much about it. The sin of unbelief is probably the most treacherous sin of all, for it opens our heart to every evil spirit.

Parallel passage: Matthew 12:43–45.

1. What happens when an unclean spirit leaves? (11:24) When it returns? (11:26)
2. What are some ways to make certain that your soul is always a believing one—that you are not caught unaware?

MAY 5
Luke 11:27–54

True Blessedness and the Light of the Body (11:27–36)

It is important to note that Jesus did not rebuke the woman in the crowd for her action. While we Protestants do not venerate Mary as Roman Catholics do, it is possible that we do Jesus' mother somewhat of a disservice by not giving her the credit due her.

The very fact that the crowds demanded signs nettled Jesus. His teachings, His life, should have been sufficient. Christ Himself is the only sign that we need.

The last four verses concern our spiritual insight, our ability to comprehend spiritual truths. As a lamp is used to light a house, as the eye was designed by God to give illumination to the body, so the soul is intended to give spiritual insight. But we allow that delightful creation to be marred by sin and unbelief. We don't have the vision we should have. Not because we do not receive signs and wonders, but because our ability to comprehend them has been dulled.

Parallel passages: Matthew 5:15; 12:38–42; 6:22–23.

1. What did the woman in the crowd say? (11:27)
2. For what were the people asking? (11:29)
3. Who will judge the people on Judgment Day? (11:31–32)
4. What is the lamp of the body? (11:34)
5. What warning did Jesus give? (11:35)
6. What steps are we taking to be certain that we do not become spiritually blind?

Woe to the Pharisees and Lawyers (11:37–54)

For an explanation of the Pharisaic rules about handwashing, see the introduction to Mark 7:1–23. Remember, the Pharisees were legalists, majoring in externals.

These people made Jesus furious, and He had harsh words for them. His words for these hypocrites were far harsher than any words He spoke against prostitutes, drunkards, even the thief on the cross.

Parallel passages: Matthew 23:4, 6–7, 23–26, 13; Mark 12:38–40.

1. What was the Pharisee upset about? (11:38)
2. What are the three "woes" to the Pharisees? (11:42–44)
3. What are the three "woes" to the lawyers? (11:46–47, 52)
4. What was the result of this encounter? (11:54)
5. In what ways are our inner selves different from that self which we show the world?

131

MAY 6
Luke 12:1–21

A Warning Against Hypocrisy; the Fear of God (12:1–12)

This passage continues along the same line as the condemnation of the Pharisees in the previous passage. Leaven is a substance used to produce fermentation in dough or liquid. The fermentation of the Pharisees was, of course, hypocrisy.

Jesus takes time in this passage to assure His followers that God will protect them.

Sparrows were among the cheapest food items on the market; seven cents was set as the maximum price for ten sparrows by an edict of the emperor Diocletian in the third century A.D.

Parallel passages: Matthew 10:26–33; 12:32; 10:19–20.

1. What will happen to things covered and hidden? (12:2–3)
2. Whom should people fear? (12:5)
3. Even what was not forgotten by God? (12:6)
4. What will be the role of the Holy Spirit? (12:12)
5. In what ways do we confess Jesus and God before others?

The Parable of the Rich Fool (12:13–21)

This is another of Luke's example parables (see the parable of the good Samaritan) and, therefore, has no parallel in the other Gospels. The obvious moral of this story is that life built on an accumulation of material things is folly.

We must be careful in the study of this story not to condemn money. Money itself represents only the exchange of values known to people. We could not operate on an honest, workable basis without it. It is the undue love of money and its acquisition that the Bible condemns, especially when it prevents our love of God.

1. What did the man from the crowd request? (12:13)
2. What did Jesus warn against? (12:15)
3. What did the rich man say to his soul? (12:19)
4. How can we use our goods to bless other lives?

MAY 7
Luke 12:22–48

Care and Anxiety (12:22–34)

In this passage, Jesus deals with worry—a most relevant subject in today's society. Jesus is simply saying that God who provided life will provide food, and that God who made a body can certainly take care of clothing that body. We could wrap this up by saying that God expects us to do the very best that we can—and then leave the rest up to Him.

God has created a planet capable of meeting the physical needs of all its inhabitants. The fact that it does not, is a sign that this is a passing age, that God's kingdom has not come, and that our worldly conditions are not in tune with God's will.

Parallel passages: Matthew 6:25–34, 19–21.

1. What does Jesus say not to worry about? (12:22)
2. What bird does He mention? (12:24) what flower? (12:27)
3. What should we seek? (12:31)
4. Where is your heart? (12:34)
5. Put the things that you are anxious about in perspective with this teaching.

Watchful Servants (12:35–48)

In this parable, Jesus warns us to be prepared for His coming. Men wore then, and still do now, long flowing robes which made working a bit difficult. So when the man got ready to pitch into the task, he gathered up his robes under his belt. That meant he was ready for work.

The lamp was a simple wick that floated in a small bowl of olive oil. The wick needed to be kept trimmed or the light would go out.

The second watch was from 10:00 P.M. to 2:00 A.M. and the third watch from 2:00 A.M. to 6:00 A.M. (see v. 38).

Parallel passage: Matthew 24:43–51.

1. What two things must a person do to be ready? (12:35)
2. What does Jesus say concerning the thief, and how does He apply it? (12:39–40)
3. Recall the recent events in your life. Are you more like the servant in verses 37 and 42 or the servant in verse 45?

MAY 8
Luke 12:49–59

Christ Brings Division; Discern the Time (12:49–59)

The first four verses are unsettling to us as we read them in the twentieth century; we can only imagine how they must have devastated the disciples and other hearers in Jesus' time. Most of them believed that Christ was the Messiah. Their concept was that the Messiah would usher in the golden age of peace and plenty. So our Lord's words were most unsettling.

The people didn't want to hear what Jesus had to say; they wanted to hear about a crown, a scepter, a throne. They wanted to see Christ acclaimed as King and destroy the accursed Romans. But Jesus said it would be the other way around.

People living in Israel are pretty good amateur weather forecasters in a country where the weather can change very rapidly. "If you can forecast the weather," Jesus said, "why can you not predict that the kingdom of God is coming?" A western cloud would be moisture-laden from the Mediterranean; a southerly wind would be blowing in from the desert.

What Jesus was saying in verses 57–59 from a spiritual sense was this: No one has a good case with God in himself. We are all condemned sinners—a point which the Book of Romans makes very clear. Since the kingdom of God is coming, it is in every person's own best interest to get a settlement with God, and the only way to do that is through Jesus Christ.

Parallel passages: Matthew 10:34–36; 5:23–26.

1. Why did Jesus come? (12:49–51)
2. What happened when a cloud came up from the west? (12:54) when a wind blew from the south? (12:55)
3. What did Jesus call the people? (12:56)
4. Why did Jesus say you should settle things for yourself? (12:58–59)
5. How perceptive are you? Are you able to "discern this time"?

MAY 9
Luke 13:1–9

Repent or Perish (13:1–5)

In this segment, Jesus gave us some very sound teaching on the subject of sin and suffering. He said they were not necessarily connected, and gave two incidents from history.

Pilate, who was the Roman governor of the province, decided that the Jerusalem water system needed a major overhaul. Pilate met resistance when he decreed that temple taxes would be used to pay for the new system. The Jews revolted; and, as a result, many of them lost their lives at the hands of the soldiers.

There is a school of teaching that would indicate to you that any suffering you may be going through is because of sin in your life. Jesus negates that idea here. It is unquestionably true that sin will bring about suffering but the fact that a person is going through a difficult time does not necessarily mean that there is sin in his life.

Then Jesus recalled the incident of the tower of Siloam falling and killing eighteen persons. The tower was part of the fortification of Jerusalem near a vital spring and reservoir.

1. What were the Galileans doing when they were killed? (13:1)
2. What will happen if a person does not turn from his sins? (13:3,5)
3. Try to determine the cost of sin in your own life.

Parable of the Fig Tree (13:6–9)

The gist of this parable was this: If a tree doesn't bear fruit, it is useless.

Christ expects the same from every believer. He expects a return on His investment in us.

Consider how much God has put into you. First of all He created you, the product of the creative genius of almighty God.

Second, Christ redeemed you. God gave the best He had for your redemption.

Third, God has given the Holy Spirit to indwell you and continue the creative processes. Creation, redemption, the Spirit of God—all gifts to you from God. To whom much is given, much is required (see Luke 12:48).

1. How long had the man had the fig tree? (13:7)
2. What did the owner want to do with the tree? (13:7)
3. What was the gardener's request? (13:8–9)
4. In what ways have you "borne fruit" lately?

A Spirit of Infirmity (13:10–17)

This is the last time we know of Jesus' being in a synagogue. Now He is teaching on the Sabbath. There was a woman in the congregation who had been disabled for many years. She may have had some kind of arthritic condition. Jesus saw her and was moved with compassion. Of course, He healed her.

1. How long had the woman been ill? (13:11)
2. How did the ruler of the synagogue react? (13:14)
3. What did Jesus call the woman? (13:16)
4. How often do we let our busyness stand in the way of helping others?

The Parables of the Mustard Seed and of the Yeast (13:18–21)

Mustard seeds are not very large, but in the Middle East they grow into rather large field plants, almost qualifying as trees.

In Jesus' day, most bread was baked in individual homes. The leaven was a small piece of dough that had been left over from the previous baking and had fermented.

Parallel passage: Matthew 13:31–33; Mark 4:30–32.

1. To what does Jesus compare the mustard seed and the yeast? (13:18,20)
2. What happens to the mustard seed? (13:19) to the yeast? (13:21)
3. These parables speak of phenomenal growth in God's kingdom. Do you see evidence of such growth today?

The Narrow Gate and the Lament over Jerusalem (13:22–35)

Our Lord has now approached Jerusalem, coming in from the eastern side, the Mount of Olives. Jesus looked over the great city and lamented it. Being the Son of God, He knew that in just forty years, the armies of Rome would be standing where He was standing. It didn't have to be that way. Had the nation turned to God and the Messiah, all could have been spared. But they didn't, and Jesus was moved with compassion and sadness.

Parallel passages: Matthew 7:13–14; 25:10–12; 7:22–23; 8:11–12; 19:30; 20:16.

1. What did the Pharisees tell Jesus? (13:31)
2. What did Jesus call Herod? (13:32)
3. With what did Jesus charge Jerusalem? (13:34)
4. How do you feel about your own nation in these times?

Healing on the Sabbath and Taking the Lowly Place (14:1–14)

Christ must have been a most versatile man because Luke notes the way He was comfortable with every kind of people. In this chapter He is enjoying a Sabbath feast in the house of a Pharisee. He must have been the center of attraction. But even in that time of rest and relaxation, Christ never forgot the reason for his being, for His ministry.

Jesus also uses this dinner as an occasion to talk about humility's place in the kingdom. He mentioned classes of uninvited guests (v. 13). Verses 8–10 are an expansion of Proverbs 25:6–7.

1. What did Jesus ask the Pharisees? (14:3)
2. When the Pharisees did not answer, what else did Jesus ask? (14:5)
3. How would Jesus feel about our Sunday observance?

Parable of the Great Supper (14:15–24)

In these verses, our Lord eloquently stated the folly of rejecting His salvation. A person can take no more foolish action. Those seated around Christ at this table were not truly His friends and Jesus, of course, knew that.

In the Middle East it is still the custom to summon those guests previously invited (see vv. 16–17). If there is still room at the table, the host tells the servant to go back out to the roads and byways and get others to come in. When the table is filled, there is a great feast.

The guests made feeble excuses, as people are still doing when invited to become a part of the kingdom of God. But none of those excuses was in itself a sinful thing. The indifference behind those excuses was the sin, a scourge in the work of God. It creeps in unaware. You must stay on top of it at all times.

Parallel passage: Matthew 22:1–10.

1. What was the response of one of those at the table with Jesus? (14:15)
2. What was the first guest's excuse? (14:18) the second guest's? (14:19) the third guest's? (14:20)
3. Who were the first replacements invited? (14:21) the second? (14:23)
4. With what things are you likely to become so preoccupied that you become indifferent to God's work?

The Cost of Discipleship and Tasteless Salt (14:25—35)

The New King James Bible uses this heading before these Scriptures: "Leaving All to Follow Christ." That's a radical doctrine in these days. There are those who would say you don't have to change a hair when you are saved. But that's not a biblical doctrine. Conversion is an about-face, an abrupt change in our lives—a total transformation by Christ.

Christ tells us that salt is no good if it has lost its flavor. We Christians are to be the flavor of the world—we are to be the ones who make it palatable.

Parallel passage: Matthew 10:37–38.

1. What is one of the costs of discipleship? (14:26)
2. What must a person do to become a disciple? (14:27)
3. What does Jesus warn his followers to do in the parables of the tower builder and the king preparing for battle? (14:28–32)
4. What has discipleship cost you?

Parables of the Lost Sheep and of the Lost Coin (15:1—10)

These two parables emphasize the importance of each individual. People are lost for any number of reasons. Regardless of the reason, they still need Christ. We must search for them until we find them and bring them to the Lord.

A flock of one hundred sheep would be considered a large flock.

Ten silver coins, or the Greek drachma (a coin roughly equivalent to the Roman denarius) was worth about sixteen cents in silver but actually had a much greater purchasing power.

Parallel passage: Matthew 18:12–14.

1. Why were the Pharisees and scribes murmuring? (15:2)
2. What does the man who has found his lost sheep do? (15:5–6)
3. What brings more joy in heaven? (15:7)
4. What did the woman who lost her one piece of silver do? (15:8)
5. What methods does your church use to bring people to Christ?

MAY 13
Luke 15:11–32

The Prodigal Son (15:11–32)

Under Jewish law, a man with two sons must leave his older son two-thirds of his estate and the younger son one-third.

The first section of the parable (vv. 11–24) deals with the joy God experiences upon welcoming the repentant sinner—much the same lesson as is found in the two previous parables.

A proverb from the Talmud says, "Cursed is the man who tends swine, and the man who teaches his son Greek wisdom!" So the younger son had sunk as low as he could go. Remember that swine were considered unclean animals under Jewish food laws.

Pods of the carob tree were fed to domestic animals, but people ate them only under the worst of conditions.

The hero of this story is really the father. There was nothing vindictive about him, nothing that demanded that his son come home on bended knee. He is really a graphic portrayal of our Heavenly Father.

The second section of the parable (vv. 25–32) rebukes those who criticize the saving of lost souls. The elder son may represent Pharasaism or Jewish Christianity in the early church. The elder son was bitter.

Bitterness—perhaps no other emotion so cripples a person. Anger usually isn't sustained for a long period of time, but bitterness seems to increase. It never really hurts the person at whom it is directed; it merely poisons the system of the bitter one.

1. What did the younger son do with his property? (15:13)
2. Why did the son end up with nothing? (15:14)
3. What kind of work did he do? (15:15)
4. How did his father react when he saw his son coming? (15:20)
5. How did he honor the returning son? (15:22–24)
6. How did the older brother react? (15:28)
7. How does your congregation show that all people are truly welcome?

MAY 14
Luke 16:1–18

Parable of the Dishonest Steward (16:1–13)

The main thought in this parable is that we are stewards of the funds God gives us. Those monies are not ours.

Jesus taught us a principle of money: It is sinful to consume more than we produce, to spend more than we make. There is value in saving and in using the portion after the tithe to help lift the burdens of others.

Verses 1–7 make it sound as if the Lord is condoning dishonesty. But remember the intent of a parable is to illustrate one truth. You get into trouble when you try to reconcile all the parts. Jesus draws some interesting conclusions from the parable in verses 9–13.

1. If children of God worked as hard at achieving righteousness as the children of Satan work at getting material goods, we could be much better off. We spend much more time and effort on our work, our jobs, our hobbies, and our own enjoyment than we do in the pursuit of God.

2. Our material possessions should be used as much as possible to effect friendships and interpersonal relationships.

3. The third lesson Jesus gave us here was that we need to learn that we are not really owners of possessions, but stewards. Everything in the world belongs to God. We are only the caretakers.

1. Of what was the steward accused? (16:1)
2. How did the steward solve his problem? (16:6–8)
3. What does Jesus say about serving both God and mammon? (16:13)
4. The first 10 percent of your income belongs to God. How do you spend the other 90 percent of your income?

The Law, the Prophets, and the Kingdom (16:14–18)

These are scattered sayings that have little relationship with each other.

Parallel passage: Matthew 11:12–13, 18, 32.

1. How did the Pharisees react to the sayings of Jesus concerning money? (16:14)
2. What is an abomination in God's sight? (16:15)
3. When did the kingdom of God begin to be preached? (16:16)
4. Who commits adultery? (16:18)
5. Reread verse 15. What things do you highly esteem in your life? Would they be considered abominations by God?

The Rich Man and Lazarus (16:19–31)

This is one of Luke's example parables—a parable that tells us some action to emulate or avoid—and appears only in Luke. In this parable Christ taught forcefully against the sin of covetousness. And the Pharisees ridiculed Jesus. They hoarded their money, using it improperly and at the expense of those who were truly in need. In this parable Jesus tells us that there will be a reversal of values in the kingdom of God.

This parable is unique in the Gospels because of its description of life after death—a pre-Resurrection life after death. All afterlife was in Hades, one part of which resembled Gehenna, the final place of fiery torment for the wicked. The other part resembled paradise, the final dwelling place of the righteous.

The rich man is often called Dives, the Latin word for *rich.*

1. How did the rich man live? (16:19)
2. How did the beggar live? (16:20–21)
3. In whose bosom did Lazarus rest? (16:22)
4. What did the rich man request of Lazarus? (16:24)
5. Was there a way to pass from one side of Hades to another? (16:26)
6. Most of us are better off than Lazarus, but we're probably not as well-to-do as the rich man. How are we using what we have?

Causing to Sin (17:1–4)

These four short verses contain two important lessons. The first one is a warning to anyone who would lead another into willful sin. The second lesson is on the necessity of forgiveness. The Jews taught that if you forgave someone for something three times you had really exhausted all necessary forgiveness. But in another passage Jesus said that was not so. We are to forgive more times than we will actually have time to forgive.

Parallel passages: Matthew 18:6–7, 15, 21–22; Mark 9:42.

1. What would be better for a person than to cause one to fall into sin? (17:2)
2. How often should we forgive? (17:4)
3. Think of the relationships in your life. How forgiving have you been in those relationships?

Faith and Duty (17:5–10)

Jesus in these verses teaches that even a small amount of faith can accomplish a great deal. Tied very much to this teaching is James' teaching in his Epistle (see 2:17) that faith without works is dead. Unless we do something with our faith, nothing will ever get done. We are the hands and feet of God on this earth.

In verses 7–10, Jesus taught the solemn lesson that we can never put God into debt. When we are faithful followers, we are doing only what is expected of us—no more.

Parallel passage: Matthew 17:20.

1. What did the apostles ask of Jesus? (17:5)
2. How much faith is necessary to accomplish a great deal? (17:6)
3. Does a servant earn extra favors for doing his job? (17:9)
4. What does Jesus' story about the servant say to those who may feel self-righteous about their good deeds?

Ten Lepers Cleansed (17:11–19)

Probably more than any ancient disease, leprosy was viewed as a curse and, because it was not understood, was greatly feared. Lepers had to stay away from healthy people, keeping a distance of at least fifty yards. This story shows how easy it is for us to *ask* for something and also how easy it is to forget to be grateful. The passage also deals somewhat with prejudice—only the Samaritan leper thanked Jesus.

1. Where was Jesus traveling? (17:11)
2. Whom did He meet? (17:12)
3. Which of the men thanked Jesus? (17:16)
4. When was the last time you thanked God for your blessings?

MAY 17
Luke 17:20—18:8

The Coming of the Kingdom (17:20–37)

This passage demonstrates the preoccupation among Jewish apocalyptic writers with looking for signs of the end time.

Although much of this material is found also in Matthew, verse 22 is found only in Luke. Christ predicts that the early Christians would be discouraged because the Second Coming had not taken place. Jesus says His coming will be unmistakable.

This Lukan passage includes Jesus' prediction about His own death and resurrection.

For the reference to Lot's wife in verse 32, see Genesis 19:26.

Parallel passage: Matthew 24:23–28, 37–41.

1. Who asked Jesus about the kingdom's coming? (17:20)
2. What does Jesus say about the disciples' expectations concerning the coming? (17:22)
3. How will Christians know when Jesus has come again? (17:24)
4. What must happen first? (17:25)
5. To what two events in the Old Testament does Jesus compare His coming? (17:26,28)
6. What do verses 20 and 21 say to you about how you should occupy yourself while waiting for the kingdom of God to come in its fullness?

The Parable of the Persistent Widow (18:1–8)

The judge in question here was a hired magistrate, paid by Herod or the Romans. These judges were a notorious lot. You could get all the justice from them you could afford.

The widow in question was poor. She could not have hired an attorney or paid a bribe if her life had depended upon it. But she had one weapon that got her through—her persistence. She wouldn't let the judge off the hook. Her persistence paid off.

Christ was teaching a principle of prayer here. James wrote that effectual, *fervent* prayer avails much. The word, *fervent*, is a key one here. It is not a simple prayer, recited quickly, but it is the continuing heartfelt cry of the supplicant.

Christ poses a mournful question at the end of this story.

1. What was the point of this parable? (18:1)
2. What did the widow request of the judge? (18:3)
3. How persistent are you in your prayers?

The Parable of the Pharisee and the Tax Collector (18:9–14)

What a difference in the prayers of those two men. One was a prayer of pride and arrogance; the other one of humility.

The Pharisee wasn't praying to God at all. He was praying to himself and those standing nearby. It was prayer for show; nothing more. There is a lot of that even in our day.

Here are some principles from this story: (1) you cannot pray when you have pride; (2) you cannot pray when you despise another person; (3) it is not your life of holiness, but God's holiness that makes it possible to pray at all.

1. How did the Pharisee pray? (18:11–12)
2. How did the tax collector pray? (18:13)
3. How do you pray?

Jesus Blesses the Children (18:15–17)

It was the custom of mothers in those days to bring their babies to a rabbi when they had reached their first birthday in order to receive a blessing. The disciples stopped the mothers from bringing babies to Jesus. Perhaps they knew the tension in Christ.

God wants parents to bring their children to Christ. The act of dedication is very important, both to the parents and to the child. Dedication does not save the child, but it sets priorities right.

Parallel passages: Matthew 19:13–15; Mark 10:13–16.

1. Why did the mothers bring their children to Jesus? (18:15)
2. What did Jesus say about the children? (18:16–17)
3. How would a child receive the kingdom of God?

The Rich Young Ruler (18:18–30)

For a person who loves Christ everything that he does is a pleasure, a privilege. We are serving the One we love more than life itself. We are laying up treasures in heaven. We have our priorities right; we know where we are headed. And so we serve the Lord joyfully. The rich young ruler mistook his possessions for his life. How terribly wrong he was.

Parallel passages: Matthew 19:16–30; Mark 10:17–31.

1. What question did the rich young ruler ask? (18:18)
2. What was the one thing the young man lacked? (18:22)
3. What did Peter say to Jesus? (18:28)
4. What are the priorities in your life?

144

MAY 19
Luke 18:31–43

Jesus Foretells His Death (18:31–34)

Jesus and His followers are slowly but surely making their way to Jerusalem for the last time, following the roadway through Perea. The word *Perea* or *Paeria* does not actually occur in the Bible. But the area was designated as the "land beyond the Jordan," that area east of the Jordan valley and slightly northeast of Jerusalem. Jews would often take this route from Galilee to Jerusalem to avoid Samaria. Israel was divided into three sections—the uppermost part, Galilee; the middle part, Samaria; and the southernmost part, Judea (which, of course, held Jerusalem). While Jews tried to avoid Samaritans at all cost, we know that Jesus had traveled through Samaria, stopping at Shechem at Jacob's well.

Jesus could not have been more than thirty or forty miles from Jerusalem when He called the Twelve and warned them for the third time of the horrendous things that should befall Him when He arrived there. Luke tells us that the disciples hadn't the vaguest notion what Jesus was saying. Have you ever wondered if, in that painful hour of knowing what lay just ahead, Jesus didn't want just a word of consolation, a pat on the back, a word of encouragement? But He didn't get any of those and therefore faced the ordeal dreadfully alone.

Parallel passages: Matthew 20:17–19; Mark 10:32–34.

1. What would happen in Jerusalem? (18:31)
2. How did the disciples react? (18:34)
3. How open are we to situations that don't turn out just as we had envisioned?

A Blind Man Receives His Sight (18:35–43)

This is the story of a man whose persistence paid off.

Jesus planned to take this time of rather slow walking to teach the disciples; but, as usual, crowds formed at the side of the road, straining to hear every word that fell from our Lord's lips.

Parallel passages: Matthew 20:29–34; Mark 10:46–52.

1. What did the blind man cry out? (18:38)
2. How did the people react? (18:39)
3. What did Jesus ask the man? (18:41)
4. What healed the man? (18:42)
5. What steps do we take to see that our bodies are at their best in order to carry out God's will?

MAY 20
Luke 19:1–27

Jesus and Zacchaeus (19:1–10)

As Jesus went into Jericho He was met by the blind beggar, a wretched creature who hadn't a farthing to his name. But he desperately needed Jesus. Then on the other side of Jericho, Jesus met Zacchaeus, perhaps the town's wealthiest man. He also needed the Lord. It doesn't matter if you are rich or poor—you still need Jesus.

Zacchaeus was rich. But he was lonely and despised. Because he was rich? No. Because he was a crook! Lonely, hated, wealthy—and wanting Jesus very much.

After Zacchaeus truly met the Lord, he was a changed man, repentant, seeking to make restitution for all the wrongs he had perpetrated.

1. Why could Zacchaeus not see Jesus? (19:3)
2. How did he manage to see Jesus? (19:4)
3. What did Jesus want from Zacchaeus? (19:5)
4. What did Zacchaeus do to make restitution? (19:8)
5. What evidence is there in your life that you have truly repented of your sins?

The Parable of the Minas (19:11–27)

Jesus and the disciples are now nearer Jerusalem than ever before. Some of His followers and the crowds believed that as soon as Jesus reached Jerusalem, the kingdom of God would appear on earth. They couldn't, in their wildest imagination, picture Calvary lying just around the corner.

Jesus tried again to get them to see by telling them a parable of a nobleman, about to depart to a far country to receive a kingdom.

This parable differs from the parable of the talents in that each servant got an equal amount, about one hundred days' wages. A *mina* was a Greek silver coin worth about twenty dollars.

The payment represents the Word of God. Note the nobleman's reward to his faithful servants. This may give us a clue to eternal life. Those who, in this life, are faithful in the tasks assigned them by God, will be given tremendous responsibilities in glory.

Parallel passage: Matthew 25:14–30.

1. Why was the nobleman leaving? (19:12)
2. How much money did he leave his servants? (19:13)
3. What did each servant do with his money? (19:16, 18, 20)
4. How did the master react to the servants' use of his money? (19:17, 19, 24)
5. How are you making use of God's Word in your life?

MAY 21
Luke 19:28—44

The Triumphal Entry (19:28—44)

What a bittersweet story: the triumphant entry into Jerusalem. The action begins in the town of Bethphage, a little town on the Mount of Olives. Try to visualize the scene. By standing on the summit of the mountain, and looking to the west, the great eastern wall of the old city of Jerusalem can be seen, directly across. Adorning the center of that wall is the Eastern Gate. To our right, farther to the north, is Saint Stephen's Gate, or Lion's Gate. Both entrances take the traveler to the temple area. Between us and that great wall is the Kidron Valley. Two great hills face each other, the Kidron Valley formed between them, the Mount of Olives on the east and Mount Moriah (of which Calvary is a part) on the west. As we ascend the Mount of Olives, we walk through a lovely, small garden area called Gethsemane. The road to the summit of the Mount of Olives winds its way upward. We crest the hill and come to Bethany, home of Lazarus, Mary, and Martha. And just beyond Bethany is Bethphage. This is the route, reversed, of course, that Jesus took for His triumphant entry into Jerusalem.

Please remember this: There was a price on Jesus' head. The leaders of the civil and religious courts wanted Jesus dead! Yet He started riding down the steep eastern slopes of the Mount of Olives, descending into the Kidron Valley.

The crowds were there! You could hear them all over the city. Only King David had ever swept into the city like that. Listen to the crowd singing: "Hosanna!" It is Victory Day—victory over the Romans, victory over all their enemies! They thought they were making Christ the center of everything. But very few caught the real drama of the moment. Luke captured it for us. There were tears standing in Christ's eyes.

Jesus knew the temperament of this crowd, any crowd. Give them a spectacle; give them a show, and they will be there. But only hours later, Christ writhed on the cross, spikes sticking through His flesh, the splinters from the instrument of torture ripping His back.

Parallel passages: Matthew 21:1—19; Mark 11:1—10; John 12:12—19.

1. Where were the disciples to find the colt and what were they to say? (19:30—31)
2. What did the people spread on the road? (19:36)
3. What did the Pharisees say to Jesus? (19:39)
4. How did Jesus answer the Pharisees? (19:40)
5. What did Jesus predict for Jerusalem? (19:43—44)
6. Do you most resemble the multitude who cried "Blessed is the King" or the Pharisees who tried to silence them?

Jesus Cleanses the Temple (19:45—48)

Every male Jew had to pay a temple tax each year. The tax was rather steep, equaling about two days' pay. To facilitate collection of this tax, approximately one month before Passover, booths were set up all over the country. The tax could be paid in these booths but most of the collection came in Jerusalem as large numbers of pilgrims journeyed to the Holy City for their most sacred religious observance. The tax had to be paid in shekels; thus, other currencies had to be exchanged. Enter the moneychangers, who charged inflated costs to make the exchange.

Then there was the practice of selling sacrificial animals to the incoming pilgrims at up to fifteen to twenty times the going rate. And it seems that one person had the monopoly.

Jesus was probably a rugged individual. He had, after all, spent His life in a carpenter's shop until He was thirty. Then He had spent three years living in the countryside, walking for miles each day.

Parallel passages: Matthew 21:12—17; Mark 11:15—19

1. What did Jesus say to the moneychangers? (19:46)
2. What was the result of His action? (19:47—48)
3. What are some times when the true purpose of our "temples" has gotten lost in other activities?

MAY 23
Luke 20:1–19

Jesus' Authority Questioned (20:1–19)

This was the day of questions. Once in the temple, having thrown out all the scoundrels, Jesus was surrounded by crowds. He was questioned by the chief priests and scribes who were trying to make a court case against Him. These men were clever. If they could get Christ to say He got His power from God, they could arrest Him for blasphemy right there. But Jesus was more clever than they, and He trapped them in their own question.

Then Jesus told the parable of the owner of the vineyard whose tenants beat his staff and killed his son. The vineyard was Israel. The tenants were the Israelites. The owner was God. The servants were the prophets. The son was, of course, Jesus.

Once again, Jesus foretold His death. He knew what lay just ahead. But despite the fact that He was alone, and the priests had all the power of Rome at their beck and call, they could not touch Jesus until He said they could. He laid down His life voluntarily; no one took it from Him. He died for you and me because He wanted to. That's how much He loved us.

Parallel passages: Matthew 21:23–27, 33–46; Mark 11:27–33, 12:1–12.

1. What question did the chief priests, scribes, and elders ask Jesus? (20:2)
2. With what question did Jesus counter? (20:4)
3. How were the religious leaders trapped by their question? (20:5–6)
4. What happened to the servants sent to the vinedressers? (20:10–12)
5. What happened when the vineyard owner sent his son? (20:15)
6. What did Jesus call Himself in this quote from Psalm 118:22? (20:17)
7. What did the scribes and chief priests perceive? (20:19)
8. Jesus comes to us in many ways and with many faces today. How do we treat Him when we meet Him?

MAY 24
Luke 20:20–44

Paying Taxes to Caesar (20:20–26)

Jesus was still being baited by the scribes and chief priests on the day of His triumphant entry into Jerusalem and the temple area. The leaders had tried to get Christ to incriminate Himself. Instead He had answered their questions in ways that made it clear who was really on trial.

The question they ask now is a deadly one. With one answer He will lose His popularity with the crowd; with another, He will come under the severest scrutiny by Roman authorities. This tax in question was not an income tax, but rather a stiff tax simply for the "privilege" of existing.

There was, of course, a legal issue that Jesus cleverly brought into the matter. The very fact that the Jews were willing to use the currency, with the inscription it bore, made their responsibility clear. For the law stated that the one who had the right to issue currency had the right to impose taxation.

Parallel passages: Matthew 22:15–22; Mark 12:13–17.

1. Whom did the chief priests and scribes send to Jesus? (20:20)
2. What question did they ask Him? (20:22)
3. For what did Jesus ask? (20:24)
4. What was Jesus' famous answer? (20:25)
5. How can we apply this passage to our feelings about taxation?

Questions About the Resurrection (20:27–44)

The Sadducees asked Jesus an interesting question based upon a ridiculous situation, and motivated by their belief that the whole idea of a resurrection was absurd.

Christ taught in verses 41–44 that a person's concept of God can be frightfully inadequate. He wanted the people to have a bigger idea of Messiah than they previously had known. We tend to make God in our image, when in truth, we were created in God's image.

Parallel passages: Matthew 22:23–33, 41–46; Mark 12:18–27, 35–37.

1. What law of Moses did the Sadducees present to Jesus? (20:28)
2. What situation did the Sadducees pose for Jesus? (20:29–33)
3. How did Jesus answer? (20:34–36)
4. How does Moses prove there is a Resurrection? (20:37–38)
5. From whom was it being said that Jesus was descended? (20:41)
6. What Old Testament book does Jesus quote? (20:42)
7. How big is your idea of the Messiah?

150

Jesus Denounces the Scribes; the Widow's Offering
(20:45–21:4)

The rabbis and scribes expected and usually received preferential treatment from those about them, for Jewish mores set rules of precedence for these men. But they didn't get preferential treatment from Jesus.

The rabbis were supposed to teach free of charge and support themselves through another trade. You remember, Paul often did that in establishing new churches. But the truth of the matter is that the people were taught that they were to give to these parasites. Consider this quotation: "Whoever puts part of his income into the purse of the wise is counted worthy of a seat in the heavenly academy." And there is no doubt that some older women who were living on pensions gave heavily to these men. The whole thing revolted Jesus, and He said so.

The woman's offering—one-twentieth of a penny—was great, because her motivation was to give of what she had.

This passage deals with a principle involving more than money. Whatever we do in the name of the Lord should be done wholeheartedly. Jesus deserves our best.

Don't be intimidated if your gift is small as long as you are giving your best. God sees it, accepts it, and uses it for His glory. And only eternity will show how great your offering was when it was placed in the hands of our creative God.

Parallel passages: Matthew 23:1–36; Mark 12:38–44.

1. Against whom did Jesus warn? (20:46)
2. What punishment would these people earn? (20:47)
3. How much money did the widow drop into the treasury? (21:2)
4. What is the motivation for your giving?

The Temple's Destruction, Signs of the Times, and Jerusalem's Destruction (21:5–24)

This chapter is Luke's version of the Olivet discourse. Matthew's account is most complete; however, Luke dealt specifically with questions about Jerusalem's end—something the other Gospel writers did not do.

In verses 7–19 Jesus prophesied Jerusalem's fall, His second coming, false christs and messiahs, and the persecution of the early church.

The catacombs—what a horrible place—are miles and miles of endless subterranean passages where the early Christians met and worshipped and were buried. We should thank God every day that we aren't called upon to pay such a price, although many of our Christian friends are imprisoned around the world at this very moment.

Jerusalem fell, just as Jesus predicted in verses 20–24. Not only did Jerusalem fall, but, as Jesus prophesied, it has not been completely in Jewish hands for any length of time since A.D. 70. Verse 24 may refer either to the time non-Jews have to repent or to the period God has foreordained for Israel's punishment.

Parallel passages: Matthew 24:1–22; Mark 13:1–20.

1. What did Jesus prophesy concerning the temple? (21:6)
2. What question did the disciples ask Jesus? (21:7)
3. What did Jesus say about wars and commotions? (21:9–10)
4. What did Jesus say about natural disasters? (21:11)
5. What would the time of persecution be an opportunity for? (21:13)
6. From where would the early Christians get the wisdom to answer their adversaries? (21:14–15)
7. What will happen to the early Christians? (21:16–17)
8. How would they know that the desolation was near? (21:20)
9. What will happen to Jerusalem? (21:24)
10. What significance does Jewish control of Jerusalem have regarding this prophecy?

The Coming of the Son of Man, the Lesson of the Fig Tree, and the Need to Watch (21:25–38)

Verses 25–26 expand upon Mark to depict the fear that people will experience just prior to the coming of the Son of Man, a term first used in the Old Testament by Daniel. These verses depict a universal judgment as opposed to the previous judgment of Jerusalem only. In verse 28, Luke encourages those who have been faithful to Christ.

As stated before, the fig tree of verses 29–31 was the most common deciduous tree in Palestine, and its budding was considered a sign of summer. The Gospel writers interpreted Jesus' teaching to mean that the end time was soon at hand (see v. 32). Whether that is what Jesus meant, we cannot know. "This generation" may just as easily refer to the race of mankind. Thus, time becomes indefinite. It is important to note that for Jesus the future "when" was never as important as the urgency of the "now." He did not intend for people to wait for the end time for His teachings to be put into effect. For Him, the kingdom of God was truly "at hand" every day.

Jesus' preoccupation with the "now" is apparent in verses 34–38 (see Mark 13:33–37).

Parallel passages: Matthew 24:29–35; Mark 13:24–31.

1. What will be some of the signs of nature preceding Christ's coming? (21:25)
2. For what does Christ say that believers should prepare when they see these signs? (21:28)
3. To what does Jesus compare the signs of the kingdom? (21:29–31)
4. What warning did Jesus give? (21:34–36)
5. In what ways are you "on watch" in your life?

MAY 28
Luke 22:1–23

The Plot Against Jesus (22:1–6)

It is not surprising that the chief priests and scribes in Jerusalem wanted Jesus dead. But why Judas? What caused him to betray the Lord for a meager thirty pieces of silver, the price of a wounded or gored slave? Luke gave us the answer in verse 3.

Parallel passages: Matthew 26:1–5, 14–16; Mark 14:1–2, 10–11; John 11:45–53.

1. What time of year was it? (22:1)
2. Of what were the chief priests and the scribes afraid? (22:2)
3. What happened to Judas? (22:3)
4. Think of a time when you thought you had gotten away with something because nobody saw you do it.

Jesus Institutes the Lord's Supper (22:7–23)

Jesus and His disciples carefully prepared for the observance of Passover. It was at Passover that Jesus had come to the Holy City to be the ultimate Lamb.

Passover is eaten by the Jewish people on the fifteenth day of Nisan, about April 15. It, of course, celebrates the deliverance of the Israelites from Egypt.

Josephus tells us that the numbers of pilgrims at Passover, besides the normal population, often approached the three million mark. Jesus' last days were played out before a packed house.

Jesus had already made provision for the Last Supper with His disciples. He had secured a room—an upper room—in a house on Mount Zion, just south of the city of Jerusalem. In those days, homeowners in Jerusalem were not allowed to charge for rooms they made available to the pilgrims. But arrangements needed to be made in advance because of the huge crowds.

Then Christ had the Last Supper with His men. We call this observance Communion. Regular participation helps us recall the deep meaning behind Christ's crucifixion and resurrection.

Parallel passages: Matthew 26:17–30; Mark 14:12–26; John 13:21–30.

1. Which two disciples did Jesus send to find the room? (22:8)
2. How did the disciples find the room? (22:10)
3. What did Jesus do with the cup? (22:17–18, 20) with the bread? (22:19)
4. How do you prepare for the Lord's Supper?

MAY 29
Luke 22:24–46

The Disciples Argue About Greatness (22:24–30)

The disciples were at the Last Supper on top of Mount Zion. It should have been a positive, memorable evening for them all except for two negative things. One was the unmasking of Judas as a traitor and betrayer, and the other was the arguing among the disciples for the prominent places at the table.

Parallel passages: Matthew 20:25–28; Mark 10:42–45.

1. About what were the disciples arguing? (22:24)
2. What was to be the nature of the disciples' ministry? (22:26–27)
3. What did Jesus promise the disciples? (22:30)
4. How can we become great in God's eyes?

Peter's Denial Foretold; Jesus in the Garden (22:31–46)

Notice the difference in this passage and Matthew's, Mark's, and John's accounts of this episode. Verses 31 and 32 express a beautiful understanding of Peter's situation and already a loving and forgiving attitude. Verse 36 shows that the attitude of the Jewish people had changed.

Most commentators view the "It is enough" (v. 38) as a Semitic saying meaning "Forget it" or something to that effect. Jesus' teaching had been misunderstood, as evidenced in the disciples' words about the swords.

After the Last Supper the party left the Upper Room and made its way across the Kidron Valley to the lovely little Garden of Gethsemane, situated on the slope of the Mount of Olives. There Jesus fought the inner battle of His life.

Parallel passages: Matthew 26:33–46; Mark 14:29–42.

1. What was to happen to Simon? (22:31)
2. What must Simon do? (22:32)
3. What did Jesus tell His disciples to do? (22:36)
4. What were the disciples to do while Jesus was praying? (22:40) What did they do? (22:45)
5. The disciples misunderstood Jesus' true mission. Try to put Jesus' mission into your own words.

MAY 30
Luke 22:47–71

Jesus' Betrayal and Arrest; Peter Denies Jesus (22:47–62)

Judas' betrayal of Christ was treacherous and cowardly. He did not lead the guards to the environs of the temple, where the crowds had gathered to hear Christ teach and to be ministered to. Instead, he knew that Jesus often went to the Garden of Gethsemane on the Mount of Olives to rest for the night, or to pray. And so Judas led the guards across the Kidron Valley to the garden at the midnight hour.

It was a custom for a disciple, meeting a beloved rabbi, to put his hands on the rabbi's shoulders and to kiss him on the cheek.

Someone has said that the greatest error Judas ever made was not the actual betrayal. His greatest mistake in judgment was in underestimating the forgiveness of Christ. Had he ever come to Christ and asked for forgiveness for his dastardly crime, divine pardon would have been his, for Judas' agony over his deed was evident.

Parallel passages: Matthew 26:36–56; Mark 14:32–50; John 18:3–11.

1. How did Judas identify Jesus? (22:47)
2. What did one of the disciples do? (22:50)
3. How did Jesus rebuke those who came to arrest Him? (22:52–53)
4. Think of a time when you have needed forgiveness. Did you ask for it and truly accept it?

Jesus Mocked, Beaten, and Taken Before the Council (22:63–71)

Jesus was taken from the garden back across the Kidron Valley to Caiaphas's house, located on Mount Zion—not far, in fact, from the location of the upper room where this whole panorama had begun hours earlier.

Parallel passages: Matthew 26:59–68; Mark 14:55–65; John 18:19–24.

1. How did those guarding Jesus mock Him? (22:64)
2. What question did the Sanhedrin ask Jesus? (22:67, 70)
3. How did Jesus answer? (22:67–70)
4. Do you believe Jesus is the Christ? Do you believe He is the Son of God? Are you telling others about Him?

MAY 31
Luke 23:1–25

Jesus Before Pilate and Herod (23:1–12)

The emperor of Rome during Jesus' life was Tiberius. He was an emotionless person and those who worked under him feared him greatly. Learning was his one great passion. His greatest unhappiness in life was his mother Livia, a vicious, cruel woman.

It should be said that Tiberius was a fair man, as emperors went. He gave the Roman senate great authority. He assumed the throne at age fifty-six and when he died fourteen years later, Rome was much better off financially.

The Sanhedrin, which had convicted Jesus in an illegal trial, had no authority under Roman law to carry out the death sentence. Only the Roman governor or procurator could do that. This is why Jesus was brought to Pilate. It is interesting that the charge on which Christ was convicted, blasphemy, was never made a matter of record before Pilate, because this man could not have cared about such a thing. So the religious leaders brought false charges.

Jesus had once called Herod "that fox." The description was a good one. Herod was a schemer. Historians believe that he was mentally unbalanced. But Jesus had no use for Herod and never opened His mouth to speak to him. He was the only man on record, I believe, to whom Jesus refused to speak.

Parallel passages: Matthew 27:1–2, 11–14; Mark 15:1–5; John 18:28–38.

1. With what was Jesus charged before Pilate? (23:2)
2. What did Pilate say to the crowd? (23:4)
3. What did Herod want to see? (23:8)
4. What does Luke record about Herod and Pilate's relationship? (23:12)
5. How does popular opinion affect your relationship with Christ?

Jesus Sentenced to Die (23:13–25)

It is made very clear that Pilate did not want to condemn Jesus. Rome was known for her impartial justice. Pilate made three separate attempts to release Jesus.

Parallel passages: Matthew 27:15–26; Mark 15:6–15; John 18:39–19:16.

1. What did Pilate intend to do with Jesus? (23:16)
2. How many times did Pilate appeal to the crowd? (23:22)
3. Think of a time when you, like Pilate, have "gone along with the crowd" because it was easier.

The Crucifixion (23:26–56)

Parts of this account are unique to Luke. In verse 30, Jesus quoted Hosea 10:8. We have more sayings from the cross in this account (vv. 34, 43, 46). And it is Luke who tells us about the penitent thief.

And now it's done. *Crucifixion.* And, sitting down, they watched Him there.

Did you ever wonder what killed Jesus? Was it loss of blood? Was it pain? Was it shock? A broken heart? No. He died of the same thing all men died of on a cross—suffocation. Hanging on the cross, the pain in His feet was so intense that they could not bear any more pressure. So Jesus would sag down and hang by His hands. But in that position, all the muscles along the arms knotted, and the pads of the shoulders became intensely painful. Then came the sudden shock— the pectoral muscles of His chest were momentarily paralyzed and He couldn't exhale. In order to exhale, Jesus painfully pulled Himself up so that His weight was again on the pierced feet.

Strip Him. Watch Him. Crucify Him.

It had now reached three o'clock in the afternoon. Jesus could bear the pain no longer. He quoted Psalm 31:5, and He died.

Parallel passages: Matthew 27:45–61; Mark 15:33–47; John 19:28–42.

1. To whom does Jesus speak on His way to the cross? (23:28)
2. What were the first words Jesus uttered from the cross? (23:34) the second? (23:43) the final? (23:46)
3. What was the inscription above Him? (23:38)
4. Who took Jesus' body? (23:50–53)
5. Who anointed Jesus' body? (23:55–56)
6. How does Jesus' crucifixion affect you?

The Resurrection (24:1–12)

There is no more carefully documented story in the Bible than the resurrection of our Lord Jesus Christ, and Luke's account is probably the most beautiful. The women who followed Jesus would not break the Sabbath even to anoint Jesus' body. So early Sunday morning they hastened to the tomb, and to their amazement, the body of Jesus was gone.

The first persons to tell the Resurrection story were these women. They looked up the disciples and told them Christ had risen from the dead. The disciples didn't believe it.

Parallel passages: Matthew 28:1–10; Mark 16:1–8; John 20:1–10.

1. What did the women find when they got to the tomb? (24:2)
2. What question did the angel ask the women? (24:5)
3. What were the women's names? (24:10)
4. Which disciple returned with the women? (24:12)
5. When faced with the good news of the gospel, are you more like Peter or the other disciples?

The Road to Emmaus (24:13–35)

These verses give us the immortal story of two disciples of Jesus who were not part of the remaining eleven. Emmaus is just a little village outside Jerusalem, about seven miles to the northwest.

These two had seen Christ in person. Perhaps they had even watched the Crucifixion several days before. They were familiar with Christ. So why didn't they recognize Him? Why didn't Mary Magdalene recognize Christ in the garden? Well, the last time Mary and these two men of Emmaus had seen Christ, He was still appearing in a man's body. But following the Resurrection, Christ was different. Now He had a glorified body, one on which time and space had no effect. He was revealed in all His glorious fullness, the eternal Son of God. Those dear people had only known Christ physically. Now they had to learn to know Him spiritually.

Parallel passage: Mark 16:12–13.

1. What was the name of one of the disciples on the road to Emmaus? (24:18)
2. What had Jesus' disciples hoped? (24:21)
3. When did they finally recognize Him? (24:30–31)
4. How did they feel when Jesus was talking to them on the road? (24:32)
5. In what form is Christ today?

Jesus Appears to His Disciples (24:36–49)

Christ, now resurrected, meets the disciples in the upper room. There are some fascinating details that Luke gives us about this particular appearance in the upper room. Apparently Jesus moved through the dimensions of time and space. Not only that, but He asked for food, proof that He was still corporeal.

Then Jesus repeated the whole gospel story to them. Christ made it plain that there is no gospel without the Cross; there is no gospel without the Resurrection. There is no gospel without repentance and remission of sins. There is no discipleship and stewardship without an ongoing missions program at home and abroad.

Parallel passages: Matthew 28:16–20; Mark 16:14–18; John 20:19–23; Acts 1:6–8.

1. How did the disciples react when Jesus appeared among them? (24:37)
2. What did Jesus say to His disciples? (24:38)
3. What did Jesus command His disciples? (24:47,49)
4. In what ways are you carrying out the Great Commission (24:47) in your life?

The Ascension (24:50–53)

Jesus again led the disciples across the Kidron Valley and up the slopes of Mount Olivet. The disciples must have been filled with wonder as they followed Christ up that mountain one last time. Calvary was past. Off to the right they could see the outskirts of Bethany. They reached the summit. Behind them they could make out the waters of the Dead Sea; to the south, the hill of Bethlehem; behind them, the awesome holy temple; to the north, the ramparts of Judea and the beginning foothills of Samaria.

There was no chariot of fire as with Elijah, no sound of trumpets filling the air. He just disappeared. He was gone—quickly, unexpectedly. That's the way He will return. And, oh, how I want to see Him.

Parallel passages: Mark 16:19–20; Acts 1:9–11.

1. Where did the disciples go after the Ascension and how did they spend their time? (24:52–53)
2. Is it possible to become so engrossed in watching and waiting for Christ's return that we neglect the work of the Lord?

JOHN

JUNE 4
John 1:1–18

The Word Made Flesh (1:1–18)

We know very little about this man John. There are very few sources regarding his life outside of the New Testament and tradition. We know that his father was Zebedee, a comparatively well-to-do commercial fisherman from Bethsaida. There is reason to believe that John's mother was Salome, the sister of Mary (Jesus' mother). If that is indeed true, then John and Christ were cousins. John had a brother named James, also an apostle, who was put to death by Herod Agrippa.

The Hebrews only had about ten thousand words in their vocabulary at that time, while the Greeks had nearly a quarter of a million words. But "the Word" meant something special to both. To the Jew, "the Word" was the personification of God Himself. "The Word of God" was a common expression to the Jew. The Greek term for *word* was *logos*, which was the principle of order under which the Greeks believed the universe existed. They believed the logos was the grand design of God, the mind of God. So John in his Gospel brought the two ideas together (see v. 1). In his very first statement, John says that Jesus Christ is the personification of God Himself. Christ is the grand design—the mind of God!

In verse 14, John makes it very plain that outside of Christ, grace and truth simply do not exist. Christ is not "a" way to God; He is "the" way. He does not teach about life; He *is* life.

1. Where and who was Christ in the beginning? (1:1)
2. What do we find in Christ? (1:3)
3. Why did John the Baptist come? (1:7–8)
4. What was given to those who accepted Christ? (1:12)
5. What was given by Moses? by Christ? (1:17)
6. How do you experience light and life through Christ in your personal life?

A Voice in the Wilderness; the Lamb of God (1:19–34)

Is it as amazing to you as it is to me that Christ could be in the midst of those people and they did not even know it? However, when we stop to think about the matter it isn't quite as amazing. Even today we often do not recognize the greatest people among us. And really Christ has been unrecognized by many in every age of time since then.

John the Baptist's father, Zacharias, was a priest. He knew well the practice of continually bringing lambs to the great altar of the temple for sacrifice. Every morning and every night the priests sacrificed a lamb for the sins of the nation. But now John is saying, "Here comes the only Lamb God will ever accept as atonement for your sins—Christ Himself. When He sees Christ in your life, He will pass over you, sparing you from eternal death."

Parallel passages: Matthew 3:1–17; Mark 1:1–11; Luke 3:1–18, 21–22.

1. Who did the priests and Levites think John was? (1:21)
2. What did the Pharisees ask John? (1:25)
3. How did John compare himself with Jesus? (1:27)
4. What did John call Jesus? (1:29)
5. What was the sign of the Spirit at Jesus' baptism? (1:32–33)
6. Who are Jesus' representatives in our lives every day? Do we recognize them?

The First Disciples (1:35–51)

There is no indication that John was upset about his disciples' leaving him for Jesus. After all, it was his mission to bring people to Christ, not to himself.

During this time at Bethabara, Jesus acquired His first two disciples. Andrew is one of the unsung heroes of the New Testament, for he brought Peter to Christ.

John's account of Jesus' calling His disciples differs completely from the account of the other three Gospel writers.

1. What did John say to his disciples? (1:36)
2. What did Jesus call Simon? (1:42)
3. Where was Philip from? (1:44)
4. What did Nathanael ask Philip? (1:46)
5. What did Jesus promise Nathanael? (1:50–51)
6. What indications of jealousy do you see among Christ's servants today?

The Wedding at Cana (2:1–12)

John called Nathanael to be a disciple in the vicinity of Cana of Galilee. While Jesus was there, He was apparently invited to be a guest at a wedding feast. It is there that He performed His first recorded miracle. Cana is quite near Nazareth. Early writings indicate that Mary, the mother of Jesus, was there because she was a sister of the groom's mother. Mary's husband, Joseph, is conspicuously absent from this narrative, probably because he had died some years earlier while Jesus was still living in Nazareth.

A wedding feast in this part of the world was quite an occasion. Jewish law decreed that a virgin should be married on a Wednesday. The festivities lasted far more than one day. The actual wedding ceremony followed the feast, late in the evening. When the ceremony ended, the couple was escorted to their new home. You can imagine the flaming torches, the bands playing, the people shouting. For a solid week, the young couple stayed at home, still dressed in their wedding finery. During that week they were treated like royalty.

The drink was indeed wine but the wine was broken down to two parts wine to three parts water. Hospitality is important in that part of the world. In this country the host would probably say, "Sorry, we are out of this or that." But in that area, it would be disgraceful to be considered in any way inhospitable.

Jesus' answer to Mary sounds rude to us; but it was simply a Jewish way of answering, "Don't worry about it; I'll take care of it."

The moral here is that whatever our Lord does, He does in abundant supply. The abundant supply He gives, however, deals with those things that have eternal merit, that prepare us for eternity. He gives grace, patience, love, peace, long-suffering. And He gives those gifts in abundance. We sing the old song, "He giveth more grace." In our thinking, we have changed that to "He giveth more goods." That's unfortunate. Primarily God is preparing the bride, the church, to meet His Son Jesus Christ at the marriage supper of the Lamb. Everything else is truly trivial by comparison.

Only John records this miracle.

1. What problem arose at the wedding feast? (2:3)
2. How did Jesus answer His mother? (2:4)
3. How much water did Jesus use? (2:6–7)
4. Who traveled with Jesus to Capernaum? (2:12)
5. In what things are you seeking a greater abundance?

The Cleansing of the Temple (2:13–25)

John dealt with Christ's life in a somewhat different chronology than the other Gospel writers. It is John, for example, who tells us that Christ visited Jerusalem on more than one occasion. These are not discrepancies in the Bible; on the contrary, they are enhancements. In verse 17, Jesus quotes Psalm 69:9.

We must take very seriously our efforts for Christ. We must constantly evaluate our motivation for service. Like the moneychangers, we can easily fall into a pattern of service that does not bless, but hinders. Let us allow the Holy Spirit to shine His light in our own hearts, seek our own minds, and get our priorities where they should be. How tragic it would be if Christ removed us from our place of ministry simply because we were not ministering at all.

Parallel passages: Matthew 21:12–13; Mark 11:15–17; Luke 19:45–46.

1. What time of year does this passage depict? (2:13)
2. How did Jesus drive the moneychangers out of the temple? (2:15)
3. What did the Jews ask Jesus? (2:18)
4. How did Jesus answer them and what did His answer mean? (2:19,21)
5. Why did Jesus not reveal Himself as the Son of God at that time? (2:23–25)
6. Out of what motivation do you operate as you do the Lord's work? When did you last stop to evaluate your motivation?

JUNE 8
John 3:1–21

Jesus and Nicodemus (3:1–21)

The story takes place in Jerusalem and the two key figures are Jesus and Nicodemus, who was a Pharisee and member of the Sanhedrin. This unusual man played a major part in the life of Christ. He is usually spoken of as the man who came to Jesus "by night." He has been, therefore, labeled somewhat cowardly because of this nocturnal visit. Was he a coward? Absolutely not. At Jesus' death he showed his colors to Pilate, Caiaphas, and the others. Perhaps he came to Jesus at dark simply because it was the best time of day to see the Master. All day long, Nicodemus would have been busy with his teaching duties, and Jesus was certainly busy in His ministry. What better time could there have been for those two men to talk?

Nicodemus was one of only six thousand persons known as Pharisees in that whole land. A man became a Pharisee at a ceremony when he took a pledge in front of three witnesses that he would spend the rest of his life observing every detail of the scribal law—the first five books of the Bible. To add one word to it or to subtract one from it was a terrible sin. The Pharisees believed that those five books contained rules and regulations to govern every single thing that could ever possibly happen to a human life. And if a law were not plainly spelled out in Genesis through Deuteronomy, the Pharisees interpreted that law. And so they compiled a huge list of do's and don'ts that had to be followed to the letter. For example, the law said to remember the Sabbath Day, to keep it holy. On that day, no work was to be done, either by man or by his servants, or even by his horses or oxen. Now that seems simple enough. But the Pharisees expanded the teaching in what they called the Mishnah, the codified scribal law. There were twenty-four chapters in that section on the Sabbath. Then they had the Talmud to explain the Mishnah.

The sad thing is that the Pharisees believed that their adherence to this type of law would bring eternal salvation. In light of all this, it is amazing that Nicodemus even came to Jesus at all.

Real conversion is supernatural. We don't know how God brings about conversion, but He divinely implants the saving life of Jesus Christ, the new birth, into a human life. There is no salvation without this second birth, this spiritual implantation of divine life.

1. To whom did Nicodemus attribute Jesus' power? (3:2)
2. What kind of birth must a man experience? (3:5)
3. How much love did God have for the world? (3:16)
4. In what ways is the second birth evidenced in your life?

165

John the Baptist Exalts Christ (3:22–36)

John the Baptist possessed many interesting character traits: charisma, leadership, speaking ability, faith, power, emotion. But there was one trait that he apparently did not have: envy, as we mentioned earlier.

Several times the apostle John tells us that followers of John the Baptist left him to become followers of Christ. Not one time did the Baptist ever rebuke them or show any hostility. On the contrary, he encouraged them to follow Jesus. He was a man of humility. He was quite willing to take a back seat to Jesus and said so in verse 30.

Have you ever wondered why John the Baptist himself did not leave the Jordan to be an apostle of Christ like Peter and Andrew? As far as we know, he never saw the Sea of Galilee or Capernaum or Tabor. He stayed in those miserable reeds near Bethabara and Salim, roaring out sermons on repentance and baptizing converts in that muddy stream. Why didn't he physically follow Jesus?

Perhaps the answer is a basic one—that was not his given ministry. He was not called to be an apostle, but a prophet. Look at 1 Corinthians 12:28–29a: "And God has appointed these in the church: first apostles, second prophets, third teachers, after that miracles, then gifts of healings, helps, administrations, varieties of tongues. Are all apostles? Are all prophets?" John the Baptist was definitely a prophet. A prophet is a special spokesman for God, usually coming with a message of repentance and condemnation.

We have never wanted ministries of repentance. We love the ministry of faith, the ministry of reconciliation, the ministry of healing. But who do you hear today calling the nation to repent? John the Baptist recognized his given ministry, and was content. He never tried to emulate someone else.

John had a deep sense of working for the overall kingdom of God. He knew that his little band on the Jordan was not the whole thing, but only a very small part. And he wanted his contribution to be for the whole, not just the part. We need that sense today. We need to shed our provincial jealousies, our denominational condemnations.

1. Why was John baptizing in Aenon near Salim? (3:23)
2. What dispute arose and between whom? (3:25)
3. To whom did John the Baptist liken himself? (3:29)
4. Who will receive everlasting life? (3:36)
5. In what ways does your church evidence the sense of working for the overall kingdom of God?

JUNE 10
John 4:1–26

The Woman of Samaria (4:1–26)

It was at Jacob's well at Shechem in Samaria, in the shadow of Mount Ebal and Mount Gerizim that Jesus touched the life of a troubled woman, known to us only as the woman of Samaria. Sychar is the modern Askar.

Israel is only a little over one hundred miles from north to south, but in that short distance there are three territories: Judea in the south, Samaria in the middle, and Galilee in the north. There was a long-standing feud between the Jews and Samaritans and, normally, Jews avoided Samaria. But to get from Judea to Galilee required either going through Samaria or crossing the Jordan valley. The latter route was much longer. So Jesus decided to go right through this hostile territory. Jesus broke down all kinds of barriers whenever possible. A viable factor of a Christian today is that he never builds unnecessary walls.

God said in Isaiah 44:3 that He would one day pour water upon those who were thirsty, and that water would be the Christ, His Son. There is total satisfaction in Jesus. In the human heart, there is a thirst for something that only Jesus can completely satisfy. After years of rough living and rock-and-roll stardom, with the attendant booze and drugs, someone told Gary S. Paxton about Christ. He was saved and wrote, "He Was There All the Time."

1. Why did Jesus leave Judea? (4:1–4)
2. For what did Jesus ask? (4:7)
3. Why was the woman surprised at Jesus' request? (4:9)
4. What kind of water was Jesus speaking of? (4:10, 13–14)
5. What did Jesus know about the woman? (4:17–18)
6. How should people worship God? (4:24)
7. Who did Jesus say He was? (4:25–26)
8. What steps have you taken to break down barriers?

The Vast Whitened Harvest Field (4:27–38)

In these verses Jesus communicated to His disciples the urgency of His work, their work, and the work of the kingdom of God. For them, it could never be "business as usual." Since the croplands near Jacob's well had recently been sowed and could not be harvested for about four months, Jesus could not have been pointing out actual fields of wheat and barley near the area to His disciples. The "fields" to be harvested were really people. Verse 35 was probably a proverb current in Galilee at that time.

1. What did the woman of Samaria do? (4:28–29)
2. What was Jesus' food? (4:34)
3. How do we express the urgency of the kingdom's work?

The Savior of the World; Jesus Finds Welcome at Galilee and Heals a Nobleman's Son (4:39–54)

These two passages draw attention to two kinds of faith. The Galileans, His own people who had earlier rejected Him, now believed because of all the miraculous events in Jerusalem. However, the Samaritan woman, the people whom she told, and the government official were not Jesus' people. The government official believed without a sign.

1. What did the Samaritan woman tell the people in the village? (4:39)
2. How long did Jesus stay with the Samaritans? (4:40)
3. Why did the Samaritans believe? (4:42)
4. What was necessary for the nobleman to believe? (4:50)
5. What time was the nobleman's son healed? (4:52)
6. What has it taken in your life to believe that Jesus is the Christ?

JUNE 12
John 5:1–23

The Healing at the Pool of Bethesda (5:1–15)

John does not say which feast Jesus was attending, but most scholars feel it was the Feast of Pentecost. During Jesus' time, all adult male Jews were required to attend Passover, Pentecost, and the Feast of Tabernacles.

The word *Bethesda* means "house of the olive." The pool was located about one hundred yards inside Jerusalem's northeast gate, known today as Lion's Gate, or Saint Stephen's Gate. The ruins of this pool are next to the church of Saint Ann. Even today it holds a lot of water. In Jesus' day the pool, fed by a subterranean stream, was extremely deep. Every once in a while, the spring would bubble up, and the pool itself would be troubled.

1. What gate in that day was the Pool of Bethesda near? (5:2)
2. What did the people believe about the pool? (5:4)
3. How long had the man been ill? (5:5)
4. What did Jesus command the man? (5:8)
5. Why did this healing cause a problem? (5:10)
6. At what time has God asked you to do something with your life that you felt was impossible?

The Authority of the Son (5:16–23)

This passage recounts one of the many confrontations Jesus had with the religious authorities. His words in verses 20–23 are very plain—a person who cannot understand Jesus cannot understand God. For the Jews of that day, such a statement was blasphemy.

1. Why did the Jews first want to kill Jesus? (5:16)
2. What was their second reason? (5:18)
3. Who is the final judge of man? (5:22)
4. What do the characteristics of Christ tell us about God?

Life and Judgment Are Through the Son (5:24–30)

In this passage, Jesus was saying that the coming age—the eschatological age when the kingdom of God would be instituted—was really at hand, in some sense. The Word (Jesus) has already come, so that the powers of the end time are already working. Once a person hears and believes the Word, that person has, in some sense, entered the kingdom of God. Those who still root their lives in worldly values are not part of the kingdom.

1. What is the future of those who believe in Jesus? (5:24)
2. What event does Jesus predict? (5:29)
3. How does Christ describe His criteria for judgment? (5:30)
4. What does it take to enter into God's present kingdom today?

Witnesses to Jesus (5:31–47)

For the Jews to ask for proof of Jesus' identity was only natural. The Jews stood on the principle that one person without evidence cannot be accepted as proof of anything. There had to be several witnesses. And a man's witness about himself could not be accepted as courtroom proof either. Therefore, Christ's claims about Himself had to be supported by evidence other than the mere fact that He claimed it.

So Jesus gave the Jews other witnesses. Jesus also intimated that His opponents loved the Word of God more than they loved God, and so they missed the whole point of the law and the Old Testament.

He was hard on these people because they had been given so much light but had never used it. Think of it: They had the Old Testament, they had the prophets, they had their profound history, they had the tradition—and all of it pointed to Christ as the Messiah. The Passover in itself is one of the greatest representations of Christ that one could ever have.

We do not walk in spiritual darkness. Before us have gone some of the greatest saints of all ages. We have their inspiration to help us.

1. What witnesses other than Himself did Jesus name? (5:33, 36–39, 45–47).
2. What did Jesus call John the Baptist? (5:35)
3. Who is the highest authority? (5:36)
4. Like the Jews, we have many witnesses—in even greater number—to Christ's authority. Why then, do we live barely recognizing Jesus' importance and rarely incorporating His authority into our lives?

JUNE 14
John 6:1–14

The Feeding of the Five Thousand (6:1–14)

Unlike most of the previous lessons from the Gospel of John, the reading in this lesson has parallels in all the other Gospels.

The Gospels tell us that Jesus often withdrew from the crowds for spiritual renewal. One of His withdrawals found Jesus leaving Capernaum for Bethsaida Julius by way of the Sea of Galilee. The crowds, however, guessed where Jesus was going and met him there—and thus we have the setting for the feeding of the five thousand. John's account is probably the one we remember best, for it is the only account that tells of the boy's role in the miracle. Has it ever occurred to you that it must have taken a great deal of courage and faith to approach Jesus with such meager provisions when there were so many people who needed to be fed?

Note the quick character study on the two disciples mentioned in this passage. Philip reacted one way to the problem; Andrew, another way.

Parallel passages: Matthew 14:13–21; Mark 6:30–44; Luke 9:10–17.

1. What feast was approaching? (6:4)
2. Which disciple did Jesus approach first? (6:5) What was that disciple's response? (6:7)
3. Who was the second disciple whom Jesus addressed and what was that disciple's response? (6:8–9)
4. How did the people who had witnessed the miracle react? (6:14)
5. What is the first thing you do when you face a difficult problem in your life?

JUNE 15
John 6:15–21

Jesus Walks on the Sea (6:15–21)

Note once again, Jesus is withdrawing. He withdrew both when the leaders wanted to kill Him and when the crowds wanted to make Him king. We do not know how Jesus brought about this miracle, but we do know that the miracle teaches us that the Christian can live without fear, that irrational emotion which renders us helpless and stranded. Jesus takes away the fear of living and the fear of dying. Jesus does not keep the storms out of our lives, but with strong hands and tender touch, He helps us weather those storms.

Parallel passages: Matthew 14:22–33; Mark 6:45–52.

1. Why did Jesus withdraw from the crowd in this lesson? (6:15)
2. Where were the disciples going? (6:16–17)
3. How far had the disciples rowed? (6:19)
4. What happened when Jesus got into the boat? (6:21)
5. Think of a difficult time in your life when you feel Jesus was watching over you or leading you.

Jesus—the Bread of Life (6:22–40)

This passage has no parallels in the other Gospels. The passage speaks to one of the ideas running through some of the current theology—that the Christian is to be the constant recipient of God's manna, or God's bounty, which is too often understood in material terms alone.

Much of today's teaching centers around how to get things from God. Have faith for this, or claim that, or make a confession in order to receive thus and so. But the issue is really this: How do we get more of Jesus Himself? How do we understand spiritual truths and attain spiritual life? Was there ever a man of more faith than Paul? Yet what did he have in his life? A few books, a cloak—once he rented a house for a couple of years, but none of these would have made him successful according to our standards, in fact, not even according to the standards of his day. Paul said, in effect, "I give them up that I might know Him" (see Phil. 3:8).

Jesus had gained the attention of the people whom He was addressing. They understood the significance of the feeding of the five thousand, for there was a rabbinical rule that a prophet who had not been recognized as a prophet but had given a sign or wonder must then be listened to.

1. From where did the people who heard this discourse come? (6:23)
2. What were the people's reasons for seeking Jesus? (6:26)
3. What did the people ask Jesus about the works of God and what was His answer? (6:28–29)
4. How did Jesus describe Himself? (6:33)
5. What do you seek from God?

Rejected by His Own (6:41–59)

In this passage, Jesus expands upon His role as the One who leads people to God. But the people have a hard time believing Him, for He was too ordinary. After all, would you be able to accept your next-door neighbor as the Messiah? In this section, Jesus refers to the Eucharist, a concept the people were unable to understand at that time. Jesus quotes Isaiah 54:13 in verse 45.

1. Why did the Jews have trouble with Jesus' words? (6:41–42)
2. How did Jesus say He fulfilled Isaiah's prophecy? (6:45)
3. What will be the future of those who eat the bread of which Jesus was speaking? (6:58)
4. Where should we be looking for divine truth today?

The Words of Eternal Life (6:60–71)

In this passage the disciples were not telling Jesus that His words were hard to understand—as they so often did in other passages. Rather, they were saying that the words of Christ were hard to accept. Acceptance is yet another step beyond belief. We can believe what Jesus taught, but accepting it means that we incorporate His teachings into every facet of our lives.

Some of the followers reacted in a predictable manner to Jesus' words, but one of the Twelve became more determined than ever before to follow Christ.

Note that Jesus predicts His betrayal at a much earlier point in His ministry than He does in any of the other Gospels.

1. What did Jesus call the words which He spoke? (6:63)
2. What did some of the disciples do? (6:66)
3. What did Jesus ask the Twelve? (6:67)
4. Which disciple answered Jesus? (6:68)
5. What did Jesus call one of the disciples? (6:70)
6. What is your reaction to Christ?

Jesus' Brothers Disbelieve (7:1–24)

Jesus' earthly ministry would last about eight more months. The approaching fall would bring the Feast of Tabernacles, which fell on about the first of October, according to our calendar. This eight-day feast, known as the Feast of Booths, was one of the three feasts that every adult male Jew who lived within fifteen miles of Jerusalem was required to attend.

An interesting note about Jesus' ministry is that the overwhelming majority of Jesus' miracles happened in Galilee. So Christ never really demonstrated His full power before the religious leaders.

When Christ arrived in the Holy City, He aroused different reactions in people. The Pharisees hated Him because He saw right through their petty rules and regulations. He didn't use the law as they did. He was diametrically opposed to their methods. If Jesus was right, then the Pharisees had to be wrong, and they were not about to change.

The Sadducees, the party from which most of the priests came, hated Jesus, too. Of course, the Sadducees hated the Pharisees as well. These were the collaborators; the priests and Sadducees had sold out to the Romans. They lived luxuriously on the bones of their victims. They did not want a Messiah. They did not want their game interrupted. And so they hated Jesus because He interfered with their vested interests.

Jesus opened Himself up to charges because He claimed personal authority in His teaching. Among the Jews, it was an accepted custom that a man who had never attended a rabbinic school would not teach in public.

1. Why did Jesus stay in Galilee? (7:1)
2. What did Jesus' brothers want Him to do? (7:3–4)
3. What answer did Jesus give them? (7:6)
4. How did Jesus go to the feast? (7:10)
5. How did Jesus answer the criticism that He was an uneducated man? (7:16)
6. How should one judge? (7:24)
7. If God is the authority for what we say and do, how do we know His will?

JUNE 19
John 7:25–36

Is This the Christ? (7:25–36)

Try to visualize the scene in this passage. To the north and the south of the temple are the great courtyards lined by Solomon's porticoes. Here are the Royal Porch and Solomon's Porch, easily recognized by the great pillared colonnades. In these areas, the common people gather for various occasions, and here the rabbis teach. Midway through the Feast of Tabernacles the city and temple areas are jammed with people. Suddenly a figure whose voice is unmatched grabs everyone's attention.

This is the moment that determines Jesus' fate in the minds of the religious leaders. Of this moment William Barclay in his commentary wrote, "This is precisely the choice which is still before us. Either what Jesus said about Himself is false, in which case He is guilty of such blasphemy as no man ever dared utter; or, what He said about Himself is true, in which case He is what He claimed to be and can be described in no other terms than the Son of God. Every man has to decide for or against Jesus Christ."

The dispersion in verse 35 refers to the scattering of the Jews following the Babylonian exile recounted in the Old Testament.

1. On what basis did the people surmise that Jesus was not the Messiah? (7:27)
2. What claim did Jesus make? (7:29)
3. Why was Jesus not arrested? (7:30)
4. What saying of Jesus did the Jews not understand? (7:35–36)
5. What does deciding for or against Christ mean in your life?

Rivers of Living Water (7:37–52)

At this point, let's look at the eight-day Feast of Tabernacles.

The people left their homes during this time and lived in little temporary booths which were everywhere—in the streets, on the flat roofs of houses, in the shopping areas. The booths were constructed of branches and palm fronds. There had to be an opening in the roof (it would not rain during this time of year) so that at night the inhabitants could see the stars to remind them that they had once been homeless wanderers on the desert without a roof over their heads. The Feast of Tabernacles was also an agricultural festival, harvesttime.

Every day of the feast, the people came to the temple with palms and willows and marched around the great altar. A priest then took a golden pitcher and walked down to the Pool of Siloam, where he filled it with water. The water was carried back to the altar while the people recited Isaiah 12:3. "Therefore with joy you will draw water/From the wells of salvation." Then the water was poured out as an offering to God, and Psalms 113-118 were sung. On the last day of the feast, a final flourish was added when the people marched around the altar seven times in remembrance of the fall of Jericho. It was in this dramatic setting that the voice of Jesus rang out from Solomon's Porch (see v. 37). Christ stated clearly that He was the fulfillment of all the longings of the human race.

1. What did Jesus say on the last day of the feast? (7:37)
2. From where did the Scriptures say the Messiah would come? (7:42)
3. Why did the officers not seize Jesus? (7:46)
4. What religious leader defended Jesus? (7:50)
5. How do you make use of the Bible in your daily life?

The Woman Caught in Adultery (7:53—8:11)

When Jesus returned to the temple to teach, the scribes and Pharisees were waiting to trap Him. The Jews considered adultery one of the three worst sins in the world. It was punishable either by stoning or by strangulation.

The situation posed a serious dilemma for Jesus. If He agreed with the Jewish leaders, He would be passing the death sentence on a woman and only the Romans had the authority to do that. Therefore, in doing so He would anger the Romans. But if Jesus didn't agree with the scribes and Pharisees, He would pit Himself against the Old Testament law.

In resolving the situation, Jesus didn't let the woman go without a lesson. He was and is quite willing to forgive sin, but not to overlook it.

The woman in this passage is often thought to be Mary Magdalene, but there is no scriptural basis for that assumption.

1. Whom did the scribes and Pharisees bring to Jesus? (8:3)
2. How did Jesus answer the accusers? (8:7)
3. How did the accusers react? (8:9)
4. What did Jesus tell the woman to do? (8:11)
5. At what times have you been willing to "cast stones" when you needed to look at your own life?

JUNE 22
John 8:12–36

Jesus, the Light of the World (8:12–29)

This segment takes place during the Feast of Tabernacles, in the temple's Court of the Women. There, there was a treasury where devout people gave their offerings for God's work and house. In this same court were four great candelabra, which were lit during a ceremony called the Illumination of the Temple. Here again is the reference to the Jewish law that required two witnesses to testify concerning a matter (see v. 17).

Here in John, as in the other Gospels, Jesus prophesied concerning His future. What Jesus told the crowd holds true for us today. There is nothing that you or I can do to merit being in a heavenly abode with God. It is only Christ's life within us that makes it possible.

1. What did Jesus call Himself? (8:12)
2. Why did Jesus say His judgment was true? (8:16)
3. Why did no one try to capture Jesus? (8:20)
4. What did Jesus predict about Himself? (8:21)
5. Who did Jesus say that He was? (8:25)
6. How did Jesus describe His relationship with God? (8:29)
7. Name some times when you have tried to take the easy way out of a situation.

The Truth Shall Make You Free (8:30–36)

Jesus spoke in words that often shocked His listeners, and the words in this passage certainly did. Sin is a binding foe that chains the unsuspecting person. The teaching about freedom had special meaning for the Pharisees, who, unlike the Zealots did not look for freedom for Rome, for they, too, believed that true freedom came from obeying God's will. Where Jesus and the Pharisees parted was in the Pharisees' belief that such freedom was their birthright because they were descendants of Abraham.

1. What makes a person Jesus' disciple? (8:31)
2. What makes a person not free? (8:34)
3. Who can make you free? (8:36)
4. To what are you enslaved?

179

JUNE 23
John 8:37–59

Abraham's Seed and Satan's (8:37–47)

The Jews answered many of Jesus' statements by saying, "We are the sons of Abraham." This great claim made the Jews spiritually and eternally secure, so they thought. But the Jews of Jesus' day were making a major mistake—one many of us continue to make today. Abraham was a great man, but his greatness, his spirituality, did not make the Jews of Jesus' day spiritual. Likewise, many of us call ourselves Christians based on our parents' or nation's spirituality.

1. What did Abraham's descendants do that Abraham would not have done? (8:40)
2. If God were truly the father of the Jews, what would they do? (8:42)
3. Why did the Jews not hear God's words? (8:47)
4. On whose commitment are you trying to enter the kingdom?

Before Abraham Was, I Am (8:48–59)

This passage contains a showdown between Jesus and His critics. Jesus gave them this chance to air their grievances. When they could not answer, Jesus explained to His critics why, and they called Him an enemy of Israel and a heretic.

In verse 51 Jesus made an outrageous claim, one that caused His critics to think Him crazy. Jesus' claim in verse 58 so angered the Jews that they sought to kill Jesus.

1. What did the Jews say of Jesus? (8:48)
2. What claim did Jesus make? (8:51)
3. What question did the Jews ask Jesus? (8:53)
4. What did Jesus say of Himself and Abraham? (8:56–58)
5. How did Jesus escape from the Jews? (8:59)
6. How do you view your short life span in terms of eternity?

JUNE 24
John 9:1–34

Jesus Heals the Man Born Blind (9:1–34)

In Jesus' day, all disease was considered the result of sin, thus the question in verse 2. This healing is one of the few in the Gospels where Jesus uses a substance to bring about the healing.

This healing brought about another clash with the Pharisees. The healed man faced the Pharisees with courage. He was not versed in the theology and issues of his day. All he knew was that he had been healed. Like the man in this passage, one of the greatest testimonies we can give is based upon our personal experience.

Often you fail to realize how many people are going through the same experiences you are. They are afraid of the future, frightened of the present. But along you come, with words telling of the same fears, the same frustrations, the same experiences. The difference between you and others can be that you have learned that you can rely on Jesus Christ to help you through such times. Your witness to this fact may be a turning point in their lives.

1. Whom did Jesus heal? (9:1)
2. What did Jesus' disciples ask Him? (9:2)
3. How did Jesus heal the man, and what did He command the man to do? (9:6–7)
4. Why did the Pharisees have a problem with the healing? (9:14)
5. What did the Jews have to do before they believed the account of the healing? (9:18)
6. What was the blind man's courageous answer? (9:30–33)
7. When was the last time you witnessed about the difference God has made in your life?

JUNE 25
John 9:35—10:21

Spiritual Blindness (9:35—41)

This passage concludes the story in the previous passage. It seems that, in spite of the man's courageous answer to the Pharisees, he still did not understand who had healed him.

1. What did Jesus ask the man? (9:35)
2. What was the man's reaction when Jesus revealed Himself? (9:38)
3. Even though the Pharisees were not physically blind, could they truly see? (9:41)
4. How deep is your understanding of who the Son of God really is and what He demands?

Jesus, the Good Shepherd (10:1—21)

In Israel, the sheep are raised for the most part for their wool, not for killing. As time progresses, a real rapport is established between a shepherd and his sheep. Every sheep is given a name. A good shepherd can look at a milling bunch of sheep and call each one by name, and the sheep respond when called. They will not follow another shepherd. They know their shepherd's voice and follow only him. (Note vv. 3—4.)

In verses 7—21 Jesus lays down principles for a shepherd's behavior. A good shepherd looks out for the good of the sheep, for their protection. He is not like a thief or robber. Down through the years, the church has been plagued by religious impostors and crafty priests and evangelists. Contrast them with the standard Jesus gave us in verse 10: "I have come that they may have life, and that they may have it more abundantly."

In many cases the shepherd is literally the door of the sheepfold. There is no door to the fold, so the shepherd himself lies across the doorway. No sheep can leave without going over his body, and no marauder can get in unless he deals with the shepherd. Christ is the door of the spiritual fold. He is the protector. And, on the other hand, if you and I wish to leave the spiritual fold, we must go over His body, broken for us on Calvary.

Note verse 16. Jesus' message is for everyone.

1. How must a person enter the sheepfold? (10:1)
2. What did Jesus call Himself? (10:7)
3. Why did Jesus come? (10:10)
4. What does Jesus say about who Christians are? (10:16)
5. Who had power over Jesus' life? (10:18)
6. How do you determine who is worthy to receive the gospel?

The Shepherd Knows His Sheep (10:22–30)

The setting for this passage is what we call Hanukkah (the Feast of Dedication). That holy time for the Jews takes place around December 25—a time of year that can be very cold and rainy in Jerusalem.

This Jewish holiday marks the cleansing of the temple following the successful Maccabean revolt.

In 175 B.C. a Syrian king named Antiochus decided to obliterate Jewish worship once and for all. When it couldn't be done through peaceful purposes or legislation, he turned to violent means. Eighty thousand Jews were butchered in the streets and a nearly equal number sold into slavery. It became a crime punishable by death to possess a copy of the Old Testament law. Circumcision also was illegal. Any mother caught with a circumcised child was crucified with her child hung around her neck. The temple was turned into a house of ill repute, and Antiochus even desecrated the great altar by offering a pig there to the god Zeus.

Antiochus' desecration of the temple was the final straw. A revolt, led by Judas Maccabeus, brought years of bloodshed but was finally successful. To commemorate the victory and the cleansing, or purification of the temple, Judas Maccabeus instituted an eight-day ceremony known as the Memorial of the Purification of the Temple. It was also called the Festival of Lights. Lights were set in the window of every Jewish home.

1. What did the Jew ask Jesus? (10:24)
2. Why did they not believe? (10:26–27)
3. What claim did Jesus make? (10:30)
4. Who or what do you follow? Are you consistent in whom or what you follow?

Jesus Rejected by the Jews (10:31–42)

Jesus' claim in the preceding passage was too much for the Jews. Jesus' irrefutable logic was beyond argument. These people who listened to Jesus had already made up their minds to go in another direction. Their minds were closed to reason.

1. What did the Jews try to do to Jesus? (10:31)
2. What was Jesus' criteria for naming Himself the Son of God? (10:37–38)
3. How open are you to reason when new situations present themselves?

The Death of Lazarus (11:1–16)

Jesus loved two cities dearly—in the north, Capernaum, right on the Sea of Galilee; and in the south on the back slopes of the Mount of Olives, Bethany. Capernaum was the home of Peter, and Bethany was the home of Lazarus, Mary, and Martha.

That Jesus loved Capernaum in His own native Galilee is understandable. It was a beautiful place, cool in summer and warm in winter. The blue of the water must have beckoned to Him again and again. However, Bethany certainly was not one of the better areas around Jerusalem. But in that town lived three people whom Jesus loved, Lazarus and his sisters. And they loved Him in return. Their house was always open to our Lord, so He came there often.

We can only guess at the nature of Lazarus' illness, but apparently the disease took life very quickly. Mary and Martha sent Jesus a very simple message, a message that shows spiritual maturity on their part. When we don't know God well, we tend to put Him in tight confines, and dictate in our prayers that we want Him to do. But Mary and Martha did not do that. Jesus would do the right thing; they knew it!

Verse 4 contains two lessons. Certainly Jesus would receive man's adulation when He raised Lazarus from the tomb, where he had lain dead for four days. But there is a far deeper message than that. John 7:39 says that the Holy Spirit would come after He, Jesus, was glorified, that is, had died upon the cross. When Jesus stated that the sickness of Lazarus would glorify Him, I believe He meant that going to Bethany and Lazarus' grave would be the first major step toward a place called Calvary and the cross.

Remember, for Jesus to return to Judea was dangerous. The authorities had already attempted to kill Jesus. Jesus told His disciples that God's work must be done in the given number of hours. Jesus' disciples must have formed a pretty solemn entourage. In their incomplete understanding of Jesus' identity and destiny, these men felt they were heading toward a funeral—not only that of Lazarus but also of Jesus.

1. How does John identify Mary? (11:2)
2. What did Jesus predict about Lazarus' death? (11:4)
3. Why did the disciples not want to go to Bethany? (11:8)
4. What kinds of phrases do you use when you pray? Do they tend to box God in?

184

JUNE 28

The Raising of Lazarus (11:17–44)

According to the ancient Jewish ritual, mourners not only went to the graveside service, but they also followed the bereaved family home and stationed themselves in a circle around the family members. There were never fewer than ten mourners and usually many more, as would have been the case here. These mourners who arrived from Jerusalem were not allowed to speak unless the bereaved asked them to. When, finally, the bereaved family members felt that they could again cope, the mourners were dismissed.

There are two accounts of Jesus' weeping in the Gospels. This, of course, is one of them. And the other is recorded by Luke, who told us that Jesus beheld the wickedness and spiritual death of Jerusalem and wept over it.

1. What did Martha say to Jesus? (11:21–22)
2. What happened when Mary met Jesus? (11:33, 35)
3. How does John describe the tomb? (11:38)
4. How did Lazarus come out of the grave? (11:44)
5. When was the last time you wept with compassion for one of Christ's "little ones"?

The Plot Against Jesus (11:45–57)

Word spread rapidly and soon there was a price on Jesus' head. Isn't it amazing? Jesus raised a man from the dead and brought life and happiness to a family, yet the world wanted to kill Him for it. It was, and still is, a strange, strange world, with upside-down values.

1. What did the Pharisees fear? (11:48)
2. Who called for Jesus' death and on what logic? (11:49–50)
3. What did Jesus do from that time on? (11:54)
4. What values are evident in the things we praise or honor today?

Mary Anoints Jesus (12:1–11)

Now the Lamb of God, the Lamb slain from the foundation of the world, is coming to Jerusalem for the Passover. He will become the ultimate passover and He will be slain.

Because Jerusalem was packed with incoming celebrants, Jesus and His disciples stayed in Bethany at the home of Lazarus, Mary, and Martha. Martha served the meal. She was a practical woman. She showed her love to Christ by working with her hands.

But Mary showed her love in a quite different manner. Spikenard was a favorite perfume, a rose-red ointment made from the dried roots and woolly stems of the spikenard plant. Imported from northern India, spikenard was expensive, and usually transported in an alabaster box to preserve the fragrance.

In that day, it was an honor to be allowed to anoint someone's head; Mary did not believe she was worthy to confer an honor upon Jesus. Mary was there not because she wanted to be exalted, but just because she loved Jesus.

William Barclay writes in his commentary of this moment: "We see how a man's view can be warped. Judas had just seen an action of surpassing loveliness; and he called it extravagant waste. He was an embittered man and he took an embittered view of things. A man's sight depends on what is inside him. He sees only what he is fit and able to see."

1. What time of year did this incident take place? (12:1)
2. What did Mary do? (12:3)
3. How did Judas react? (12:5)
4. What was Judas' role among the disciples? (12:6)
5. What is your attitude toward the money you give for Christ's ministry?

JUNE 30

The Triumphal Entry (12:12–26)

The next day Jesus and His disciples headed for the city of Jerusalem, a relatively short walk down the western slopes of the Mount of Olives, across the deep Kidron Valley, and up the steep road that entered the temple area via the beautiful Eastern Gate. It is the way of the triumphant entry of our Lord. The view is absolutely staggering. And in Jesus' day, when the temple mount was adorned by Herod's magnificent temple, it must have been the most beautiful walk in the world!

In the city itself, many of Jesus' followers heard that Christ was coming. They went out to meet Him, taking branches of palm trees. There were really two crowds converging there in the Kidron Valley, those who were coming with Jesus from Bethany and those who were coming from Jerusalem to meet them. Jesus was riding upon the colt of an ass. He was making a deliberate claim of being the Messiah. Zechariah wrote: "Rejoice greatly, O daughter of Zion!/Shout, O daughter of Jerusalem!/Behold, your King is coming to you;/He is just and having salvation,/Lowly and riding on a donkey, A colt, the foal of a donkey" (Zech. 9:9).

Throughout the Old Testament, great leaders came into cities riding upon one of two animals. Usually, if they were riding a horse, they were coming for war. But if they came on an ass, they were coming in peace.

The crowd completely misread Jesus' approach to Jerusalem. They wanted Him to destroy the authority structure as it presently existed. They wanted Him to grind Rome into the dust. But he did not come to do that. He came in peace.

The fact that Philip and Andrew were the two disciples with Greek names may explain why they served as intermediaries between Jesus and the Greeks.

Parallel passages: Matthew 21:1–11; Mark 11:1–11; Luke 19:28–40.

1. What did Jesus quote after finding the donkey? (12:15)
2. What did the Pharisees say among themselves? (12:19)
3. What answer did Jesus give the Greeks? (12:23–26)
4. What are you attempting to gain in your life?

Jesus Predicts His Death on the Cross (12:27–36)

Again, Jesus told His followers the real reason for His coming into the world; but, as usual, His disciples didn't appear to grasp His message.

Although John's Gospel does not include Jesus' struggle in the Garden of Gethsemane, it does make it clear that Jesus wrestled within Himself. No one wants to die. Although Jesus was God's Son, He had human desires and fears. The closer He came to the Cross, the more He seemed to fight the battle within Himself.

1. What saying echoes the Gethsemane prayer? (12:27–28)
2. What did the people around Jesus hear? (12:29)
3. To what was Jesus referring in verse 32? (12:33)
4. Have there been times when God has spoken to you but you have failed to realize what was happening?

Who Has Believed Our Report? (12:37–50)

John quoted the Old Testament prophet Isaiah in this passage. Was Isaiah saying that God causes men to rebel against Him? No. God is saying to the people, "For all the good I have done for you through miracles and signs and wonders, I might as well have done nothing for you at all, because you have refused to believe, refused to heed my words. Your hearts have grown increasingly blasé about it all, no matter what I have done for you."

1. Why did some of the rulers believe but not confess? (12:42–43)
2. To what does Jesus compare Himself? (12:46)
3. Where does Jesus get His authority? (12:49–50)
4. For what aspects of your life will you be held accountable before God?

JULY 2
John 13:1–30

The Master Becomes a Servant (13:1–20)

In his book, *The Christ Commission,* Og Mandino describes what that upper room probably looked like that night (far from the romanticized concept made popular by Leonardo Da Vinci): "Dominating the large, cluttered chamber was a huge table, rising no more than a foot above the mat-covered floor. It was at least ten feet long and four feet wide, and its dark polished surface [shone in the light]. Piled high along one wall were bundles of clothing and crates filled to overflowing with sandals of countless variety. Wicker baskets beneath the room's three small windows were bulging with squash, ears of corn, figs, grapes, and other fruits. Rows of thick round cheeses, wrapped in cloth and decidedly pungent, towered high in another corner."

Only John records the incident in verses 3–11 and the subsequent teaching. Unfortunately our generation seems to have replaced this servant model with a "star" mentality about those in the ministry. We introduced them as "God's man of the hour," complete with orchestral fanfares and drum rolls. What do you suppose God thinks about that?

1. What had already happened when the supper ended? (13:2)
2. What unusual act did Jesus perform? (13:3–5)
3. What was Peter's reaction? (13:6, 8–9)
4. Why did Jesus perform this act? (13:14–15)
5. In what areas of your life do you carry out the servant model?

Jesus Foretells His Betrayal (13:21–30)

Have you ever wondered what Judas might have been had he allowed Christ control of his life? He must have had some gift of intellect and insight. Perhaps that was his downfall. A person can be so gifted that he doesn't think he needs the Lord. Judas wanted his own way; he wanted to control Christ. But a disciple knows that that can never be.

Parallel passages: Matthew 26:20–25; Mark 14:17–21; Luke 22:21–23.

1. Which disciple asked Jesus to identify the betrayer? (13:23–25)
2. How did Jesus identify the traitor? (13:26)
3. What did Jesus say to Judas? (13:27)
4. What did the disciples think Jesus was saying to Judas? (13:29)
5. What are some ways we betray Jesus today?

JULY 3
John 13:31—14:18

The New Commandment (13:31–35)
This passage records the commandment that is the basis of Christianity. Christ gave the standard of how to love at a later point in John (15:12): "You love one another as I have loved you." We are to love our neighbor with the same kind of love that God shows toward us.

1. How long would Jesus be with His disciples? (13:33)
2. How will people recognize Christ's disciples? (13:35)
3. How do you demonstrate your love for your neighbor?

Peter's Denial Foretold (13:36–38)
These are sad verses, for Peter did not understand how deep a commitment was required of him.
Parallel passages: Matthew 26:31–35; Mark 14:27–31; Luke 22:31–34.

1. What did Peter claim? (13:37)
2. What did Jesus predict? (13:38)
3. If you were in Peter's situation today, how would you react?

The Way, the Truth, and the Life (14:1–18)
This well-known passage is usually misread or misquoted. Nowhere in Scripture does it say we are going to get a mansion. It says "a place" (v. 2). "A place" with Christ is far, far better than a mansion somewhere else.

Christ is "the way" by His teaching. His words show us the way to God. He is also the way by His example. He went before, enduring all that we will ever be called upon to endure. He is the way by His work of mediation: dying, rising, and ascending.

Christ is the truth in all the prophecies in Scripture; He is the truth of all the promises of God; He is the truth of all the typology: the ark, the ladder, the tabernacle, the mercy seat. Christ is the truth as the teacher and expounder as the actual embodiment, and as the dispenser through us.

1. What did Jesus promise His disciples? (14:2–3)
2. What did Thomas ask Jesus? (14:5)
3. What did Philip say to Jesus? (14:8)
4. For what would Jesus pray to God for His disciples? (14:16–17)
5. What promise did Jesus make? (14:18)
6. In what ways do you see God's Spirit at work today?

190

JULY 4
John 14:19—15:8

Indwelling of the Father and the Son; the Gift of His Peace (14:19–31)

In this passage, Jesus gave the hallmark of a disciple. Jesus makes it very clear that discipleship involves obedience. "To obey is better than sacrifice" (1 Sam. 15:22) and Jesus' teaching does not refute this. Jesus also promises help to His disciples when He is no longer with them.

1. What promise does Jesus make? (14:19)
2. Who are the ones who love Jesus? (14:21)
3. Who is the Helper that Jesus will send? (14:26)
4. What gift will Jesus leave His disciples? (14:27)
5. Jesus said that it is important to obey His Word. How familiar are you with His Word?

Jesus, the True Vine (15:1–8)

Three vital lessons can be found in these verses about the vine, the branches, and the fruit.

1. The vine is good for nothing if it does not bear fruit. This familiar theme runs through all the Gospels. There isn't a thing you can do with a fruitless vine. A vine can only do one thing, and that is bear fruit. If it doesn't do that, it has no reason for being.

2. The branches grow out of the vine. They are really an extension of the main vine. As Christians we receive our sustenance and character from Christ. We are to be an extension of our Lord. If that branch somehow gets severed from the vine, there is no more life.

3. The vine doesn't bear fruit; the branches do. Christ expects us to bear fruit. He will bear us; He will sustain us, but we are to be the fruit-bearers. What kind of fruit? The fruit of the Spirit. But also in a very real way, we are to bear others into the kingdom.

This promise regarding answered prayer is in direct response to being a fruit-bearing branch on the vine. Such a branch is not going to ask something amiss. Every action will bear further fruit for the kingdom, for Christ. And prayers will be in relationship to the bearing.

1. To whom did Jesus compare Himself and God? (15:1–2)
2. What happens to those who do not live according to Christ's will? (15:6)
3. How do your prayers reflect that you are a fruit-bearing vine?

191

JULY 5
John 15:9—16:4

Love and Joy Perfected (15:9–17)

In this passage Jesus describes the kind of love Christians must express. We must look at Christ's love as the pattern, even though we know that we cannot love with the same divine intensity.

How did Christ love us?

Certainly we did not deserve that love. In many cases we didn't even want it. And our love for others, as Christ's for us, does not begin with the other person's doing something for us. That love does not have to be stimulated or bought. It is spontaneous.

Our concept of love is rather superficial. To read of the love Christ had for you and me and to read further that He expects us to love others in the same way is staggering. We cannot fulfill this commandment through our own strength and devices.

1. What did Jesus command? (15:9, 12, 17)
2. Who are Jesus' friends? (15:14)
3. What would Jesus no longer call His disciples? (15:15)
4. What do we need to remember when we feel we are falling short of the kind of love Christ wants us to demonstrate?

The World's Hatred (15:18—16:4)

This is a difficult passage and one we don't want to hear in this generation. We want to be accepted and appreciated. We want the world to applaud, but Jesus said it wouldn't happen.

Why? The values of today's world are far different from the values Jesus taught. To try to live according to Jesus' values marks one, at the very least, for ridicule. Some of our current literature would make you think that when you become converted, people will fall all over themselves to touch you. Not so. This world hates Jesus. So it will hate the one in whom Christ lives.

Further, Jesus said the world system would hate you because it does not know God and, in fact, hates God. Why? No reason. Jesus said, "They hated Me without a cause" (v. 25). It is a blind hatred of everything that is holy and pure.

1. What did Jesus mean when He said, "A servant is not greater than his master"? (15:20)
2. Why does the world have no excuse for sin? (15:22)
3. Why was Jesus hated? (15:25)
4. Why did Jesus tell His disciples these things? (16:4)
5. How popular are you in the eyes of the world?

JULY 6
John 16:5–33

The Work of the Holy Spirit (16:5—15)

These verses form a treatise on the ministry of the Holy Spirit in our generation. Jesus said that a part of the Holy Spirit's work was that of moral conviction. Knowing about sin and being convicted of sin are two different things. When the Spirit shows us God's concept of sin and then convicts us of it, we cannot help being shocked. We indeed desire the cleansing that comes from Christ.

The Holy Spirit convicts the world of righteousness—Christ's standard of rightness. The more we know of Christ, the more awful sin becomes. The more we compare our world with the works of God, the greater that chasm grows.

The second great work of the Holy Spirit is that of spiritual guidance in the life of the believer. Think how much the disciples could have learned from Jesus had they been able to grasp His teachings! But they could not. You and I today have so much more light. If we are spiritually ignorant, it is because we have chosen to be that way. The Holy Spirit *will* teach us.

1. Why was it to the disciples' advantage that Jesus go away? (16:7)
2. Why could Jesus not say more to His disciples? (16:12–13)
3. Name several ways in which the ways of our world do not match God's ways.

Jesus Christ Has Overcome the World (16:16—33)

Jesus again predicts His death and resurrection, but this time He goes on to say that the tables will be turned.

In verses 25–33, Jesus told His disciples an important truth, for without it, they could not have carried on His work. From that point, a person no longer needed a priest or advocate to act as an intermediary between himself and God. The disciples had one more step to go, however. They had to be filled with the Holy Spirit. That would happen at Pentecost.

1. What did the disciples ask one another? (16:18)
2. To what does Jesus compare the sorrow and joy to come? (16:21)
3. How did Jesus' teaching change at this point? (16:25)
4. How can we have peace and tribulation at the same time? (16:33)

JULY 7
John 17:1–19

Jesus' Prayer for Himself and His Prayer for His Disciples (17:1—19)

This prayer comes at the end of the Last Supper. Only John records the teachings following the Last Supper. Jesus' prayer is for glorification— both for Himself and for God (see vv. 1—5).

In verses 6–19, Jesus' prayer, was for His disciples. Jesus never asked God to take the disciples out of the world. Rather they should put themselves in the center of worldly activity. It is important to note that Jesus prayed that the disciples be unified, for there is nothing worse than division in the work of God.

The question naturally follows, "What about denominations?" Thank God for them. God made each of us as individuals. You might not like my church; it may be too noisy. On the other hand, you might think it's too quiet. We all enjoy different worship styles, but we are united in our love for God, for Christ, for each other, and in the need for the Holy Spirit to do a work in our lives.

1. What is eternal life? (17:3)
2. What had Jesus done on earth? (17:4)
3. How did the disciples come to Jesus? (17:6)
4. What did Jesus call Judas? (17:12)
5. What was Jesus' prayer for His disciples? (17:15,17)
6. How does that prayer apply to us today?

Jesus' Prayer for All Believers (17:20–26)

Jesus' prayer for all believers is among the last words the disciples heard Him say in His incarnate form. He prayed here for you and for me.

In His prayer, Jesus spoke of glory. In the first chapters of Relevation (especially chapters 4–6) we read of a partial glimpse of that glory. We get glued down to the mundane things of life so easily. We come to see the work of God as a mimeographed bulletin or a scrubbed Sunday school floor. But those are only tools, imperfect tools.

If only we could see with spiritual eyes the glory of Christ! If only we could be motivated by higher instincts than the desire to have a perfect attendance button or another worthless trophy! If, like Isaiah, we could see Him high and lifted up, His train filling the temple, then we could rise above the mediocrity that so often engulfs us.

I know that I will never see Christ's full glory while I am on this earth in a mortal body. But through the creative touch of the Holy Spirit sometimes I can get a partial glimpse and I am elevated to new heights of worship and adoration. I don't worry much about people being so heavenly minded that they're no earthly good. Usually it's just the opposite; we are so earthly minded that we are not much heavenly good.

When I see Christ in all His glory, then my day-to-day living takes on new meaning.

1. For what two things does Jesus pray in this passage? (17:21, 24)
2. Why does He pray this prayer for us? (17:23)
3. When was the last time that you had a glimpse of Christ's true glory?

Betrayal and Arrest (18:1–14)

John has taken four chapters to tell us of the proceedings in the upper room on Mount Zion where Jesus had His Last Supper with the disciples. Now, in chapter 18, John gives us a quickly changing scenario. The Lord Jesus leaves the upper room for the Garden of Gethsemane, where He is arrested and taken to Annas. From there He is taken to Caiaphas and to the governor's residence (ironically, right back on Mount Zion again).

Only John records that soldiers were among those who came to arrest Jesus. Og Mandino, in his book *The Christ Commission,* suggested that Pilate had sent along two hundred soldiers with the temple party to show his utter contempt for Caiaphas and the Sanhedrin. After all, if there were a budding king in that garden, one should take all precaution in dealing with this "impostor."

Parallel passages: Matthew 26:47–56; Mark 14:43–50; Luke 22:47–53.

1. Where did Jesus go after His Last Supper teaching? (18:1)
2. How did Judas know the place? (18:2)
3. What did the crowd do when Jesus first identified Himself? (18:6)
4. What did Peter do? (18:10)
5. What was the servant's name? (18:10)
6. How were Annas and Caiaphas related? (18:13)
7. What advice had Caiaphas given the Jews? (18:14)
8. Jesus visited Gethsemane often. Do you have a special place where you go to be alone with the Lord?

Peter's Denial (18:15–27)

There isn't a person reading this section who can't identify with Peter. All of us have made mistakes. All of us have done something we would like to erase. But Jesus' love casts a long shadow, and it reaches out to us just as it did to Peter.

Parallel passages: Matthew 26:59–75; Mark 14:55–72; Luke 22:55–71.

1. Who followed Jesus? (18:15)
2. Who first recognized Peter? (18:17)
3. Whom did Jesus say to call as witnesses? (18:21)
4. What did an officer do? (18:22)
5. Who else recognized Peter? (18:26)
6. What would you like to erase from your life? Have you opened yourself up to Jesus' healing love in that situation?

JULY 10
John 18:28—19:16

Jesus Before Pilate (18:28—40)

The leaders of the Sanhedrin were quite powerless to do anything with Christ. They wanted to kill Him, but only the Roman governor Pontius Pilate had the authority to mete out the death sentence. So very early in the morning, they led Jesus to the Praetorium, Pilate's Jerusalem headquarters, near the temple and adjacent to Herod's palace.

Excavations have unearthed some of this palace, called "Ecce Homo," or "Behold the Man." Visitors to Jerusalem can stand on the actual pavement where Jesus was severely beaten by the soldiers. It is truly a holy place, and its authenticity is historically documented.

Parallel passages: Matthew 27:1–2, 11–14; Mark 15:1–5; Luke 23:1–5.

1. Why did Jesus' accusers not enter the Praetorium? (18:28)
2. What reason did the Jews give for bringing Jesus to Pilate? (18:31)
3. How did the Jews respond when Pilate offered to release Jesus? (18:40)
4. Jesus said His kingdom was not of this world. What evidences do you see of the existence of Jesus' kingdom?

Jesus Sentenced to Die (19:1—16)

After giving in to the Jews' demand, Pilate had Jesus scourged. The person who carried out the scourging was called a *lictor.* The whip was a short, circular piece of wood, to which were attached several strips of leather. At the end of each strip was a chunk of bone or a small piece of iron chain. There was no set number of stripes, and the law said nothing about the parts of the body to be assailed. The bits of bone and chain would have flung around the sides of the body and raised small hemorrhages under the skin or torn off bits of flesh.

The emperor at that time was Tiberius Caesar, a brooding, suspicious man who had a morbid fear of disloyalty. During his administration, history records a number of treasonry trials. At the time of Christ's trial, Tiberius had become senile and suffered other mental disturbances.

Parallel passages: Matthew 27:1–2, 11–14; Mark 15:1–20; Luke 23:1–5, 13–23.

1. How did the soldiers mock Jesus? (19:2–3)
2. What did Jesus say to Pilate about earthly power? (19:11)
3. What did Pilate want to do? Why was he afraid to do so? (19:12)
4. What areas of our lives are equivalent to convicting Christ?

The Crucifixion and Burial (19:17–42)

Historically, a person was never beaten the way Jesus was, in addition to being crucified. It should be pointed out here that a person to whom such punishment was administered was in critical condition for days afterwards. However, Jesus was forced to carry His cross to Golgotha, halfway across the city. Christ must have been in incredible physical condition to take such punishment and still be able to bear that heavy burden.

As Jesus agonized on the cross, below Him the soldiers parted His garments and gambled over them.

Only John records Jesus' words in verses 25–27 and also verses 28–30.

Sabbath was just a few hours away, and no body could remain on a cross once Sabbath began. The Romans had a practice of breaking the victims' legs with huge clubs so their bodies would sag, and their arms would have to bear the full weight of the body. In that position, the pectoral muscles in their chests would involuntarily become paralyzed so the victims could not exhale.

The Old Testament prophecies referred to in verses 36 and 37 are from Exodus 12:46; Numbers 9:12; Psalm 34:20; and Zechariah 12:10.

Parallel passages: Matthew 27:32–61; Mark 15:21–47; Luke 23:26–56.

1. What title did Pilate place above Jesus' head? (19:19)
2. What displeased the chief priests about the title? (19:21)
3. What did Jesus' garment look like? (19:23)
4. Who stood by the cross? (19:25)
5. What instructions did Jesus give concerning His mother? (19:26–27)
6. Who buried Jesus? (19:38–39)
7. The multitudes Jesus helped were not present at the Crucifixion. Have there been times in your life when you haven't been there when Jesus needed you for His work?

John 20:1–31

The Empty Tomb (20:1–31)

It was now the first day of the week, Sunday. Jesus' friends had observed "Shabbat," or Sabbath, and thus had stayed home on Saturday. Now they are coming out in the streets again. The first one to the tomb was Mary Magdalene. It was still dark when she arrived. It is possible that no one ever loved Jesus as much as Mary Magdalene did, for He had done so much for her.

Why didn't Mary recognize Christ when He appeared to her? No longer could Jesus be recognized by the flesh. He was no longer God in a man's body. Now His form was glorified; it was eternal. He was now revealed in His true form. And to recognize Him was a spiritual exercise, not just a physical one. That is why the new birth is essential to salvation. It is not enough to know the historical Jesus. We must know Him in the fullness of His present glory.

Verses 24–31 tell the well-known story of doubting Thomas. There are few of us who cannot identify with Thomas. Until we've seen, it is difficult to believe.

Parallel passages: Matthew 28:1–20; Mark 16:1–18; Luke 24:1–12, 36–49.

1. What did Mary Magdalene do when she found the tomb empty? (20:2)
2. Which disciples went to the tomb? (20:3)
3. Who stayed at the tomb and what did she see? (20:11–12)
4. What did Jesus warn Mary about? (20:17)
5. Why were the disciples hiding? (20:19)
6. What did Jesus give the disciples and how? (20:22)
7. What proof of Jesus' resurrection did Thomas need? (20:27)
8. How do the Resurrection appearances help your faith?

Final Encounters with Disciples (21:1–25)

The disciples must have been very confused, dismayed men. From their homes, they could look to the northwest of the sea, just above Capernaum and see the great hillside where Jesus had given the Sermon on the Mount. Just below that was the place where Christ broke the loaves and fishes and fed the multitudes. To the east was Gadara where Christ had performed miracles. Nearly everything they saw was evidence of Christ's life. What would they do now? Where would they go? Would they ever see Jesus again?

What was Christ asking in verses 15–17? It could have been two things. Looking around the beach there, at the boats, at the fish, at Peter's home, Jesus may have been asking, "Peter, do you love Me more than all these things? Are you willing to give up your job of fishing, your reasonable comfort, and give yourself to My work?"

Or Jesus might have been looking at the other disciples in the area and asked, "Peter, do you love Me more than these men do?" Remember Peter had once bragged to the Lord, "Though they all fall away because of You, I will never fall away" (see Matt. 26:33).

Jesus must have been pleased with Peter's answer.

This Gospel closes on such a touching and poignant note.

John did indeed live a long time, the only one of the original twelve to die a normal death. He died in Ephesus, where he pastored that great Spirit-filled church for so long.

1. What were the disciples doing? (21:3)
2. What did Jesus tell them to do? (21:6)
3. Who recognized Jesus? (21:7)
4. What did Jesus command Peter? (21:15–17)
5. What did Jesus say about John? (21:23)
6. What did John say about Jesus' other acts? (21:25)
7. Do you love Jesus more than any or all of your possessions? Are you willing to follow Him though all others forsake Him?

ACTS

JULY 14
Acts 1:1–26

The Promise of the Holy Spirit (1:1–8)

The Book of Acts tells the story of brave men and women, filled with the power of the Holy Spirit, who faced incredible obstacles in taking the gospel of Christ to the known world.

Both the Gospel of Luke and the Acts are addressed to the same man. We do not know exactly who this Theophilus was. The name means "friend of God" in Greek. "The former account" (v. 1) was Luke's Gospel, in which he told Theophilus the things that Jesus began to do and teach before He ascended to the Father.

1. What did Jesus command the apostles? (1:4)
2. What did the disciples ask Jesus? (1:6)
3. What did Jesus say about human knowledge of God's will? (1:7)
4. How does this passage speak to us today about our attempts to witness?

The Ascension; The Upper Room Prayer Meeting (1:9–26)

The Ascension, described in verses 9–11, emphasizes Jesus' eternal character. For three years Jesus had been teaching His disciples that His kingdom was not of this earth. They could not comprehend that teaching. Just moments before, one of them had asked, "Lord, will You at this time restore the kingdom to Israel?" (v. 6). It was in the upper room that the disciples chose a successor to Judas.

1. Who appeared at Jesus' ascension? (1:10)
2. Who, besides the disciples, entered the upper room? (1:14)
3. Who took the leadership among the disciples? (1:15)
4. What happened to Judas, according to this account? (1:18)
5. Whom did the disciples propose for discipleship and how was he selected? (1:23, 26)
6. By what methods do we choose our own church leaders today?

The Coming of the Holy Spirit (2:1–13)

The Feast of Pentecost or the Feast of Weeks (see Lev. 23:15–21) was perhaps the most popular of all the Jewish feasts, coming fifty days after the Passover Sabbath. During this harvest festival the participants presented loaves prepared from the newly ripened wheat as offerings to God. Jerusalem was packed with worshipers at this time.

It was at Pentecost that the Holy Spirit was given by Christ for a new dimension of service and ministry. Jesus had often promised such an outpouring. It does not mean that the Holy Spirit had not been on earth previous to that; for, indeed that Spirit had ministered in all ages. But now the Spirit came to give truth concerning the resurrected and glorified Savior. He ordained the church with divine power to declare the message of Christ.

Note that Luke makes it clear that the disciples were in one accord, or united for a common purpose. No church body will experience the ministry of the Holy Spirit without such unity of the Holy Spirit. Jesus had told Nicodemus, "The wind blows where it wishes, and you hear the sound of it, but cannot tell where it comes from and where it goes. So is everyone who is born of the Spirit" (John 3:8).

The matter of speaking in tongues presents a problem for many people. This manifestation occurs today, but the problem comes when people seek God solely to speak with tongues. The first believers at Pentecost made no such request. They were glorifying God and worshiping Christ when the miracle happened. The filling of the Spirit and the resulting miracle of tongues are the direct result of a person's seeking God and wanting to be touched by God's Holy Spirit. It is the Spirit that we seek; not the manifestation.

1. What two signs of the Holy Spirit appeared to those gathered in the room? (Acts 2:2–3)
2. Who lived in Jerusalem at the time? (2:5, 9–11)
3. How did Jerusalem's inhabitants react? (2:7–8)
4. What was the cause of this phenomenon, according to some onlookers? (2:13)
5. What is your motivation for seeking the Holy Spirit in your life?

JULY 16
Acts 2:14–47

Peter's Sermon (2:14–41)

This passage contains perhaps the greatest recorded sermon of all time. It is the first Christian apology with the aim of proving that Christ was the Messiah. Every preacher and teacher would do well to note two aspects of this sermon: Peter preached Christ, the risen Messiah; He effectively used Scripture, not taking part of a verse and building a whole case around it, but using chapters to prove the validity of his case.

Note particularly verses 37–40. They record the church's first true altar call.

Note also that the supreme argument for Christ's messiahship is the Resurrection, and it continues to be the central thesis of our faith today.

1. What Old Testament prophet did Peter quote? (2:16)
2. What did David say concerning Jesus? (2:25–28)
3. What did Peter say that everyone should know? (2:36)
4. What was the result of Peter's preaching that day? (2:41)
5. What place does the Resurrection play in your own faith?

Life Among the Believers (2:42–47)

The Book of Acts gives us the scriptural pattern for our conduct in church matters, so it is important that we see what happened to these new converts; They *continued* (salvation was not the whole walk) in the apostles' teaching. The act of conversion or the new birth is only the first step in the Christian walk, certainly not the culmination. It is more like a physical birth.

One writer has summed up the Jerusalem church like this: 1. It was a learning church. 2. It was a church of fellowship. 3. It was a praying church. 4. It was a reverent church (v. 43 gives us the feeling of the "awe" these people had for the Lord). 5. It was a church where things happened, where signs and wonders were present. 6. It was a sharing church. The people had feelings of care and responsibility for each other. 7. It was a worshiping church. 8. It was a happy church. 9. It was a church filled with people that others could not help liking.

1. What did the first believers do? (2:42)
2. How did the believers deal with their possessions? (2:44–45)
3. How much like this first church is your congregation of believers?

JULY 17

Acts 3:1–26

A Lame Man Healed; Preaching in Solomon's Porch (3:1–26)

Devout Jews had specific times to pray at the temple: 9:00 A.M., noon, and 3:00 P.M. This healing incident would have taken place during the afternoon prayer time. This first major miracle brought the new church to the attention of the religious leaders.

The miraculous healing was the occasion of Peter's second great sermon, which carried the same theme as his first sermon—that Jesus is the Christ. Peter stressed the enormity of rejecting Jesus Christ but held out hope in the form of a call to repentance—a positive call that carried no dire threats but rather a positive promise.

While it is true that there are terrible ramifications to rejecting God's grace and saving love, fear is no reason to come to the Lord. It is far better to motivate a person to come to the Lord from a positive perspective.

The commandment from the Lord, as given by Peter in this third chapter, is to repent. The Bible gives us this teaching over and over again. This is not some shallow repentance brought about by the fear of being caught in sin. Rather, it is an abhorrence of sin much like God's. Repentance involves change of thinking and attitude. It also involves restitution, making things right.

1. What two disciples carried out this first healing? (3:1)
2. Who was healed? (3:2)
3. What caused Peter to begin this second sermon? (3:11–12)
4. Whom did Peter credit with the healing? (3:12–16)
5. What did Moses prophesy? (3:22–23)
6. How does your repentance compare with the repentance of which the Bible speaks?

JULY 18
Acts 4:1–31

Peter and John Before the Sanhedrin (4:1–31)

Peter's sermon resulted in his and John's arrest. It is important to note that the new church's first clash with Judiasm came from the Sadducees rather than the Pharisees. Throughout the Gospels, Jesus was confronted primarily by the Pharisees, who were concerned that Jesus was not following Jewish law. But the new church clashed with the Sadducees, the party that denied any kind of resurrection and the party whose primary concern was to preserve their political power.

In verse 7, the authorities asked Peter the question intended to condemn him, and Peter took a lesson from the Master Teacher. He took no credit for the healing and asked: "If we this day are judged for a good deed done to the helpless man, [isn't this whole hearing a bit out of hand?]" (v. 9).

The disciples' response to the authorities demand in verse 18 was a complete severance of the Christian movement from the government and social state. Such a response is often needed in our day.

1. Who arrested Peter and John and why? (4:1–2)
2. How many people were converted as a result of Peter's sermon? (4:4)
3. What question did the authorities ask Peter and John? (4:7)
4. What did the disciples, quoting from Psalm 118:22, call Jesus? (4:11)
5. What quandary did the authorities find themselves in? (4:16–17)
6. What did they command the disciples? (4:18)
7. What did Peter and John answer? (4:19–20)
8. At what time, if any, have you felt it necessary to act out of your Christian belief rather than your government's official stance?

JULY 19
Acts 4:32—5:11

All Things in Common; Ananias and Sapphira (4:32—5:11)

Luke gives us a brief insight here into the cultural pattern the early Christians established. It was a sort of communal living, much like the present-day *kibbutzim* in Israel, where the people own nothing privately, but have all things in common. Such a pattern is truly only a cultural pattern, certainly not a leadership mold for spiritual truth. The spiritual principle to be found here is that the people cared for each other. Jesus had said that the notable thing about believers would be their love for each other. No one went without.

Perhaps one of the reasons our government has to be involved heavily in welfare is that the church has abandoned it altogether. The early Christians cared for one another's physical and material needs.

The story in verses 1–11 is a tragic one. It is the New Testament equivalent of the story of Joshua and Achan. You will recall that story. Joshua and the children of Israel had just conquered Jericho and were now embattled with the little fortress of Ai. They suffered a horrendous defeat there because one man, Achan, had coveted some of the conquered goods dedicated to God. The essence of idolatry is *the private use of property that has been devoted to God.* Achan had hidden booty from the other Israelites. His act cost them a victory, and Achan and his family their lives.

The great sin of these two was worldliness, an attitude that blinds people to the presence of God. Their every dream, every vision, every thought is carnal and filled with worldly desire. Ananias was trying to impress the people of the church. He may have indeed done so for a while. But he certainly did not impress God.

1. What did the people do with their possessions and land? (4:35)
2. What particular believers evidently made a large donation? (4:36–37)
3. What did Ananias do? (5:2)
4. With what charge did Peter confront Ananias? (5:4)
5. What happened to Ananias? (5:5)
6. What happened to Sapphira? (5:10)
7. How much of our time do we spend trying to impress others?

206

Many Signs and Wonders Performed; the Apostles Freed and Persecuted (5:12–32)

Much of the teaching and ministry of the young church was carried out right in the temple courtyard—an area of twenty-six acres.

Peter now was a very different man, for he had placed himself in God's hands. His shadow became the equivalent of Jesus' robe. The term "the rest" in verse 13 is confusing. It may refer to people who were afraid to join the Christians publicly.

Verses 17–21 record a miraculous deliverance. After reading this passage, meditate on the delivering hand of God in your life.

When Peter and the other apostles were rearrested, Peter gave the same defense he had previously given (see v. 29).

1. How were the sick brought to Peter? (5:15)
2. How were the apostles freed? (5:19)
3. Where did the authorities find the apostles? (5:25)
4. What was Peter's defense? (5:29)
5. How have you experienced God's deliverance in your life?

Gamaliel's Advice (5:33–42)

One man who saved the apostles at this point was an older teacher named Gamaliel. This development is fascinating, because Gamaliel was a renowned doctor of Jewish law and was at that very time the instructor of a fellow named Saul of Tarsus, later to become Paul the apostle. Gamaliel was of the house and lineage of David, the grandson of Hillel, who founded the very best school of thought among the Pharisees.

There are some who believe Gamaliel had been influenced by other leaders such as Nicodemus and Joseph of Arimathea and was one of the secret believers in Christ. That theory seems rather farfetched in light of the fact that Paul reflected none of those feelings until he personally encountered Christ on the road to Damascus. But no matter what the state of his heart at the time, Gamaliel's tolerant and liberal attitude saved the apostles from death at this juncture.

1. What was the basis of Gamaliel's argument? (5:36–39)
2. What did the authorities do to the apostles? (5:40)
3. What was the attitude of the apostles? (5:41)
4. At what time, if ever, have you suffered because of your Christian stand?

JULY 21
Acts 6:1–15

The Appointment of the Seven (6:1–7)

The church was comprised of two kinds of Jews, Aramaic-speaking Jews and Greek-speaking Jews (Hellenists). There was tension between the two groups, which is revealed here by a rather insignificant matter. The Hellenistic Jews thought their widows were receiving less than the Aramaic Jews in the daily distribution of food. The apostles were right in the middle of this. The matter was important to those involved, but let's face it, the apostles had more to do than to parcel out food every day. And none of them wanted to supervise the financial arrangement of the church community. So it was their desire that the members select seven men who would be responsible for the distribution of charitable allocations.

1. What qualifications did the seven men need to have? (6:3)
2. What did the Twelve intend to do after the seven were appointed? (6:4)
3. Who were the seven? (6:5)
4. How are the leaders in your church chosen?

Stephen's Arrest (6:8–15)

Stephen was the first Christian martyr. Dr. Alexander Wyte wrote, "In the stoning of Stephen, there was lost to the Pentecostal Church another Apostle Paul. Stephen was a young man of such original genius and of such special grace that there was nothing he might not have attained to had he been allowed to live. His wonderful openness of mind; his perfect freedom from all prepossessions, prejudices, and superstitions of his day; his courage, his eloquence, his spotless character; with a certain sweet, and at the same time majestic, manner; combined to set Stephen in the very front rank both of service and of risk."

The synagogue mentioned in verse 9 was apparently attended by Jews from a number of lands of the dispersion. Some believe that Saul of Tarsus was a member of that synagogue. The members were fiercely loyal to Judaism. The fact that this young preacher carried the Greek name of Stephen probably didn't help him.

1. What synagogue was angered by Stephen's preaching? (6:9)
2. With what did they charge Stephen? (6:11)
3. What did the false witnesses report? (6:14)
4. What stand has your congregation taken that had made it unpopular with some group?

JULY 22
Acts 7:1–16

Stephen's Defense (7:1–16)

Give yourself time to read Stephen's words slowly and to take them in fully. What the young deacon did was to give a defense of Christianity, not a defense of himself. Stephen probably knew his fate was a foregone conclusion and that he would be with the Lord before the day was over.

Stephen's points were valid ones. He admonished his accusers not to restrict God to one land or one building or one locality or even to one people. Those were difficult words for Stephen's critics to swallow. For a long time they had believed they were the sole possessors of God's promise. Anyone else or anyplace else was only an impostor. That's why they had such a difficult time accepting Christ. They could only see their great temple, the massive altar, the priests, the sacrifices. Anything beyond that was impossible for them to understand or rationalize. They had truly put God into the proverbial box.

Stephen's name in the Greek is *Stephanos,* which means a garland or a crown. The record of Stephen's death is the longest account of any death in the Bible next to that of our Lord's.

Stephen was the first Christian preacher who was not a rough Galilean. He was the first truly educated preacher. He was foreign-born and spoke Greek. With Stephen, the Christian message was thrust outside Jerusalem and the Sea of Galilee into the cultural, political, social, economic, and academic life of the known world.

But there is another fascinating thing about this man Stephen. With all his culture and breeding, his insight and learning, he was a man of conviction. He really believed the things he said.

Peter admonished us to be able to give a reason to anyone who asks us about our faith. When Caiaphas demanded an answer from Stephen concerning his faith, he got far more than he ever bargained for. Stephen was able to verbalize his faith in exquisite detail.

1. How did Stephen defend himself generally? (7:1–16)
2. What did God say to Abraham? (7:3)
3. How well can you articulate your faith?

JULY 23
Acts 7:17–43

Stephen Before the Sanhedrin (7:17–43)

In his defense, Stephen used the basic Jewish teachings—teachings agreed upon by all those in the synagogue—to point to Jesus Christ as the Messiah.

Stephen recalled the Israelites' delivery from Egypt. Have you ever wondered why the Jews hated Egyptians so? History tells us that in 2000 B.C. Egypt was quite advanced culturally but that its government was fragmented.

Because Egypt was split into five divisions, each with a ruler and separate government, the nation was ripe for invasion. Those invaders were called the Hyksos kings or shepherd kings, who swept in from Syria and conquered the country. Those kings were ruthless and brutal in their takeover. They burned the cities and razed the temples, exterminating the male Egyptian population and making slaves of the women and children.

Small wonder then, that when the native Egyptians finally gathered the strength to recapture their government after four centuries of foreign rule, they hated all outsiders, including the vast number of Hebrews in their midst, and made slaves of them.

Into this chaos, Moses was born, the great Old Testament deliverer. Just as Jesus was born in due season, in the fullness of time, to become the great deliverer of the New Testament. In his defense before the Sanhedrin, Stephen was building a solid basis for his belief that Christ was the Messiah.

Stephen's reasoning drew hostility from his listeners. They could not reject his debating procedures, but his conclusions were like waving a red flag in front of a bull. Stephen had taken the great names of Abraham and Moses and used them as forerunners to this Christ, whom they had just killed on Calvary. Not only did this man present an executed man as the Messiah, but he was using their national heroes to do it. And that was just too much for them to take.

1. How did the Egyptians treat the Israelites? (7:19)
2. How was Moses educated? (7:22)
3. What happened when Moses was forty? (7:23–25)
4. How did the Israelites react to Moses' action? (7:26–28)
5. Where did Moses go? (7:29)
6. Where did Moses meet God? (7:30)
7. How did Israel rebel against God? (7:40–43)
8. What kind of "gods [do we have] to go before us" today?

God's True Tabernacle (7:44—60)

In this passage Stephen concludes his defense—a defense that so angered the religious authorities that Stephen became the first Christian martyr. Stephen said that the Jews had killed all of the prophets. There is no historical basis for that statement, but it was legendary that nearly every prophet did indeed become a martyr.

1. How did the Jews worship God in the wilderness? (7:44)
2. Where did Stephen say God dwells? (7:48—50)
3. What did Stephen call the authorities? (7:51)
4. What did Stephen see? (7:56)
5. What were Stephen's last words? (7:59)
6. Name a time in your life when you've felt Jesus' presence in extreme situations.

Saul Persecutes the Church (8:1—8)

Luke gives us here a graphic portrayal of the reactions of men when confronted with the Christ.

Verse 1 describes one reaction; verse 2 describes another. There was no middle ground, and there never can be. One is either fully for Christ and therefore committed to Him, or he is totally opposed to Him.

So we are introduced to this man, Saul of Tarsus, who becomes the dominant figure throughout the rest of the New Testament.

1. What happened following Stephen's death? (8:1)
2. In what activity did Saul engage? (8:3)
3. Where did Philip go and what were the results of his ministry? (8:5—8)
4. What steps have you taken to see that you continue growing in the faith after your conversion?

JULY 25
Acts 8:9–40

Simon the Sorcerer (8:9–25)

Simon Magus evidently had messianic ambitions. He had quite an ego and a reputation as a sorcerer, or practitioner of black magic. He no doubt was a horoscope reader, and he had the attention of the city.

Simon tried to buy the healing powers the apostles possessed. Had Simon been alive today, he would have doubtless gone on TV with "miracle meetings."

There is perhaps a little of Simon in all of us: Most of us seek the praises and adulation of men. Herbert Lockyer calls it "the perils of popularity.

1. Why did the people listen to Simon? (8:11)
2. What was Simon's reaction to Philip? (8:13)
3. What were the people in Samaria lacking? (8:15–16)
4. What was Simon's sin? (8:18–19)
5. What was Peter's evaluation of Simon? (8:23)
6. Think of some ministries today which might be very much like Simon's in that they are lacking in the influence of the Holy Spirit.

Philip and the Ethiopian Eunuch (8:26–40)

Most of this eighth chapter deals with the ministry of a remarkable deacon named Philip. Philip was a man who loved to evangelize. Whatever God told him to do, he did. He was expressly obedient. He preached all over Israel, from the desert country near Gaza (where he met the eunuch) to Caesara in the north. He must have been a marvelous father; his four daughters loved him and followed in his steps. They, too, were excellent preachers of the gospel. Paul said that he loved to stay in Philip's home.

The Ethiopians, from the region of the Nile south of Egypt, were Nubians. Ordinarily a eunuch, being imperfect, would have been excluded by the law from worship, but Isaiah 56:3 shows a more charitable attitude.

Azotus (v. 40) is the Ashdod of the Old Testament.

1. What did the angel instruct Philip to do? (8:26)
2. Whose official was the eunuch? (8:27)
3. What was the eunuch reading? (8:28)
4. What did the eunuch want? (8:36)
5. How does this passage speak to the notion that only certain kinds of people qualify to worship God?

JULY 26
Acts 9:1–30

The Conversion of Saul (9:1–30)

Saul's home city, Tarsus, was famous for two things: It was a commercial center and the site of a well-known university. Although Paul was a Jew, he was a Roman citizen. Since citizens of Tarsus were not automatically Roman citizens, Paul's father probably received his citizenship as a freeman, serving some Roman family.

Paul was doubtlessly well educated and, as a result, bilingual. He would have studied at the University of Tarsus; but, as a Jew, his education would not have been a purely Greek one. We know that he went to Jerusalem to study under the rabbis—something every well-off, devout Jew would have done. The Jewish historian Josephus said of the rabbis that "the only wisdom they prize is a knowledge of our laws and the correct interpretation of the Scriptures."

Verse 2 probably refers to an event recorded in the intertestamental book 1 Maccabees (15:15). The Romans allowed the high priest to extradite to Jerusalem Jewish wrongdoers who had fled to other parts of the empire. Such a practice would have affected Jewish Christians who fled to other parts of the empire, including Damascus, following the stoning of Stephen.

"The Way" was one of the earliest names given Christianity.

Parallel passages: Acts 22:4–23:11; 26:12–18.

1. What was Paul on his way to Damascus to do? (9:2)
2. What did the voice say to Saul? (9:4)
3. How did Saul get to Damascus? (9:8)
4. How long was Saul blind? (9:9)
5. Who was to go to Saul? (9:10–11)
6. What was Ananias' reaction? (9:13–14)
7. What did Saul do after he received his sight? (9:19)
8. How did the people who heard Saul preach react? (9:21–23)
9. Who brought Saul to the disciples? (9:27)
10. When have you, like Ananias, been sent by Christ to a very unlikely candidate?

Aeneas Healed; Dorcas Restored to Life (9:31–43)

This passage begins the account of the first mission to the Gentiles. While Paul was beginning his ministry, Peter was spreading the good news of the gospel throughout the land. *Lydda*, a town located about thirty miles northwest of Jerusalem, apparently already had a large Christian colony. Lydda was well-known for its purple-dyed materials. After Jerusalem's destruction, Lydda became a center of rabbinical instruction. *Sharon* refers to a fertile plain that ran the length of the coast.

Joppa is the modern Jaffa and is Jerusalem's port city. *Tabitha* (or *Dorcas*, in Greek) means "gazelle."

1. What was wrong with Aeneas? (9:33)
2. What words did Peter use to heal Aeneas? (9:34)
3. What kind of woman was Tabitha? (9:36)
4. Where did Peter stay? (10:43)
5. Dorcas was described as "full of good works and charitable deeds." How would fellow believers describe you?

Peter and Cornelius (10:1–16)

This chapter is a very crucial one. The time had come for the gospel message to cross the barrier which separated Jews from Gentiles. Caesarea was a cosmopolitan city where the Roman governor was headquartered.

It is important to note that although Cornelius would have had no problem with Peter's presence, Peter, as a Jew—even a moderate Jew—would not have willingly entered the home of a Gentile.

God intended that Peter be the initial agent in bridging some of the natural barriers that separate people from each other, but the gospel allows no hatred among races.

1. What was Cornelius's position? (10:1)
2. What did Cornelius's vision instruct him to do? (10:5–6)
3. Describe Peter's vision. (10:11–16)
4. How does Peter's vision address the racial and ethnic differences we experience today?

JULY 28
Acts 10:17—48

Peter and Cornelius (10:17—48)

Of all the miracles recorded in the Book of Acts, the miracle recorded in this passage may truly be the greatest. It is one thing for God to heal a person's body, but to heal that person's attitudes and personality is something else again.

Peter's statement in Acts 10:34—35 was a very unusual statement for a Jewish preacher of that time.

Verses 44—48 describe the Pentecost of the Gentile world. What happened in Cornelius's home was very similar to what happened in the upper room in Jerusalem to the one hundred twenty believers. The rushing wind and the cloven tongues of fire were absent, but the spectators heard the people praising the Lord in unknown tongues.

1. How did Peter respond to Cornelius's request? (10:23)
2. How did Cornelius greet Peter? (10:25) And what did Peter say to him? (10:26)
3. How did the Jews react to the Holy Spirit's presence? (10:45)
4. What did Peter do after the Holy Spirit's presence became known? (10:47—48)
5. When was the last time you intentionally sought God's will, and then attempted to interpret it and carry it out?

JULY 29
Acts 11:1–30

Report to the Church at Jerusalem (11:1–18)

When the word of the miraculous event at Cornelius's home reached Jerusalem, the church authorities were beside themselves with anger. They were upset that Peter had gone beyond their narrow concepts of right and wrong. By this time, much of the opposition to the Christian church had disappeared in Jerusalem itself. They were quite accepted by the Hellenists. But the Jews feared that if the news about their leader fraternizing with Gentiles got out the persecution would start all over again. By this time the church leader in Jerusalem was James, the brother of Christ, and not one of the twelve original apostles. In fact, James didn't believe in his own brother until after the Resurrection.

1. What did the Jerusalem church say to Peter? (11:3)
2. What question did Peter ask those leaders? (11:17)
3. What did the leaders conclude? (11:18)
4. Cite some examples of this same kind of "hands off" attitude in present-day attempts at evangelism.

The Church at Antioch; Relief to Judea (11:19–30)

Antioch, a gorgeous place called "the beautiful and golden," was situated north of Israel, about fifteen miles inland from the sea. The Romans captured it about 50 B.C. and turned it into a huge cosmopolitan city of some half-million residents. Many of its inhabitants were Jews who were given privileges similar to the Greeks. It was an aggressive, commercial, and wicked city. The first Gentile church was founded there.

Agabus is mentioned again in Acts 21:10. A prophet was usually ranked next to the apostles in the new church. The Roman historians Tacitus and Suetonius relate that there were several famines during Claudius's reign (A.D. 41–54).

1. What happened after Stephen's stoning? (11:19)
2. Whom did the Jerusalem church send to Antioch? (11:22)
3. Where did this man go from Antioch? (11:25)
4. What first happened in Antioch? (11:26)
5. What did Agabus prophesy? (11:28)
6. What did the church at Antioch do? (11:29–30)
7. What kind of relief work is your church involved in?

JULY 30
Acts 12:1–24

Herod's Violent Death (12:1–4, 20–24)

James, the brother of John, was the second Christian martyr (Stephen being the first). His father, Zebedee, was a prosperous Galilean fisherman; his mother was Salome, who was believed to be a sister of Jesus' mother, Mary. James had spent seventeen years in the work of the Lord. He apparently was content to be a "helper" and never sought any special place in the kingdom.

While in Rome, Herod (also known as Agrippa) became close friends with Gaius, the grandnephew of the Emperor Tiberius. When Gaius succeeded Tiberius to the throne, he bestowed special favors on Herod. He made him the king of southern Syria, and two years later added Galilee and Perea to the territory. When Claudius was made emperor (following the assassination of Gaius), he further increased Agrippa's realm by adding Judea.

Agrippa sincerely wanted the favor of the Jewish people. When he perceived that the general populace did not favor the Christians, he took action against the Christians.

The "set day" in verse 21 was a feast in honor of the emperor, according to the Jewish historian Josephus. Josephus tells us that Herod died five days later from a severe, loathsome disease affecting his digestive tract.

1. What happened to James? (12:2)
2. Why was Peter not killed immediately? (12:3–4)
3. What was the occasion for Herod's speaking to the people? (12:20)
4. How does the scriptural account describe what happened to Herod? (12:23)
5. Are there people today who come close to claiming the power of God for themselves?

Peter Freed from Prison (12:5–19)

Aside from recounting a miraculous delivery, this passage tells us one of the truly humorous incidents in the Bible. Tradition has it that the house of Mary in verse 12 held the upper room of the last supper and was the headquarters of the Jerusalem church.

1. What did the church do while Peter was imprisoned? (12:5)
2. How did Peter escape? (12:7–10)
3. Who answered Peter's knock and why did she not open the gate? (12:13–14)
4. Under what circumstances have you (or your church) engaged in intercessory prayer?

The Work of Barnabus and Paul (12:25—13:15)

The church at Antioch was evidently a remarkable church full of prophets, teachers, and people with vision. These Christians at Antioch were the first Christians to send out missionaries to foreign lands.

Cyprus was a major island in the Mediterranean. Salamis is on the eastern coast; Paphos, the seat of the provincial government, was west of Salamis.

Pamphylia was a small province located in what is today the southern area of central Turkey. The present port city of Antalya was probably where the apostles entered the country.

In his commentary, William Barclay had this to say about Mark's action:

> Mark was very young. His mother's house seems to have been the center of the church at Jeruslam and he must always have been close to the center of the faith. Paul and Barnabas took him with them as their helper, for he was kinsman to Barnabas; but he turned and went home. We will never know why. Perhaps he resented the deposition of Barnabas from the leadership; perhaps he was afraid of the proposed journey up into the plateau where Antioch in Pisidia stood, for it was one of the hardest and most dangerous roads in the world; perhaps, because he came from Jerusalem, he had his doubts about this preaching to the Gentiles; perhaps at this stage he was one of those many who are better at beginning things than finishing them; perhaps the lad wanted his mother. At any rate, he went.

Note that at this point Paul, rather than Barnabas, becomes the leader.

1. Who did Barnabas and Saul take with them? (12:25)
2. What did the Holy Spirit ask of the church at Antioch? (13:2)
3. What false prophet did Paul and Barnabas encounter? (13:8)
4. What was the prophet's fate? (13:11)
5. Who was converted? (13:7, 12)
6. How does your community of worship react to a sudden change in leaders?

AUGUST 1
Acts 13:16–52

At Antioch in Pisidia (13:16–52)

This Antioch is located in central Turkey. Near this city today one can enter a cave where the early church met during times of persecution. Etched into the walls are writings about Christ, and there is a series of escape tunnels leading from the rear of the cave.

Paul's sermon in this passage is a very important one, for it is the first recorded sermon we have of Paul's and the only one to be recorded in its entirety. In his sermon, which followed the same basic outline as Stephen's defense had many years previously, Jesus Christ was the focal point.

The social and religious situation in Antioch was a flammable one. The Roman city was filled with a great mixture of races and cultures. The Jewish faith impressed Gentile women there because of its strict moral codes. The women saw in this faith a restraint against the eroding family life in the city. Thus, the Jewish leaders could use the women to incite their influential husbands against the new faith.

1. What one event did Paul keep lifting up in his sermon? (13:30, 33–34, 37)
2. How did the Jews feel about the apostles' reception? (13:45)
3. What did Paul and Barnabas tell the Jews? (13:46)
4. What happened to Paul and Barnabas? (13:50)
5. Our nation often takes the stance that it has all the right answers—much like the New Testament Jews. How would we react to leadership from another nation?

AUGUST 2
Acts 14:1–28

Paul and Barnabas in Iconium, Lystra, and Derbe (14:1–28)

Iconium is also in Turkey. Here, the opposition did not come as quickly or in as organized a manner as it had in Antioch, so the missionaries were able to continue preaching for a longer period of time.

In a book from the second century called *Acts of Paul*, a man named Onesiphorus, a resident of Iconium, gave the best description of Paul available: "And he saw Paul approaching, a man small in size with meeting eyebrows, with a rather large nose, bald-headed, bowlegged, strongly built, full of grace, for at times he looked like a man, and at times he had the face of an angel."

Lystra, modern Zoldera, was about twenty miles from Iconium. The remains of the ancient city were discovered in 1885.

Zeus was the chief of the gods. Evidently Barnabas was still the nominal head of the expedition. Hermes was the patron god of oratory; thus the reason for mistaking Paul as Hermes (see v. 12).

The site of Derbe is still unknown, but it probably was not far from Lystra.

Paul's reappearance in Lystra, Iconium, and Antioch must have given the Christians there tremendous encouragement. After the treatment he received in those cities, the believers no doubt thought he would never return.

1. Why did Paul and Barnabas leave Iconium? (14:5–6)
2. Why did the people of Lystra mistake Paul and Barnabas for gods? (14:10–11)
3. What did the chief priests intend to do? (14:13)
4. What happened to Paul in Lystra? (14:19)
5. How easy is it for us to return to a place where we have been ridiculed for our beliefs? Would we?

The Conflict over Circumcision (15:1–29)

This chapter is a vital one; Luke looks upon it as a turning point. Apparently, nothing Paul and Barnabas had said had made an impression on the legalists. Paul and Barnabas were fighting battles similar to those Jesus fought with the legalistic Pharisees.

Jesus never once referred to the matter of circumcision as a necessary qualification for salvation, but nearly twenty years had passed since Jesus' earthly ministry, and many of His teachings had been forgotten.

James' letter, which reflected the outcome of the Jerusalem Council, has been called the Magna Charta of Christian liberty. The letter had three main points:

1. *Liberty.* The law of Moses was not the criteria for New Testament salvation. If, indeed, keeping the law is the only way to be saved, then nobody can be saved. Only the saving life of Jesus Christ can bring a man or woman into the presence of a holy God.

2. *Purity.* Liberty is not license, however. Just because we are "free" does not mean we can live any way we choose. There is still a life of holiness that must be kept and believed. *Holiness* comes from the word *wholeness* and encompasses moral, mental, and spiritual health. God wants His children to be healthy. The world system pollutes and destroys.

3. *Charity.* We should not heedlessly offend those who prefer to observe certain forms and ceremonies. God puts some things on some people's "off-limits" lists and not on others'.

The Jerusalem Council was a terribly important event in the New Testament, for the ground rules for missions were established, rules that we live by to this very day. Also, it freed the hands of Paul and Barnabas and Silas and Timothy to continue their historic and creative enterprises for the Lord.

1. What was the issue at stake between the Jewish Christians and Paul and Barnabas? (15:1–2)
2. Who first spoke against the legalist viewpoint? (15:7)
3. Who put the matter into perspective? (15:13)
4. What did this person decree? (15:19–21)
5. What things did the Jerusalem Council deem necessary to be a Christian? (15:29)
6. When a church is too wrapped up in the trappings of its religion, what does that usually say about the church's ministry?

Division over John Mark; the Macedonian Call (15:30—16:15)

You can imagine how delighted the Gentile Christians were to receive news of the Jerusalem decree. This marks the end of the first missionary journey.

Verse 36 begins the description of the preparation period for the second missionary journey (Acts 15:36—18:23).

Evidently, Paul's feelings against Mark eventually mellowed, for Paul, in prison in Nero's Rome years later, asked Timothy to come and bring Mark with him, "for he is useful to me for ministry" (2 Tim. 4:11).

After covering much of the same territory covered in the first missionary journey, Paul was called to enter Europe. Neapolis is today the Greek city of Kavala. It is located on the north end of the Aegean Sea, very near the northwest corner of Turkey.

Early in this second journey, Paul returned to Lystra. Here is where we first encounter Timothy, although extrabiblical sources claim that it was Timothy's family who took Paul in when he was stoned and left for dead while preaching in Lystra the first time.

Thyatira was known for its trade unions and for the scarlet cloth produced by the city's dyers.

1. What did Barnabas want to do? (15:37)
2. How was the dispute between the two resolved? (15:39–40)
3. What did Paul ask that Timothy have done before he joined him? (16:3)
4. What role was the Holy Spirit playing in Paul's itinerary? (16:6–7)
5. What was Paul's vision? (16:9)
6. Whom did Paul baptize in Europe? (16:14–15)
7. How aware are we of the Holy Spirit's guidance in our ministry?

AUGUST 5
Acts 16:16–40

Imprisonment in Philippi; the Jailer Saved (16:16–40)

The girl following Paul and Silas was known as a Pytho, a person who gave oracles to guide people in the future.

The ruins of the old prison mentioned in this passage still exist. The dungeon was a brutal place. Paul and Silas would have been situated so that their backs were resting against the jagged stone wall of the pit, and the blood and dirt could drip from their arching bodies into a trench below. A spring flowed through that trench, keeping the place reasonably clean. Can you imagine singing in that place?

This is the first passage in which it is evident that Paul's Roman citizenship could be a help to him in his ministry. Note that Paul could have insisted upon the jailer's death, for anyone who whipped a Roman citizen was liable to such a fate.

1. Why were the slave girl's masters unhappy that she had been healed? (16:19)
2. What was the mob's charge against Paul and Silas? (16:20–21)
3. What freed Paul and Silas? (16:26)
4. Why was the jailer frightened? (16:27)
5. Why did Paul refuse to leave secretly? (16:37)
6. How did you react the last time you had a chance to "get even" with someone?

AUGUST 6
Acts 17:1-34

Paul at Thessalonica, Berea, and Athens (17:1-34)

Verse 1 tells us that Paul, Silas, and Timothy traveled to Thessalonica in northern Greece. The trip took them over one hundred miles of treacherous roads. Amphipolis, Apollonia, and Thessalonica were on a major military road, the Eglatian Way. Along with Ephesus and Corinth, Thessalonica was one of the busiest cities of the Aegean. The military road gave it a means of direct communication with Rome. A "free city," Thessalonica had its own democratic constitution and its own magistrates, called politarchs. These are referred to in verse 6.

Berea was a smaller city about forty-five miles west of Thessalonica. Cicero described Berea as a town "off the road."

Athens is the only city in which Paul's preaching did not stir up controversy. The city was not a commercial or a military center but a center of learning. It is possible that Paul's listeners were more interested in what he had to say from a philosophical standpoint. The thinkers of Athens held two basic philosophies. The Epicureans believed that everything happened by chance, that there was no afterlife, and that, at best, the gods were unsympathetic to people's needs. Their main aim was happiness. The Stoics believed that everything was God and that whatever happened was because God had ordered it. Both philosophies, however, resulted in the same lifestyle.

All in all, Paul probably had less success in Athens than any place in which he ministered.

1. Whose house did the Jews attack because of Paul? (17:5)
2. How did the people at Berea receive Paul and Silas? (17:11-12)
3. What about Athens upset Paul? (17:16)
4. Where did Paul address the philosophers? (17:19, 22)
5. Who believed Paul's teaching? (17:34)
6. What should be the place of philosophy in Christian thought?

AUGUST 7
Acts 18:1–28

Ministering at Corinth (18:1–17)

Paul had now reached Corinth, Greece. It is probably safe to assume that there was not a more wicked city on earth at that particular time. Overlooking the city is a huge bluff on which stood a temple built to Aphrodite. It contained one thousand priestesses, each one a prostitute. Each night they came down to the city. One doesn't need much imagination to conjure up their activities.

Apparently during this time in Corinth Paul went through a personal spiritual crisis. Verses 9–10 indicate that he became severely discouraged. That isn't hard to understand. We can only imagine the loneliness he felt. He was also forced to spend more time providing for his material needs than he would have liked. Another contributing cause to his depression was the hostile attitude of his fellow Jews. And the general atmosphere of Corinth itself, a blatantly wicked city, must have added to his discouragement.

Gallio was a brother of Seneca, the well-known philosopher. He was a popular person among the Romans, but about twelve years later Nero had him killed just to satisfy a whim.

1. With whom did Paul live while in Corinth? (18:2)
2. What did Paul do to support himself? (18:3)
3. How long did Paul stay? (18:11)
4. What happened to the ruler of the synagogue? (18:17)
5. Cite examples of perseverance in the face of tribulation on your part or on the part of your worshiping community.

Ministry of Apollos (18:18–28)

At this time Ephesus was perhaps the most exciting city in the world, the greatest commercial city in all of Asia Minor. The harbor there has since silted up, leaving the ruins of the five cities of Ephesus some miles from the water's edge. But in Paul's time, Ephesus was right on the ocean. Ephesus was built around one of the ancient "seven wonders" of the world, the temple to the goddess Diana, said to be seven times larger than the Parthenon in Athens.

Verse 18 indicates that Paul may have taken a Nazirite vow (see Num. 6:5, 18).

1. Why did Paul leave Ephesus? (18:21)
2. Where was Apollos from? (18:24)
3. What did Priscilla and Aquila do for Apollos? (18:26)
4. What opportunities are you giving yourself to grow in the faith?

AUGUST 8
Acts 19:1–20

Paul at Ephesus (19:1–20)

Luke, in Acts, in reality gives an incomplete picture of Paul's ministry at Ephesus. The Epistles tell us more, particularly those to the Corinthians. Paul was apparently troubled by the problems in the church at Corinth throughout his Ephesian ministry (see 2 Cor. 12:14). Paul seems to have made a hurried visit from Ephesus to Corinth (see 2 Cor. 2:1) and to have followed that visit with an anguished letter (see 2 Cor. 2:4).

These same letters also talk about afflictions Paul suffered in Asia (see 2 Cor. 1:8; 4:8–12; 6:4–5; 11:23–27). Ephesus was probably the site of Paul's imprisonment with Andronicus and Junia, as recorded in Romans 16:7.

Paul, as usual, used the synagogue as the base for his ministry. Note that in verse 9, Luke reports that "some were hardened." This was always the case. It was never the entire Jewish community.

Paul was probably seen as a traveling sophist—a common figure in that day. Thus, the radical nature of his teachings may have gone unnoticed longer than in other cities.

Verses 11–20 show that Paul's ministry in Ephesus was not just academic; his words were substantiated by supernatural works. Because Paul could not be everywhere at once, and because Ephesus was a city with a population of nearly one million, many sick persons requested handkerchiefs from the apostle. Paul sent these cloths to be used as a point of contact with the sick, and many of them were healed. This appears, of course, to be highly psychosomatic; however, remember that Luke, a doctor, said that many diseases were healed.

1. What did Paul ask the followers at Ephesus? (19:2–3)
2. How many men received the Holy Spirit? (19:7)
3. Who tried to call out evil spirits in Jesus' name? (19:13–14)
4. What happened to them? (19:16)
5. What did the people of Ephesus do when they heard what happened to the sorcerers? (19:19)
6. When have you attempted a ministry without the guidance of the Holy Spirit?

AUGUST 9
Acts 19:21—20:6

The Ephesian Riot and Journeys in Greece (19:21—20:6)

Ephesus was a religious center, the seat of the "Asiarchate," the religious confederacy of the cities of Asia. The Asiarchs (see v. 31) were officers of the province. Their special duty was to arrange for the festival in honor of the emperor. Each Asiarchate tried to outdo the preceding one.

"The image which fell down from Zeus" (v. 35) was probably some symbol for Artemis (Diana). It may have been a rough image, which may have had a supernatural origin, according to devotees of the cult.

That riot in Ephesus was the last major incident of Paul's ministry in that city. Acts 20:1–6 tells of Paul's journeys in Greece. He bade the Christians there farewell and left for Macedonia. He probably took a freight carrier northward up the coastline to Troas, the coast of present-day Turkey. Troas was located near what we call the Dardanelles. In this place, the apostle hoped to rendezvous with Titus, whom he had sent to minister in Corinth.

Titus did not get to Troas, so Paul left there and continued north-westerly toward Macedonia. Titus met him there and gave him good news from the Corinthian church. Later Paul wrote of Titus' message, "For indeed, when we came to Macedonia, our flesh had no rest, but we were troubled on every side. Outside were conflicts, inside were fears. Nevertheless God, who comforts the downcast, comforted us by the coming of Titus, and not only by his coming, but also by the consolation with which he was comforted in you, when he told us of your earnest desire, your mourning, your zeal for me, so that I rejoiced even more" (2 Cor. 7:5–7).

Paul probably spent the better part of a year in Macedonia, happy in spirit, and increasing the kingdom of God in that province.

Then Paul went south into Greece for the winter months of A.D. 56–57. Biblical scholars believe that Paul wrote the Book of Romans during that time.

1. What was Paul's ultimate goal? (19:21)
2. Whom did Paul send to Macedonia? (19:22)
3. What Ephesian craftsman incited the riot and what was his occupation? (19:24)
4. Whom did the Ephesians seize? (19:29)
5. Who quieted the crowd? (19:35)
6. Who accompanied Paul to Asia? (20:4)
7. Examine your life to see if your occupation or hobby is hindering your carrying out the gospel's message.

AUGUST 10
Acts 20:7–38

Ministering at Troas; Exhorting the Elders of Ephesus (20:7–38)

The trip from Philippi to Troas took five days. Paul's party must have been sailing against the wind, for the first such trip took only two days. It was at Troas, during a long preaching service, that Paul performed one of his miracles. After the service, Paul sent his companions on by sea while he traveled part of the way overland to Jerusalem. Possibly, Paul wanted to attend the Jewish festival in Jerusalem in order to show the Jewish Christians that he was still loyal.

Since Paul did not have time to stop at Ephesus, he asked the Ephesian elders to meet him at Miletus. Verses 18–35 record Paul's deeply moving last words to those elders. Apparently, some of Paul's adversaries in Asia had been undermining Paul and his teachings. Paul set the record straight by appealing to his listeners' personal knowledge of him.

Verse 31 is intriguing—"with tears." When the passion and intensity leave our churches, nothing is left but meaningless recitals that stir no one. Paul was not afraid to let the Ephesians know how deeply he cared about them and about the message he was giving them.

In verses 36–38, Luke gives us one of the most poignant scenes in all the Bible.

1. What happened to Eutychus? (20:9)
2. At what ports did Paul stop? (20:14–15)
3. What Jewish festival did Paul want to attend? (20:16)
4. What awaited Paul in Jerusalem? (20:23)
5. Would Paul see his Ephesian friends again? (20:25)
6. What did Paul predict for the Ephesian church and what advice did he give them? (20:29–31)
7. What words of Jesus did Paul commend to the Ephesians? (20:35)
8. When was the last time you let someone know how much you appreciated that person's life?

AUGUST 11
Acts 21:1–25

Paul's Journey to Jerusalem (21:1–25)

This chapter of Acts is the one that Dr. W. A. Criswell calls "the beginning of the end" in the life and ministry of Paul. From this chapter until the final day of his life Paul was a prisoner for Christ.

This visit to Jerusalem was Paul's last. Five times following his conversion, Paul went to Jerusalem: the first, after he was saved on the road to Damascus; the second, after Agabus predicted an international famine and Paul and Barnabas raised money for the saints there; the third, at the conclusion of his first missionary journey when he took Titus, a Gentile convert, with him; the fourth, at the end of his second missionary journey. As his final missionary trip ended, Paul went once again to the Holy City, bringing the offering that the Gentiles had collected for the poor saints in Jerusalem.

Paul's friends begged him to stay away from the Holy City, but he was adamant about going. Many believe that Paul's obstinancy cost him his life, but I believe that God was leading Paul in the way that would enable him to evangelize Rome. Paul knew he was expendable.

While in Jerusalem Paul was asked to underwrite the cost of four Nazirites' taking their vows. Nazarite men abstained from meat and wine for thirty days, and allowed their hair to grow. The last seven days of this time were spent in the temple, after which special offerings were brought, including a year-old lamb for a sin offering. When the lamb was sacrificed and burned on the altar, the men would shave their heads, and the hair was also burned. This whole ordeal was expensive. Many men could not go through the rite at all because of lack of funds.

It is quite a mark of Paul's greatness that he was willing to help these brothers take a vow he probably personally believed was unnecessary in order to win those who believed it was necessary. He told the Corinthians: "... to those who are under the law, [I became] as [one] under the law, that I might win those who are under the law" (1 Cor. 9:20).

1. Where did Paul and his companions spend seven days? (21:3–4)
2. What did Philip's daughters do? (21:9)
3. Who depicted for Paul what would happen if he went to Jerusalem? (21:10–11)
4. What was Paul's answer? (21:13)
5. What in our lives and the lives of our congregations witnesses to our willingness to put issues in their proper perspective, as Paul did, in our attempts to carry out the gospel message?

229

AUGUST 12
Acts 21:26—22:21

Paul's Arrest and Defense (21:26—22:21)

Remember that Jews had come for this feast from all over the world, including the region around Ephesus. Earlier in Ephesus, Paul had reaped the hatred of many of the Jewish leaders for his teachings. They were unable to do much about it in Ephesus, but now some of them had come to Jerusalem and had seen him there.

Trophimus, a Gentile, would not have been allowed in the temple. For Paul to have taken him there would have been a capital offense. A Gentile could enter the Court of the Gentiles, but between that court and the Court of the Women was a clearly posted barrier. One of those warnings (written in Greek) has been found by archeologists: "No foreigner may enter within the barricade which surrounds the temple and enclosure. Anyone caught doing so will have himself to blame for his ensuing death."

An indication of the seriousness of such an offense was that the Romans actually acknowledged this law and carried out the death penalty. Evidently the Jews thought one of the four men with Paul was a Gentile and a riot ensued.

Apparently the captain of the Romans mistook Paul for an escaped leader of a rebel band. In A.D. 54, an Egyptian rebel had led a band of desperados to the Mount of Olives. The Romans had slaughtered the rebels, but the leader got away. He must have looked like Paul.

What power in the man Paul! Of verse 40, William Barclay said, "Nothing in all the New Testament so shows the force of Paul's personality as this silence that he commanded from the mob who would have lynched him. At that moment the very power of God flowed through him."

Paul's defense in 22:1–21 was really more of a story, his own story of salvation and fellowship with Jesus Christ.

The Jews believed that God loved only them and that God's salvation was for them only. Paul knew that God loves all persons—red, yellow, black, and white. He laid down his life for that principle.

1. With what did the Asian Jews charge Paul? (21:28)
2. What was the Roman commander's purpose? (21:32, 34)
3. In what language did Paul speak to the commander? (21:37)
4. Paul died because he believed God loved all people. What is your feeling about that belief?

AUGUST 13
Acts 22:22–23:22

Paul's Roman Citizenship (22:22–23:22)

When the crowd again turned against Paul, the soldiers quickly took him into the lower dungeons. There, by the light of flickering torches, they stripped him and secured his ankles and his wrists. His ankles were tied to a bar on the floor and his wrists were pulled by thongs toward a beam in the ceiling until his body was as taut as a drum. The apostle knew what was coming—the dreaded flagellum, the brutal whip of heavy rawhide strips loaded with bits of iron and bone, sharp as a razor. The use of the barbaric implement often did irreparable damage to the kidneys and nerves, and often killed its victim. This was the same beating that Jesus endured.

To use the flagellum on a Roman citizen was illegal. The mere fact that Paul, a Roman citizen, had been tied up could have led to terrible repercussions for the soldiers.

The president of the Sanhedrin, Ananias ben Nedebaeus, was a disgrace to the office. Paul, who didn't see very well, unintentionally reviled him, not knowing the speaker was the high priest (see 23:3–4). Paul, being sensitive to his Jewish brethren and true to his upbringing would not have knowingly done such a thing. He apologized, quoting Exodus 22:28.

At this point, Paul made a brilliant move by turning one of the groups comprising the Sanhedrin in his favor.

Paul's deliverance was short-lived, for the Jews were determined to kill him and plotted to do so.

Verses 11–22 tell us why Paul had to leave the holy city of Jerusalem for the very last time. It had been Paul's great goal to reach that city with the gospel, but he never did. It would take someone else to do that. God had called Paul to reach the Gentiles, not the Jews, and he was more than successful in evangelizing Gentiles across his known world.

1. What angered the Jews? (22:21–22)
2. How did Paul come by his Roman citizenship? (22:28)
3. What did the high priest command be done to Paul? (23:2)
4. How did Paul divide the Sanhedrin? (23:6)
5. How did the Sadducees and Pharisees differ in their beliefs? (23:8)
6. What message did Paul receive from Jesus? (23:11)
7. What was the plot against Paul? (23:14–15)
8. Who warned Paul? (23:16)
9. To what specific work on earth has God called you?

AUGUST 14
Acts 23:23—24:21

Paul Before Felix (23:23–24:21)

The magnitude of the threat to Paul's life becomes apparent when we read of the preparations made to get Paul out of Jerusalem (vv. 23–24). We think Antipatris (v. 31) was about forty miles from Caesarea, or two-thirds of the way from Jerusalem. However, the exact site is unknown.

Governor Felix was a scoundrel. He had been born a slave, but through a long twisting path, led by his brother (a freedman named Pallas and a favorite of Emperor Claudius), Felix was given his freedom and began his climb to power. Perhaps because of his poor beginnings, Felix was consumed by greed. His moronic leadership had caused terrible bloodshed throughout the province. Tacitus summed up this man with one terse sentence: "He exercised the power of a king with the mind of a slave."

As usual, Paul's defense was brilliant, and there was no question that the case should be dismissed. Felix knew of the earlier decree by Gallio that under Roman law no legal disposition could be made in regard to followers of Christ. The legal precedent had already been set. Felix should have ended the whole matter at that point, but he loved to agitate the high priest. So he made some pretense of legal delay.

There is another historic factor here to keep in mind. At any time, Paul could have purchased his release from Felix. As judge and head of the Roman court, Felix acquitted people, not on the basis of their innocence or guilt, but upon their ability to pay bribes.

Even the high priest Ananias was crooked. He had obtained office by overseeing the assassination of the former high priest Jonathan. Once in power, he used the office for personal gain and profit. He organized a group of killers known as the *Sicarri*—men who mingled in the crowds and used their daggers quietly and efficiently to kill the enemies of the high priest. The Jewish historian Josephus tells us that this man was finally tried before Claudius himself on a charge of cruelty, and bribed his way to acquittal. When the great revolution against Rome started in Judea, the first thing the Jews did was murder Ananias.

1. How many Romans accompanied Paul to Caesarea? (23:23)
2. Who came to Caesarea to accuse Paul? (24:1)
3. Who, according to Paul, should have been in the hearing to accuse Paul? (24:18–19)
4. When in your life have you felt the need to "keep going"? Did you sense God's presence with you?

AUGUST 15
Acts 24:22—25:12

Felix Procrastinates; Paul's Appeal to Caesar (24:22—25:12)

Quite possibly, a long period of time passed between verses 23 and 24. During that time Paul was under arrest, always chained to, or at least in the presence of, a centurion. By the summer of A.D. 58, Felix still had made no final decision in Paul's case, and was hoping for a lucrative bribe (see v. 26).

During these spring and summer months, Timothy left for the mission fields of Europe and Asia Minor. If Paul wrote the Book of Hebrews, which he may or may not have done, it could well have been written during this time. Paul didn't waste his time, but kept witnessing to Felix and his third wife, Drusilla, a fascinating personality. She has been described as one of the more beautiful woman in the Roman Empire. She was the youngest of King Herod Agrippa's (Acts 12) three daughters and she married, at sixteen, King Azia of Emesa, a minor king in northwestern Syria. An ambitious socialite, she later left her husband and married Felix.

Felix was succeeded by Porcius Festus, who, like his predecessor, saw through the charges against Paul. At this point, Paul's Roman citizenship played an extremely important role.

1. When did Felix say he would make his decision? (24:22)
2. What did Paul teach Felix about, and what was Felix's reaction? (24:25)
3. What was Felix waiting for? (24:26)
4. What did the chief priest ask of Festus concerning Paul and what was Festus' response? (25:2–5)
5. What did Festus suggest to Paul? (25:9)
6. How did Paul respond? (25:10–11)
7. Felix missed a chance at a turning point in his life. At what time might you have overlooked a chance to turn your life toward Christ?

AUGUST 16
Acts 25:13—26:32

Paul Before Agrippa (25:13—26:32)

Before Paul was sent to Rome, he stood before King Agrippa and Queen Bernice. The young king was only thirty-two years old. Bernice, Drusilla's sister, was not Agrippa's wife, but his sister with whom he lived in an incestuous relationship.

Festus really wanted the king to circumvent Paul's desire to go to Rome. It was a very costly procedure to appeal to Caesar and, if the case displeased the emperor, it could go badly for the governor. However, the whole procedure went contrary to Festus' hopes and Paul used the opportunity to witness to the royal couple.

Paul's statement was divided into three categories: (1) his life before his conversion; (2) his conversion; and (3) his ministry following his conversion. We gain some insight into the apostle's life in this chapter. The account of Paul's speech has probably been cut short. In verse 3 Paul asked Agrippa to indulge him patiently, so, in all probability, his speech was considerably longer; and Luke merely summed it up for us. Paul wanted Agrippa, who was a Jewish sympathizer, to understand that his ministry was never meant to undermine the Jewish faith, but merely to complete it.

He thought Agrippa, who understood Jews, would see why those leaders had such animosity toward a former rabbi who offered Gentile believers spiritual privileges on the same basis as the chosen people themselves.

After Agrippa parried Paul's challenge to become a Christian (see 25:28), the king went back to his throne, Festus went back to his duties as governor, and Paul went back to his cell and to his chains. No, the king didn't want him executed; but that isn't what mattered to Paul. He wanted Agrippa to accept Christ and become the man that God intended him to be.

Paul must have been depressed as he went back to his cell. Though others might have considered the encounter a tremendous success, Paul saw it only as a failure, for there were no spiritual results.

1. Why did Festus say he was hesitant to send Paul to Rome? (25:25–27)
2. What was Festus' opinion of Paul? (26:24)
3. How did Agrippa respond to Paul? (26:28)
4. Why could Agrippa not set Paul free? (26:32)
5. Are the things we are living for worth Christ's dying for?

AUGUST 17
Acts 27:1–38

Paul Sails for Rome (27:1–38)

In this chapter, Paul the prisoner left the land of Israel for the final time. He would never see it again. He left Caesarea on his way to Rome for his confrontation with the emperor, and eventually, the headsman.

The whole prisoner corps was to have been in Rome by the end of October A.D. 59. They set out from Caesarea the last week of August, heading for Sidon, a mere sixty-seven miles north.

The winds dictated that the ship sail directly between the island of Cyprus and the Cilician (or Turkish) shore on their way westward. The seas in that area can be ferocious. Off to the north Paul would have been able to see the Taurus Mountains.

It was a rough trip for Paul's vessel because of absent or contrary winds. For fifteen days they never set into a harbor. It was nearly mid-September by the time they reached Myra. In that important port city, they changed ships, transferring to an Alexandrian ship headed for Italy. They headed southwest around the southern coast of Crete, well below Greece.

By this time, all hopes of reaching Rome by October had ended. By mid-November all open-sea navigation would cease because the sun and stars would be overcast for days on end, preventing the crew's getting their bearings. The captain wanted to get as far as he could before that November deadline. Once they left the coast of Crete, they had to head into the open sea between Crete and Malta—a vast expanse of ocean.

Evidently a strong wind roared down from Mount Ida, the highest point on Crete. The storm was a northeaster; Luke described the wind as one with the strength of a typhoon.

For fourteen days the ship rode out the storm. Miraculously, and unbeknownst to the crew, God must have been directing the ship, for the place where they finally ran aground was of such a nature that no lives were lost.

1. To whom was Paul delivered? (27:1)
2. Who accompanied Paul? (27:2)
3. What did Paul advise the crew? (27:10)
4. What was the headwind called? (27:14)
5. What was Paul's vision? (27:23–26)
6. What did Paul do on the fourteenth day? (27:33–36)
7. How many persons were on the ship? (27:37)
8. Think of a time when you were in a crisis situation. Did you remember that God was with you?

Shipwrecked at Malta (27:39—28:10)

On the fifteenth day the ship lay at the entrance to a bay. "No one recognized it; not knowing the rate or direction of drift, they might be anywhere off Sicily or Tunisia. Ahead stood a rocky shore, but they could see a creek with a sandy beach. The captain carried out a complicated maneuver. The crew, in Luke's description, slipped the anchors and let them go; at the same time they loosed the lashings of the steering paddles, set the foresail to the wind, and let [the ship] drive to the beach. The captain had her completely under command and half a mile to go. Soon she would be beached and they could wade ashore. He could not have realized when he gave the order that the rocky spit of land close on their starboard beam was, in fact, a little island linked to the mainland by a shoal, a place where two seas meet. Because of this, the vessel was caught in a crosscurrent and swept onto the shoal until the forepart stuck fast in a bottom of clay and mud while the breakers began to pound the stern to pieces." (John Pollock, *Life of Paul*, pp. 216–217.)

God directed that ship in that fifteen-day storm! The ship wrecked at Malta, due south of Italy and Rome. Luke was thrilled with the reception of the Malta natives.

Can you see the picture? Over two hundred sailors and prisoners coming into land, swimming and riding on debris, shivering, some sick.

Jesus had told the original disciples that snake's poison would not hurt them. There are some who act presumptuously by handling snakes in their services. Paul's experience is not to be used to vindicate such intentional handling. Paul was accidentally bitten.

Apparently the crew and passengers stayed for the winter on Malta—a far cry from reaching Rome by the end of the previous fall.

1. What did the soldiers plan to do? (27:42)
2. How did the natives welcome Paul and the others? (28:2)
3. What happened to Paul? (28:3–5)
4. What did the natives think of Paul? (28:6)
5. In what areas of your life might Jesus be able to use you more fully?

Paul's Arrival and Ministry at Rome (28:11–31)

At long last, Paul reached Rome, about six months after his journey began. The ship's figurehead would have been Castor and Pollux, the patron deities of sailors.

Paul was still technically under arrest, although he was given great liberty, while accompanied by a Roman soldier.

Two full years passed before Paul was summoned before the Court. During that time Paul openly preached the gospel throughout Rome without any hindrance at all.

Finally, the Emperor Nero, now growing quite insane, had Paul summoned to his court. And, amazingly, the emperor repeated the verdict of Gallio in Corinth years earlier that Christianity was not an illegal cult. The gospel could be preached freely. So Paul was set free. Nero would change his mind, but five years would elapse during which Paul had free run of the whole Roman Empire. We don't know his exact movements, but it is possible he went as far as Spain. It is almost certain he returned to the eastern Mediterranean, visiting Titus in Crete and Timothy in Ephesus. Possibly, he journeyed to Colossae to visit Philemon and Onesimus.

Then in A.D. 64, Nero went completely berserk and burned the great city of Rome, blaming the Christians for the fire. Tacitus wrote of that period: "A vast multitude were not only put to death, but put to death in insult, in that they were either dressed up in the skins of beasts to perish by the worrying of dogs or else put on crosses to be set on fire, and when the daylight failed, to be burnt for use as light by night."

We know that Paul was tried as one of those who had caused the great fire of Rome. He was acquitted of that charge but found guilty of propagating a forbidden cult, a capital offense. Paul spent the final two years of his life in the Mamertinium Prison. Then in A.D. 67, Peter was nailed upside-down to a cross at Nero's Circus on the Vatican. Paul, because he was a Roman citizen, was beheaded north of Rome on the Ostian Way.

1. How much time passed before the second attempt to reach Rome? (28:11)
2. What did Paul do when he got to Rome? (28:17)
3. How did the Roman Jews react to Paul? (28:24)
4. What words of Paul caused a dispute among the Jews? (28:28–29)
5. How faithful are our churches in spreading the gospel beyond their own walls or membership?

ROMANS

AUGUST 20
Romans 1:1–17

Introduction

Paul's authorship of the Book of Romans is not questioned. It was written somewhere in Greece near the end of the third missionary journey. How the church at Rome was established we do not know. Possibly some of those present at Pentecost traveled back to Rome and spread the Word. It is also possible that some of Paul's converts in his missionary travels came to the city of the seven hills and started the church.

Paul's Desire to Visit Rome (1:1–17)

Throughout his missionary travels, Paul was primarily in the east—that is, the continents east of Rome, the capital of the world. He wrote numerous times of his desire to go to Rome and preach the gospel.

This letter to the church at Rome was Paul's way of preparing the Christians there for his visit. He wanted to give them a full statement of the gospel as he believed and proclaimed it.

In verse 1, Paul uses the phrase "a servant." The word Paul used for *servant* was *doulos,* which really means slave. Often Paul spoke of Jesus as *kurios* or *Lord,* meaning someone who had undisputed possession of a person or thing. In other words, Paul considered Jesus to be his owner, his master.

In verse 2, Paul connected this gospel of Christ very clearly to the Old Testament, saying that the Old Testament contained the promises and that the New Testament showed how these promises were being fulfilled in Christ Jesus.

The word *debtor* (see v.14) refers to Paul's sense of his commission.

Verse 16 holds Paul's great declaration. What a statement! The tribulations had made Paul even stronger in the faith. The gospel he preached was the very power of God.

1. What two things did Paul consider himself? (1:1)
2. Why did Paul want to visit Rome? (1:11–12)
3. What is the basis of Paul's existence? (1:17)
4. Is the basis of your existence the same as Paul's?

The Guilt of Mankind (1:18–32)

Verse 18 is the basic, overriding law in the world—the soul that sins shall die. God hates sin, and He created the world in such a manner that if we break His law, we do so at our own peril.

William Barclay summarizes Paul's teaching this way: "It is Paul's argument—and it is completely valid—that if we look at the world we see that suffering follows sin. Break the laws of agriculture—your harvest fails. Break the laws of architecture—your building collapses. Break the laws of health—your body suffers. Paul was saying, 'Look at the world! See how it is constructed. From a world like that you know what God is like.' The sinner is left without excuse."

Paul deals with the subject of man's reaction to this knowledge of God and His laws. Mankind rebels, not so much concerned with the will of God as with their own opinions.

The essence of idolatry is selfishness. When a person creates an idol, he prays to it and brings it offerings. He does this in order to advance his own dreams and hopes. His worship is for his own sake . . . and not for God's.

Verses 24–25 tell us God's reaction to the idolatry and foolhardiness of people.

Paul speaks of idolatry and then in verse 24 he swings the subject into immorality. The close connection between idolatry and immorality can be found throughout the Bible. Idolatry breeds immorality. In the Book of Wisdom, King Solomon wrote, "For the idea of making idols was the beginning of fornication, and their invention was the corruption of life."

Remember that Paul was writing this Book of Romans from one of the most immoral cities in history, the city of Corinth, the city whose main temple was the house of a thousand prostitutes.

1. What brings about God's wrath? (1:18)
2. What sins does Paul list under immorality? (1:29–31)
3. Think of some instances in your life when you have rationalized some behavior that Paul would consider sinful.

AUGUST 22
Romans 2:1–29

God's Righteous Judgment (2:1–16)

In these verses, Paul is addressing Jews. Chapter 1 was primarily concerned with the Gentiles and paints a distressing picture of the heathen world. When he wrote it, Paul knew that the Jew would wholeheartedly agree with that picture. God would judge the heathen, but He would protect the Jew—automatically. But in chapter 2 Paul pointed out to the Jew that he is just as much a sinner as the Gentile.

The Jewish people of that time did not believe that. They had a saying, "God will judge the Gentiles with one measure and the Jews with another." They believed the Jew was exempt from divine judgment.

In Ephesians 2:9, Paul wrote that salvation is "not of works, lest anyone should boast." But the fact that salvation is not attained by doing good things does not mean that God will not judge sin or that He won't reward good works. Every person, regardless of race or background, ultimately will be judged by God according to the knowledge that he has, according to the deeds that he or she commits against the light he or she has received.

1. What does Paul say about our judging others? (2:1)
2. How will God's judgment manifest itself and to whom? (2:7–8)
3. Compare your everyday actions with what you know of the gospel message. How do you measure up?

The Jews as Guilty as the Gentiles (2:17–29)

Here Paul was quite specific and brought out a double standard that his people continually perpetrated: The law of sound moral conduct is for the Gentiles; it may or may not be necessary for Jews.

Paul wraps up the second chapter by saying that all of our outward ordinances and teachings are in vain if we are not obedient to the Word of God. The ordinances and teachings should be kept, there is no question about that, but they must be in addition to our obedience to God's principles.

God looks not only on the outward trappings, but also upon the inner condition of the heart. God sees inside.

1. What three examples of unheeded teaching in the law did Paul give? (2:21–24)
2. What did Paul say about circumcision? (2:25)
3. Who is a Jew? (2:29)
4. In what areas of your life do you sense that you operate on a double standard?

AUGUST 23
Romans 3:1–20

All Have Sinned (3:1–20)

In this passage, Paul deals with this question: Because the Jews have the oracles of God, because they have been given the Commandments, because they practice circumcision, are they in a better position to be saved than the Gentiles?

Oracles is translated from the Greek work *logia,* and means, basically, the Word of God.

In his commentary on Romans, William Barclay suggests we remember that Paul is carrying on an argument with an imaginary objector:

> The objector: The result of all that you have been saying is that there is no difference between Gentile and Jew and that they are in exactly the same position. Do you really mean that?
>
> Paul: By no means.
>
> The objector: What, then, is the difference?
>
> Paul: For one thing, the Jew possesses what the Gentiles never so directly possessed—the commandments of God.
>
> The objector: Granted! But what if some of the Jews disobeyed these commandments and were unfaithful to God and came under His condemnation? You have just said that God gave the Jews a special position and a special promise. Now you go on to say that at least some of them are under the condemnation of God. Does that mean that God has broken His promise and shown himself to be unjust and unreliable?
>
> Paul: Far from it! What it does show is that there is no favoritism with God and that He punishes sin wherever He sees it. The very fact that He condemns the unfaithful Jews is the best possible proof of His absolute justice. He might have been expected to overlook the sins of this special people of His but He does not.
>
> The objector: Very well then! All you have done is to succeed in showing that my disobedience has given God an opportunity to demonstrate His righteousness. My infidelity has given God a marvelous opportunity to demonstrate His fidelity. My sin is, therefore, an excellent thing. It has given God a chance to show how good He is.
>
> Paul: An argument like that is beneath contempt. You have only to state it to see how intolerable it is.

1. What is the advantage of circumcision? (3:2)
2. What Old Testament passages does Paul quote to show that all have sinned? (3:12–18)
3. How do these teachings of Paul bear upon our tendency to judge others?

241

AUGUST 24

Righteousness Through Faith (3:21–31)

Paul uses the word *propitiation*. What is that? Under the Old Testament law, when a person sinned he brought a sacrifice to God, in hope it would turn away the punishment for his sin. The sinner was in a wrong relationship with God; to get back into proper relationship he offered his sacrifice. But the system did not do entirely what it was supposed to, for people instinctively knew that the earthly sacrifice did not truly make matters right.

We are told today that there are many doors to Christ. But there is only one door to salvation and that is through Jesus Christ. It doesn't matter what your racial, academic, moral, or material background is.

1. What does Paul say about all of us? (3:23)
2. What frees us from our sin? (3:24)
3. What justifies us apart from the law? (3:28)
4. Who establishes the law? (3:31)
5. Try to express in your own words the relationship between faith and law in today's world.

Abraham Justified by Faith (4:1–12)

In the second and third chapters of Romans, Paul sought to convince the Jews that salvation was not attained through an arduous keeping of the law, but through unshakable faith in God. This was a most preposterous concept to the Hebrews, who had long ceremonial methods of keeping even the most minute laws. Then this Pharisee, Paul, said that all of that was to no avail. It is relationship, not regimen, that saves a person. To prove his point, Paul used Abraham as his choice illustration. And he could not have made a better selection, for the Jewish people regarded Abraham as their founder.

Paul reasoned that Abraham had not been given a special relationship with God because he meticulously performed the demands of the law, but because he put his complete trust in God.

Remember that Paul was debating in this Book of Romans with an imaginary Jew who questioned Paul's reasoning at this juncture. Verses 9–12 based this imaginary opponent's argument again on circumcision.

1. Who, besides Abraham, was justified by faith? (4:6)
2. When was Abraham considered righteous? (4:10–11)
3. Name some outer trappings of religion upon which we rely that may cover up a shallow faith.

The Promise Granted Through Faith (4:13–25)

Another question with which these two debaters dealt was the difference between "law" and "promise." The law refers to the law given us through Moses. The promise refers to God's covenant with Abraham that his seed would be the beginning of a great nation. Abraham's acceptance of God's word, no matter how preposterous it might seem, put him into this marvelous relationship wth his Creator. If Abraham's children had that same propensity for faith, they would inherit the Abrahamic covenant. The essence of the covenant relationship was believing that God could make the impossible possible.

You see, many of the things God calls us to are simply impossible by our standards and efforts. But in our believing that the God who called us to them will place within us the divine power to achieve those goals, we, like Abraham, put ourselves in line for God's promises.

Perhaps you can begin to see the basic differences in people here. There are legalists, the Pharisees of our day, who put forth all sorts of external manifestations as signs that they are doing God's will. Based on this marvelous Book of Romans, we must believe that it is not the externals that mark you; it is the internals, those feelings of belief and trust in God that enable you to embark upon impossible ventures for His glory.

The promises of God are to those who dare to believe God and the Word. That's the kind of person Abraham was. That's the kind of person Paul was. And that's the kind of person we all must try to be.

1. On what basis was the promise to Abraham made? (4:13)
2. For whom was the promise also given? (4:24)
3. Think of a time when you dared to believe God's Word enough to take some action.

AUGUST 26
Romans 5:1–21

Faith Triumphs in Trouble (5:1–5)

Romans 5:1–8:39 has often been called not only the most important section of Romans but also the most important section in all of Paul's Epistles.

In previous chapters, Paul has made a case that we are justified by faith, not by a painstaking keeping of Mosaic law. He opens this fifth chapter by declaring that there are some wonderful benefits to this justification.

The first of these is the peace of reconciliation with God through our Lord Jesus Christ.

Second, through Jesus' sacrifice we have access by faith to God's grace.

Third, we can glory in our tribulations and difficulties because they build character in us. Today's shallow theology completely ignores Paul's third and fourth verses by telling us that we should never have any difficulties if we know the Lord.

1. What does tribulation produce? (5:3)
2. Why are we not disappointed in hope? (5:5)
3. What do you consider a proper relationship with God?

Death in Adam and Life in Christ (5:6–21)

This passage relates one of the greatest truths, but usually the least taught, in the Bible—that it is Christ in us that makes us good, not our trying to imitate Christ.

Paul had a rather "maddening" habit at times—that of starting a long sentence and never ending it, but rather going right from it into another long sentence. That's what he does here, beginning in verse 12. It looks complicated, but it isn't. He says basically the same thing in 1 Corinthians 15:21–22: "For since by man came death, by Man also came the resurrection of the dead. For as in Adam all die, even so in Christ all shall be made alive."

Verse 20 gives us one of the most priceless treasures given to mankind.

1. How did God demonstrate His own love toward us? (5:8)
2. How did sin enter the world? (5:12)
3. What is available to us in abundance because of Jesus' death? (5:15)
4. Which abounds more, sin or grace? (5:20)
5. In what ways have you experienced God's grace in your life?

AUGUST 27
Romans 6:1–23

Dead to Sin, Alive to God (6:1–14)

In the first five chapters of Romans, Paul has made an air-tight case for imputed righteousness, for justification by faith, for that marvelous unmerited favor of God known as grace.

Here is where the libertine gets excited. "Well," he says, "since that grace is so great, always abounding above and beyond our sin, why not just keep sinning? We are predestined; we are covered by grace. So let's just do as we please."

How quickly Paul puts the skids to that heresy—as if the apostle recoiled at such a repugnant thought. In Colossians 3:3 Paul put it like this: "For you died, and your life is hidden with Christ in God."

This passage does not mean that the Christian is perfect. The Bible does not teach that a person can reach a state in which he does not commit sin. But there is a great difference between committing a sin and constantly sinning and then delighting in that sin.

Verse 14 means that while God's law is not the means to salvation—"it is the gift of God, not of works" (Eph. 2:8–9)—the law is still God's standard of conduct and behavior.

1. Is it acceptable for the Christian to continue to sin? (6:2)
2. How are we united to Christ? (6:5)
3. What should not have dominion over us? (6:14)
4. Describe your feelings when you know you have sinned.

From Slaves of Sin to Servants of God (6:15–23)

More and more we hear Christians talking about "rights," the right to do this or the right to do that. That is not a scriptural premise. Nowhere have I found verses that tell me I have personal rights. Our rights are valid as long as they are exercised in our role as a servant of Jesus Christ and a servant of righteousness.

The whole subject of sin seemed to fill the apostle Paul with horror. He could not tolerate it in his own life and he sought every way possible to persuade others. We preach so many positive things today that we have lost sight of the terrible effects and ravages of sin. But Paul brings sin clearly into focus in verse 23.

1. What does Paul call us? (6:17–18)
2. Why did Paul speak in human terms? (6:19)
3. What is the result of sin? the gift of God? (6:23)
4. Try to chart your spiritual progress. At what points do you feel sin has impeded that progress?

Law and Sin (7:1–25)

Verses 1–6 are built upon a specific premise: Death concludes a contract. For example, when a man and woman are married, they are bound to each other "till death do them part." If one leaves the other mate and remarries, that person is said to be living in a state of adultery. There are several considerations that need to be added to that, of course, but the basic fact remains. Paul says, should one of the marriage partners die, then the other mate is free to remarry and such a remarriage does not constitute adultery. Why? Because death concluded the previous contract.

Prior to Calvary, the human race was bound to Satan and sin. But Jesus died on the cross, defeated Satan, and killed the effects of sin in our lives. That death ended the contract, and now we are free to live for Christ.

The same premise holds true for the law. Once we were married to the law, but we have died to the law and come alive to grace and mercy. So, we serve God in the newness of the Spirit and not in the old way of the letter.

It is my love relationship to Christ that causes me to live a holy life—not a long list of do's and don'ts that have been established by another person. The whole process of sanctification is a delightful one, a lovely one—not negative, strict, or harsh. Sanctification comes about through my love relationship to Jesus Christ. Because I love Him, there are some things I do not want to do.

Verses 7–12 tell us that we would not have known anything about sin had it not been for the law.

In verses 13–25, a well-known passage, Paul opens his heart to reveal his total humanness. Until we have incorruptible bodies, we are going to have the conflict that Paul so eloquently described. Therefore, don't be discouraged because you have inner conflict. Even Paul had it. The glorious truth is that Christ is sufficient to meet that need.

1. How does sin affect us while we are in the flesh? (7:5)
2. Which commandment did Paul quote as an example of knowledge of the law? (7:7)
3. What is the relationship between law and commandment? (7:11–12)
4. What conflict does Paul describe? (7:15–23)
5. What conflicts are you experiencing as you attempt to become a better Christian?

AUGUST 29
Romans 8:1–17

Free from Indwelling Sin (8:1–11)

Verses 1 and 2 are two of the most exhilarating verses in the Bible.

There is no way to appeal to a Christian on the basis of guilt; he has been freed from guilt. The believer who actively pursues the things of God, who does not walk according to the flesh (the human desires that are negative), but walks in the Spirit of God—that person has no guilt.

There are few things in life that are as blessed as being freed from the overwhelming burden of guilt and anxiety. Only God knows how much psychosomatic sickness is caused by guilt and condemnation. But Christ sets us free from that. The person who is free from this anxiety is the person who saturates himself with the things of God (see vv. 5–6).

We must simply become dead to sin. We become dead to the world and its system. We are alive to God. We hear God's voice. Other voices mean nothing.

1. What has freed us from the law of sin and death? (8:2)
2. Why was the law not sufficient? (8:3)
3. To what does Paul equate the carnal mind. (8:7)
4. How do you deal with the concept of guilt in your life?

Sonship Through the Spirit (8:12–17)

Most people would tell you they live with some type of fear: fear of dying, fear of social rejection, fear of failure. Rather than risk failure, it is easier to hold back the effort. Fear is man's most disruptive activity.

In verses 12–17, Paul deals with fear, an unnatural circumstance in the lives of men and women. Fear does not come from God. It is interesting to note that when angels visited this earth, they opened their conversations with mankind by saying, "Be not afraid." God does not want us to fear; we receive other feelings from God: joy, comfort, peace, love, warmth, and freedom from anxiety. Fear produces bondage; God sets us free. We cannot function in the way God intends if we are tied up with doubts and tension.

1. What spirit have we received through God's action? (8:15)
2. If we suffer with Christ, what do we become? (8:17)
3. What fears in your life keep you from a full relationship with God?

From Suffering to Glory (8:18–39)

Verse 18 is perhaps the greatest verse of encouragement in the whole Bible. That is no small claim for Paul to make, for he suffered as few men have ever suffered. He gave a short recital of some of those sufferings to the Corinthians:

> In labors more abundant, in stripes above measure, in prisons more frequently, in deaths often. From the Jews five times I received forty stripes minus one. Three times I was beaten with rods; once I was stoned; three times I was shipwrecked; a night and a day I have been in the deep; in journeys often, in perils of waters, in perils of robbers, in perils of my own countrymen, in perils of the Gentiles, in perils in the city, in perils in the wilderness, in perils in the sea, in perils among false brethren; in weariness and toil, in sleeplessness often, in hunger and thirst, in fastings often, in cold and nakedness—besides the other things, what comes upon me daily.
>
> (2 Cor. 11:23–28)

Now we need to spend some time on verse 26. We often pray amiss. Paul intimated this very thing about his own life in 2 Corinthians 12:7–10 when he talked about his thorn in the flesh. He said in verses 8 and 9: "Concerning this thing I pleaded with the Lord three times that it might depart from me. And He [God] said to me, 'My grace is sufficient for you.'"

Christian believers have two intercessors—Christ and the Holy Spirit. Jesus gave us this assurance in John 14:16–17: "And I will pray the Father, and He will give you another Helper, that He may abide with you forever, even the Spirit of truth, whom the world cannot receive, because it neither sees Him nor knows Him; but you know Him, for He dwells with you and will be in you."

Verse 28 contains a gracious promise, one that is a bit hard to grasp—especially when everything appears to be going wrong. A very wise pastor taught me something early in my ministry. It was this: "Always give God adequate *time* to work things out in your life. Don't rush Him."

Verses 38–39 mark the end to this great section of Romans.

1. What does Paul say about suffering? (8:18)
2. How does Paul describe our desire to become adopted by the Spirit? (8:22)
3. How do things work for those who love God? (8:28)
4. What can separate us from the love of Christ? (8:38–39)
5. For what kinds of things do you pray?

Israel's Rejection of Christ (9:1–33)

In chapters 9 and 10 of Romans, Paul injects a parenthetical thought regarding the Jews' rejection of Jesus Christ as the Messiah.

Paul wrote these two chapters not from an angry heart, but from a broken one. He makes it clear that he would have been more than willing to give him life if it would bring his brethren to Jesus, for Paul never forgot that he was a Jew.

In verses 6–13 Paul makes a point that is difficult for a Gentile to comprehend, although the Jews to whom Paul addressed this book would certainly understand it.

Paul claims that there is more to being a Jew, being a part of the "chosen people," than just physical descent. The chosen people are those whom God uses in the continuing propagation of His plan of salvation and redemption.

This ninth chapter of Romans has been called by some the most difficult chapter in the Bible, and it is true that one has to be very careful in teaching it. Verse 15, in which Paul quotes God's statement to Moses, and verse 18, which goes along with it, are difficult to deal with.

Do these verses mean that God arbitrarily picks out the ones to be saved and discards the others? Some believe that, and there are certainly some verses of Scripture that would seem to swing the argument in their favor. But a shallow and hasty handling of the Bible can be dangerous. We must take into account the whole Word and not make a theology on just a few verses. The Bible still promises that "whosoever will, may come."

Those who say that God can do anything He wants are overlooking an important point; that is, God will not do anything which contradicts His own nature. God will not, for example, commit any act which is unjust, because God is a just God.

1. How does Paul describe his emotional state while writing this letter? (9:2)
2. What two Old Testament examples does Paul give of Israel as God's chosen people? (9:7, 11)
3. What two Old Testament prophets does Paul quote? (9:25, 27)
4. What was the stumbling stone for Israel? (9:32)
5. Can you think of a time in your life when you have grieved, as Paul does here, over unbelief, or some other thwarting of God's will for His world?

SEPTEMBER 1
Romans 10:1–21

Israel's Need for and Rejection of the Gospel (10:1–21)

Paul's heart ached for his fellow Jews because they served God with great zeal, but with misunderstanding and ignorance of some vital issues. They tried to lift themselves into God's presence with their feasts, ceremonies, and laws. Paul uses this chapter to emphasize the necessity of faith in bringing about salvation.

The Jews were ignorant of their desperate plight, that they were in a lost condition. When they cried out concerning Christ, "His blood be on us" (Matt. 27:25), they didn't really know what they were saying; they didn't understand the enormous historical portent of their cry.

Paul said that his people's sincerity needed to be coupled with right action.

Paul's people were ignorant of how to gain salvation. Unfortunately, we equate that aestheticism, ceremony, and ritual with salvation; and that is a tragic mistake. That's what the Jews did with their legalism.

Then how are you saved? Look at Romans 10:12–13. Paul, in his writings to the Romans, anticipates the arguments of his readers and answers them. In verses 14 and 15 he does this again.

Paul has anticipated the argument: "You (Paul) say that salvation comes through trust in God? Well, how can we trust God unless we hear about this gospel—unless someone is sent to us to proclaim this good news?" To answer their argument, Paul says that the Jews cannot say that they never had a messenger given to them, because Isaiah described those very messengers hundreds of years earlier.

Then Paul anticipates another argument: "But how could God hold us accountable for this gospel? We never understood it properly." Paul's answer was quite pointed (see vv. 18–21).

God will condone no excuses that reject God's plan of salvation.

1. Who is the end of righteousness? (10:4)
2. What questions are unworthy of our concern? (10:6, 7)
3. What Old Testament prophets does Paul quote to show that the Jews have indeed heard? (10:16, 19, 20)
4. What excuses do we attempt to give today in pleading ignorance to God's will for our world and our lives?

Israel's Rejection Neither Total nor Final (11:1–36)

At this juncture Paul addressed the Gentiles of Rome. Prior to this Paul's remarks had been aimed at the Jews. Here the apostle gave a couple of object lessons. The first has to do with a lump of dough. According to Numbers 15, when dough was being prepared, the first part of it was offered to God. That being accomplished, the entire lump of dough was sacred from that moment on. It was similar to the planting of a tree. When the sapling was planted and dedicated to God, every branch that came from it thereafter was sacred to God.

What Paul was saying was this: "Our forefathers were sacred to God. Think of those great people—Abraham, Jacob, Isaac, and the like. Our whole nation sprang from them. The fact that they were given to God and were faithful to their call, in a way, makes all of our race sacred. We are the sum total of our forefathers."

That is true up to a point, for each person must make his own commitment to the Lord.

Paul continued with an allegory. Throughout the Old Testament, the prophets pictured the nation of Israel as the olive tree of God. Now, as Paul addressed the Gentiles, he told them they were wild olives that had been grafted into the tree of God. By an act of God's grace they were brought into the tree.

Paul warned the Gentiles against developing an attitude of contempt toward the Jews for their nonacceptance of Christ.

Paul really began to unburden his heart in the next few verses. Although his people had rejected Christ, and most of Paul's sufferings for Christ were at the hands of his own people, he believed the situation was temporary and that a spiritual awakening would come. Paul believed the promises of God. And he knew that, no matter how bleak the present situation looked, nothing could ever change the overall will of God for the Jews. God wanted to save His people, not destroy them. So Paul remained optimistic.

The last few verses of this chapter, beginning with verse 33, are a cry of love for God from this great man. Through all this man's questions, his persecutions and his difficulties, he never loses his faith in God. He never doubts his great God!

1. Has God written off all the Jews? (11:1, 5)
2. If the root is holy, what are the branches? (11:16)
3. What warning did Paul give the Gentiles? (11:19–22)
4. How does Paul characterize God's gift and calling? (11:29)
5. What is your attitude toward the Jews?

SEPTEMBER 3
Romans 12:1–13:7

How Christians Were to Live (12:1–13:7)

Paul just completed a lengthy theological treatise, one that has fascinated students for centuries. Now in a typical Pauline maneuver, he changed abruptly to a very practical matter—how to live a Christian life in the secular world.

Paul realized that the Christian faith was new in Rome, and it was being watched closely. His desire, like that of Jesus, was for the believers to be the light and salt of the earth.

Of verse 1, the Romans and Greeks would have said, "Present your state of mind or your inner being to the gods, but let your bodies revel in whatever state you wish." Not so with Christianity. It is considered "reasonable" by God to give our bodies in continuing sacrifice to His work.

Romans 12:3–8 is another listing of spiritual gifts. These differ from those Paul listed in 1 Corinthians.

These gifts are valueless without a sound Christian life. So Paul simply taught us here to behave like Christians. His teachings appear simple: avoid hypocrisy; abhor evil and do good; be kind, consistent, hopeful, patient, humble, and peaceable (see vv. 9–21).

In 13:1–7 Paul continued this practical teaching.

Today many of us live by the maxim "Do your own thing," but Scripture teaches us that we should come under authority.

Paul made this teaching extremely practical—right down to paying taxes. Of all people in the world, the Christian should recognize his need to be obedient to civil rulers. It is our moral obligation to do so. The "fear" that Paul mentioned really means reverence. Give honor or reverence to those in places of authority over you.

1. How should we regard ourselves? (12:3)
2. What does Paul say about our use of our gifts? (12:6)
3. What does Paul say about the Old Testament "eye for an eye" teaching? (12:17–19)
4. In what ways do you live out the teachings in verses 17–20?

SEPTEMBER 4
Romans 13:8–14:23

Love Your Neighbor (13:8–14)

The spiritual fulfillment of the infilling of the Holy Spirit is the God-given capability to live up to Christ's expectations of us as members of the kingdom of God. Matthew 5—7 (the Sermon on the Mount) outlines His expectations. Paul bears this out remarkably in this passage.

Psychologists would call Christ's teaching about loving yourself "being comfortable" with yourself. Without respect for yourself, you can't have a proper relationship with someone else.

In verse 11, aside from referring to the shortness of life, Paul was reminding us of the return of Christ to take His church away. Paul sensed an urgency in regard to the coming of the Lord. Then he listed five sins which should certainly not be a part of the Christian life.

1. List the sins Paul named. (13:9)
2. How does Paul tell the Roman Christians to live until Christ returns? (13:13–14)
3. What is your concept of living under the expectation that the day is "at hand"?

The Law of Liberty (14:1–23)

In this somewhat difficult chapter, Paul dealt with our obligation to be proper examples to others. Although an action may or may not have anything to do with our own salvation, it may affect another person who may be watching.

This passage speaks of a two-way tolerance. The person who understands true Christian freedom is tolerant of another person who is still living in some kind of condemnation; on the other hand, the person who is under condemnation must be tolerant of the person who knows the victory of freedom. This is an almost "utopian" position, but it needs to be stressed.

1. What does Paul say about acceptance into the faith? (14:1–3)
2. What is Paul's advice about judging others? (14:4)
3. What is unclean? (14:14)
4. What activities should we pursue? (14:19)
5. Think of some areas in your personal life or in your congregation's life that need more tolerance.

253

Christian Community; Paul's Plan to Visit Rome (15:1–33)

In this chapter Paul continues to stress that believers must be considerate of one another, particularly of those whose faith is less mature. This teaching demonstrates Paul's own greatness and maturity in the faith, for he could understand and accept the fact that others may not have been able to reach the same level of discipleship that he had.

Verses 7–13 contain a principle with which most of those who specialize in church growth would disagree. Generally, churches that accept all classes and races do not grow as much as churches that are more exclusive. This unfortunate fact is an indictment of our society.

Verses 14–21 give us another insight into Paul the apostle. He was a complicated man, yet, strangely enough, a common one. His cherished dream was to visit the church at Rome. He accomplished that dream later, but first he prepared the people for his coming. He let them know what kind of man he was, what his aspirations were, and what his goals and his background were. But above all, Paul remained the humble servant of Christ.

All of us, no matter what our ministry may be, are there to be used simply for the cause of the Lord. If God wants us to go, we go. If God wants us to stay, we stay. As an epitaph, Paul wanted "This man was a servant of Jesus Christ."

Paul planned to go to Spain with an intermediate stop in Rome. Paul told us over and over that he would never build on another person's foundation. He was, in other words, a pioneer, a trailblazer.

Why go to Spain? At that time Spain was a cultural, political, and professional center. Some of the greatest leaders of the world were Spanish. Paul reasoned that if he could reach these people for Christ, the influence worldwide would be tremendous.

To reach the largest number of people in the shortest possible time, Paul went to the great population and political centers. This is a principle that Christians should always remember.

1. For what did Paul ask God for his fellow believers? (15:5)
2. To what did Christ become a servant? (15:8)
3. What was Paul's goal? (15:20–21)
4. Why was Paul going to Jerusalem? (15:25)
5. Examine your community of worship. How alike or different is it in both class and race?

Greetings and Benediction (16:1–27)

We have only about fifty words to tell us of Phoebe, but from those words we can deduce that she was very active in the early church. Cenchrea was the port city of Corinth.

Prisca (Priscilla) and Aquila appeared earlier in Acts 18. Paul then sent greetings to twenty-four other persons, about whom we know virtually nothing. Of the twenty-four persons, six are women. Paul is often accused of disliking women. While Paul may have reflected some of the social values of his time, they were tempered by God. At all times Paul elevated women to a far higher status than they normally enjoyed in those days.

Tryphena and Tryphosa were probably twin sisters.

Many scholars believe that Rufus was the son of Simon of Cyrene, the man who was compelled to carry Christ's cross. If so, and there are certainly valid historical reasons to support this belief, a large part of the missionary movement of the early church was led by this man.

In verses 17–20 Paul seems to have remembered some other things he wanted to share. Here he warns Roman believers to stay clear of improper influences and expresses his concern about dissenters and hinderers.

Paul never waited until trouble had wrecked a church before he tackled the problems. When he realized that difficulties loomed on the horizon of a church, he had the courage to deal with them at that very moment. That's the mark of a great pastor.

Verses 21–23 show clearly that it takes a lot of people with different ministries to do the work of God. Tertius would have been the scribe who actually wrote Paul's letter to the Romans.

Paul closes this magnificent book with two points: the gospel is completely sufficient to make men and women able to stand firm, and the gospel has as its source the Lord Jesus Christ.

1. Who was the first Christian convert in Asia? (16:5)
2. Whom do those who seek to divide serve? (16:18)
3. Who was Paul's host? (16:23)
4. What is your concept of ministry? Does it reflect the breadth of Paul's concept?

1 CORINTHIANS

Greetings; the Sin of Sectarianism (1:1–31)

Because of its location, Corinth was a melting pot of humanity. Seamen and merchants came from all parts of the Roman Empire. As might be expected in such a port of call, immorality and drunkenness were rampant.

First Corinthians is Paul's answer to the Christians regarding their conduct in this fortress of dissipation.

Sosthenes, whom Paul mentions here, is the chief ruler of the synagogue at Corinth (see Acts 18).

Verse 2 gives us one of the most challenging definitions of the church in the entire Word of God. *Sanctified* means "being set apart and made holy in order to accomplish His specific good pleasure."

Four or five years had transpired since Paul had established the church at Corinth. News had reached him at Ephesus of difficulties in the church, and so he wrote to correct those situations. But first he commended the church for the good things they had done.

Verses 10–17 address the sectarianism that was dividing the church at Corinth. Paul pleads for the church's unity under Christ. Years earlier, an eloquent preacher named Apollos had ministered in Corinth, and his fiery oratory had produced many personal followers. Others liked the plain preaching of Paul. Some believers had heard Peter preach somewhere, and they were followers of the big fisherman. All this favoritism had produced some terrible divisions.

The "foolishness" of the gospel (see v. 18) refers to the fact that the Christian faith for the most part was based on beliefs, events, and teachings that the world's value system did not hold in high regard.

Paul did not belittle knowledge; he was himself a scholar. But Paul did maintain that we gain access to God through Christ, not through human insight.

1. For what did Paul plead with the Corinthians? (1:10)
2. Why did Christ send Paul? (1:17)
3. How does the message of the Cross appear to those who are perishing? to those who are being saved? (1:18)
4. What facets of the gospel might be called stumbling blocks in today's society?

SEPTEMBER 8
1 Corinthians 2:1–16

Christ Crucified; Spiritual Wisdom (2:1–16)

Even Paul's preaching was on a simple plane. Do verses 1 and 2 mean that Paul was unprepared, boring, or insulting to the human intelligence? Not at all. His preaching was demonstrative of the Spirit and power, but it was not based on Paul's wisdom or training. It was based on the power of God.

Paul was certainly not condemning education. He was one of the better trained ministers of all time. He was a Pharisee, a man gifted in numerous languages, and a trained Roman. But Paul didn't come to Corinth to impress the people with his lofty knowledge and superior education. He came to give them Jesus Christ on the simplest level he could, so that not even a child could say he did not understand the gospel.

In verse 6 Paul called for believers to mature in the faith continually. Things that caused difficulty last year should not be causing difficulty this year. We should be making continual progress.

How?

We are continually taught by the Spirit of God. There is a seeking after knowledge on the part of the believer. That means the great Teacher, the Holy Spirit, ministers to us.

In verse 9 Paul is not talking about heaven. He is talking about "now." He is talking about spiritual maturity and growing in the things of God. He is not talking about the acquisition of things, but about discipleship. Paul says that the average person on the street knows nothing about this kind of vital relationship with the Creator.

1. How did Paul describe himself when he came to Corinth? (2:1, 3)
2. What made Paul the great man he was? (2:2, 4)
3. What Old Testament prophet does Paul quote? (2:9)
4. From where does our knowledge come? (2:12)
5. How does your spiritual life this year compare to your spiritual life a year ago?

257

SEPTEMBER 9

1 Corinthians 3:1–23

Sectarianism Is Carnal (3:1–4)

Carnal means "given to crude, bodily pleasures." Paul, in verses 1–4, says that some of these Christians are not spiritually minded, but spend much more time in pursuit of bodily pleasures.

1. How did Paul first teach the Corinthians? (3:2)
2. What makes for carnality? (3:3)
3. In what areas of your life do you find the characteristics listed in the above question?

Watering, Working, Warning (3:5–15)

In verses 5–15 Paul says there are six materials we can use to build the structure of our life. Of those six, three are hard to find. They are precious, sought underground. Fire refines, but does not destroy them. But the other three are abundant and not particularly valuable, quickly consumed by fire, leaving only ashes.

Paul is saying that when we believers stand before the Judgment Seat of Christ, we will have our Christian works tried. Paul says the unfortunate, lazy, carnal Christian will be saved, as by fire.

1. Who should get credit for the ministry of Apollos? (3:6–7)
2. What warning does Paul give? (3:10)
3. How will one's work be tested? (3:13–15)
4. Name some ways you can treat yourself as God's temple.

Avoid Worldly Wisdom (3:16–23)

What of this matter of Christian liberty? Are we free? Yes! Does that mean we can do anything we want? No, because our bodies are the temple of God. How can any person yield his or her body, which is the temple of God, to adultery or fornication? "The [marriage] bed [is] undefiled," (Heb. 13:4) the Bible says. A believer can and should enjoy a healthy sex life within the confines of the marriage vow.

Now look at verse 21. We live in a temporary setting; everything that can be shaken will be shaken. So Paul admonishes us not to glory in worldly values. We should only glory in God's values.

1. How does the wisdom of the world compare with God's wisdom? (3:19)
2. What Old Testament passages does this passage quote? (3:19–20)
3. What part of the world's wisdom of today might contradict God's wisdom?

The Ministry of the Apostles; Fools for Christ's Sake (4:1–21)

Most of the difficulties experienced by the Corinthian church came about because of pride and presumption.

Verses 4:1–2 contain the standard of our conduct and work.

A steward was a slave who cared for the goods of his master. The main requirement of a steward was faithfulness. A steward was expected to sacrifice his own interests and to act faithfully on behalf of his master.

Verses 6–21 speak of the arrogance and pride of the Corinthian church. The Corinthians charged that those who were going through tribulations did not have much faith. They boasted of their spiritual gifts as if they were something they had merited. Because they had been blessed materially and enjoyed reasonably good health and a good standard of living, they felt they were superior to the apostles.

There are people today who claim that if Paul had the revelation they have, he never would have been in prison or had difficulties in life. Such teaching is blasphemy. The role of an apostle was difficult and few could have succeeded in it. Paul said, "Even to the present hour we both hunger and thirst, and we are poorly clothed, beaten, and homeless. And we labor, working with our own hands. Being reviled, we bless; being persecuted, we endure it; being defamed, we entreat. We have been made as the filth of the world, the offscouring of all things until now" (1 Cor. 4:11–13).

Many Americans desire the dramatic, the far-out, the spectacular. But much more important to the kingdom is that man or woman who labors patiently in the power of God, building slowly but surely for the kingdom's sake.

Paul was writing to the Corinthians to correct the spirit of dissension and dissatisfaction in the church and to bring the Christians into a feeling of unity. The church must be united behind its leadership and philosophy in order to be effective. In any church where there is a spirit of suspicion or pride or where we have factions and special interest groups, that spirit has to be eradicated before there can be any true furthering of Christ's cause.

1. How should we want people to think of us? (4:1)
2. Who is the only one qualified to judge us? (4:4)
3. What does being "fools for Christ's sake" mean? (4:10–13)
4. What did Paul warn the Corinthians? (4:14–16)
5. Why did Paul send Timothy? (4:17)
6. What factions can you discern in your worship community?

SEPTEMBER 11
1 Corinthians 5:1—6:20

Immorality Defiles the Church; Lawsuits Against the Brethren (5:1—6:20)

Paul had learned that an incestuous relationship within the Corinthian church was not being dealt with by the leadership. This chapter is a call for discipline within the church. The difficult matter, for the sake of the body, had to be dealt with.

Note that while this incestuous sin was the main cause for the letter to the Corinthians, Paul did not deal with this problem first. He began with the problem of unity. Once the church knew its purpose, then it would be possible for the body to deal with the discipline matter.

Paul said that such sin should have filled them with shame. Dr. Charles Erdman wrote that the Corinthians "should have understood that the true glory of the Christian Church consists not in the eloquence and gifts of its greatest teachers but in the moral purity and the exemplary lives of its members."

Paul even says that a believer is not to have unnecessary relationships of any kind with impure Christians. In the next letter he will deal with the matter of being unequally yoked with unbelievers.

In this chapter Paul deals primarily with three sins: sexual sin or lax morality, greediness for the world's goods, and idolatry— the worship of anything other than the one true God.

In the first part of this sixth chapter, Paul deals with the growing problem of Corinthian Christians' going to court against each other. He stated emphatically that such a practice must not continue.

Does this mean that a Christian can never appeal to the civil courts for justice? No, for the Bible says that the authoritative powers are given to us by God. But quarrels between two believers must not be brought into such surroundings.

1. What was the Corinthians' attitude toward their sinfulness? (5:2)
2. To what does Paul compare the sinful person in the Corinthian church? (5:6–7)
3. With whom should Christians not associate? (5:11)
4. What does Paul say about secular judges? (6:2, 4)
5. To what does Paul compare the body? (6:15)
6. In what ways does your life glorify God?

SEPTEMBER 12
1 Corinthians 7:1–24

Marriage and Divorce (7:1–24)

Paul wrote the letter to the Corinthians because he had received word that various problems faced that particular church. Apparently, one of these problems was marriage.

Paul has often been criticized because of his treatment of marriage and women. However, we must remember that he was answering specific difficulties in a specific situation, all the details of which we do not know. Paul treats four basic areas: marriage and sexual relationships within it, divorce, marriage and Christian service, and marriage relating to Christ and His church.

Verses 1–7 dealt with believers who apparently considered celibacy to be virtuous, even if the abstainers were married to each other.

Even today, many believers consider sexual relations somehow to be wrong in marriage. That is an unhealthy attitude. Others believe that the sexual union is for reproductive purposes only. That also is an unhealthy mental attitude. The Bible is not a primer on sex, but it does put forth a balanced concept that sexual relations are not everything to marriage, but are a very important part.

But what about divorce? This passage deals with a specific issue: There were those in Corinth who believed that when one accepted Jesus as Savior, he broke all former ties, including the marriage vow. And they believed that a married believer should divorce an unbeliever.

Verse 14 is a difficult verse. Does it mean that the unsaved person *automatically* becomes holy in the sight of God? No. William Barclay wrote about that verse: "There is an infection about Christianity which involves all those who come into contact with it. A child born into a Christian home, even into a home where only one of the partners is a Christian, is born into the family of Christ. In a partnership between a believer and unbeliever, it is not so much that the believer is brought into contact with the realm of sin, as that the unbeliever is brought into contact with the realm of grace."

The remainder of this segment is a beautiful one in which Paul teaches that becoming a believer does not necessarily change our circumstances, but allows us to live victoriously within them.

1. What does Paul say about sexual relations in marriage? (7:5)
2. What word does Paul give to the unmarried and widows? (7:8–9)
3. Paul says that we should live as we are called (7:17–24). In what areas of your life do you feel you are successful at this? Are there areas where you feel as if you need to reexamine your calling?

SEPTEMBER 13
1 Corinthians 7:25—8:13

To the Unmarried and Widows (7:25–40)

Here again, Paul answered the Corinthians' specific questions regarding marriage. Although Paul had no direct commandment to fall back on, he did offer his own advice.

Paul believed that Jesus' return was imminent; thus all other pursuits ought to be laid aside. It was not that he opposed marriage. When he wrote to the Ephesians, he compared the relationship between the believer and Christ to a man and his wife.

The danger of taking one verse or even several verses out of context is very real. Isolated verses may make it look as if Paul opposed the home, but that is not true. When you take all his writings as a whole and read them within that context, you find that Paul considered the home to be important.

1. What was Paul's authority? (7:25)
2. What was his advice? (7:28–29, 38)
3. How does this passage relate to those today who feel their call is to remain celibate?

Be Sensitive to Conscience (8:1–13)

In this chapter Paul deals with a thorny problem. Unfortunately there are some things that some people believe are fine and that others believe are wrong. In other words, the consciences of some are offended by the action, while the consciences of others remain free.

We have some of the same types of differences today. Paul's whole thesis in this eighth chapter is that the matter cannot be settled on the basis of right or wrong. It must be settled on the basis of love, one for the other.

In the Christian walk, while I am absolutely free, I still have responsibilities. I am my brother's keeper and have an obligation to his betterment. A vital part of the principles of Christ's kingdom have to do with my regard for my brother and sister. If I hurt them, I hurt my Lord.

1. How does Paul differentiate between knowledge and love? (8:1)
2. What was the particular problem Paul was addressing here? (8:4)
3. Think of one situation where your action, although all right for you, may have a detrimental effect on another.

SEPTEMBER 14
1 Corinthians 9:1–27

A Pattern of Self-Denial; Serving All Persons (9:1—23)

Verse 12 of this chapter gives insight into Paul's character and motivation.

The secret of Paul's life was that he could take personal affronts, deprivation, threats against his health and against his very life, but he would not do anything that could be construed as a hindrance to the work of his beloved Lord. Paul would never have asked, "What do I get out of this?" His conviction was, "For to me, to live is Christ" (Phil. 1:21).

His teaching here should not be taken to mean that one should not be supported by the ministry. Rather, Paul was trying to teach the people that while they had a responsibility to him, he had a responsibility as well—that of being a proper example.

Verses 19–23 indicate Paul's desire to be all things to all men in order to gain some for Christ. That does not mean he was a compromiser in any way, but that he could minister to all levels of society in a way they could understand.

1. What issue was Paul addressing in this passage? (9:6–7)
2. What was Paul's answer? (9:9–12)
3. What was Paul's reward? (9:18)
4. It is necessary that we be remunerated for our work in order for us to live in our society. However, where should the reward lie in our work? How can you apply that principle to your job?

Striving for a Crown (9:24—27)

In Paul's writings, he used easily understood word pictures to make his teachings clearer. Here he talked about running the race. The Corinthians could understand that because of the nearby Isthmian Games. Many participants would enter the race, but only one could win the wreath of honor. A person had to run with all his strength in order to achieve that victory.

Paul's point is that some of the Corinthian Christians only wanted to jog along in the spiritual race. They were not even trying to succeed. Perhaps the cost was too high.

1. How should one run a race? (9:24)
2. What does Paul say about the crown? (9:25)
3. How and why should one train for the race? (9:27)
4. What personal desires and appetites do you have that do not further God's goal for you?

SEPTEMBER 15
1 Corinthians 10:1–11:1

Old Testament Examples (10:1–13)

Lack of personal discipline has negative results. Paul has already given us two examples: (1) It can cause other believers to stumble and fall, and (2) it can hinder the work of God in subtle, damaging ways.

Now Paul gives a third serious result: Indulgence can destroy your own soul. Paul lists some of the indulgences that destroy our faith and witness:

(1) *Idolatry.* Numbers 11:4–34 tells us that Israelites who wished to follow Egyptian ways were stricken with the plague.

There may be no greater danger for the church in America than this one. In a time when we feel that a church building is not complete without a gymnasium, I suggest we are missing the mark.

(2) *Fornication (sexual sin).* Verse 8 refers to the story in Numbers 25:1–9. Today sexual messages from thousands of sources scream at us and give us a false impression of the real values. More and more we see brothers and sisters succumbing to these twisted messages.

(3) *Tempting Christ.* This sin refers to doing evil with the purpose of seeing what God's reaction will be. The Israelites did this in Numbers 21:5–9. We do the same thing to God. We know what His Word says, but we go ahead and do the opposite. Then we watch to see what God's reaction will be.

(4) *Complaining, or displaying a bitter, negative spirit.* Such a spirit characterized the Israelites through the entire Book of Numbers. We are admonished in the Word to have a sweet spirit of thanksgiving.

1. What happened to most of those who escaped from Egypt? (10:5)
2. How did Paul describe idolaters? (10:7)
3. What is God's role when humans face temptation? (10:13)
4. Think of a time when you were tempted but resisted that temptation. Did you feel God's presence in that?

Flee Idolatry (10:14–11:1)

This passage is a passionate plea to flee from idolatry. Idolatry involves an inordinate love of the world, or the world system. Paul stuns us with verse 21. We have been called to be a separate people. There must be a mark of distinction between believers and nonbelievers.

1. What is the cup of blessing? (10:16)
2. What is a good test for our behavior? (10:31)
3. How do you and your fellow church members support one another?

SEPTEMBER 16
1 Corinthians 11:2–34

Head Coverings; Conduct at the Lord's Supper (11:2–34)

Here begins a fascinating portion of Scripture—one often misunderstood. Many criticize Paul as a male chauvinist. These critics are not viewing what Paul says in light of the culture of his day.

The question here was a purely local one that had to do with Corinthian culture.

Some of the Corinthian women had mistakenly decided that, once they were saved, their relationship with their husband changed; they were independent. In light of that, they defied local custom and threw the veils away. To them the veil was a symbol of submission and dependence which, they said, was done away with upon their conversion. However, nonbelievers in the community were offended by this disregard for custom, and thus the gospel was hindered.

In verses 17–34 Paul turns to another serious situation in the Corinthian church. In those days, the church had what is known as a "love feast." Everyone brought food according to his ability. Usually the rich brought a lot, and the poor, little or nothing. But all the food was pooled and everyone joined together in fellowship and love, partaking of the common table. But in Corinth there were so many factions that this was not possible. The rich folks got together in one corner, like gluttons, and shoveled down their food, while the poor folks huddled together eating what little they had. As a result, the social differences among the believers were accentuated to an alarming degree. The cliques were not just material in distinction but were theological as well. The Apollos crowd sat in one place, while the Paul crowd sat in another. And they were calling this "the Lord's Supper."

Paul's warning in verse 27 is a solemn one.

Paul is not saying that a person cannot take Communion unless he is worthy, for none of us is. He is not speaking so much of character here as he is of conduct.

The fact that we are unworthy is what makes Calvary precious. That is the marvel of grace. And Communion is such a valid object lesson of that grace that each time we partake of it we are reminded of our debt to the Savior.

1. Who is the head of every man? (11:3)
2. Did a man have to have his head covered? (11:4, 7)
3. What is the relationship between man and woman? (11:11–12)
4. What is Paul's warning concerning the Lord's Supper? (11:27)
5. What is the place of the Lord's Supper in your worship life?

Spiritual Gifts: Unity in Diversity (12:1–11)

The people of Corinth believed that the more a person was bereft of his own senses and controlled by some unknown spirit, the more effectively that spirit was using him. The Greek soothsayers and cultists had cultivated this teaching. So when they became Spirit-filled believers and received various spiritual gifts, some of them used the same reasoning—that is, the more "far-out," wild, and hyper-emotional, the more of God it was. And such is not so.

Paul mentions nine of the gifts of the Holy Spirit in this chapter. Throughout the New Testament we are taught that we are to employ spiritual discipline in the use of these gifts; for, while their proper use will edify the church and touch the unsaved, their improper use will repulse outsiders and breed disharmony within the church.

1. How can the people of Corinth tell who is speaking by the Holy Spirit? (12:3)
2. What manifestations of the Holy Spirit are listed here? (12:8–10)
3. All persons have a gift, or gifts, of the Spirit. What do you feel your gift is? How are you using it?

Unity and Diversity in One Body (12:12–27)

Take a good look at your own body for a moment. You have hands and legs that are visible. But there are vital parts of your body down deep inside that you cannot see. You cannot see your heart, although your hands and legs would be useless to you if it were not for your heart. We have thousands of parts, seen and unseen, big and small, beautiful and not so beautiful.

The body of Christ, the Church, is the same. It is composed of the lovely and the unlovely. But all of these parts work together for the good of the entire body.

Be careful how you tolerate other members of the body of Christ. You are eternally connected with their welfare. Treat them kindly. We are all different, but functioning for the same purpose, the health of the body of our Lord.

1. How were we baptized? (12:13)
2. What does Paul say about the weaker members of the body? (12:22)
3. What signs in your congregation indicate that all members of Christ's body do not respect each other as they should?

The Best Gifts; the Greatest Gift (12:28–13:13)

We are approaching Paul's classic thirteenth chapter of 1 Corinthians, the noted love chapter. The apostle has just finished a major discourse in which he discusses three major problems facing the Corinthian church: (1) the conduct of women in the church, (2) the sacraments, and (3) spiritual gifts. All of the teachings he had given them now come under the umbrella of love in chapter 13.

Love, true spiritual love, must permeate all the actions of a Christian. Paul taught firmly that love and its practical application in each human heart are more vital than any other teaching he had given them. Now he lists fifteen characteristics of Christian love and behavior.

The Greek word for patience here is one that connotes patience with people. We are to be as patient with each other as God is with us.

William Barclay points out that there are two kinds of envy: one covets the possessions of other people; the second begrudges others their possessions and wishes they couldn't have them.

Take the list of fifteen characteristics of love and place them beside every situation you face. This is God's test. Do you give forth manifestations of the Spirit? Tongues? Prophecy? What about love?

Our Christian witness and life are tempered by Christ's love. Does that mean we compromise? No. It means that we demonstrate the life and love of our Lord Jesus Christ to everyone we touch.

1. What are we like if we do not have love? (13:1)
2. What are the fifteen characteristics of love? (13:4–8)
3. How does Paul describe our spiritual journey? (13:9–12)
4. What are the three things a Christian should possess? (13:13)
5. Take just one of your current life situations and apply Paul's fifteen characteristics of love to your actions in that situation.

SEPTEMBER 19
1 Corinthians 14:1–40

Gift of Tongues (14:1–25)

This chapter gives us a view of Gentile worship, which was far different from that of the Jewish synagogue. Jewish Christian worship would be considered "high church," by today's standards, while Gentile worship in Corinth would be considered Pentecostal.

Tongues is speech that originates with the Holy Spirit and is directed toward God.

Mysteries in verse 2 refers to the fact that the uttered speech is unintelligible.

Prophecy, like tongues, is an ecstatic utterance that came from the Holy Spirit. It is different from tongues, however, in that the speech of prophecy is intelligible. Paul regarded prophecy as superior to tongues precisely because prophecy was intelligible.

1. What spiritual gift did Paul admonish the Corinthians to pursue particularly? (14:1)
2. Why is a person who prophesies greater than one who speaks in tongues? (14:2–6)
3. What must happen before speaking in tongues becomes a valid gift of the Spirit? (14:12–13)

Order in Worship (14:26–40)

In verses 26–40 Paul goes into some detail on the conduct of the Spirit-filled worship service.

First of all, it is not a spectator situation. Everyone is involved. And Paul puts a limit on the number of messages in tongues, for there are other parts of the worship service that are equally important.

Verse 34 is a touchy one for us today. I am convinced that the issue is a purely local one, for God has used women in marvelous ways throughout history and is still doing so today. In the church at Corinth, womanhood was at a very low level and, in general, the people were immature. Paul would not permit anything to come into the congregation that would become a stumbling block.

Look at verse 40. Ours is a God of order. The universe itself operates with a precision that is marvelous. The worship service should reflect the nature of that very God.

1. How should speaking in tongues be carried out? (14:27)
2. Of what is God the author? (14:33)
3. What was Paul's order concerning women? (14:34)
4. What is the manner of worship in your community of worship?

SEPTEMBER 20
1 Corinthians 15:1–28

The Risen Christ—Faith's Reality, Our Hope (15:1–19)

Let us remember that Paul is writing to Corinthians, who were Greeks. The Greek mind could hardly comprehend the concept of a physical resurrection from the dead. The very idea of it was ridiculous to them. Remember that Paul faced this same kind of contempt for the message of the Resurrection when he spoke on Mars Hill in Athens. The Greeks believed in the eternal aspect of the soul; it was the *physical* resurrection which they could not accept.

In this chapter, Paul treats two principles of resurrection: (1) the fact, and (2) the manner in which it would happen.

Without the reality of Christ's resurrection there is no validity to the Christian message. Our salvation, our eternal destiny, our forgiveness for sins depend completely upon the resurrection of Christ.

Paul summarizes the historical proof of Jesus' resurrection.

Could this overwhelming proof of the Resurrection be pitched out and ignored? No. One historian has declared that the resurrection of Christ is one of the best documented facts of all human history.

Apparently there was a faction in the Corinthian church that denied the resurrection of the saints and possibly even questioned the resurrection of Jesus (vv. 12–19).

1. Who is the first witness to the Resurrection? (15:5)
2. How does Paul describe himself? (15:9)
3. If Christ is not risen, what naturally follows? (15:14–19)
4. What place does resurrection hold in your own faith?

Last Enemy Destroyed (15:20–28)

In the beginning of the redemption plan, God gave Christ the responsibility of defeating sin and death and bringing complete victory and life to the human race. Jesus has been doing that work ever since, and the day is rapidly coming when the work will be completely finished. Jesus will return to the Father, a conqueror, and God's victory over all His foes will be complete. The resurrection of His only begotten Son from the borrowed tomb was merely phase 1; the resurrection of all God's adopted children through grace will be the completion of the redemptive plan.

1. To whose life does Paul compare Christ's life? (15:22)
2. What will be the last enemy to be destroyed? (15:26)
3. What must happen before God's rule is established? (15:28)
4. What are some victories you have won in Christ?

269

Effects of Denying the Resurrection (15:29–34)

Verse 29 has puzzled many people for a long time. Paul asks why the Corinthians continue to baptize for the dead when they don't believe in the Resurrection.

What is the practice of baptizing for the dead? If a person who was not yet a member of the church died suddenly, the Corinthians were uncertain that he would go to heaven, even if he had been saved. Water baptism to them was the final assurance that they would be secure for eternity. So someone would stand in for the deceased and be baptized for him. There was no Christian dogma to substantiate it.

In verse 32, Paul quotes the philosophy of the hedonist: "Let us eat and drink, for tomorrow we die." Apparently even some of the Christians had fallen prey to his Epicurean view of the future because of their pagan associates. So Paul warned them against such fellowship.

1. What question is Paul dealing with in this passage? (15:29)
2. What would be useless if there were no afterlife? (15:32)
3. What signs of espousing an Epicurean lifestyle do you see in today's society?

A Glorious Body; Our Final Victory (15:35–58)

Having established the doctrine of resurrection, Paul deals with questions regarding it. When does the resurrection take place? What is its nature?

The most glorious hope of the church is the moment when Christ takes us home. "For the Lord Himself will descend from heaven with a shout, with the voice of an archangel, and with the trumpet of God. And the dead in Christ will rise first. Then we who are alive and remain shall be caught up together with them in the clouds to meet the Lord in the air" (1 Thess. 4:16–17). That's when death will be once and for all defeated.

1. What is the body like after it is resurrected? (15:42–44)
2. What cannot inherit the kingdom of God? (15:50)
3. What is the famous statement in this chapter regarding death? (15:55)
4. What is Paul's final advice to the Corinthians? (15:58)
5. How does the belief in an afterlife affect the way you set goals for your earthly life?

SEPTEMBER 22
1 Corinthians 16:1–24

Collection for the Saints (16:1–12)

Paul's mind was constantly churning. He has been giving the Corinthians some of the loftiest theology ever put to paper; but as he wraps up this first letter, he suddenly does an "about-face" and shifts into the very practical.

Notice the last verse of chapter 15 and the first verse of chapter 16. The offering Paul is talking about here is a collection for the saints in Jerusalem, who were going through a rough time materially. Everywhere he went, Paul asked the Christians he met to contribute to this collection. He taught them the spirit of generosity. Paul was concerned about the people at home.

This brings to mind the families right in our own churches who are hurting and who could be richly helped and blessed if we would take time to notice them. At one point Paul admonished us to be good to all men, but especially to those who are in the household of faith.

1. How was the offering to be collected? (16:2–3)
2. When did Paul plan to go to Corinth? (16:5)
3. How long was Paul to remain in Ephesus? (16:8)
4. Whom did Paul commend to the Corinthians? (16:10)
5. How generous are we to those around us?

Final Exhortations (16:13–24)

Paul begins this segment like a drill sergeant, barking out five commands. Then he gives us a brief insight into some of the wonderful personalities around him. Notice Stephanas. He was an important believer in that time. He had joined Fortunatus and Achaicus at Ephesus to work with Paul. He had apparently come to know Christ while living in Corinth, so the people to whom Paul was writing would have known him quite well.

Notice verse 20. That was a lovely custom in a world filled with hatred and strife. As the church becomes less and less a fellowship and more and more a corporation, we often have less affection for the individuals around us. A Christian church should be filled with love and fellowship, laughter and joy.

1. What were Paul's five commands? (16:13–14)
2. What early Christian phrase did Paul use in bidding the Corinthians farewell? (16:22)
3. In what way, if any, do you use your home as Priscilla and Aquila used theirs?

271

2 CORINTHIANS

SEPTEMBER 23
2 Corinthians 1:1–24

Comfort in Suffering (1:1–11)

The church at Corinth was about five years old. Its founder, the apostle Paul, was laboring in Macedonia, far to the north. There he met Titus, who brought him news of the work at Corinth. Paul felt it necessary to write the church a letter and send it back with Titus.

In all his Epistles, except Galatians, Paul included a lengthy thanksgiving at the outset. Even when he had to address matters of grave importance—doctrinal issues, conduct lapses, perils, and imprisonments—Paul had a thankful spirit.

Through all of Paul's suffering, God's wonderful presence covered him, keeping him from becoming bitter. Paul's comfort did not have its source in a lovely motel room or a pleasurable place to minister. His comfort was in God.

1. For what two things did Paul thank God? (1:3–7, 8–10)
2. How were the people of Corinth helping Paul? (1:11)
3. For whom or what has your church practiced intercessory prayer?

Paul's Sincerity (1:12–24)

Most ministers, at one time or another, have had their motives questioned by parishioners. It hurts, but it happens. So once in a while a minister feels it necessary to open his heart and defend his own character. This is usually not a good idea, but at times there is no other option. Paul had reached such a point in his ministry. The church at Corinth had grown suspicious of Paul's motives and had questioned his sincerity. The reasons for it are threefold: He had promised the people there that he would come to them soon, yet he had delayed for a long time; when he came, he was going to use a different route than he had told them he would take; and, finally, in 1 Corinthians he had dealt with the problem of incest.

1. Of what could Paul boast? (1:12)
2. Who directed Paul's ministry? (1:21–22)
3. In what ways can your community of worship help lighten the workload among its leaders?

SEPTEMBER 24
2 Corinthians 2:1—3:6

Sparing the Church; Forgive the Offender (2:1—11)

Some scholars believe that Paul had made an interim visit to Corinth between the founding of the church and the time of this writing. It must have been a dramatic and traumatic time, for Paul said, "I would not come again to you in sorrow" (v. 1). He was staying away deliberately until he could return to them in joy.

One of the church members in Corinth had been severely disciplined. It may well have been the brother who was living in incest in 1 Corinthians 5. After he had been disciplined by the church, they were unwilling to forgive him. Paul had apparently indicated to them that they must forgive him.

There are several vital lessons here. No church can just sit idly by while its members trifle with sin. The church must take a stand of some kind, both for the sake of the church and for the sake of the one who sins. But when true repentance has been shown and any wrong corrected, the sinning brother or sister must be received with full welcome and restoration—the sin is never to be remembered against the person.

1. What brought Paul joy? (2:3)
2. How did Paul write to the Corinthians? (2:4)
3. What happens if we fail to forgive? (2:11)
4. Whom have you failed to forgive?

Triumph in Christ; Christ's Epistle (2:12—3:6)

One of Paul's greatest concerns was for the church at Corinth. In this passage Paul even passes up an opportunity to spread the gospel in order to get word from Corinth sooner.

In verses 1–6 either or both of two things had happened: False evangelists have come into Corinth with alleged letters of commendation from Jerusalem Christians, or Paul has again been forced to answer the charge that he is simply an egotist who furthers himself through his ministry.

By "letter," Paul means the written law. He is referring to the deadly effect of that law in contrast to the life of becoming what the gospel offers.

1. Why could Paul not minister in Troas? (2:13)
2. What is Paul's epistle of commendation? (3:2)
3. What kills and what gives life? (3:6)
4. What does this passage say about any feelings of insecurity we have?

SEPTEMBER 25
2 Corinthians 3:7–4:18

Glory of the New Covenant (3:7–18)

The heretical teachers from Jerusalem insisted that the Corinthian Christians, who were mostly Greeks, were only saved if they believed on Jesus Christ *and* kept the Jewish ceremonial law. They told the Corinthians that Paul was not to be accepted among them because he denied the Jewish faith entirely.

Paul said all of us who believe in Christ are like Moses, who was privileged to gaze upon the glory of the Lord. The veil that would hide that glory has been taken from our hearts. In the face of Christ, as in a mirror, we see the glory of the Lord. We gaze upon Him in faith and in love. Before the brightness of His face, the fading glory of our old life of self-righteousness and self-dependence, of legalism and ritualism, of weakness and bondage and failure, grows dim and disappears. Instead of merely reflecting the glory of the Lord in our faces, as Moses did, we experience an inner transformation of character by the presence and indwelling of the Spirit of Christ.

1. Why could the people of Israel not look at Moses? (3:7)
2. What takes the veil away? (3:16)
3. In what ways are you aware of the indwelling of Christ's Spirit?

The Light of Christ's Gospel; Cast Down but Unconquered (4:1–15)

In verses 1–6 Paul asks, in effect, why anyone would ever want to be dishonest or to "use" other human beings. Paul said the gospel is so marvelous that it can stand alone without anyone's having to be "phony" in order to present it.

1. To whom is the gospel veiled? (4:3)
2. What does Paul preach? (4:5)
3. How do you live out the spirit of faith Paul speaks of in verse 13?

Seeing the Invisible (4:16–18)

Look at verse 16. Oh, that we might live with the same kind of spiritual intensity as this man Paul—beaten, persecuted, hurt, imprisoned, shipwrecked, ignored, mocked, stoned, lied about, slandered, maligned—no matter. None of those things moved him.

1. What happens to the inward and the outward person? (4:16)
2. For how long is our affliction? (4:17)
3. What parts of your life do you see as temporary? eternal? (4:18)

SEPTEMBER 26
2 Corinthians 5:1–6:10

Assurance of the Resurrection (5:1–11)

Paul has shared with the Corinthians some news of his sufferings. He never had it easy. Yet he brimmed over with hope.

His body probably was never very strong. We don't know what his thorn in the flesh was, but in all probability it had to do with his health. But Paul wasn't going to quit just because he didn't always feel well.

But in verse 10 he inserts a sobering note. Paul did not want to be ashamed before Christ at His coming. He lived his life in the light of that upcoming event.

1. What do we have if our bodies are destroyed? (5:1)
2. What does Paul call our bodies? (5:1, 4)
3. Why do we groan in our bodies? (5:4)
4. What must every person do? (5:10)
5. Everyone has a "thorn in the flesh." What is yours, and what are you doing to overcome it?

Be Reconciled to God; Marks of the Ministry (5:12—6:10)

Paul had another motivation that superseded all his personal hurts and discouragements (see v. 14). For no other reason could he have labored under such pressure.

In verses 18–21 Paul teaches us the doctrine of reconciliation. Prior to Calvary, God and man were estranged by our sin and rebellion and His justice and condemnation of our sinful lives. But Jesus Christ brought us together at Calvary.

It is doubtful that anyone can work in the kingdom of God without coming under character attacks similar to those Paul experienced. Satan uses whatever he can to abuse us. But as we grow closer to God, drawing on His very nature within us, we become like Him. Our reactions to the abuse are changed. Instead of being self-serving, our reactions are ones of forgiveness and love.

1. What was Paul's motivation? (5:14)
2. What should be the purpose of our lives? (5:15)
3. What was God doing through Christ? (5:21)
4. How does a Christian manifest himself or herself in the face of tribulation? (6:4–10)
5. Look at the list of characteristics in verses 4–10. Think of a problem area in your life. How can you apply these characteristics to your handling of your situation?

The Unequal Yoke; Be Holy (6:11—7:1)

In this passage the apostle Paul makes an impassioned plea to the Corinthians (and to us) for separation from the world, from unbelievers. He is urging that we not allow unbelievers to influence us.

Verses 14 and 15 have been preached many times with special regard to marriage. But there is more than marriage to this verse. Paul is talking about all unnecessary social contact—including business relationships, secret orders, social activities, and other fellowships.

Holiness really means "wholeness," or "health." Holiness is a positive walk with the Creator of the universe, allowing His divine love and life to fill your soul.

The first verse of chapter 7 is Paul's great summation.

1. What restricts the Corinthians? (6:12)
2. To what does Paul liken associating with unbelievers? (6:14—16)
3. Where can we apply this call to separateness in our own lives?

The Corinthians' Repentance (7:2—16)

Verse 2 is a heartbreaking verse. Here is Paul, perhaps the greatest Christian of all time, asking believers to believe his ministry.

Paul must have spent many lonely days. Even today there are believers who attack the apostle, putting wrong accents on his teachings, creating a stern, hard, difficult man out of this most tender and affectionate apostle. What a man! What a preacher and teacher! And how lonely he often must have been.

Paul always carried a great concern for the churches that he had pioneered. The heart of a great minister is not that he is alert and effective on the platform alone; it is also manifested the rest of the day in the concern he has for his flock.

Every believer should carry that same burden of really caring about the church. What is the church? It is, of course, the great mystical worldwide body of Christ. But in its most practical form, the church is a local body of believers. Every one in that church needs to feel a deep heart-wrenching concern for it.

1. What was Paul's state of mind when he got to Macedonia? (7:5)
2. What brought Paul comfort? (7:6—7)
3. What was the result of Paul's letter? (7:9)
4. In what ways do you show your concern for your own church?

Excel in Giving; Christ, Our Pattern (8:1–24)

Chapters 8 and 9 give us a volume of teaching on Christian benevolence. A true Spirit-filled believer is a giver, and the giving goes beyond tithing which, of course, should be considered the absolute minimum.

The collection for Jerusalem is the same collection mentioned earlier in the New Testament. The dispute in the Corinthian church had sidetracked Paul for a while.

The Jerusalem Christians were primarily persons of small means. They were right in the center of persecution and social ostracism.

What else shows more clearly the love of Christ than our concern for the needs of those about us? As Paul wrote earlier, "Though I speak with the tongues of men and of angels, but have not love, I have become as sounding brass or a clanging cymbal" (1 Cor. 13:1).

This may sound like a social gospel, and it is—one that shows you have been saved and that you care.

In this passage Paul tells the Corinthians that there is another grace they need.

John told us that we are children of God. As His children we take on His characteristics. How generous and liberal God is to us! He manifests that love to us in a thousand and one tangible ways. Now we are to be liberal as well. We are to be giving, generous people!

As we respond in love by giving to others, we need to realize that our gifts may not always be received with the gratitude we expect. But that should not matter. Christ is the motive for a generous church, for a generous believer.

1. What churches had excelled in giving? (8:1–2)
2. What other graces did the Corinthian church possess? (8:7)
3. What was Paul's advice concerning the Jerusalem offering? (8:10–11)
4. What is your philosophy of giving and how does it compare to Paul's?

SEPTEMBER 29
2 Corinthians 9:1–10:6

Administering the Gift; The Cheerful Giver (9:1–15)

As we studied in the preceding lesson, Paul is encouraging the Gentile churches to give a generous offering to help the suffering Christians in Jerusalem. To stimulate their giving, he encourages the Corinthians by citing the example of the Macedonians.

Why do people give? Some people give because they feel obligated. That's a poor way to give—motivated by guilt or a feeling of "have-to."

Some folks give because it makes them feel good. There really is some validity to that motivation. It is fun to give.

Some people give to the Lord because their giving is posted somewhere for others to see. They give for the attention they receive.

But the motive behind true Christian giving is love for the Lord. We aren't investing in raffle tickets. We give to God because we love Him and desire to please Him.

1. Why did Paul send the brethren to Corinth? (9:3–5)
2. What kind of giver pleases God? (9:7)
3. What was Paul's prayer concerning God's treatment of the Corinthians' gift? (9:10–11)
4. What is your attitude toward giving?

The Spiritual War (10:1–6)

This is an important paragraph of Holy Scripture because we learn what we are up against in our spiritual battle and how we can win.

The weapons of the flesh are not much good in this war! But the weapons God gives to us—love, patience, the gifts of the Spirit—are mighty weapons in this battle.

Paul warns us to attune our every thought to Christ. This has to be one of the most important teachings ever given us. The mind is God's access to us—the antenna for spiritual reception. So it becomes very important what thoughts we allow to go through our minds!

We cannot be responsible for thoughts that flit through our minds, but we are responsible for the thoughts we dwell on.

1. How does Paul plead with the Corinthians? (10:1)
2. What do we battle against? (10:5)
3. What are the sources from which we are daily filling our minds?

SEPTEMBER 30
2 Corinthians 10:7—11:15

Reality and Limits of Paul's Authority (10:7—18)

Paul makes reference here to his outward appearance, which apparently wasn't very impressive. We have some descriptions handed down to us through the centuries, although we don't know how accurate they are, since they are not found in Scripture. Apparently he had weak, watery eyes, a rather prominent nose, a somewhat bent body—totally unimpressive in outward appearance.

Paul's response to his critics in verse 11 is powerful. Paul is saying, "I will be weighty and powerful when I get there."

Paul then turns around in verses 12—18 and says that there are limits to his capacities, for when a person is measured against Christ Himself—that person can never measure up.

1. What basic question does Paul deal with here? (10:7)
2. What were Paul's detractors saying? (10:10)
3. How is it unwise to measure ourselves? (10:12)
4. Who receives approval? (10:18)
5. By what standards do you judge accomplishments?

Concern for Their Faithfulness; Paul and False Apostles (11:1—15)

Verse 2 is significant for any believer.

We are the bride of Christ. We will be eternally given to Him at the marriage supper of the Lamb. Now we are betrothed or engaged to Him. An engagement may not seem to be a very lasting type of commitment, but that's because we live in a civilization two thousand years removed from the time of Christ.

At the time Paul wrote, an engagement was a deep commitment. Thus, in this binding agreement, Christ has every right to expect us to remain faithful to Him.

Can you imagine that? The Corinthians once had Paul for a pastor, and they were not satisfied. Paul defended his ministry against these self-serving critics, but in so doing he always lifted up Jesus.

1. Why was Paul jealous for the Corinthians? (11:2)
2. What was Paul's fear for the Corinthians? (11:3—4)
3. How can false apostles appear to be apostles of Christ? (11:14)
4. How deep do you consider your commitment to Christ and His church to be?

OCTOBER 1
2 Corinthians 11:16–12:10

Reluctant Boasting; Suffering for Christ (11:16–33)

Paul is not trying to carve out a niche in Corinthian history for himself, but is desperately trying to save the Corinthians from false teachers and false doctrines. Of necessity he has to get personally involved in the matter, so Paul meets his opponents on their own turf.

Apparently, the false apostles were Jewish men who prided themselves on their Hebrew heritage. They came from Jerusalem, the very heart of Judaism. They reasoned that, since Paul came from Tarsus, he must be an impostor.

Paul intimates that to think of those men as ministers involves a bit of insanity. The apostle itemizes some of the costs of real ministry and catalogs sufferings he had to endure.

1. Why does Paul allow himself to boast? (11:18)
2. What validates Paul's ministry as opposed to the ministries of the false apostles? (11:23)
3. What was with Paul daily? (11:28)
4. How did Paul escape from Damascus? (11:32–33)
5. What kind of boasting do our churches engage themselves in?

The Vision of Paradise (12:1–10)

In this passage Paul tells about a very sacred and personal moment in his life. Because he did not achieve this moment of his own doing, he preferred to speak of it in the third person. Something happened at a key time in Paul's life to transform him. It was as if his spirit left his body and he was given a brief glimpse into paradise.

In light of such an experience, it is not hard to understand why Paul could do all that he did; he had no interest in the things of life beyond the bare necessities. After all, he had been given a glimpse of eternity, and everything else paled by comparison.

He also had a thorn in the flesh (see v. 7) that kept his priorities straight. There has been much conjecture about what that thorn was. Some say it was his eyesight; others claim it was his physical presence. Others say it was a wife, a grim domestic situation.

1. When did this experience happen to Paul? (12:2)
2. What kind of words did Paul hear? (12:4)
3. How can you apply your belief in God's grace to your "thorn in the flesh"?

OCTOBER 2
2 Corinthians 12:11–13:14

Signs of an Apostle; Love for the Church (12:11–21)

It seems that, in this segment, Paul has taken a deep breath, exhaled wearily, and leaned back in his chair, so spent is he from the effort of the ordeal he has just gone through—that of defending his ministry. He sighs, "You have forced me to act like a fool—this defense of my ministry. I shouldn't have to do any of this. I am not inferior to those so-called super preachers who have invaded Corinth. My work as an apostle was evident among you. The only thing I would change was being a financial burden."

Paul had built the work at Corinth. He had poured out his life there and left behind a growing church. He needed no other defense of his ministry. Yet his love for the people and the work itself was such that he felt compelled to answer the charges against him in love and tenderness. Never once did he rail against the people. He would do nothing, even at this critical juncture, to injure the work of God. It is the mark of a Spirit-filled believer that he or she would do nothing negative toward the church—only positive, constructive, words and actions.

In verses 19–21 Paul listed the marks of a carnal church.

1. What was Paul's attitude toward the church at Corinth? (12:15)
2. Whom did Paul send to the Corinthians? (12:18)
3. What did Paul fear for the church at Corinth? (12:20)
4. How have you handled (or seen handled) dissension in your community of worship?

Going with Authority (13:1–14)

Paul ends 2 Corinthians with a flourish. He warns of a showdown upon his return to Corinth.

As we see from verse 7, Paul hoped that the Corinthians would do the honorable thing even before he got there. For us, his words mean that we should live the life because we are motivated to from inward glory, not outward discipline.

I love verse 11. Great Christians are well-rounded. Not excessive in one thing and lacking in another. Heresy is usually built on a measure of truth, but the truth has been pushed to a ridiculous extreme. So be a complete believer, lacking in nothing.

1. What proof did the Corinthians seek? (13:3)
2. What quality did Paul prefer for himself? (13:9)
3. What is Paul's advice to the church at Corinth? (13:11)
4. What is your motivation for being a Christian?

281

GALATIANS

OCTOBER 3
Galatians 1:1–24

Paul's Authority; Only the Gospel (1:1–10)

On his third missionary journey, Paul learned that the church in Galatia was under attack. Critics were maligning the apostle Paul and undermining the solid theology of the church. The main problem was that there were those who wanted to prolong the age-old theory that the gospel was only for the Jews, God's chosen people. Therefore, if a Gentile wanted to become a Christian, he would, first of all, have to become a Jew to be eligible for salvation. That meant he would have to undergo the rite of circumcision and shoulder the impossible weight of the Mosaic law. In other words, they were teaching that a person's salvation depended largely upon his ability to keep the law. Paul preached just the opposite—that a person has been granted salvation because of God's mercy and grace.

The simplicity of the gospel is the greatest hurdle an unbeliever has to overcome. It is ingrained in us that religion is a matter of dotting all the i's and crossing all the t's. This is not the case.

1. What did Paul marvel at? (1:6–7)
2. What does Paul say about pleasing men? (1:10)
3. The Jews perverted the gospel in the early church. What are some of the ways we pervert the gospel today?

Call to Apostleship (1:11–24)

In this passage Paul gives us a brief autobiographical sketch of his life that is helpful in our understanding of him, especially for those years immediately following his conversion in Damascus.

Sometimes we don't stop to consider that, between Paul's conversion and his ministry, a number of years intervened. Like Moses, Paul spent time alone with God in the desert. He had much to learn, and to unlearn. New believers need to follow Paul's example.

1. How did Paul receive the gospel he preached? (1:12)
2. Where did Paul go immediately following his conversion? (1:17)
3. Which two apostles did Paul see in Jerusalem? (1:18–19)
4. In what ways are you continuing your training in the gospel?

OCTOBER 4
Galatians 2:1–21

Defending the Gospel (2:1–10)

Paul was a rugged individualist, a man of strong principles, a creative thinker, and an achiever. In spite of all those characteristics, Paul never went outside the system to accomplish his work.

Paul had a healthy respect for authority—even when he didn't agree with it. He knew that eliminating the authority of duly appointed leadership was inviting anarchy.

But, balancing that position, Paul was never overawed by human authority to the point of changing his beliefs and convictions. He was courteous and polite to those who opposed him, but also firm and determined.

1. When did Paul go to Jerusalem the secomd time and who accompanied him? (2:1)
2. What mission had been given to Paul? to Peter? (2:7)
3. Who gave Paul the right hand of fellowship? (2:9)
4. What did the Jerusalem leaders request of Paul? (2:10)
5. Paul was given a ministry to the Gentiles. What ministry has God given you?

Issues of the Law; Crucified with Christ (2:11–21)

Paul related the story of the love feasts at Antioch in which Peter made a substantial error in judgment. The love feast was a common meal, held each week. All the believers came together for a very special time in which everyone mingled and ate together. The common denominator was Christ.

A true believer does not allow class distinction, whether racial, economic, or social, to be a part of his life. None of these distinctions is appropriate in a true Christian body.

Verse 20 gives us the whole gospel in a nutshell. When we are born again, we die to the world system. We are crucified with Christ. We don't belong to ourselves any longer. We belong to Christ. Our lives will be what He wants them to be.

1. What behavior of Peter caused Paul to confront him? (2:12)
2. Who else played the hypocrite? (2:13)
3. By what are we justified? (2:16)
4. What follows if salvation is gained by observance of the law? (2:21)
5. Name two ways in which you feel you have died to the world system.

OCTOBER 5
Galatians 3:1–29

Justification by Faith (3:1–9)

No one receives the Holy Spirit by keeping the law; rather, we receive the Spirit when we hear the gospel and believe it by faith. We find it hard to believe that the gift of the Holy Spirit is offered freely by God. Why not accept the offer with thankfulness?

There are those who claim that people will never do anything worthwhile if salvation is a free gift. That is not the case. Paul said that when a person really tunes in to God, he becomes an instrument of righteousness. And that righteousness is an effect, not a cause.

1. Why does Paul call the Galatians foolish? (3:3)
2. Who are the sons of Abraham? (3:7)
3. To whom did God preach the gospel beforehand? (3:8)
4. What are you doing with your free gift of salvation?

The Law Brings a Curse; the Purpose of the Law (3:10–29)

The Bible says there is a curse—or a sentence—on all who are under the moral law that God gave to Moses. But Christ has redeemed us from death. He has given us liberty. We never need to be afraid again! Paul implores the Galatians not to turn back to the law from which Christ redeemed them; not to turn from the blessing of faith to the curse of the law.

Then is the law useless? No. The law still has an effect on us even today by showing us the standard of living that God expects of us. Even though we cannot keep those standards in our own strength, Christ will keep them through us.

In verses 23–29 Paul compares the law to an old slave found in a Grecian household. He had the task of taking the children to school each day. He saw that they arrived safely and brought them home at evening. He was not a teacher or schoolmaster. His job was to take the children to the teacher.

1. By what are we justified? (3:11)
2. From what has Christ redeemed us? (3:13)
3. Who confirmed God's covenant with Abraham? (3:17)
4. What was the purpose of the law? (3:19)
5. How are we related to Jesus? (3:28) to Abraham? (3:29)
6. How does verse 28 relate to your feelings about the many ethnic groups in the world?

284

OCTOBER 6
Galatians 4:1–31

Sons and Heirs (4:1–7)

In ancient times, a boy had no rights until he reached a certain age. He then took on the responsibilities and privileges of manhood.

Paul told the Galatians that if they listened to the false teachers and reinstituted the Judaic law to run in tandem with the gospel, they would be regressing from fullblown sons of God to mere servants of the law.

1. Who had control of the child until he became of age? (4:2)
2. To what were we in bondage before we knew the gospel? (4:3)
3. If we have passed from servanthood to sonhood because of the gospel, what are we to God? (3:7)
4. At what point in your life do you feel you passed from servanthood to childhood and thus became God's heir?

Fears for the Church (4:8–31)

The Galatian church was regressing, Paul says, because they were turning their backs on true freedom to become servants of a law that is impossible to keep. Verse 10 refers to the seasons of the Jewish calendar.

When Paul, Barnabas, and Mark left Antioch on the first missionary journey, they traveled to the island of Cyprus, then headed north across the sea into Phrygia (present-day Turkey). Paul did not preach there even though there was a large population. Why? Many believe it was because he was ill.

The region of Pamphylia along the coast was rampant with malaria, and Paul probably did not stay there in his weakened condition; rather he traveled to the central plateau toward Antioch in Pisidia. This was one of the most dangerous routes in the world. Perhaps it was this danger that caused Mark to quit the team and return to Jerusalem. At any rate, when Paul came into Galatia, he was not feeling well, but the people did not turn from Paul's infirmity with loathing.

1. Like whom did Paul want the Galatians to become? (4:12)
2. How did the Galatians receive Paul? (4:14)
3. What are the two covenants? (4:24–26)
4. Paul has referred several times to his thorn in the flesh. How does our society treat persons with an infirmity or with a handicapping condition?

OCTOBER 7
Galatians 5:1–26

Christian Liberty; Love Fulfills the Law (5:1–12)

The whole Book of Galatians boils down to this: The way of the law spotlighted human achievement, but the way of grace spotlights Christ's mercy.

Paul ends his argument with a rather brutal illustration. Near Galatia was Phrygia, where the people worshiped Cybele. The priests had a barbaric ceremony in which they mutilated themselves by castration. It is to this act that Paul probably refers in verse 12. Paul, in effect, told the Galatians, "If you are going to make salvation dependent upon circumcision, you might as well end up like the heathen priests by castrating yourselves."

1. What happens when a man allows circumcision to be imposed upon him? (5:3)
2. Paul, as Jesus often did, refers here to leaven. What does he say about leaven? (5:9)
3. Think of something either in your own life or in the life of your worshiping community that might act as leaven.

Walking in the Spirit (5:13–26)

If we are not going to be saved by the law, but by grace, does that give us license to sin? Of course not (see vv. 16–17).

We live in a free society in America. And yet, in order to remain free, we have certain restrictions. You would not want to live here if those restrictions were lifted. This chapter records a list of restrictions.

Although these words seem restrictive and harsh, Paul is really pointing out that a life devoid of such fleshly sins gives us the freedom to carry out God's will for us and thus achieve a fuller life.

In verses 22–26 Paul lists attributes of that fuller life. The believer is a disciplined person. Even with all our freedom, we are not our own property. We are Christ's. We belong to Him. We have been redeemed by Him. He is living His life in and through us.

These manifestations of spiritual fruit in our lives are not options. They are to be standard equipment on all of us. They are to be the hallmark of believers.

1. How can we avoid the lust of the flesh? (5:16)
2. What are the works of the flesh? (5:19–21)
3. What is the fruit of the Spirit? (5:22–23)
4. Examine your own life. Which fruits of the Spirit are at work in your life? Which are lacking?

OCTOBER 8
Galatians 6:1–18

Share the Burdens; Be Generous and Do Good (6:1–10)

Paul wraps up his letter to the Galatians with some very helpful Christian advice in verse 1. Paul is not talking about repeated abuse of the grace of God. He is talking about the person who "slips up." Any person can make a mistake. We are not to gloat or feel more spiritual than the fallen person. We are to restore that person.

Verse 7 is one of the most profound verses of all Scripture. We usually have this in mind when we think about sinful living, but Paul's teaching here affects a far greater part of living than that. It is easy to grow weary in well-doing. But here is a blessed promise: If we do not lose heart, if we keep at it, faithful in season and out of season, we will one day reap bountifully.

Again, Paul advises us to take special care in our treatment of those in our family of believers (see v. 10).

1. What attitude should we take toward those who sin? (6:1)
2. What will fulfill the law of Christ? (6:2)
3. What does Paul say about pride? (6:3)
4. How can we relate Paul's teaching in 6:3–4 to our tendency to be judgmental toward others?

Glory Only in the Cross; Blessing and a Plea (6:11–18)

Paul adds a postscript in his own handwriting. Verse 11 has often been used to support the theory that Paul's eyesight was a problem. The apostle says that those who wanted the Galatians to be circumcised had three motivations for this heretical teaching: (1) it could be used as a kind of protection should Rome begin another vigorous persecution of the church; (2) they could prove they were Jewish; (3) they were trying to impress God by this great show of ritual and ceremony (an impossible task). These legalists weren't nearly as concerned with a convert's salvation as they were in furthering their own cause.

Look at verse 17. There were too many cities in which to build churches, too many people to tell about Jesus, to worry about little things. Paul could say that Christ's grace and peace attended his spirit. He was at peace with the world.

1. How did Paul write his postscript? (6:11)
2. In Christ Jesus, what is the only thing that counts? (6:15)
3. What things get in the way of your becoming a new creation in Christ?

EPHESIANS

Redemption in Christ (1:1–14)

The theme of this Epistle, written by the apostle Paul, is that the church is the body of which Jesus Christ is the Head. Paul teaches us that we are seated with Christ and that we should live accordingly.

Paul probably survived many of his afflictions by not allowing self-pity to gain possession of him. Far better, he reasoned, to count his blessings. And so he began to enumerate them.

1. God has known us from the very beginning, before the foundation of the world. He has chosen us. It is not a matter of our making a decision about God, but that God has made a decision about us.

2. We have been forgiven of our sins.

3. God has revealed His will to us.

4. We have obtained an inheritance—eternal life, infinite value, divine wisdom, Holy Ghost power, the joy of healings.

1. To what have we been predestined? (1:5)
2. What is God's will? (1:10)
3. Who guarantees our inheritance until we redeem it? (1:13–14)
4. How does God's view of humanity affect how we regard each other?

Prayer for Spiritual Wisdom (1:15–23)

In these verses Paul goes beyond the lofty beginning of a person's salvation and calls for a maturing process that in no way minimizes that initial experience. Without salvation there is no eternal life, just as there is no physical life without birth. But a person cannot go through life just glorying in the fact that he or she was born. There is a life to be lived and enjoyed. There is the growing up, the maturing. And so it is in the Christian life.

Paul tells us in verses 20 and 21 that Christ sits at the right hand of the Father and that He is in control of the universe.

1. What did Paul keep doing? (1:16)
2. What did Paul want the Ephesians to know? (1:18–19)
3. What is the body of Christ? (1:22–23)
4. What are you doing to mature in the faith?

OCTOBER 10
Ephesians 2:1–22

By Grace Through Faith (2:1–10)

Salvation is more than mental assent that Jesus Christ is who He says He is. Salvation is quite literally life from death. "And you He made alive, who were dead in trespasses and sins" (v. 1).

This kind of salvation demands a change. Some lives may be more dramatically changed than others because of prior circumstances, yet there is an inner transformation in each one.

Do not distort verses 8–9. Some will say, "You see, works are not important." But they are important. James made that clear when he wrote, "Faith without works is dead" (James 2:20). After we are saved we will want to begin doing the works of Him who saved us. Those works do not in themselves save us, but without those works the salvation process remains incomplete.

1. How does Paul describe our life before the reality of salvation? (2:2–3)
2. What motivated God to send Christ to us? (2:4)
3. For what purpose are we created? (2:10)
4. Reread verse 10. What import does that verse have on your daily life? Might it change the way you do anything?

Brought into Peace and Security (2:11–22)

Paul addresses an important matter in these verses. Remember that Paul was a Jew. The Jews, for the most part, believed that the promises of salvation were primarily their birthright and that the Gentiles were at best interlopers, and, at worst, fodder for hell. But here is this Jew, Paul, saying that we are in the same boat, drawn into fellowship with God with the same promises and blessings as the original children of Abraham. Paul takes the study even further by saying that there should be no enmity between the Christian and the Jew.

Every person has as much potential for God as any other person. The difference does not lie in ability, but in love, dedication, zeal, and availability!

1. What has broken down the dividing line between Gentile and Jew? (2:14)
2. How do we have access to God? (2:18)
3. What is Jesus Christ in the household of God? (2:20)
4. What are some things you can do to make yourself more receptive to God?

OCTOBER 11

Ephesians 3:1–21

The Mystery Revealed (3:1–13)

Paul paid a price for his high calling, for his ministry was not a bed of roses. Yet he never complained about the deep valleys through which he journeyed. He was a missionary—the first one to take the glorious gospel to the Gentiles. And, rather than receiving the plaudits of the world for this courageous mission, he took undeserved beatings and other abuses.

Even as he is writing this Epistle, probably from Rome, Paul is under arrest, awaiting a hearing from Nero.

In these next verses Paul makes it clear that, even though he has had to pay dearly for his calling and ministry, he has never doubted for even one moment that he is carrying out the will of God. A person in the work of God needs that kind of solid assurance. We need to know that it was God who called us, that we are not teaching or preaching or singing the gospel for any reason other than the fact that we have been divinely called. Paul had that kind of assurance.

1. How did Paul learn the mystery of Christ? (3:3)
2. What was not known in other ages? (3:5–6)
3. What is the purpose of the mystery? (3:10–11)
4. In what ways does your life demonstrate the assurance that you have been called by God?

Appreciating the Mystery (3:14–21)

In these precious verses we read Paul's prayer for the Christians in Ephesus—that they continually experience inner growth.

God expects constant maturing on our part. God's righteousness is imputed to us, and the sins that so easily beset us a year ago should not still have dominion over us today. We gain new ground, day by day and little by little. Always advancing (although sometimes failing), but never standing still.

Prayer, worship, and study—study of both Scripture and other Christian resources—are our primary tools for growth in the faith.

1. What did Paul want the Ephesians to be able to comprehend? (3:18–19)
2. In what ways are you more firmly grounded in the faith than you were at this time last year?

OCTOBER 12
Ephesians 4:1–24

Walk in Unity (4:1–16)

In the first three chapters, Paul has reminded us of Christ's lofty position at the right hand of God and of the task to which we have been called. In this chapter, which begins the second section of Ephesians, he tells us emphatically that there are certain requirements expected of a follower of Christ. And one of the primary requirements is to love each other in the Spirit of the Lord, living together in unity.

You and I do not belong to ourselves; we belong to Christ. Perhaps there are things we feel justified in doing, but we do not have the right. We have been bought with a price, and we belong to God.

This passage should not be seen as an indictment of denominations. Denominations are a good thing, for we are not all alike. We do not have the same tastes in worship. What appeals to one might not appeal to another. But denominations should live together peaceably and in love and, hopefully, even in fellowship.

In verse 11, Paul gives us a partial list of God's gifts to the church.

In verses 14–15 Paul again makes a plea to the believer for new depths of spiritual maturity—a maturity that will result in unity, in each person's carrying his or her share of the load.

1. How should we conduct ourselves to be worthy of God's calling? (4:2–3)
2. How does Paul emphasize the unity of which he writes? (4:4–6)
3. What does Paul no longer want us to be like? (4:14)
4. Look at the list of spiritual gifts. What do you see as your spiritual gift and how do you carry it out?

The New Man (4:17–24)

This passage echoes Paul's earlier call to become a new creation by putting aside Gentile ways. Paul in this letter has previously addressed the Ephesians as "Gentiles." Here, he separates them from the Gentiles and, by the term, obviously means "pagans." Paul's summary of the moral status of the pagan world closely matches Romans 1:21–32.

Vanity is often associated with idolatry.

1. Why are the Gentiles alienated from God? (4:18)
2. What does Paul say we should "put off"? (4:22) "put on"? (4:24)
3. In what ways have you put away the "old man"?

Don't Grieve the Spirit; Walk in Love (4:25–5:21)

In this section Paul is pleading with the Ephesian Christians to learn about spiritual growth, to become more and more Christlike.

In verse 25 he makes a call for telling the truth. You see, a lie is only an evidence of a dishonest spirit inside. As a person is inside, so his mouth speaks.

Paul's teaching in verse 26 is especially good for husbands and wives. To allow an angry spirit to fester is a dangerous thing.

He warns of sexual sin; that is, intimacy outside of the marriage bed. A man and his wife who are intimate in commonly accepted activities are not sinning. The Bible says that the marriage bed is undefiled. Sex was not given by God only for procreation; it was also given for the pleasure of the husband and wife.

Children should learn sound, basic principles of sex from mothers and fathers who are loving to each other and understand what God truly established. Sex is not bad in the marriage bed; it is wholesome and beautiful, given by God. So maintain a healthy balance in this matter.

The word *goodness* in verse 9 is a powerful one. A Christian should be committed to principles of goodness. Anything that is not good, anything that leads to hatred or strife or discrimination should not be tolerated by the believer.

In verse 16, "redeeming the time" means putting to good use opportunities as they present themselves.

Verse 18 is a well known one. We Pentecostals see this as an important verse; we believe in abstinence from drinking. But there is more to this verse. Look at the second phrase, "but be filled with the Spirit." It is good for a Christian to be sober, but if that Christian isn't a Spirit-filled person, has he truly fulfilled the Scripture here? No.

1. Why should we speak the truth? (4:25)
2. What should we put away from us? (4:31)
3. How should we treat one another? (4:32)
4. What sins does Paul list here? (5:3–4)
5. How should we speak to one another? (5:19)
6. How do you define *goodness* in your life?

OCTOBER 14
Ephesians 5:22–6:4

Marriage—Christ and the Church; Children and Parents (5:22—6:4)

It is not stretching the truth to say that if Christianity does not work in your home, then it does not work anywhere. Paul sets up the husband-wife relationship as a means to spiritual growth and maturity. In reality, if a man and woman do not have a proper relationship to each other, then all the rest of their professions of faith do not have a great deal of sincerity.

The principle of submission in verse 22 is not a matter of a meek, mousy woman, lowering herself to the role of the family dog. Any man who would expect that from his wife is not much of a man. But someone in the family unit has to make the final decisions, and a wife is to defer to her husband in these matters.

I am not nearly as concerned about a wife's submission to her husband as I am the husband's obedience to God's command to be the kind of husband he should be. The woman will respond properly to that kind of husband almost every time.

In this section Paul takes all the dogma and puts it into practical truth and talks about husband-wife relationships. That's where Christianity really has to start. There is probably no part of our lives that is more susceptible to worldly attack than our domestic lives. A good marriage relationship is hard work—and just about impossible unless we hold to the truths of the Word of God.

Verse 4 is interesting. Paul has just emphasized obedience on the part of the children, but here he says that there is such a thing as being firm enough that the child never senses the deep feeling of love he or she requires. Tell your children every day of their lives that you love them. And show them in tangible ways. I am not talking about giving them a lot of *things*. Rather, give them love, direction, understanding, time, sympathy. That's the training that will bring them into a delightful adulthood.

1. What comparison does Paul make between the church's relationship to Christ and a wife's relationship to her husband? (5:25)
2. How should a husband treat his wife? (5:28)
3. How should children relate to their parents? (6:1–3)
4. What warning does Paul give to fathers? (6:4)
5. Do you feel your marriage is a fitting example of the church's relationship to Christ? How could your marriage be strengthened?

OCTOBER 15
Ephesians 6:5–24

Servants and Masters (6:5–9)

These five remarkably interesting verses point out a principle of Bible study that we should dwell on for a few moments.

The Word of God never called for society-wide changes. In this case, for example, Paul does not lash out at slavery, devilish though the system is. He does not believe in slavery, but he knows that change has to come from within the hearts of men and women.

One way of changing the world is to be Christlike, to allow His saving grace to be exhibited by the way we walk and talk. And that teaching obviously worked, for the whole Roman Empire collapsed while Christianity grew and flourished.

1. How should we show respect to our superiors? (6:6–7)
2. How does the Lord treat slave or free? (6:8)
3. How should masters treat slaves? (6:9)
4. What does the last phrase of verse 9 say to those of us whose goal it is to move toward unity with God?

The Whole Armor of God (6:10–24)

To think that the work of God can be done by conventional, man-conceived plans is a mistake. If we were opposing a human force, that would be one thing. But the enemy, Satan, is not human. He is a fallen angel with far more power and ability than we have. So to go against him with our limited resources is a pathetic exercise in futility. Our strength and wisdom come from the Lord; God blesses only that which comes from Himself.

The fact that the word *perseverance* (v. 18) is in Scripture is indication enough that we should not be shocked when we have trials and tribulations. Don't be misled by those who tell you the Christian walk is a mere flit from one mountaintop to another. We often go through extremely severe tests, but we can persevere through Christ who strengthens us.

1. Against what are we wrestling? (6:12)
2. What clothing symbolism does Paul use in this passage? (6:14–17)
3. What should we be doing constantly while battling the "powers" and "principalities"? (6:18)
4. When was the last time you admitted that you could not handle a situation and turned it over to God?

PHILIPPIANS

OCTOBER 16
Philippians 1:1–11

Greeting; Thankfulness and Prayer (1:1–11)

Ancient Philippi was the first city Paul visited on the continent of Europe—at least a city of any real dimension. He entered Europe by way of Neapolis (current city of Kavala) in northern Greece and made his way some eight to ten miles inland over the mountains to Philippi. The city was named after Philip of Macedon, the father of Alexander the Great. This major city was the gateway to Europe.

Many tremendous things happened in Philippi for the Lord. Just outside the city, Lydia and her entourage were saved and baptized in water. And inside the city, after Paul and Silas were beaten and imprisoned, God shook the city with an earthquake while the prisoners sang at midnight.

Much later, while imprisoned in Rome, Paul wrote this letter to the church at Philippi. It is perhaps the most personal of all his writings and does not contain a great deal of doctrine. It does show, however, that even in his imprisonment and ordeal with Rome, Paul could still keep his joy and radiance.

In the Book of Ephesians, Paul told the church over and over again that salvation was only the beginning of the spiritual maturing process. Here, he is telling the Philippians the same thing. We are in a constant state of growth, and that which God has begun in us He will complete. He hasn't brought us this far to let us down. There are two key words in that sixth verse—*begun* and *complete*. And even with that great commendation, Paul says there is still distance to be gained in their spiritual journey (vv. 9–10).

1. For what did Paul ask in every prayer? (1:4–5)
2. What did Paul wish for the Philippians' love? (1:9)
3. What can you do to ensure that your very memory prompts gratitude to God?

Christ Is Preached; To Live Is Christ (1:12–30)

Now Paul shows what spiritual maturity really is. No sorrow for himself, no grumbling, no self-pity. Paul was willing to take any burden, pay any price, go any number of miles, if in so doing Christ could be preached. Paul never asked, "What's in this for me?"

Note the sharp condemnation of the self-seekers in verse 16: "[They] preach Christ from selfish ambition, not sincerely."

Verse 21 is one of the most priceless treasures in sacred truth, and it is posted over the stocks in the remains of the prison at Philippi.

There is nothing left of Philippi. The ruins of the prison stand on the hillside overlooking the *agora* or marketplace. The main prison was destroyed in the savage earthquake that occurred at midnight as Paul and Silas were singing. The inner prison or dungeon area still remains. You can see where the stocks were secured to the stone walls, where the blood and gore dripped from prisoners' backs into a trough through which spring water ran, emptying into a cistern beneath the prison. The sign has been posted just over the stocks.

Paul tells them in verse 28 not to be consumed by fear because of persecution. Paul realized that persecution might come, and he addresses that possibility in verse 28. You see, the believer is truly expendable. If you don't feel that way, then you can never achieve the quality of service that Christ taught. After all, He considered Himself a servant. Are we greater than the Master? No, never!

1. How did Paul view the things that had happened to him? (1:12)
2. What effect did Paul's imprisonment have on the brethren? (1:14)
3. What are two motivations for preaching Christ? (1:15–17)
4. What was Paul's struggle between life and death? (1:21–25)
5. Name some ways in which you carry out the servant attitude in your life.

OCTOBER 18
Philippians 2:1–30

Unity Through Humility; the Humbled and Exalted Christ (2:1–11)

There were not a lot of distracting dangers confronting the church at Philippi; however, there was one potentially crippling difficulty that Paul dealt with in this second chapter—disunity (or disharmony) among members of the church.

If Christ is worth knowing and loving and serving, then the believers must live together in love and unity. In verses 3 and 4 Paul listed those things that can cause disunity.

In verses 5–11 Paul admonishes us to have the mind of Christ, the thinking of Christ, who considered Himself a servant.

1. What would bring Paul joy? (2:2)
2. What should our motivation for action be? (2:3–4)
3. Describe Christ-mindedness. (2:5–8)
4. Think of some ways others may have seen you as serving God. Was your service for God's benefit or for your own?

Light Bearers; Timothy and Epaphroditus Praised (2:12–30)

The subject of the believer's attitude is paramount in this segment. Our whole lifestyle really changes around if our attitude is what it ought to be. Christ is the One who should receive all the glory and honor. If our lives honor Him, then are they not successful?

Timothy was Paul's faithful helper, his virtual son in the faith. How Paul must have loved him! Paul could not come to Philippi at this time, since he was a prisoner in Rome, so he was sending Timothy. He wanted to be sure that Timothy would be well received in Philippi.

Here we learn more of another trusted worker with Paul—Epaphroditus. Paul told the Philippians he would have sent Epaphroditus to them earlier but he had been ill, so they had to hold back on their plans. Here is one of Paul's right-hand men who is ill, right in the work of the Lord. Our bodies betray us even when we work for God. We should not feel guilty if we happen to be ill.

1. How should we do all things? (2:14)
2. How does Paul describe Timothy? (2:20)
3. Why did Paul ask the Philippians to receive Epaphroditus with extra gladness? (2:29–30)
4. What is your attitude when asked to do something?

OCTOBER 19
Philippians 3:1–4:1

All for Christ (3:1–11)

Verse 2 is interesting. In it Paul is obviously telling the Philippians that he is about to cover ground he has covered before.

Dogs may refer to the Jewish term for heathen; *evil workers* refers to the ceaseless activity of such people in trying to make believers conform. *Mutilation* is a pun on the Greek word for circumcision.

In the latter part of this section, Paul's mind is on two things—his present fellowship with God and his future life in the kingdom. Note verse 10. To *know* implies much more than an intellectual knowledge. It implies a willingness to carry out God's work and a love of God that springs from the heart.

1. How does Paul characterize Christians in reference to circumcision? (3:3)
2. How does Paul now view the things that seemed important to him before he came to know Christ? (3:7–8)
3. What things have taken on either more or less meaning since you have come to know Christ?

Pressing Toward the Goal; Our Citizenship in Heaven (3:12–4:1)

Every believer should memorize verses 12–14 and say them aloud every day. We should key in on a couple of phrases:

"I press on." I haven't got it made yet. Yes, I am saved; I know that I am saved. But there is still much, much ground to cover. I may get knocked over, stepped on, passed by, but I will get back up and press on. I will not be sidetracked.

"One thing I do." Many unfortunates have been left by the wayside because they did not keep their primary and singular commitment of pressing on toward Jesus Christ.

"Forgetting those things which are behind." Past mistakes and failures should not blot your future. Every person in the world has made serious blunders, unreasonable mistakes. And Satan reminds you of them often, as perhaps do those around you. But so what? Forget your past and be motivated by Christ the King.

1. What kind of Christian is like-minded with Paul's statement in verses 12–14? (3:15)
2. What does Paul say that lets us know that there is room for growth in Christian life? (3:16)
3. What things get in the way of your keeping a primary and singular commitment to Jesus?

OCTOBER 20
Philippians 4:2–23

Be United, Joyful, and Prayerful; Meditate on These Things (4:2–9)

This chapter is packed with drama and mystery. We are introduced to two women of Philippi who apparently were not getting along. We don't know what the issue was, but Paul's concern was that they be of the same mind.

Now it is altogether possible that the "true companion" of verse 3 is a proper name, which would have been "Sunzugos." It is also possible that it is a common noun, as the King James suggests. If so, who is the companion? Some writers say it was Paul's wife, some say it was the husband of either Euodia or Syntyche, and others say it was the pastor of the church at Philippi.

The thought life of the believer is something to take into careful consideration. Proverbs 23:7 reads: "For as he thinks...so is he." You are the sum total of what you think.

1. What two women are introduced briefly in this chapter? (4:2)
2. What should a Christian's attitude be? (4:4)
3. How should we deal with anxiety? (4:6–7)
4. Think of something you are anxious about in your life. How can you apply verses 6–7?

Philippian Generosity; Greeting and Blessing (4:10–23)

Learning contentment must be one of the cardinal virtues of our faith. We live in a society of ever-increasing want. Television commercials, I'm sure, add to our distress in this area.

Paul never got involved with this ever-increasing want. No anxiety. Note verse 18. The man is a prisoner; still he can have inner peace and contentment.

Note verse 22. Even in Nero's palace of insanity, even in his government of iniquity, there were men and women who were living for Jesus Christ. This verse demonstrates that circumstances are not of great importance. The hope of glory is Christ in you. A man or woman can serve God anywhere, anytime, and under any circumstances.

1. Where did Paul derive his strength? (4:13)
2. Why was Paul glad that the Philippians had sent him aid? (4:17)
3. Note what Paul says in verse 14. How can we apply this verse to opportunities to help others?

COLOSSIANS

OCTOBER 21
Colossians 1:1–18

Their Faith in Christ; Preeminence of Christ (1:1–18)

Colossae was a city on the river Lycus, about one hundred miles from Ephesus (in present-day Turkey). Paul did not found this church (in fact, we have no record of his ever having been in the city). The church was begun during those three years when Paul ministered in Ephesus. Epaphras may have been the pioneer who began the work in Colossae. Most of the converts there were Gentiles.

In this letter, Paul deals with a heresy that had sprung up in Colossae which attacked the total adequacy of Jesus Christ. It emphasized astrology and the power of demons, it insisted on observing special days and rituals, and it laid down strict laws about food and drink. Apparently followers even worshiped angels. This heresy was a mystery cult based upon a knowledge revealed only to a selected few. It is commonly known as Gnosticism.

Paul doesn't begin by condemning the Christians at Colossae. His approach is positive.

We can learn a lesson from Paul here. As bad as a given situation may be, it is always well to count our blessings first before tearing into the problem. A healthy mental attitude is the key to change.

In verses 9–18 Paul talks about his prayers for the church. He was able to pray healthy prayers because his attitude toward the church was healthy. He was not the avenger. He was a man whose burdened heart was expressed in fervent prayer.

1. From what has God delivered us? (1:13)
2. Of what is Christ the image? (1:15)
3. How does Paul describe creation? (1:16)
4. On the basis of verse 16, what should be the level of our awareness of and activity in ecological concerns?

OCTOBER 22

Colossians 1:19–29

Reconciled in Christ; Sacrificial Service for Christ (1:19–29)

Now Paul deals with the great gap that has been spanned by the love which Christ manifested on Calvary.

The Gnostics didn't believe that God had created the world, but that God's enemy, Satan, had played a major role in bringing all things into existence. So the Gnostic truly believed that creation was from evil material. Further, they taught that while Jesus might be good, He was only one of many good emanations from God. Paul said that was not true, that Jesus was the fullness of the Godhead in bodily form. Gnosticism isn't of major consequence in our generation, but the theme of Colossians is paramount—the preeminence of Christ.

Paul says that Christ is for every man, regardless of background or race. I must quote a paragraph from Barclay's commentary on Colossians, which summed it up so beautifully: "The fact is that the only thing in this world which is for every man is Christ. It is not every man who can be a thinker. There are gifts which are not granted to every man. Not every man can master every craft, or even every game. There are those who are colorblind and to whom the loveliness of art means nothing. There are those who are tone deaf and for whom the glory of music does not exist. Not every man can be a writer or a student or a preacher or a singer. Even human love at its highest is not granted to all men. There are gifts a man will never possess; there are privileges a man will never enjoy; there are heights of this world's attainment which a man can never scale; but to every man there is open the good news of the gospel, the love of God in Christ Jesus and the transforming power which can bring holiness into life" (*Colossians*, p. 127).

We do people a disservice when we treat them as if they are all alike and should react to everything in the same manner. We are not all alike—we have individual preferences; we have different abilities. All of this is truly manifested in the church, but the common denominator is Jesus Christ!

1. How does Christ's reconciliatory act enable us to appear before God? (1:21–22)
2. What is the qualifier to the above verse? (1:23)
3. What is the mystery of which Paul speaks? (1:27)
4. To what end did Paul work? (1:28–29)
5. What ministries in our congregations affirm our uniqueness?

OCTOBER 23
Colossians 2:1–23

Not Philosophy but Christ (2:1–10)

Verse 1 gives us great insight into the heart of Paul. Paul had never seen or met these people in his life, yet he felt a tremendous concern for them. Mission begins here. It is the burden of those you will never meet that causes you to give of your substance to missions at home and abroad.

Paul gives the Colossians a brief outline concerning what a great church should be.

1. *The church should be courageous*—courageous leadership and courageous membership. The battle does not go to the faint-hearted.
2. *The church should be loving.*
3. *The church should be spiritually wise*—wise in the Word and in the constant unfolding of truth by the Holy Spirit.
4. *The church should be of sound doctrine and resistant to heresy.*
5. *The church should be disciplined.*

1. What did Paul wish for the Colossians? (2:2)
2. What assurance does Paul give the Colossians? (2:5)
3. What is Paul's warning to the Colossians? (2:8)
4. How does your church measure up to the five qualifications Paul outlines?

Not Legalism but Christ (2:11–23)

The Gnostic heretics propounded a strange gospel.

1. They wanted to make it very difficult by adding to the simple gospel very elaborate systems of pseudophilosophical thought.

2. The Gnostics introduced astrology to the church. Astrology is a heresy because it undermines Christ as our Leader, our Master. No other force can control our destiny.

3. The Gnostics wanted to add circumcision to their heresy. Once again Paul faces the works-salvation theology.

In verse 23 Paul summed up his opinion of the Gnostic philosophy: "These things . . . are of no value against the indulgence of the flesh."

1. What kind of circumcision did the Colossians receive? (2:11)
2. What does Paul say about the trappings of the heresy? (2:23)
3. Name some ways we make the gospel difficult today.

OCTOBER 24
Colossians 3:1–25

Not Carnality but Christ (3:1–11)

This third chapter deals with carnality—the preoccupation with anything characteristic of the world system. It is amazing how many things fall under this broad category of carnality. Hebrews tells us that everything that can be shaken will one day be shaken, so that those things that cannot be shaken will remain. Anything that can be shaken, torn apart, and left on this doomed planet is carnal.

Our instructions from the Lord as Paul interprets them in verse 2 are very clear: "Set your mind on things above, not on things on the earth." The standard by which all things must be judged is whether they are worth Christ's dying for.

The word *members* in verse 5 refers to parts of the body.

Paul emphasizes that we are new creatures in Christ Jesus and there is to be a manifested change in our character. He reiterates the theme that God does not recognize the distinctions in people that we make.

1. What did Paul admonish the Colossians to "put to death"? (3:5, 8)
2. What is the new person like? (3:10)
3. Look at the lists in verses 5 and 8. Which of those things are a part of your life? Which things have you managed to gain ground in conquering?

Character of the New Man; the Christian Home (3:12–25)

In this section Paul switches from the negative to the positive and tells us some of those things that should characterize our lives.

Paul also touches on the gospel as it relates to the home, saying that, if your Christian faith doesn't work in your home, then it doesn't work anywhere.

In verse 23, Paul lays down an eternal principle of Christian service.

Why do we look to people to reward us for our Christian work? Do we do our work for the human recognition? Paul suggests another motivation.

1. What is the character of the new person? (3:12–13)
2. Above all things, what should the new person demonstrate? (3:14)
3. What advice does Paul give to wives? (3:18) husbands? (3:19) children? (3:20) fathers? (3:21)
4. How does your home reflect the Christianity you profess?

Christian Graces; Final Greetings (4:1—18)

Paul continually emphasizes prayer.

The Bible tells us to pray without ceasing. Prayer is an attitude as well as an action. It is a constant communion with God. Aside from that time on your knees at the church altar or in a private place of prayer, it is also that attitude of communion that exists between you and God as you work, as you go about your many duties during the day. It is a beautiful relationship that exists between the Creator and the creation.

Paul tells us how to pray. What ingrates some of us are! The average American lives far better than the wealthy in some other lands. We have more comfort, more conveniences, more luxuries than most of the world has ever dreamed of. Yet many of us want more, more, more—we have not learned to be thankful for what we have.

Note Paul's request in verses 3 and 4. He did not ask that the Colossians pray for the obvious—his release.

Verse 6 tells us that a Christian doesn't need to be dull. The Christian should know a lot of heartfelt laughter; the Christian should be an exciting person.

Verses 7–15 give us a minigallery of who was who in Paul's life.

Tychicus was an important man in Paul's ministry. He was the one who hand-carried the letter to the Ephesian church. He was also chosen as a representative of his church in Rome to carry the offering to the saints in Jerusalem, so he must have been a trusted saint.

Onesimus was a runaway slave who had reached Rome. There he was touched by Paul and the gospel. Paul was sending him back to Colossae to his master. Notice what Paul calls this slave.

Aristarchus, a Macedonian, was in the arena at Ephesus during the riot and he was present when Paul set sail for Rome.

Mark had evidently made a remarkable comeback. Remember how he had left the missionary team of Paul and Barnabas after they evangelized Cyprus?

Epaphras was probably the pastor of the Colossian church.

Luke never left Paul's side. "Only Luke is with me" (2 Tim. 4:11), wrote the apostle from his death cell in Rome. What a man Luke was!

1. How does Paul say we should pray? (4:2)
2. For what does Paul say to pray? (4:3–4)
3. How should we treat nonbelievers? (4:5)
4. Pay more attention to your prayers. How full of thanksgiving are they?

1 THESSALONIANS

OCTOBER 26
1 Thessalonians 1:1–2:12

Their Good Example (1:1–10)

Thessalonica is the current Greek city of Saloniki. Probably no other ancient city, outside of Rome, has kept its original character and importance as much as this city. Thessalonica was founded in 315 B.C. by the Macedonian king, Cassander, and was named after his wife, the sister of Alexander the Great. Because the Thessalonians sided with Antony and Octavian (the winning side) in the second Roman civil war, it was given the status of a free city. This meant the people there could pick their own local leadership.

The founding of the church at Thessalonica, recorded in Acts 17, took place during Paul's second missionary journey. After he and Silas were beaten and imprisoned at Philippi, they continued along the Egnatian Road (which extended from Istanbul to Rome) into Thessalonica. As a result of Paul's ministry there, a potpourri of Christians came into being.

1. What three virtues does Paul mention? (1:3)
2. How did the gospel come to the Thessalonians? (1:5)
3. How can you incorporate into your life the virtues Paul lists?

Paul's Ministry (2:1–12)

These twelve verses are truly a guide for pastors today, for they describe the way ministers of local churches should conduct themselves. Apparently, there had been some unrest in the church because Paul had not returned to Thessalonica. Some of the less spiritual began attacking Paul's ministry. Paul never retaliated; he simply reminded the people of the standards by which he ministered to them there.

1. How did Paul describe his preaching of the gospel? (2:2)
2. Paul preached to please whom? (2:4)
3. What was the purpose of Paul's preaching? (2:12)
4. Verses 5 and 6 can be addressed to all Christians, not just pastors. Try to apply them to your daily life. How well do you meet those standards?

305

The Thessalonians' Conversion; Longing to See Them (2:13—3:5)

Paul's preaching the gospel to Thessalonica, where many people believed, brought not only the joy of salvation but also trouble and difficulty. Only an immature Christian thinks that the church will never encounter any trouble in this world. Nothing could be further from the truth. The Thessalonians went through severe tribulation because of their faith.

One of the reasons Paul wrote this letter was because some of the Thessalonians had been hurt when Paul did not return to them. In 2:17–3:5 he tells them why he could not return and instead sent Timothy to them. We are not told what Satan did to keep Paul from returning to Thessalonica, but it must have been something pretty stunning to keep a man of Paul's character and resolution away.

True Christianity is directly opposed to the world system. Our God has sworn to destroy the whole system and replace it, yet we are surprised when the enemies of the faith strike and wound us. We are so success oriented that we cannot handle setbacks. That the church today is far more comfortable with motivators than with prophets is a tragic indictment.

1. Why did Paul fail to come to Thessalonica? (2:18)
2. What does Paul call the Thessalonians? (2:20)
3. Whom did Paul send to the Thessalonians? (3:2)
4. Name some ways the church is persecuted openly today. What are some more subtle forms of persecution we might face?

Encouraged by Timothy; Prayer for the Church (3:6—13)

In both 1 and 2 Corinthians Paul wrote about our accountability to God, and he does so again here. He could take the physical attacks, the beatings, the imprisonments, the stonings, the shipwrecks. The one thing that mattered was that he would stand before God one day. For Paul it wasn't a matter of finding out whether he was saved or not; he knew he was saved. "For I know whom I have believed and am persuaded..." (2 Tim. 1:12). It was a matter of being found worthy of honor in the ultimate kingdom of God.

1. What brought Paul comfort? (3:6–7)
2. What was Paul's prayer for the Thessalonians? (3:12–13)
3. How do you incorporate the idea of accountability to God into your everyday life?

Plea for Purity: a Brotherly and Orderly Life (4:1—12)

The first three chapters of 1 Thessalonians contain Paul's *personal* message to the church. Now we come into the *practical* section of the book.

Verse 6 has caused interpreters trouble. Some feel that in this verse Paul changes subjects—from sexual conduct to conduct in business. The evidence for the view that Paul is still addressing sexual conduct is very strong, particularly in light of the fact that Thessalonica was a center for cults that contained strong phallic symbolism.

In verses 9–12, Paul encourages the believers to have proper relationships with each other and to maintain a good reputation by working hard. One of the greatest virtues of the Christian ethic is that of work. We are to be industrious about God's business and in taking proper care of our families.

In verse 11 Paul adds three characteristics of the Christian's life.

1. What does Paul teach about sexual immorality? (4:3–6)
2. When we are sexually immoral, whom are we really offending? (4:8)
3. What are three characteristics of the Christian life? (4:11)
4. Apply the above three characteristics to the way you live your life.

The Comfort of Christ's Coming (4:13–18)

Remember that the Rapture and the Second Coming are two separate events. At the Rapture, we believers will meet our Lord in the air. Christ does not return to the earth at the Rapture—we go to meet Him. But at the Second Coming, the event that ends the Battle of Armageddon and starts the Millennium, Christ does indeed return to the earth.

The next major event in the prophetic calendar is the Rapture of the church. It will happen in an instant, the twinkling of an eye. It will come at an unexpected time. And it will set the stage for Antichrist.

1. What will happen to those who have already died? (4:14)
2. How will Jesus descend from heaven? (4:16)
3. What should the Thessalonians do with words concerning the Rapture? (4:18)
4. How should belief in the Rapture affect our daily lives?

OCTOBER 29

1 Thessalonians 5:1–28

The Day of the Lord (5:1–11)

Paul continues his teachings here on the return of Christ. Apparently the Thessalonians made two basic errors concerning the Rapture—two errors that are probably common today. The first belief was that day-to-day living could be neglected since Christ's return was imminent. The second error was that such an expectation allowed total neglect—a blasé attitude. Paul teaches that we are to expect that Christ will come at any time, yet continue to live as if He will delay.

1. How will the day of the Lord come? (5:2)
2. To what does Paul describe the suddenness of the coming of the day of the Lord? (5:3)
3. What are Christians as compared to non-Christians? (5:5)
4. In what way does your worshiping community demonstrate its belief that the day of the Lord could come at any time?

Various Exhortations; Blessing and Admonition (5:12–28)

We are to esteem our pastors and those who labor with us in the Lord (see vv. 12–13). We are to support and encourage them—not hinder them or shoot at them with words.

"Warn those who are unruly" (v. 14). There should be discipline in our churches, for conduct both in and out of the church.

"See that no one renders evil for evil to anyone, but always pursue what is good" (v. 15). Vengeance belongs to the Lord.

"Rejoice always" (v. 16). Count your blessings. Be a positive person, not a negative one. See the good, not the bad.

"Pray without ceasing" (v. 17). Prayer is an attitude as well as an action. We are to be in a constant state of prayer, communicating with God.

The exhortation in verse 21 reflects a recurring theme in Paul's Epistles: that the believers not allow themselves to be misled.

The "holy kiss" in verse 26 is mentioned in three other letters of Paul (see 1 Cor. 16:20; 2 Cor. 13:12; Rom. 16:16). In the early church, the kiss became a symbol of Christian fellowship.

1. How should believers act among themselves? (5:13)
2. What does Paul say about returning evil for evil? (5:15)
3. As we have done with previous lists of Paul, compare his exhortations in verses 12–22 with your own life. Where are you strong? Where are you lacking?

2 THESSALONIANS

OCTOBER 30
2 Thessalonians 1:1–2:12

God's Judgment and Glory (1:1–12)

Only a few months have elapsed since Paul dispatched his first letter to the Thessalonians. Apparently many of the people there had not taken Paul's letter to heart.

Paul commonly began his letters—right after his greeting—with an extended thanksgiving. He listed the great attributes of those to whom he wrote. Yes, there are severe problems he must address in this letter; but he understands that these people are going through bitter persecution and don't need his vitriolic dressing down.

Verses 9–10 hint at something we often have trouble accepting—that God's wheels of justice grind more slowly than ours—but that they grind surely and exactingly.

1. Of what did Paul boast among the churches? (1:4)
2. What will happen to those who persecute the Christians? (1:6)
3. When have you sought revenge, rather than leaving it to God?

The Great Apostasy (2:1–12)

Now we come to a fascinating segment of Scripture which deals with Christ's return and the coming of the Antichrist.

The "man of sin," or "man of lawlessness" in some translations, appears for the first time here. Some scholars think Paul saw the Roman Empire and its emperor as the man of lawlessness. Others feel some teacher of Judaism was this personage. Probably two figures served as models for Paul's "man of sin"—the Syrian Antiochus Epiphanes, of whom Daniel wrote, and the Roman emperor Caligula, who about A.D. 40 had tried to set his statue up in the Jerusalem temple as an object of worship.

1. What must happen before Christ comes again? (2:3)
2. What will happen to the lawless one? (2:8)
3. What will happen to those who follow the lawless one? (2:12)
4. What are some ways we can guard against being "taken in" by the Antichrist?

OCTOBER 31

Stand Fast; Pray for Us (2:13—3:5)

In the preceding passage, Paul spent time talking about the man of sin and those multitudes who would be deluded enough to follow him. Now he turns his attention to giving thanks for the Thessalonian converts who have received salvation through faith in Jesus Christ. What a contrast!

Sanctification refers to our being set apart to follow God. We are all given tasks to perform. *Sanctification* simply means "given to God, set apart for God's purposes, dedicated to God's will." Following salvation we are sanctified to work for God's kingdom. And there is never an excuse for not doing the work to which we are called.

1. What two things did Paul ask the Thessalonians to do? (2:15)
2. For what two things did Paul ask the Thessalonians to pray? (3:1–2)
3. What did Paul wish for the hearts of the Thessalonians? (3:5)
4. What place do religious traditions play in your life?

Warning Against Idleness; Benediction (3:6—18)

Paul now returns to a call for continued discipline, this time among the Thessalonian believers. Paul is not asking the believers to be snobs, but to be very careful about their close affiliations. Negativism is highly contagious; therefore, Christians should associate with those who will elevate their faith.

Paul sets a good example for us. He was actively engaged in ministry far to the south in Corinth; yet he had a real burden for the work in Thessalonica. Even if we are involved in that which God has called us to do, let's not forget our brothers and sisters in Christ who labor in other fields at home and abroad; remember them in our prayers and, when possible, provide help.

1. What was Paul's command to the Thessalonians? (3:6)
2. Why did Paul minister as he did? (3:9)
3. How should the Thessalonians treat those who do not heed Paul's words? (3:14–15)
4. How do you balance the work ethic of which Paul speaks with the Christian ideal of building strong relationships in your family?

1 TIMOTHY

NOVEMBER 1
1 Timothy 1:1–2:7

No Other Doctrine; Glory to God for His Grace (1:1–17)

We come now to the letters of Paul to Timothy and Titus. There is an immediately obvious difference in these letters from the former ones we have studied: The others were written to churches, while these are written to individuals. These letters, therefore, are highly personal, yet they carry messages that are relevant for you and me today.

In the days of the young pastors, Timothy and Titus, the church was besieged with what Barclay called "speculative intellectualism." That simply means some of the people would rather have talked about the ins and outs of various worthless theologies.

Another problem that had cropped up again was that age-old one of legalism. Some church members taught only for monetary gain. So Paul wrote these young pastors to help them.

Paul exhorted Timothy as a pastor to teach sound doctrine, and reminded Timothy throughout these writings that his beliefs and his manner of teaching were vital!

1. To what should Timothy not give heed? (1:4)
2. What is the purpose of the commandment? (1:5)
3. Why, according to Paul, was he able to obtain grace? (1:13)
4. How well can you express your faith in a consistent way?

Fight the Good Fight; Pray for All Men (1:18—2:7)

Paul encouraged Timothy to keep on going, to continue his ministry despite all obstacles.

In verse 20 Paul briefly mentions two men who evidently gave the apostle a great deal of trouble. We do not know what the problem was.

Verses 1–7 show clearly that all men can be reached with the gospel. We are to pray for all persons.

1. What two men had given Paul trouble? (1:20)
2. What is God's desire? (2:4)
3. What does Paul call Jesus Christ? (2:5)
4. Think of some people you have written off as unable to be saved. Should you reconsider?

Men and Women in the Church (2:8–15)

This is a rather controversial segment of Pauline Scripture—the roles of men and women in the church. It is believed by some, I am afraid, that Paul was rather chauvinistic in his approach. The truth of the matter is that Paul was probably one of the more liberated males of his day. A woman's place in his time was very low. She was treated not as a person but as a thing.

The Greek customs were just as difficult. Most women in Greek temples were prostitutes, as in the great Temple to Diana in Ephesus. A married Grecian woman lived in her own quarters, which were off limits to any person but her own husband. So Paul was facing a strictly local cultural problem here. If you take his teaching as more than that, you are doing violence to the gospel, for Paul's overall view of the matter is recorded in Galatians 3:28: "There is neither Jew nor Greek, there is neither slave nor free, there is neither male nor female; for you are all one in Christ Jesus."

1. How should a woman adorn herself? (2:9–10)
2. What is the woman's role in learning and teaching? (2:11–12)
3. How can we deal with Paul's teaching about women in light of women's active role in the church today?

Qualifications of Overseers, of Deacons (3:1–13)

Paul lists qualifications for church leadership, and he starts right at the top—the bishop or overseer. Some would call him a superintendent. The qualifications are stringent and not all can fill them.

1. What are the qualifications of a bishop? (3:1–7) of deacons? (3:8–10) their wives? (3:11)
2. Do your church's ministry and laity reflect these qualifications?

The Great Mystery; the Great Apostasy (3:14–4:5)

Paul tells Timothy, in verses 15–16, how to conduct himself in the house of God.

In verses 1–5 Paul once again lets us know that the early Christians looked for the reckoning to come soon.

1. What is the mystery of godliness? (3:16)
2. What does Paul say about all of God's creation? (4:4)
3. In light of verses 4–5, how should we view ourselves?

NOVEMBER 3
1 Timothy 4:6—5:16

A Good Servant of Jesus Christ (4:6–16)

In verses 6–10, Paul tells us how important it is to teach others the faith.

In verses 11–16 Paul writes about how a minister should behave. The Christian minister, like the Jewish rabbi, would have had more than an ordinary education. He would have been constantly engaged in reading both the Old Testament Scriptures and the new Scripture writings. As preacher, he would also have been involved in interpreting what he had read.

1. What should the minister reject? (4:7)
2. What comparison does Paul make between bodily exercise and spiritual exercise? (4:8)
3. To what should Timothy give attention? (4:13)
4. What does Paul's emphasis on teaching say to the difficulty we have enlisting church school teachers today?

Treatment of Church Members (5:1–16)

In verses 1–2, Paul deals with the generation gap in the church. Yes, it was a problem even then! Paul emphasizes that church members should be like a family to one another.

In verses 6–16, "widows" refer to those who have no children, grandchildren, or relatives to care for them. The woman who is left thus can devote all her time to furthering God's work and, therefore, has a right to ask for protection and support from the church.

Verse 8 is very strong in its language about those who do not care for their elders.

Verse 9 indicates that there was an official order of widows in the church. The qualifications for entering such an order were stringent enough to keep the numbers small. The passage seems to indicate that there were problems with widows leaving the order. Perhaps those under sixty had previously been admitted and had then remarried, forgetting their vow to remain single.

1. Why should children or grandchildren care for widows? (5:4)
2. What does Paul say about believers who do not care for their elders? (5:8)
3. What qualifications did a widow have to possess to be taken into the order? (5:9–10)
4. In what ways does our society follow or go against these teachings of Paul?

313

Honor the Elders and the Masters (5:17—6:21)

Paul deals with the work ethic throughout 1 and 2 Thessalonians and also here in 1 Timothy. A person is to work to sustain life, and the rule is, the harder he works, the more he should receive.

Paul also deals with church discipline in this section. Those who persist in causing unrest in a church or in living selfish, sinful lives must be dealt with by a disciplinary board.

Verse 22 may be telling us not to take newborn Christians and put them in places of responsibility right away. Let them get some teaching. Let them sink some roots. Let them prove themselves. Look at the biblical examples. Paul stayed in Arabia an undetermined length of time before God used him. God prepared Moses for forty years, and Jesus Himself didn't begin ministry until He was thirty.

In verses 1–2 we again encounter the issue of slavery. Because it was such a common element of life at that time, the New Testament never really questions the institution itself. Instead it calls for fairness and brotherhood within the institution.

In verses 4–5 Paul has some sharp words for the grandstanders in the church—for those proud persons for whom godliness becomes a means, or at least an aid, in becoming wealthy. Christianity is a means of making great gain—other than financially. It is in contentment that the gain lies. Paul says that wealth is not essential to our well-being.

1. What are the elders worthy of? (5:17)
2. How can an accusation against an elder be heard? (5:19)
3. For what purpose did Paul allow the use of wine? (5:23)
4. What things should make us content? (6:8)
5. What does Paul call the love of money? (6:10)
6. What should those who are already rich be taught? (6:17–19)
7. Where do you find your contentment?

2 TIMOTHY

NOVEMBER 5
2 Timothy 1:1—2:13

Timothy's Faith and Heritage; Not Ashamed of the Gospel (1:1–12)

Because Timothy had everything going for him, he had a great spiritual fight throughout his life. The greater your ability, the greater your call and your spiritual fight. Paul could sense the battle going on continuously in this young man's heart. Listen to the pathos in his heart as you read verses 3 and 4.

There was no way Paul could see Timothy again. In a few short hours, the executioner's axe would sever Paul's head from his shoulders. But he could at least write one more letter to Timothy, expressing his belief in him and his anticipation of the great spiritual victories the young man would gain.

1. Who were Timothy's mother and grandmother? (1:5)
2. How did Timothy receive the gift of God? (1:6)
3. Why is Paul not ashamed of the gospel? (1:12)
4. Name some signs that our culture is "ashamed" of the gospel.

Be Loyal to the Faith and Strong in Grace (1:13—2:13)

Paul encourages Timothy to hold fast to the gospel he knew Paul preached. Verse 14 is a challenge to every preacher.

Notice the verb in verse 3: *endure!* Some people today don't believe in that doctrine, but it is still a biblical one. We as Christians are not going to be delivered from everything on earth. We will face suffering of one kind or another. Even in his chains, even in his imprisonment, even in his trials and tribulations, Paul knew that the inconveniences of the moment were not worthy to be compared to the glory that awaited him.

1. What two men turned away from Paul and his teachings? (1:15)
2. Who sought out Paul when the apostle first came to Rome? (1:16–17)
3. What does Paul want Timothy to do with the things he has learned from Paul? (2:2)
4. Relate Paul's teaching about endurance to your view of why bad things happen to people.

NOVEMBER 6
2:14–3:17

Approved and Disapproved Workers (2:14–26)

Historically, one of the ways the church has been weakened is in the dilution of preaching. The most important part of any church service is the preaching, for it is still the "foolishness" of preaching that changes the heart.

I am intrigued by Paul's pleading in verses 23 and 24. Paul advises the preacher to stick to the pure gospel. Not only is he trying to avoid distortions of the gospel from secular sources, but he is also talking about distortions that come from within.

1. What should workers shun? (2:16)
2. Who are two men whose message has strayed from the truth? (2:17)
3. How does Paul describe the hypocrite? (2:20)
4. Around what is the service in your worshiping community built?

Perilous Times and Perilous Men; the Man of God and the Word of God (3:1–17)

In these verses Paul gives us a sure sign of the end times, especially in verse 5. We see again the expectation on the part of the early church that the "last days" were near. The description of vices in verses 2–5 could apply to any time of extreme change in history. Verse 5 departs from traditional vices in including a reproof against heretics. The heresy to which Paul refers may be one which denied the Resurrection.

Jannes and Jambres (see v. 8) are not identified in the Scriptures or by early historians, but early church literature names them as two of Pharaoh's magicians who tried to outdo Moses with their magic.

In verses 10–17 Paul makes a plea for the sanctity of the Word of God—for its preeminence in the church and for the individual Christian. Paul tells us why Timothy is qualified to preach the faith. The Greek expression for *Scripture*, which is often translated "sacred writings," is not found elsewhere in the New Testament, but it is found in Jewish writings. These sacred writings are believed to be the Old Testament writings.

1. What are the characteristics of people as the end time approaches? (3:2–4)
2. Why is Timothy qualified to preach? (3:10, 14–15)
3. From where does Scripture come and what is its use? (3:16)
4. How do you make use of the Scriptures in your daily life?

Preach the Word; Paul's Valedictory (4:1–8)

Writing shortly before his execution, Paul was pulling every stop in this Epistle, exhorting his son in the faith, Timothy, to new heights and dimensions of service. Look at the way Paul begins this fourth chapter.

Verses 2–3 tell the preacher how to preach and warn that the churches will not always accept the truth. That is certainly true of today's churches and is probably why there is very little real preaching.

Paul's words reach their loftiest heights in the valedictory message in verses 6–8. He is steps away from death, but it means nothing to him. He is ready. The crown was a symbol in the Greco-Roman world of the winner of an athletic contest.

1. How does Paul say to preach the gospel? (4:2)
2. What should the minister do when people turn from him because of his preaching? (4:5)
3. How does Paul describe his ministry? (4:7)
4. Paul urges preachers to be outspoken in preaching the gospel. What does that say to us as listeners?

The Abandoned Apostle; the Lord is Faithful (4:9–22)

Paul abruptly switches the tone of his writing here as he begins to talk about personal relationships. He mentions three people who forsook him or treated him wrongly. He also gives instructions regarding people who have remained faithful in their ministry.

Historians generally agree that Paul stood trial once in Rome, was acquitted (vv. 16–17), and spent several years in a Gentile mission before he was rearrested and condemned to death.

Paul urges Timothy to come quickly (v. 21), either because he is lonely or because he needs the supplies desperately. Ships did not sail for Rome during the winter.

1. Who forsook Paul? (4:10) Who did him harm? (4:14)
2. What did Paul ask Timothy to bring? (4:13)
3. Are you more like Demas or Mark? Do you love this present world? Are you a useful minister?

TITUS

The Elder's Qualifications and Task (1:1–16)

We don't know a great deal about Titus, but what we do know assures us that he was an unusually fine man and a trusted coworker of the apostle Paul. He was apparently converted through Paul's ministry. He quickly learned the ways of the Lord, and Paul trusted him to assist him in the ministry.

Look at verse 5. In that verse Paul tells Titus why he left him in Crete. What a challenge to Titus and to us!

The purpose of the body of elders in each local church was to enable the churches to resist inroads being made by unorthodox teachers. That is, the elder is to be a keeper and perpetrator of the teachings of the Word of God, an example to the rest of the flock.

"Jewish myths" refers to Gnostic speculations based on Old Testament writings.

1. Why did Paul leave Titus in Crete? (1:5)
2. What are the qualifications of an elder? (1:6–9)
3. Which people sought particularly to subordinate Christian teachings? (1:10)
4. How much attention is given to whether the officials of your body are well-versed in Christian teaching?

The Qualifications of a Sound Church (2:1–10)

According to this letter to Titus, the qualifications of a sound church involve a knowledge of sound doctrine, strong interpersonal relationships, and "sound speech." In the Epistles to Timothy and Titus, sound speech refers to preaching that stays within the norm of Christian teaching.

1. Describe the proper behavior of older men in the church. (2:2)
2. Describe the proper behavior of older women. (2:3–4)
3. How should younger women behave? (2:4–5) younger men? (2:6)
4. How should church members who are servants behave toward their masters? (2:9–10)
5. Measure your church by the three qualities of a sound church.

NOVEMBER 9
Titus 2:11—3:15

Trained by Saving Grace (2:11–15)

The opening verse in this passage summarizes the Christmas story. The grace of God has appeared in the form of the Christ child.

Has the Christ child been born in you? If so, then there will be some easily recognized results, such as those in verse 12.

In verse 14 Paul says that believers are Christ's own special people, or as it says in the King James, a "peculiar people." How are we "peculiar"? There have been some strange interpretations of this "peculiar people." Jack Shuler wrote:

> It is at the point of our peculiarity that some have stumbled. They have supposed that we are to affect a peculiarity in dress and custom which our Lord never intended. There are many ways to be peculiar. Wherein, then, is our peculiarity to be found? God's people are to be different in the way they react to adverse world conditions. Joseph was peculiar when he fled the advances of Potiphar's wife. Moses was peculiar when he abandoned the ease and luxury of an Egyptian court for a desert rendezvous with God. Daniel was peculiar when he forfeited the favor of the king to seek the approval of heaven. Paul and Silas, with bloody backs, were peculiar when they sang hymns at midnight in a Philippian jail. God's people have always been peculiar in the way they have faced and overcome their difficulties (*Shuler's Short Sermons*, pp. 56, 57).

1. How should we live in the present age? (2:12)
2. What are believers awaiting? (2:13)
3. In what ways do you demonstrate that you are a special person?

Graces of the Heirs of Grace; Avoid Dissension (3:1–15)

Believers live within a definite discipline; hence, the word *disciple*. In this section Paul outlines the attitudes of that discipline.

Again Paul treats a subject with which he has dealt over and over—the relationship between faith and works. What saves us, and how will we react to that salvation?

1. How did Paul describe himself before he accepted Christ? (3:3)
2. What has saved us? (3:5)
3. What should believers be careful to maintain? (3:8)
4. What are some areas of dissension in your church? How can you work to smooth over those areas?

PHILEMON

NOVEMBER 10
Philemon 1–25

Greeting: Philemon's Love and Faith; Paul's Plea (1–25)

This letter was written by the apostle Paul to his good friend in Colossae, a man named Philemon. Philemon's wife was Apphia, named in verse 2, and his son was Archippus.

Notice that in the opening verse Paul makes no mention of the fact that he is an ordained apostle, as he usually does in his other letters. This intensely personal letter pleads for Philemon to spare Onesimus.

Having escaped to Rome, in a bizarre set of circumstances, the runaway had met the apostle Paul, who was himself a slave, a slave of Jesus Christ. Onesimus was caught up in the fervor of the apostle and gave himself to the Lord. He quickly became a favorite of Paul's, who knew down deep in his soul that the issue regarding Onesimus' return had to be dealt with sooner or later. Under normal circumstances, when the slave returned, the slaveowner could do anything to him he wished, including beating him or even taking his life.

Paul decided to personally intercede on the slave's behalf. Verse 10 outlines the main issue.

Note that Paul *requested* Philemon's help; he did not *demand* it!

Note verses 15–16. Paul asks for a drastic change in Philemon's thinking. Christ does change our ways of thinking, doesn't He?

In verses 17–19 notice Paul's involvement. Paul was willing to pay any damages, even though he had nothing to do with the business.

Now, with a flash of humor, in verses 19 and 20, Paul says in effect, "Philemon, you have got a lot out of me during your lifetime; now let me get something from you. Do what I ask in regard to Onesimus." We have no reason to believe that Philemon did anything other than that which Paul requested. Paul had given much, and now he was reaping the benefit of his generosity.

1. How does Paul describe himself in this letter? (9)
2. Why did Paul send Onesimus back? (14)
3. How should Onesimus return to Philemon? (16)
4. If Philemon was to receive Onesimus as a brother, what does that say about the way we treat others?

HEBREWS

NOVEMBER 11
Hebrews 1:1—2:9

God's Supreme Revelation; the Son Exalted (1:1—14)

Hebrews is a complicated, yet glorious, book. We do not know for sure who wrote this volume, although there is some indication that Paul did. It was written to the Jewish Christians in Jerusalem, who had grown very discouraged by the oppression and persecution. Perhaps, they reasoned, they had lost everything in their pursuit of Christ; the temple, the sacrifices, the atonement. But the author tells them clearly that in Christ they have everything better than ever. In fact, the key word in this book is *better.*

The Jewish Christians had lost their glimpse of the glory of the Lord, for the oppression of life had been too severe. They got caught up in their humanity, rather than Christ's divinity. *Perhaps the old legalistic approach was better after all,* some of them reasoned. But the Hebrew writer put the spotlight squarely on the Christ again.

1. How does the writer of Hebrews describe Christ? (1:3)
2. How is Christ better than the angels? (1:4)
3. How do we demonstrate that we have not lost the glimpse of the glory of the Lord?

Do Not Neglect Salvation; Made Lower than Angels (2:1—9)

The old covenant message, delivered by angels, was kept to the letter and proved steadfast and sure. Knowing that Christ is greater, we can ill afford to ignore the salvation He offers.

Only Christ can ever elevate us to the lofty ideal of this passage and its parallel, Psalm 8. We have allowed the humanists to saddle us with degrading principles and sadly inferior ideals—far, far from what God wants us to be. In Christ we again begin to see those ideals and to realize that, in Him, we can indeed be what God wants us to be.

1. What do we need to do with the news of the gospel? (2:1)
2. What bears witness to the gospel? (2:4)
3. How does Psalm 8 describe humanity? (2:7—8)
4. How do you view humankind? As inherently good or inherently evil? Why?

Bringing Many to Christ (2:10–18)

In this Scripture, we see Jesus revealed as the great "trailblazer" of salvation and righteousness. Christ was the one who cleared the way for you and me to have access to God Himself. Without that, you and I would have been left in our sins forever.

Some of the cults teach that Christ is only one of the ways to God—that the leaders of their heresies are just as efficacious, if not more so, than Christ Himself. I have heard some believers in Christ say that the Moslem teaching is not unpalatable for, after all, Moslems believe in Jesus, too. Yes, they do believe in Jesus— as a prophet, and no more. They have many prophets. But contrast that to Jesus' claim, "I am the way, the truth, and the life. No one comes to the Father except through Me" (John 14:6). Now if that claim is not true, then Jesus perpetrated a fraud and could not possibly be the Son of God. But if it is true, where does that put the heresies and cults that are rampant today? You cannot have it both ways—it is either one way or the other.

This passage also forces us to remember Christ's sufferings. Look at verses 14 and 18. Christ not only came to earth, He came as a human being, subject to the same powers and frailties as everyone else.

Look at what Barclay says about this suffering: "The basis of the Greek idea of God was detachment; the basis of the Christian idea is identity. Through His sufferings Jesus Christ identified himself with man."

1. Why is Christ not ashamed to call us brothers and sisters? (2:11)
2. What made us subject to bondage before Christ's death and resurrection? (2:15)
3. What is Jesus called in this passage—a name that will be repeated throughout Hebrews? (2:17)
4. If Jesus needed to identify with humanity in order to become our Savior, what does that say to us in our attempts to help others?

The Faithful Son; Be Faithful (3:1–19)

Please remember the basis for this book. The writer is encouraging Christian Jews who are being persecuted for their faith. He begins by saying that Jesus Christ is the ultimate in life, yes, even better than the angels. Now having established that fact, he goes on to his second point: that Jesus is even greater than Moses.

In verses 7–19 the writer gives an impassioned plea to the saints to remain in faith, to persevere, to endure to the very end.

Look at the phrase in verse 13: "the deceitfulness of sin"! My friend Jimmy Sowder calls it "the deceptiveness of the gradual." Sometimes I am asked why I am such a stickler for church attendance, why I constantly encourage believers to be in the house of God. Because, as this chapter says, sin is deceitful and Satan is clever. He can find many ways to take my attention off the Lord and the things of God. He knows that the only way I will have peace is to be constantly aware of God. In and through the church, I learn discipline.

It is vital to the believer to maintain a soft and kind spirit. Don't ever allow the cynical, blasé attitude of the world to come into your heart. Remember that the Holy Spirit is gentle and speaks softly. Are you in a spiritual condition that will allow you to hear His Voice? Or are you tuned in to the din and uproar of the world?

1. Why was Christ greater than Moses? (3:3–6)
2. What must we do to become partakers of Christ? (3:14)
3. Is your spiritual condition such that you can hear the "still, small voice" of God in the din and uproar of today's world?

The Promise of Rest (4:1–10)

The grand gift of God, salvation, is more than forgiveness of sins alone. Do not misunderstand me; I would not for a moment depreciate the fabulous aspect of forgiveness. But, on the other hand, I would seriously impair the teaching if I did not tell you there are blessed by-products of salvation. Among them is rest.

The writer deals with rest in three contexts: First, there is the rest of spirit and soul in knowing God; second, the rest promised the Jews with the takeover of the Promised Land; and third, the rest that God enjoyed on the seventh day of Creation when He ceased from His labors.

1. Why did some not profit from the gospel message? (4:2)
2. How does the author of Hebrews describe the rest? (4:10)
3. How is it possible to experience God's rest during the stressful times in our lives?

Our Compassionate High Priest; Qualifications for High Priesthood (4:11—5:11)

Verses 11–13 need to be proclaimed from housetop to housetop. They describe the Word of God.

If the Word is that important, then why is it not featured in every worship service?

The warning aspect of these verses should not be overlooked. The author gave us reassurance in the previous verses, but there now follows a warning to those who take no heed.

In verses 5:1–10 the author deals with the qualifications of the earthly priesthood which Jesus, of course, fulfills. He then deals with Jesus' bitter experience on earth and what that signifies for us. It is this latter idea that is the main theme of the remainder of Hebrews.

Verse 6 simply signifies that Jesus' priesthood was different from the Levitical priesthood.

1. What kind of High Priest do we have? (4:15)
2. What are the qualifications of an earthly high priest? (5:1–4)
3. To what order of high priesthood does Jesus belong? (5:10)
4. How can we apply the characteristics of an earthly high priest to our own ministries—clerical or lay?

Spiritual Immaturity; the Peril of Not Progressing (5:12—6:8)

What a cry for spiritual maturity! The author is addressing the faults of indifference and laziness rather than any particular heresy. The rebuke in verses 12–13 is followed by a warning in 6:1–8. The author summarizes the most elementary of principles that he feels every Christian should know and puts them in three pairs, all having to do with different stages of faith; repentance and faith, baptism and the laying on of hands, and resurrection and judgment.

The warning comes in verses 4–6, and it is a harsh one. Whether the impossibility of salvation comes from God or whether it comes from the hardness of the human heart, the author gives no hint.

1. How does the author describe the mature in faith? (5:14)
2. What is the warning? (6:4–6)
3. Compare this warning to your ideas concerning what Jesus taught about forgiveness.

A Better Estimate; God's Infallible Purpose in Christ (6:9–20)

In verses 13–20, the writer of Hebrews reminds us of one of the promises God made to Abraham—that all his descendants would be blessed. The fulfillment of all God's promises to the patriarch were made complete in Jesus Christ. What is that blessing, that ultimate hope that we have?

Prior to Calvary, only one man, the high priest, had access, once a year, to the literal presence of God. He would go cautiously behind the great veil of the temple that separated the Holy of Holies. When Jesus died on Calvary, at that precise moment, the veil of the temple was torn in two from top to bottom. Now that sequence is important because it shows that no man could have done it. The tearing was done by God Himself, opening up His presence to everyone who would come by way of Calvary. It is our great hope and reality that in Jesus Christ we have access to God, not because of our righteousness or our merit, but because of what Jesus Christ accomplished on the cross.

The two unchangeable ("immutable") things in verse 18 are the promise and the oath.

1. What example of patient endurance is given? (6:13, 15)
2. What does the author call the hope God has given us? (6:19)
3. What does it mean to you to know that you yourself have access to God?

The King of Righteousness; Need for a New Priesthood (7:1–19)

The author of Hebrews has stressed that Jesus Christ was far superior to the law, to the angels, even to Moses. In the fifth chapter he set forth the qualifications of high priesthood. And in this seventh chapter he points out that the accepted priesthood, that of the Levitical order (or those who came from the tribe of Levi), was not enough because it had never solved the sin problem. And he lifts up Jesus Christ as the ultimate High Priest and King.

Hebrews now reintroduces an extraordinary biblical character, Melchizedek. You will remember that Abraham and his servants were involved in a battle with a five-king coalition and won that skirmish overwhelmingly. On the way back to their camp, as they neared Salem, a man named Melchizedek greeted the patriarch warmly, and we have record now of Abraham's giving him a "tenth part of all" (v. 2).

The writer of Hebrews says that Melchizedek was so great that Levi himself (yet unborn), in effect, paid tithes to him. So Melchizedek was far greater in himself than the entire Levitical priesthood—and Jesus Christ is greater than Melchizedek.

1. How does the writer of Hebrews describe Melchizedek? (7:3)
2. If the priesthood changes, then what of necessity changes? (7:12)
3. Why was the former law annulled? (7:18)
4. How do we communicate through our own lives the hope that Christ brings to everyone?

Greatness of the New Priest (7:20–28)

The priests of Levi, who had long served in both the tabernacle and temple worship as the mediators between God and men, became priests by birth. But the writer of Hebrews reminds the Jewish believers that Christ became High Priest, not through succession at birth but through a sovereign act and oath of God. Again he quoted David in Psalm 110:4.

1. Why were there many priests? (7:23)
2. What can Christ do for us that others could not? (7:25)
3. What is the difference between Christ and the Levitical priests? (7:27)
4. What are we holding back from Christ?

New Priestly Service (8:1–6)

This chapter opens with a brief summary of what the writer has been stressing all along.

Dr. F. F. Bruce in his sterling commentary on Hebrews wrote: "As the (old) priesthood gives place to the priesthood after the order of Melchizedek, so the old covenant (between God and man) gives place to the new, the earthly sanctuary gives place to the heavenly, and sacrifices which were but temporary tokens give place to one that is effective and of eternal validity."

So, Christ is our High Priest. That being the case, what is His priestly ministry to you and me? A priest, as a mediator between God and men, had to have something to offer God from men—a sacrifice, if you will. That sacrifice was made at the great altar inside the tabernacle and temple enclosures, and once a year the blood was offered inside the Holy of Holies by the high priest. Now where does Christ, our High Priest, minister and what does His ministry offer? He ministers at the right hand of God, the ultimate sanctuary, and that which He offers is Himself, His death on the cross. When God sees me, a sinner, His sinless nature is violated and He judges me severely; but Christ, who is my High Priest, offers Himself again, afresh, reminding God, in effect, of His atonement, and as always, when God sees the blood, He passes over us. Hallelujah!

These passages in Hebrews are a good example of why it is necessary to have a working understanding of the Old Testament. The Old Testament will give you the foundation you need for proper interpretation of the New Testament.

1. What does the author of Hebrews call the law? (8:5)
2. What does the author call Christ? (8:6)
3. What makes the new covenant better? (8:6)
4. How versed are you in Old Testament Scriptures and their relationship to the New Testament? What steps can you take to further your understanding?

A New Covenant; the Earthly Sanctuary (8:7–9:5)

Evidently, some Jewish believers were considering a return to the old law, perhaps because they were being persecuted for their faith. Some of them no doubt thought, *Is it worth it? Why not go back to the old law and be like everyone else?* The writer of Hebrews responds in verse 7. And then he quotes Jeremiah 31:31–34, in which God promises the people a new testament or covenant far superior to the law. The substance of this new agreement, or covenant, that God makes with us involves three ideas.

In the Old Testament, God wrote His laws *to* the people. In the New Testament or covenant, He will write His laws *in* the people. Their very lives will be the transcript of this covenant.

Verse 10 states the second idea. Unfortunately, many pseudo-believers think they can take the Savior without making God, God! But that cannot happen. It is only when we accept the mastery and headship of God that we can even begin to fathom what it means to accept the Savior.

The third idea is stated in verse 12.

In 9:1–5 the author gives us a brief overview of the actual tabernacle interior, excluding, of course, the courtyard enclosure. The tabernacle was not very big—about fifteen feet wide and forty-five feet long (the whole enclosure was roughly seventy-five feet wide and one hundred fifty feet long). The tabernacle was divided into two rooms. Only the priests could enter the first room, and only the high priest could enter the inner room, or the second room. The first room was called the Holy Place and was about fifteen by thirty feet. There were several articles in it: the lampstand, an elaborately-wrought menorah (seven-branched candlestick, made of pure gold); a small gold-covered altar table about two feet long, which held little cakes, or shewbread. Twelve cakes of shewbread were placed on this table each week. Then, behind the ornate veil or curtain, was the second room called the Holy of Holies.

1. Why was a new covenant necessary? (8:7)
2. How will God give the new covenant? (8:10*b*)
3. For what reciprocal action did the new covenant call? (8:10*c*)
4. What did the ark of the covenant contain? (9:4)
5. To what extent have you accepted God as the sovereign of your life? What areas of your life might need reevaluation in this light?

NOVEMBER 19
Hebrews 9:6—10:18

Limitations of the Earthly Service; the Heavenly Sanctuary (9:6–15)

Beginning with verse 6, the author of Hebrews describes what happens in the sanctuary.

The author then describes how Christ made that ultimate atonement.

Note verses 13 and 14. They summarize very well the difference between the Old Testament sacrifices and the ultimate sacrifice.

1. What was the place of the tabernacle in the whole scheme of things? (9:9–10)
2. Of what is Christ the High Priest? (9:11)
3. Is what you are living for worth Christ's dying?

Greatness of Christ's Sacrifice and Insufficiency of Animal Sacrifices (9:16—10:18)

Verses 16–22 are a beautiful teaching about Christ's great will and testament, or covenant. A last will and testament is not in effect until the death of the one who made the will.

Verses 23–28 continue to compare the ultimate sacrifice of Christ with the animal sacrifices of the Old Testament.

Those sacrifices in the Old Testament had to be offered again and again. Why? Because they could never perfect a human being. But Calvary can! The sacrifice of life that Jesus made can bring a man or woman, once filthy in sins, right into the very presence of a holy God!

And just as the penalty of sin does not need to be paid again on the cross, once a person has accepted Christ as Lord and Savior and that process of regeneration has started in his life, it need not be repeated either.

Verses 5–7 quote Psalm 40:6–8, but as Christ's words, not the psalmist's.

Verse 18 of chapter 10 is a clarification of verse 17 and as such sets the stage for the warning that appears in verse 26.

1. With what was the first covenant dedicated? (9:18)
2. Why was Christ's sacrifice necessary? (9:23)
3. What does the author of Hebrews say about the finality of death? (9:27)
4. What is the hint of the warning to come? (10:18)
5. How do you view your own salvation—recurring, ongoing, temporary? How does Hebrews address this question?

NOVEMBER 20
Hebrews 10:19–11:7

Hold Fast Your Confession (10:19–25)

The privileges you and I have in Christ! Most of us live far beneath those rights. No, we are not talking about acquisition of things here. It is increasingly frustrating to hear and read today that godliness is equated with material gain. But look at the blessings the author of Hebrews outlined for us here:

1. We have boldness to enter the very presence of God.
2. Christ is our access, and through Christ we are eternally linked with the Savior.

But with the blessings come responsibilities. Tozer once wrote that you and I are as close to God at this moment as we want to be. God doesn't set the limitations; you and I do. How close to God are you right now? Well, that's as close as you want to be.

1. What makes a true heart? (10:22)
2. How should we deal with one another? (10:24)
3. How does verse 25 address the idea of those who say church attendance is unnecessary?

The Just Live by Faith; by Faith We Understand (10:26—11:7)

Here is an excellent description of the sin of apostasy. *Apostasy* means "sinning willfully after we have received the knowledge of the truth." Now this doesn't refer to stumbling or making mistakes. This involves the person who shakes his fist in God's face and cries out, "Leave me alone" after he has once been saved. How terrible are the implications of verses 26 and 27. All that is left is to await the final judgment of the God he forsook. What was the crime of the apostate? Look at verse 29.

Hebrews 11:1–7 begins a catalog of the heroes of faith. Verse 1 is one of the best known in all the Bible.

Two words leap out at us: *faith* and *hope*. They go together. Yes, Christianity is positive. A nonbeliever is left with verse 31 of the previous chapter, but the believer is immediately hit with the positive—faith and hope.

1. What happens if we commit the sin of apostasy? (10:26–27)
2. What sufferings had the recipients of this letter endured? (10:33–34)
3. What do we need to please God? (11:6)
4. In what areas of your life do you need to reflect the more positive aspects of Christianity?

NOVEMBER 21
Hebrews 11:8–40

By Faith We Understand; the Heavenly Hope (11:8–16)

Everything promised to the Old Testament pilgrims of faith pointed to the reality of Jesus Christ. Someone has said that the Old Testament points forward to Christ, and the New Testament points back to Christ. Christ is the focal point.

Many teach today that faith has to do with acquisition of things on this earth. Not so. In this classic chapter on faith, the author was inspired of the Holy Spirit to remind us that these stalwarts knew full well that this world was not their home and that their great promises from God had to do with eternity. That is the key—you and I are eternal beings. Verse 16 describes God's response to their faith.

1. How did the Old Testament examples of faith demonstrate their faith? (11:13)
2. How did God respond to their faith? (11:16)
3. What kind of "country" (v. 14) do you seek?

The Faith of the Patriarchs; By Faith They Overcame (11:17–40)

Hebrews continues with its catalog of Old Testament persons of faith. All of their stories are fascinating, but let's touch on just one—Jephthah (see Judg. 11).

He was born an illegitimate child and was expelled from his family early in life. He never had a chance in that society to amount to anything. Yet he became a great judge of Israel and delivered the people from their archenemies, the Ammonites. His story is that of an outcast who became a national leader. You and I are not limited by heredity and environment; we are limited only by our lack of faith in God.

Notice that not all of these stories are success epics. Look at verses 36 through 38. Here again is evidence against the spiritually immature habit of equating faith or spiritual success with acquisition of material things.

1. What was Abraham's greatest act of faith? (11:17–18)
2. What harlot demonstrated great faith? (11:31)
3. A person is successful if he or she has been used by God in the manner God intended. What has God planned for your life? Are you obedient to that divine plan? Or have you mapped out your own ways?

331

The Race of Faith; the Discipline of God (12:1–29)

Chapter 12 opens with a heavenly challenge based upon the witnesses we have had in the previous chapter.

To what do the characters in chapter 11 witness? They tell us daily that, although people may fail, God never does. They assure us that God's grace is always sufficient, regardless of the circumstance. They tell us over and over that God always remains faithful to His promises. And they are cheering us on from the heavenly grandstand.

The sin mentioned in verse 1 is different for each one of us. I have no justification for pointing to the sin in someone else's life; I must take care of the sin problem in my own heart.

Verses 3–29 form a fascinating segment on the discipline that God gives us. Verse 6 tells us why God disciplines us. There is a real need today for renewed teaching and preaching on discipleship, on discipline. As Christians, we are not free to "do our own thing." Look at verses 8 and 9.

The writer of Hebrews compares the relationship an Old Testament believer had with God with the relationship of a New Testament saint. God was unapproachable in the old covenant, the frightening God of Mount Sinai. But in the new covenant we come to Mount Zion, to the new city of God, to the protection of holy angels, to the companionship and good will of every saint who has ever lived. And, of course, we come to Jesus.

This chapter closes, in verses 27 and 28, with the warning that one day God will say, "Enough!" and will speak the word that will shake the earth—so that only those things that absolutely cannot be shaken will remain. What is unshakeable? Our souls, those treasures that we have laid up in heaven, our commitment to God and God's work, our investment of time and effort in God—those are unshakeable attributes.

1. Why did Jesus endure the Cross? (12:2)
2. If God chastens us, what are we to God, and conversely, if God does not chasten us, what are we? (12:7–8)
3. What is the result of chastening? (12:11)
4. What does the author call God? (12:29)
5. What is the sin in your life that holds you back from fulfilling the Lord's potential for you?

Concluding Moral and Religious Directions (13:1–25)

This chapter may be the continuation of the list begun by the author in 12:14 before he apparently became diverted.

In verses 1–6 the author addresses fellow Christians and, if Hebrews 10:32–34 is any example, outlines treatment of fellow Christians, without extending his exhortations beyond that.

The author of Hebrews was probably referring in verse 2 to several Old Testament stories, for example, Abraham and Sarah (see Gen. 18), Lot (see Gen. 19), and Manoah (see Judg. 13), all of whom found themselves with sudden company in the form of angels.

Verses 7–16 appear unrelated to the previous six verses. In the passage the author tells believers that the teachings of Jesus Christ are forever and that believers should watch out for false teaching—a warning that is sounded throughout the New Testament.

In verses 20–21, the author introduces for the first time a different picture of Christ.

1. What should believers continue doing (see 13:1) and whom should they remember? (13:2–3)
2. What should our conduct reflect? (13:5)
3. What is Jesus called? (13:20)
4. Apply the moral directions in verses 1–6 to your own life.

JAMES

NOVEMBER 24
James 1:1–11

Profit from Trials; the Perspective of Rich and Poor (1:1–11)

This Epistle was written by the "man with camel's knees." James, the brother of our Lord Jesus, was a prayer warrior, an intercessor constantly on his knees. Legend has it that his knees became calloused like a camel's. It is most interesting that while Jesus was still living, James did not follow Him. Neither did he believe that his brother was the Son of God. But when he became a witness of the Resurrection, all was changed. Following his conversion, he became an active member of the church in Jerusalem and finally emerged as its leader. He was martyred when the scribes and Pharisees pitched him from the pinnacle of the temple onto the rocks of the Kidron Valley.

James clearly identifies the people to whom he is writing as the Jews who have been scattered abroad. The Jews were scattered on various occasions, the first time when the people of the Northern Kingdom (or Samaria) were taken captive by the Assyrians. Ten tribes were involved in that dispersion. Then the Babylonians conquered the Southern Kingdom (or Judah). General Pompey of Rome also scattered the people about sixty years before Christ was born.

The Bible never suggests that being a Christian is easy. Look at verse 2. Does that make any sense? Why should a person thank the Lord for testings? The answer is in verse 3.

James comments on the way we pray—those things we ask God to give us. God provides our material needs; there is no question about that, but we are to ask for an abundance of spiritual blessings.

"Double-minded" in verse 8 refers to trying to divide our allegiance.

Christ affects men in different ways. A poor man understands that the fact he is not wealthy in no way keeps him from serving God. A rich man understands the fact that even though he is blessed materially he still must be subject to the will of God for his life.

1. For what reaction to bad situations should we strive? (1:2–3)
2. For what should we ask God? How? (1:5–6)
3. What will happen to the person who pursues riches? (1:11)
4. For what do you pray? Is your prayer backed up by faith?

NOVEMBER 25

James 1:12–27

Loving God in Trials; Doers—Not Hearers (1:12–27)

James gave us some of the finest teaching on temptation that exists in the Bible. It is vital material because everyone is tempted. Everyone has a vulnerability in some area (or areas) of life; however, the fact that we are tempted does not mean we must succumb to it. And the person who resists temptation will be rewarded with a crown of life at the Judgment Seat of Christ. There are five basic crowns that are promised to the believer: (1) the "crown of life" (James 1:12); (2) an "imperishable crown" (1 Cor. 9:25); (3) a "crown of rejoicing" (1 Thess. 2:19); (4) a "crown of righteousness" (2 Tim. 4:8); and (5) the "crown of glory" (1 Pet. 5:4).

A believer must, by an act of his own will, determine to set aside every bit of unrighteousness in his life. You and I cannot do it without God's help, but God will not intervene in our lives until we have made a determination to follow Him. Not only are we to study the Word—to know what it says—but we are to *do* what it says as well.

Someone may say, "Well, I do what the Word says; I don't steal or lie or cheat or commit adultery." But there is more to it than that. Much more. For example, look at verse 26.

1. Who tempts us? (1:13–14)
2. What is the result of sin? (1:15)
3. From where does the good come? (1:17)
4. What is our responsibility to the Word? (1:22)
5. How can we keep ourselves "unspotted from the world," as James puts it in verse 27?

NOVEMBER 26
James 2:1–26

No Personal Favoritism (2:1–13)

If there were one key word in the Epistle of James, it would be *practicality*. James must have been a good pastor. His teachings were sound and highly usable in everyday life. And our faith in Christ must relate to day-to-day living.

The first verses of chapter 2 deal with snobbery in the church, and they are very explicit.

James reminded us of one of Jesus' principal teachings: "You shall love your neighbor as yourself" (Matt. 19:19). A truly spiritual church treats everyone alike, for they realize all Christians are brothers and sisters of our Lord Jesus Christ.

Note verse 13. If we show mercy, we can turn God's condemnation into favor.

1. For what has God chosen the poor of the world? (2:5)
2. What will you do if you fulfill what James calls "the royal law according to the Scripture"? (2:8)
3. What happens if we stumble in one part of the law? (2:10)
4. What role can mercy play? (2:13)
5. What kind of church is your church? What is the role of partiality and mercy in your church?

Faith Without Works (2:14–26)

We come here to a marvelous treatise on works. Remember that Paul taught clearly that works could not save us: "Therefore we conclude that a man is justified by faith apart from the deeds of the law" (Rom. 3:28). "A man is not justified by the works of the law but faith in Jesus Christ . . . for by the works of the law no flesh shall be justified" (Gal. 2:16). Now here we have James' writing in verse 17. Were Paul and James at odds on this matter of faith and works? No. They were in total agreement. We are not saved by our works but by the mercy of God; however, when a person is saved, that salvation will be clearly evident by the works in his or her life.

1. How does James reduce his faith-works teaching to practical Christianity? (2:15–16)
2. What is faith without works? (2:17)
3. What two Old Testament examples of faith borne out by works did James give? (2:21, 25)
4. In what areas of your life do you carry out the works that your faith requires? Try to be specific.

NOVEMBER 27
James 3:1–4:10

The Untamable Tongue (3:1–12)

The author's premise here is that the area of greatest potential slip-up has to do with the words we speak.

The Book of Ecclesiasticus, one of the apocryphal books, has some sharp thoughts on this subject: "Cursed be gossips and the double-tongued, for they destroy the peace of many./A meddlesome tongue subverts many, and makes them refugees among the peoples;/It destroys walled cities, and overthrows powerful dynasties./A meddlesome tongue can drive virtuous women from their homes and rob them of the fruit of their toil. . . ./A blow from a whip raises a welt, but a blow from the tongue smashes bones;/Many have fallen by the edge of the sword; but not so many as by the tongue" (28:13–18NAB).

1. To what does James liken a loose tongue? (3:5)
2. What does James call the tongue? (3:8)
3. Think of some instances when loose tongues (gossip) have caused problems in your church.

Heavenly Wisdom, Pride, and Strife (3:13–4:10)

In verses 13–18 James taught that our lives must undergird the words we say.

In verse 4 of chapter 4, James made a statement that has almost been forgotten in the church today. Today we want the best of both possible worlds—the blessings of God and the pleasures of the world. The Bible still teaches, "Come out from among them/And be separate, says the Lord" (2 Cor. 6:17).

Look at verses 7 and 8. James reiterates Jesus' teaching that you can't serve "two masters." Slovenly Christianity is a problem today, even though we can study the Word and find clearly written standards that God expects every believer to meet. A man once said to me, "I would like to be a faithful disciple, but I just can't seem to do it." The truth of the matter is that we do exactly what we want to do.

1. From where do envy and self-seeking come? (3:14–15)
2. What causes wars and fights? (4:1)
3. What is friendship with the world? (4:4)
4. In what areas of your life do you feel that you might be trying to serve two masters?

NOVEMBER 28
James 4:11–5:20

Do Not Judge a Brother;
Neither Boast About Tomorrow (4:11–17)

Two powerful verses, verses 11–12, condemn the sin of slander, that is, speaking evil of one who is not even there to defend himself.

It is the law of God (the "royal law" as James calls it) that we should love our neighbors as ourselves. It stands to reason that when a person is slandering another person, he cannot possibly love that one as he loves himself. Therefore, he is breaking one of God's greatest laws. James said that the slanderer, in effect, sets himself above God's edicts and says, "I can do what I choose; so I will speak evil of this person if I desire to."

There is another great danger in slander: The slanderer becomes judge. Only God has the right to judge actions and motivations.

1. What do you do if you judge the law? (4:11)
2. How should we deal with tomorrow? (4:14–15)
3. What concerns you about tomorrow?

Judgment of Rich Oppressors; Patience and Perseverance;
Meeting Specific Needs (5:1–20)

James makes a strong case in verses 1–6 against two kinds of wealth: (1) wealth from illegal and immoral means; and (2) indulging in materialism to the point of forgetting one's responsibility to God.

James also condemned the rich who use their wealth wantonly.

Look at verse 11. We are living in the day of "instant" everything. (There is something suspicious about a society that invents "instant potatoes.") In the spirit world, of which believers are a part, the great victories are accomplished by enduring to the end. Look at David, who was anointed king years and years before he ever took the throne.

Verses 13–18 have the blessed promise of healing for those who will call for the elders of the church, who, in turn, pray the prayer of faith.

1. What do gold and silver do? (5:3)
2. What virtue does James extol while we await the Lord? (5:7)
3. What does James say about the reliability of our word? (5:12)
4. What should those who are sick do? (5:14)
5. How do you determine priorities for spending your money?

1 PETER

NOVEMBER 29
1 Peter 1:1—2:3

A Heavenly Inheritance (1:1—12)

The theme of Peter's writing is endurance. Peter wrote to Christians who were being horribly persecuted by Rome. Something had happened to turn Rome against believers during Nero's rule.

Historians have pinpointed July 19, A.D. 64, as the day the great fire broke out in Rome. For three days and nights the fire raged. No one seemed to doubt that Nero himself had set the fire and, indeed, kept it going. When the fire appeared to be about out, it suddenly resumed its ferocious blazing, and the second outbreak was worse than the first. By this time the people of Rome intensely hated Nero. But Nero cunningly directed their hatred toward the Christians. After all, hadn't they preached of a day when the world would go up in flames? A horrible persecution of the Christians ensued in which the believers were crucified, burned alive, or thrown to wild animals.

Peter reminds the faithful that this world is not their home, for God had promised them a heavenly inheritance far exceeding anything this world could ever offer.

1. To whom was Peter writing? (1:1)
2. How does Peter refer to the persecution? (1:6—7)
3. What is the end of our faith? (1:9)
4. What would your reaction to persecution be?

Living Before God; the Enduring Word (1:13—2:3)

Despite persecution and deprivation, Peter reminds believers that they are still to maintain a standard of holy living.

Finally, the Christian life is remarkable in its fulfillment of brotherly love. Yes, even when persecutions abound and times are tough, love is manifested, one toward the other.

1. For what should we hope? (1:13)
2. Why should we be holy? (1:16)
3. With what did we obtain redemption? (1:18—19)
4. What should we lay aside? (2:1)
5. Why do you conduct or attend worship services?

NOVEMBER 30
1 Peter 2:4—3:6

The Chosen Stone and His Chosen People (2:4—12)

This is a truly beautiful passage that teaches us some basics about the church. First, Christ is the cornerstone. You and I, as believers in Christ, give it strength and durability. We are active in the church as a royal priesthood, bringing people to God.

1. How are we being used as living stones? (2:5)
2. What does Peter call the people of his time and to what purpose are they called? (2:9—10)
3. How do you carry out your obligation to live differently from the world?

Submission to Government, Masters, Husbands (2:13—3:6)

One of the ways in which the believer will honor Christ is in his reaction to authority. To put this passage into perspective, we must understand that in that day there were over sixty million slaves in the Roman Empire. Most of the actual work done in the Roman Empire was done by slaves.

Why didn't Peter or Paul or other early Christian leaders cry out for the abolition of slavery? Because it would have caused the whole known world to collapse. Does that mean they believed in slavery? No, they didn't believe in it, for in the Christian faith there is neither slave nor free. But Christianity is not a subversive religion. It is a faith that creates new people who are headed for eternity. And even today, ofttimes our circumstances are not changed when we meet the Lord. We are not saved *from* the circumstances, but saved *in* the circumstances.

To understand 3:1—6, we must again look at the culture of the time. A woman of that day had no rights. She was not much more than a slave. What happened if she became a Christian while her husband remained a nonbeliever? Peter answers that question. The submission of which Peter speaks is a Christian one, for it is a submission born of love.

1. What do we do by submitting ourselves to laws? (2:13—16)
2. Why should servants submit to masters? (2:19—20)
3. Who serves as an example for slaves? (2:21—22)
4. What should a Christian wife do if her husband refuses to become a believer? (3:1—2)
5. What is your view of authority? Are there times when it should be called into question? If so, how?

DECEMBER 1
1 Peter 3:7—4:11

A Word to Husbands; Called to Blessing (3:7–17)

Peter had a full set of instructions for husbands in verse 7, and in verses 8–17, he outlines some general principles of behavior for Christian men and women.

Demonstrating unity does not mean we agree in all things; but once a conclusion is reached, the Christians must dwell in unity.

Verse 15 is difficult. *Sanctification* means "to set apart" or "to make holy." Certainly God sanctifies us, but how do we sanctify God? Paul gave us the answer when he said, "For to me, to live is Christ" (Phil. 1:21). Sanctification is actually Christ's life that dwells within us. It was the will of Christ to show forth God in all that He did. And Christ's life being manifested in us will do the same thing.

1. How should a husband treat his wife? (3:7)
2. How should we treat others? (3:8–9)
3. What should we always be ready to do? (3:15)
4. When have you suffered for doing good, as Peter writes in verse 17?

Living God's Will and Serving God's Glory (3:18—4:11)

Verses 18–22 contain some of the most marvelous teachings ever given on the atonement of Christ.

Peter's contention that Christ went into the world of the dead means that every person who ever lived has heard the gospel story. There is not a place in the universe over which our Lord does not have control.

Conversion means an about-face. It is turning from darkness to light, from an old way of living to a new.

Verse 7 is a shocker, isn't it? Some of us may think that those early writers who said such things were dreamers, for two thousand years have passed and we are still living. But Peter was correct. He had only a few days left to live on this earth. In the light of history's length and the shortness of our lives, comparatively speaking, the end of all things in our lives *is* at hand. We need to be ready to meet the Lord right now, today.

1. Why was the gospel preached to those who are dead? (4:6)
2. What does Peter say we should do, in anticipation of the end of time? (4:7)
3. What will happen if we partake in Christ's sufferings? (4:13)
4. What is your attitude when you help others?

DECEMBER 2
1 Peter 4:12–5:14

Suffering for God's Glory (4:12–19)

In this passage Peter deals with suffering for Christ—quite different from anything you and I know. As we mentioned earlier, the Christians of Peter's day were being bitterly persecuted by the insane Roman Emperor Nero.

The sense of the word *commit* that Peter uses here refers to the kind of faith in God that would enable you to trust Him with everything in your life—your family, your job, your possessions.

1. To what future happening does Peter refer? (4:12)
2. What behavior does Peter condemn? (4:15)
3. How should we react if we suffer as a Christian? (4:16)
4. What have you committed to God?

Shepherd the Flock: Submit to God and Resist the Devil (5:1–14)

In verses 1–4 the old apostle had some valuable advice to give the elders in the church. The concept of "elders" went back to Moses. You will recall that when the children of Israel were tramping around the wilderness for forty years, Moses was overburdened with his duties. God told him to set apart seventy elders (see Num. 11:16–30) who were given a special place of leadership in the nation. They served as advisors in key areas and were marvelous administrators. They were not preachers, nor did they usurp the authority of Moses; but they were invaluable assistants to the advancement of that nation.

What do elders do in the church? They serve as shepherds of the flock. The motive for being an elder must be carefully examined. An elder should be a willing vessel in the hands of God. He must not serve only to make money. And he must live an exemplary life before the believers. A reward awaits the faithful elder.

How do you resist Satan? First of all, you must take the voluntary step of acknowledging that he must be resisted. You cannot be passive about Satan. He is your adversary. The Word of God gives us the strength to overcome Satan.

1. How should an elder serve? (5:2–3)
2. What does Peter call Christ? (5:4)
3. What advice does Peter give young people? (5:5)
4. What ways can you prepare yourself to resist the devil?

2 PETER

DECEMBER 3
2 Peter 1:1–2:11

Growth in the Faith (1:1–15)

Second Peter was written to prevent deterioration of the Christian ethic, which was under attack by a number of critics. Verse 4 gives one of the clearest descriptions of a Christian in all the Bible.

Christ's life is manifested in us in some practical ways: *faith*—the certainty in our hearts that everything Jesus said is factual; *virtue*—excellence of character, the inner you that will not be swayed from Christ's life; *knowledge*—wisdom in the things of God, implying a depth of commitment and experience that goes beyond the possibility of years, God-given insight into the meaning of life.

Peter adds to this list *self-control*, which means literally to "get a grip on yourself"; *perseverance*, which means sticking to the task until it's completed; and the list continues.

What is the result of these manifestations in your life? "For if these things are yours and abound, you will be neither barren nor unfruitful in the knowledge of our Lord Jesus Christ" (v. 8).

1. What does Peter exhort the people to add to their faith? (1:5–7)
2. What is the person who lacks these things? (1:9)
3. Describe what the phrase "For to me to live is Christ" means to you.

The Trustworthy Prophetic Word; the Test of Knowing Him (1:16—2:11)

In verses 16–21 Peter remembers the experience on the Mount of Transfiguration.

Now Peter warns the believers against false doctrines—another theme that runs frequently through the New Testament.

1. How did Peter himself know of the power of Jesus? (1:16)
2. From where does prophecy come? (1:21)
3. How does Peter demonstrate that God can deliver people out of temptation and punish only the unjust? (2:4–9)
4. What steps could we take to guard ourselves against false doctrines?

Depravity and Deceptions of False Teachers (2:12–22)

In the previous lesson, Peter warned the believers against the words of false prophets. In this segment of Scripture, Peter described in some detail those who would corrupt your faith for their own benefit.

Every preacher, every teacher, every writer, and every witness has an obligation to the truth of the gospel. Every believer has an obligation to know the Word of God for himself so that he knows when the truth is being distorted. Furthermore, the believer must be so in tune with the Spirit of God that his own spirit will bear witness when he is not being told the truth of the gospel.

Note verse 20. This is another theme that runs throughout the New Testament—those who fall away from God, once having known Him, are in far greater danger than they were before their conversion.

1. How does Peter describe false teachers? (2:12)
2. What kept Balaam from committing further wrong? (2:16)
3. What happens to those who accept the gospel and then choose to live contrary to it? (2:22)
4. What might characterize false teachers today?

God's Promise Is Not Slack (3:1–18)

Remember that Peter wrote this second Epistle as a warning to Christians against heretics. One of the heresies spawned was that Christ was not returning to earth (see vv. 3–4).

The argument of these scoffers was that their fathers, and their fathers before them, had come and gone and nothing had changed; everything had remained the same. Not so, claimed Peter. The scoffers were forgetting some important considerations, and Peter outlines these.

One of the marks of a mature believer is consistency, a characteristic Peter emphasizes in verses 14–18.

1. What were the scoffers forgetting? (3:5–7)
2. How does the human calendar compare with God's calendar? (3:8)
3. How will the Day of the Lord come? (3:10)
4. In what way should we be diligent? (3:14)
5. In what ways do you live in awareness that the Day of the Lord is near?

1 JOHN

DECEMBER 5
1 John 1:1–2:14

The Basis of Fellowship with Him (1:1—2:2)

First John is vastly different from 1 Peter. Peter wrote his letter to a church that was being persecuted by the Roman authorities. But John, as a heartbroken shepherd, writes to the last of his wolf-torn lambs. He is writing to a church that has been seduced by the world system. By this time, the believers were second- and third-generation Christians. The fervor was gone; the passion was missing.

Verses 1–4 are a call to return to that joy of knowing Christ. John wanted the saints to have true fellowship with the Lord out of contentment.

Fellowship with God cannot be maintained unless we walk in the light of God's Word and Christ's example. John tells us why (vv. 5–7).

1. How do we know that John had a personal relationship with Jesus? (1:1–3)
2. What was Jesus' message? (1:5)
3. Why is confession necessary? (1:8–9)
4. How willing are you to confess the sins in your life?

The Test of Knowing Him; Their Spiritual State (2:3–14)

The tough question is, "Who is really a Christian?" John answers that question in verses 3 and 4.

Beginning with verse 7, John reminds us of an eternal principle of practical living: If we say we are walking in the light of God's Word, yet we have something against another person, we are still in darkness, despite our testimonials. It is absolutely essential for Christians to love each other.

John calls us to draw near to God. Such an act implies our own volition, doesn't it? No one can do it for us. If you are away from Him today, it is because you have chosen to be.

1. What of those who say they love God but do not keep His commandments? (2:4)
2. What new commandment did John write? (2:8–11)
3. In what ways do we demonstrate a willingness to draw near to God?

345

Do Not Love the World; Deceptions of the Last Hour (2:15—23)

The sins that war against the human heart can be classified in three basic areas.

1. *The sins of the flesh, or desire.* Immediately we think of sexual sin in this sense, and, of course, that is truly a part of it. But Christians who never think of committing sexual immorality still succumb to sins of the flesh, whether the sin be gluttony, excessive pleasure, or extravagant spending.

2. *The lust of the eyes.* This sin refers to those who want everything they see. Many Americans want anything that is packaged right and presented with the proper appeal, whether the item is needed or not. Such lust reveals an unbridled, covetous destructive spirit.

3. *The pride of life.* This sin can be summed up easily: boasting.

Oh, the warning expressed in these verses 18–23—a warning about the Antichrist and the spirit of antichrist! To learn about the Antichrist, read the Book of Daniel thoroughly. The rather sobering fact is that the world is already waiting for this person with open arms.

1. What do we lack if we love the world? (2:15)
2. Why has John written the letter? (2:21)
3. Who is a liar? (2:22)
4. What examples of sins of the flesh, as defined here, do you see in your worshiping community?

Let Truth Abide in You; Children of God (2:24—3:9)

The privileges of the believer could fill a library. We are children of God; therefore, we may have confidence in living and not be worried about the coming of the Lord, for we will be ready to meet Him. We are privileged because we are recipients of His love.

Our possibilities are also endless. The final result, of course, is our glorification with Christ, according to 3:2.

I cannot live the life that God wants me to. It is impossible. But Christ can—and will. So I ask Him to run my life. And I surrender my body to Him. He begins to live in me, and to break the power of sin.

1. What has God promised us? (2:25)
2. What do we know about those who practice righteousness? (2:29)
3. What will we be like as children of God? (3:2)
4. Why did God become manifest in Jesus? (3:5)
5. How do we open ourselves up to let Christ be born in us again?

DECEMBER 7

1 John 3:10–4:6

The Spirit of Truth and the Spirit of Error (3:10—4:6)

If you should wander down a country road and see an orchard with every tree within sight bearing apples, what kind of orchard do you suppose it would be? You say, "Well, that's silly; it would be an apple orchard, of course."

By their fruit, you know what kind of trees they are. And by the fruit in the life of a person, you can tell whether or not he or she is a believer—a theme that runs consistently through the New Testament.

John adds his amen to this teaching.

In verses 16–23 John lays down a very practical standard of love. He then brings this standard down to the most practical, everyday level.

How many of us have been blessed in many ways yet never stop to consider what we can do to help another person in need? Didn't Jesus say that we were to be the "salt of the earth" and the "light of the world"? If we never go outside ourselves to bless other people's lives, how can we be salt and light?

In 3:24–4:6 John tells us how to spot heresies or the spirit of the Antichrist. He warns us to "test the spirits" to see if they are of God.

So how do we test these spirits?

1. A true godly spirit will acknowledge that Jesus is Christ, the Messiah.

2. The spirit must acknowledge that Jesus Christ was incarnated (born in the flesh, of Mary) two thousand years ago. Jesus Christ was not just a good man, as many say. He was God.

1. Who is not of God? (3:10)
2. How do we recognize love? (3:16)
3. How do we overcome the false prophets? (4:4)
4. Why does the world listen to false prophets? (4:5)
5. How do we discern truth from error? (4:6)
6. How does the love of God dwell in your actions toward your brothers and sisters?

Knowing God Through Love; Obedience by Faith (4:7–5:21)

John tells again the marvelous story of God's search for man. In verse 11, John comes back to an oft-repeated theme. It must be very important, wouldn't you say, to be repeated so often?

One of the greatest advantages of being loved is that fear is driven out (v. 18).

A believer has tremendous respect for the majesty of God. We realize that God is the divine Creator. Yet, our fear has been tempered by our love for God and God's love for us. I cannot say that I fear the wrath of God, for I don't expect it. I am God's child. What kind of parent would bring down wrath upon a child? Chastisement at times, yes. But not wrath. Not vicious beatings and judgment. God loves me, so the fear is gone.

It is difficult to relate to the question, "What do you have to give up to follow Christ?" I only gave up that which gave me ultimate grief and that which sought my destruction. Everything I gained was for my benefit and eternal satisfaction. The life Jesus offers satisfies completely. His commandments are not burdensome.

Verses 6–13 teach about the reality of the Trinity—God the Father, God the Son, and God the Holy Spirit. This does not mean we have three Gods. It is a blessed thought to know that God the Father, God the Son, and God the Holy Spirit all reach out to minister to us in a thousand ways. We are not alone. The blessed Trinity of God lives within us.

Verses 18–21 remind us that a Christian keeps himself from sin. He flees it. He resists Satan. He does not flirt with disaster. He stays as uninvolved in worldly pursuits as is humanly possible, and he cleaves to God with all his might.

1. What is the relationship between God and love? (4:7)
2. How did God manifest love? (4:9)
3. How do we see God? (4:12)
4. Where is your satisfaction in today's world?

2 JOHN

DECEMBER 9
2 John 1–13

Walk in Christ's Commandments; Beware of Antichrist Deceivers (1-13)

This short book contains only thirteen verses. Although brief, it warrants our attention. Written by John the beloved apostle, about A.D. 85, probably from Ephesus, it is addressed either to a specific woman or to the church, designated an "elect lady."

Some believe that the "elect lady" was Mary, the mother of Jesus. You will remember that in one of His last words on the cross Jesus placed the care of His mother upon John—the only apostle at Calvary during the Crucifixion. It is possible that John wrote this letter to Mary; however, she would have been very, very old by this time—almost one hundred. The other possibility is that the elect lady was Martha of Bethany. But by this time she had a thriving ministry of her own in Marseilles, France.

There were in the church at that time three distinct kinds of ministers: the apostles, the prophets (who were wandering ministers or evangelists), and the ordained church elders. By calling himself "the elder," John is referring to his age—past seventy.

The first section of the book deals with following Christ's commandments, not any new commandments. Then in verses 7–11 John changes his emphasis and warns of the Antichrist. John makes a powerful charge here—that anyone denying the Incarnation is an antichrist. In his first Epistle John stressed the same spirit: "By this you know the Spirit of God: Every spirit that confesses that Jesus Christ has come in the flesh is of God, and every spirit that does not confess that Jesus Christ has come in the flesh is not of God. And this is the spirit of the Antichrist" (1 John 4:2–3).

1. Why did John rejoice? (4)
2. For what did John plead? (5)
3. How should we receive those who do not believe in the Incarnation? (10)
4. In what ways are you letting the Antichrist's message creep into your home unawares? Through some of the current television programs, perhaps? Name some other ways.

349

3 JOHN

DECEMBER 10
3 John 1–14

Gaius Commended; Diotrephes and Demetrius (1–14)

There are only fourteen verses in this little book, but what powerful ones they are! John wrote this book about A.D. 85 to address a troubling situation in a local church. We don't know anything about the person to whom the letter was written other than his name.

Verse 2 has been taken by so many radio and television preachers and distorted beyond all reason. This verse has been one of the main texts for the prosperity gospel. We have had it drummed into us that God wants us rich. After all, doesn't John declare it? But John wrote that he prayed we would prosper and be in health *as our souls prosper.* There is the key. The truth of the matter is that if we prospered materially the way we have prospered spiritually, we would starve to death! We would dry up and blow away.

There is no way you would ever get me to believe that Jesus died on that horrible cross of torture just so you and I could drive a little better car or have a little larger house or a few extra pairs of shoes in the closet. I don't believe it for a moment. He died for our eternal benefit. And that eternal benefit must be the first thing we look out for in this life. The other things don't matter.

This third Epistle was written about a church that had allowed an antimissionary spirit to pervade it, a movement headed up mainly by a renegade named Diotrephes. We don't know a lot about him, but John gives us a few clues: This man loved to have preeminence in the church, he was a malicious gossip (but then all gossips are malicious), and he actively hindered the mission work in the church.

The only churches that are worth their salt in the kingdom are those that are mission-minded. You see, when God's people start looking outside themselves to the world around them, they begin to view things as God views them.

1. To whom was this letter written? (1)
2. What is John's greatest joy? (4)
3. How have you grown spiritually since this time last year? How have you grown materially?

JUDE

DECEMBER 11
Jude 1–25

Contend for the Faith; a List of Apostates (1–11)

Jude and James grew up in the same house as Jesus. Jude was our Lord's half brother. You will remember that neither he nor James accepted Christ as Messiah while Jesus lived. But following the Resurrection, they both believed and became ardent defenders of the faith. Jude's great premise in this short book is that believers must contend for the faith.

As the church entered its second and third generation, false teachers abounded. Their goal was either money, power, or both. And they were enormously successful. These false teachers had led some to believe that the grace of God was so encompassing that the believer could engage in sin and still be the recipient of Christ's salvation.

Jude called for the believers to put a halt to this kind of evil heresy—to contend for the faith, to return to the teachings of Jesus.

1. What kind of men had become active in Christianity? (4)
2. What happened to former angels who did not keep their appointed place in the heavenly hierarchy? (6)
3. What are Jude's seven examples? (7–11)
4. How well versed are you in church history? Try relating what is happening today to Jude's premise that, once corruption sets in, disaster follows.

Depraved and Doomed; Maintaining Spiritual Life (12–25)

Then in verses 12 and 13, Jude described these heretics—again using seven examples. In verses 14 and 15, Jude issued a stern warning about God's vengeance.

What is the defense of the believer against these apostates and corrupt merchants of spiritual poison? Look at verses 20–21. How do you get faith? Faith comes by hearing the Word of God.

1. How did Jude describe the heretics? (12–15)
2. Who are apostates? (16)
3. What are the readers to do? (20–23)
4. In what ways are you making time for God in your life?

351

REVELATION

DECEMBER 12
Revelation 1:1–20

Greeting the Seven Churches; Vision of the Son of Man (1:1–20)

We come now to one of the most exciting adventures of all time—the Book of Revelation, written by the apostle John concerning the visions he received on Patmos. John was banished to die on Patmos by the Roman Emperor Domitian. John would doubtless have perished there, probably of starvation, had not the emperor died first. His successor freed the old apostle.

Note John's opening, for it doesn't come from him alone. That greeting is to us today. The seven local church congregations addressed in this book serve as "types" of the church today.

Verses 9–20 relate John's vision of Christ. John was on the Isle of Patmos, a Roman concentration camp. All around him were dying men. Yet, in spite of all the despair of that place, John could write verse 10. A true believer reacts differently from a nonbeliever to outside stimuli. While other men were cursing their fate and blaspheming God, John was in the Spirit on the Lord's Day.

Just think how many years had passed since John had last seen Jesus—perhaps as many as fifty years. John knew the Lord well. No one had ever been closer to Jesus than John. But Jesus was different. Look at the description beginning in verse 14.

When Christ ascended to the Father and took His rightful place at the right hand of the throne, He was changed. John hardly recognized his Lord. The Jesus with whom we deal today is not the lowly Nazarene of Galilee—He is King of Kings.

1. From whom does John's greeting come? (1:4–5)
2. How does the Lord describe Himself? (1:8, 11)
3. Where were the seven churches? (1:11)
4. What did Jesus look like? (1:13–16)
5. How did John react? (1:17)
6. What were the seven stars and the seven lampstands? (1:20)
7. John's great vision came to him at a dark moment in his life. How can we apply that knowledge to our efforts to deal with some of the rough times in our own lives?

352

DECEMBER 13

Revelation 2:1–7

The Church at Ephesus (2:1–7)

This was the very church John was pastoring at the time of his banishment to Patmos. Perhaps in the time he had been gone, the people had grown lukewarm in their pursuit of God. First John mentions the good things about the church, but then in verse 4 is Christ's condemnation. The Lord didn't say they had *lost* their love; He said they had *left* their first love. It was an act of their will to do so. Church became a business. It had the corporate image. And those things they were doing were not out of love for God, but for other reasons.

How would I feel if I came home today and my wife Darlene said to me, "Dan, I will continue to live with you and take care of the children, clean the house, prepare the meals. But I don't love you. Now don't worry—I am not going to leave you." That would be the most heartbreaking thing in the world to me. I would rather have her love than anything else. I wonder how the Lord feels when our service to Him becomes perfunctory, just business as usual. Christ called upon the Ephesian church to repent of this lack of love. He said that if they did not repent, He would remove them from their place.

1. What characteristics of the Ephesian church did the Lord commend? (2:2–3)
2. What did the Lord have against the church? (2:4)
3. What does the Lord command the church to do? (2:5)
4. Who will receive eternal rewards and what are the rewards? (2:7)
5. Our service to the Lord can easily become mechanical and lacking in love. What steps can you take to guard against this danger?

The Churches at Smyrna, Pergamos, and Thyatira (2:8–29)

Unbelievers in Smyrna were not interested in Christ or the church, and the saints there were vigorously persecuted. Yet you will notice that Christ did not have one word of reproach for them. You see, persecution cannot stamp out the church.

It is also interesting to me what the Lord said about these Christians in verse 9. In the middle of a wealthy society, these people were poor. They couldn't get jobs because they were Christians. Their faith cost them all material gain. Yet they didn't lose their faith. Today we tend to equate Christianity with lovely sanctuaries and stained-glass windows and marvelous pipe organs. All those things are fine, in the proper perspective. But there is a certain attraction to the facade of our faith. What if that facade were removed? What if our worship areas were reduced to old barns in the country or to somebody's basement or to unlighted river banks at night? How strong would our faith be then? What if the gospel were outlawed in this nation? What if serving Jesus were punishable by death?

The church at Pergamos is known as the compromising church. What persecution could not do, permissiveness accomplished. Persecution slowed, and a new age entered in. Little by little, paganism began to encroach, in little spurts here and there, with just enough truth thrown in to make it palatable. The city worshiped Zeus Soter. The "white stone" (v.17) may refer to an amulet with the secret name of Jesus written on it.

The church at Thyatira was the corrupted church—as far removed from the original gospel as it was possible to get. Citizens of Thyatira worshiped the sun god, Apollo Tyumnaios, and the current Roman emperor. Probably this had bled over into the Christian community.

Two things had happened in this church: 1) A false teacher had apparently come in and begun teaching heresies and false doctrine, which the church accepted, and 2) the church had never repented even though the Lord had given it opportunity to do so.

1. What will happen to the Christians at Smyrna? (2:10)
2. To what other doctrines did the church at Pergamos hold? (2:14–15)
3. To whom had the church at Thyatira listened? (2:20)
4. How much could you lose and not lose your faith?

DECEMBER 15
Revelation 3:1–22

The Churches at Sardis, Philadelphia, and Laodicea (3:1–22)

Sardis was the dead church! Non-Christian citizens of Sardis were strongly involved in emperor worship, possibly because the city had been heavily damaged by an earthquake in A.D. 17, and Emperor Tiberius had been quick to rebuild it.

"White garments" (v. 5) symbolize righteousness and immortality. Other sources tell us that white garments actually cover the immortal bodies of the saved.

The church at Sardis was dead. Many of us are, too—dead in our relationship with Christ. It's a form only, a name only, nothing more.

We are dead in our relationship to the Word of God. We are dead to the needs of the world.

Oh, to have belonged to the church at Philadelphia! You will not find one word of condemnation from Jesus' lips regarding this church. Every word was positive. The church at Philadelphia was known as the faithful church. Look at some of the accolades from our Lord regarding these people.

Like Sardis, this lesser city was also heavily damaged by the earthquake in A.D. 17 and was restored by Tiberius. From then until Nero's reign, it was called Neo-Caesarea.

The reference to the "key of David" (v. 7) is a quote from Isaiah 22:22. The key symbolizes authority in office.

The reference to Christ's "new name" (v. 12) is uncertain, it may refer to Christ's name at His second coming.

It seems that once a church becomes "on fire" for God, so many things enter in to cool it off. So while it does not become cold like the church at Sardis (cold in death), it becomes lukewarm, mediocre, like the one in Laodicea. Read what Jesus said to the Laodicean church in verses 15 and 16. This church receives the harshest condemnation of all from our Lord.

The Laodiceans, like some of the others, were involved in emperor worship. Evidently Christians at Laodicea were trying to compromise their worship of Christ with this emperor worship.

1. What will happen if the people at Sardis do not repent? (3:3)
2. What does Christ promise the church at Philadelphia? (3:10)
3. How will Christ demonstrate His wrath at the church at Laodicea? (3:16)
4. One of these churches was faithful, one was "dead," one was "lukewarm." Compare your congregation to what Christ says about each one of these churches.

355

DECEMBER 16
Revelation 4:1–5:14

The Throne Room of Heaven (4:1–11)

Beginning with chapter 4, we focus on the end-time events. Immediately John was in the throne room of God Himself—the place where each Christian will be right after the Rapture. Sinners who were never saved by grace will also find their way to this same room.

The first thing John saw was God sitting upon the immense throne. John describes God in terms of light and later will tell us that God *is* the light.

The rainbow mentioned in verse 3 is God's sign of mercy, referring to Noah and the covenant made with him following the Flood. Later on, when the sinners are brought to the same place, the rainbow is conspicuously missing.

The creatures in verses 6–8 are a combination of the cherubim in Ezekiel and the seraphim in Isaiah.

Verse 11 is a song of assurance that God continues to exercise control over the universe and will soon show His power.

1. To what stones was God compared? (4:3)
2. Who surrounded the throne? (4:4)
3. What lay before the throne? (4:6)
4. What were the living creatures like? (4:7)
5. Combine the concept of God's majesty with the concept of a loving God. How are you able to combine the two images?

The Lamb Takes the Scroll (5:1–14)

The scroll in verse 1 tells of the future of earth's inhabitants. Compare Ezekiel 2:9–10 with this verse. Note verse 5. The lion (symbolic of the Messiah) can defeat the eagle, the symbol of the Roman Empire.

Note verse 6. Jesus changes from a lion to a lamb—a favorite designation of John for the Messiah. The lamb here is a victorious lamb; its seven horns tell of the lamb's complete power.

1. What question did the angel ask and what was the response? (5:2–3)
2. How did John respond? (5:4)
3. Who opened the scroll? (5:5)
4. How did Christ look? (5:6)
5. Are you prepared if the Rapture should take place today?

DECEMBER 17
Revelation 6:1–7:17

Six of the Seals Broken (6:1–17)

In chapter 5 Jesus takes the great scroll from the hand of God. The scroll is closed by seven seals. One by one, Jesus breaks them open.

The first seal (see vv. 1–2) symbolizes an invading conqueror. For those of John's day, the conqueror was perhaps the Parthians, who were a threat to Rome's eastern border and were expert horsemen and users of the bow and arrow. The conqueror is the Antichrist, Satan's masterpiece of deception who will rule the world during the Tribulation.

The second seal (see vv. 3–4) also symbolizes war with its special horrors. The third seal (see vv. 5–6) symbolizes scarcity on earth, an imbalance in supply and demand.

The fourth seal (see vv. 7–8) was death.

The martyrs of the fifth seal (see vv. 9–11) are the Tribulation saints—those who have turned to God during the Tribulation.

The sixth seal (see vv. 12–17) predicts cosmic disturbances (cf. Joel 2:10).

1. What were the colors of the four horses? (6:2, 4, 5, 8)
2. For what did the martyrs cry? (6:10)
3. What did the martyrs receive? (6:11)
4. What were the cosmic disturbances? (6:12–14)
5. Where will you and your loved ones be during this terrible time?

The Seal of Israel; a Multitude From the Great Tribulation (7:1–17)

The woes cease until those who have been martyred during the Tribulation are sealed. John uses symbolism from Babylonian cosmology to describe how this is done. Compare Ezekiel 37:9 for an Old Testament use of the four winds.

The seal may have been a sacred name inscribed on the white stone given to the martyrs (2:17).

The number one hundred forty four thousand signifies Christians of every nation who are the true Israel (cf. James 1:1; 1 Peter 1:1). Note that the tribe of Dan is omitted, for it committed idolatry.

1. What kept the four winds from blowing? (7:1)
2. How many people stood before the Lord to sing praises? (7:9)
3. What will be the future of those standing before the Lord? (7:16–17)
4. Revelation 7:9 speaks of people of all nations. What does this say about our racial prejudices and cultural biases?

DECEMBER 18
Revelation 8:1–9:21

The Seventh Seal and the Six Trumpets (8:1–9:21)

Now we come to the seventh seal. Earlier in this book John had heard all the redeemed church and the angels (numbering over a billion) singing praises to God. Now suddenly, there is total silence. The first six seals were terrible judgments, although largely through the hands of people against people. But in this half hour of silence, God is preparing to send down the trumpet judgments, which are His divine punishments on earth. The trumpets were recognized symbols of heralds of the Day of the Lord.

With the fifth trumpet, imprisoned demons from the very blackest haunts of hell were released. There are two basic types of demons: One group has been on earth since the Garden of Eden, and the other group has remained imprisoned in the bottomless pit (as Peter says) reserved in chains of darkness. These demons are, I believe, the fallen angels who sinned with Lucifer in commanding a rebellion against God. Now with the fifth trumpet the imprisoned demons are set free to torment those who have the mark of the beast.

When the sixth trumpet is sounded, four angels (who had been bound, so they must have been evil angels) are released to wreak havoc on mankind. They are from the great river Euphrates—or the East. Some students of prophecy think this is the army of China which, including reserves, currently numbers about two hundred million; but I believe these are demonic creatures. The Euphrates River is not in China.

These creatures kill one third of the earth's remaining population. Remember, the fourth horseman of the apocalypse killed one fourth or one billion of earth's people. Now these demonic creatures kill another billion people. Those who still will not repent will be killed.

1. What happened when the first trumpet sounded? (8:7)
2. The second trumpet? (8:8–9)
3. The third trumpet? (8:10–11)
4. What happened when the fourth trumpet sounded? (8:12–13)
5. What was given the fifth angel? (9:1)
6. What did the demons look like? (9:7–10)
7. Who led the demons? (9:11)
8. Describe the army of horsemen. (9:17)
9. What three plagues killed how many? (9:18)
10. What is so attractive about sin that people do not repent?

DECEMBER 19
Revelation 10:1–11:19

The Mighty Angel with the Scroll; John Consumes the Scroll (10:1–11)

This passage speaks about a time approximately midway through the Tribulation period.

Some have indicated that this mighty angel is Jesus, but others believe it could well have been the archangel Michael. Verses 2–3 establish the angel's power over all the world.

Verses 8–11 resemble parts of Ezekiel 2:8—3:3.

The little book obviously was the prophecy of God regarding more events to come. It would be sweet to the taste because the news would be welcome, but it would be bitter to digest when the full horrors of interim happenings were comprehended.

1. Describe the angel. (10:1)
2. Where did the angel plant his feet? (10:2)
3. What happened when he cried out? (10:3–4)
4. When will the end come? (10:5–7)
5. What command was given John? (10:11)
6. What are you doing about *digesting* God's Word?

The Two Heavenly Witnesses; the Seventh Trumpet (11:1–19)

Israel's outlook will be radically changed during the seven-year Tribulation period. Also, the temple will be rebuilt. To begin building something on this property now would set off a *jihad*—a holy war. But midway through the Tribulation, still rejecting Messiah, Israel will begin to rebuild.

Two people will then emerge on the scene with fantastic power. Who are these two men? We don't know. Some writers say Elijah and John the Baptist. Others say Enoch and Moses.

Are we going to know what's going on while we are with God during this time? Absolutely! Look at verses 16–19. John saw the believers who had earlier been raptured (thus missing all the tribulation) fall on their faces and worship God.

1. What task was given John? (11:1–2)
2. How long would the witnesses prophesy? (11:3)
3. What power will the witnesses have during their mission? (11:6)
4. What will initially happen to the witnesses when they have completed their mission? (11:7–10)
5. What is the final end of the witnesses? (11:11–12)
6. Think of some of your second-best efforts, wasted hours.

DECEMBER 20
Revelation 12:1–12

Visions of the Dragon's Kingdom (12:1–12)

Chapters 12 through 15 are what we call parenthetical chapters of Revelation—a break in the action during the seven trumpet judgments. And in them, God gives us a keen insight into the future state of Israel during the Tribulation. It should not be surprising to any student of prophecy that the world lines itself up so vehemently against this tiny state of Israel, or that the United States finds itself further and further removed from the Jewish government. Satan knows that if he could destroy Israel, he could destroy the whole prophetic implications of Revelation. His attack on that little nation will grow more and more vitriolic, leading right up to Armageddon.

Let's briefly remind ourselves of what has happened: When Christ opened the seals of the scroll, Antichrist was released, along with the other horsemen of the apocalypse—war, famine, and death. We have studied the fact that one hundred forty-four thousand sealed witnesses (all Jews) will preach the gospel of Christ all over the world, and a revival will follow. We have studied the two special witnesses who have power like Elijah and Moses, who absolutely frustrate Antichrist until he is finally able to kill them. He leaves their bodies in the streets where, after three days, they come back to life and ascend to heaven.

The woman symbolizes the church during the 1,260-day persecution by Satan. The numbers seven and ten are used throughout eschatological (end-time) writings. Remember the ten-horned beast of Daniel 7:7. Seven was a sacred number.

The second and third visions (verses 7–12) record a fantastic drama. Sometime during all this chaos on earth, Satan is going to make war on heaven itself. The Trinity does not even directly become involved. God sends out Michael, the great archangel, and his forces against Satan and his forces. Verse 9 gives us the outcome.

1. Describe the woman in the first vision. (12:1)
2. What appeared with the woman? Describe him. (12:3–4)
3. To whom did the woman give birth? (12:5)
4. What happened to the dragon? (12:13)
5. Satan is an awesome opponent. What is the best way to fight him?

The Woman Persecuted; the Beast (12:13–13:10)

In the fourth vision (vv. 13–17) the woman again is symbolic, this time of those who escape for a while. Now, completely infuriated, Satan launches war on Israel. Israel has long since been disarmed, as we are told in Ezekiel 38 and 39. In fact, earlier in this drama, when Russia and her allies attacked Israel, the Jewish state was already neutralized. Antichrist had cunningly caused Israel to disarm for both political and economic reasons. And Israel would have been destroyed by Russia and her friends, had not God sovereignly intervened and destroyed the invaders. So when Satan causes the final anti-Semitic attack on the nation, Israel has no way to defend herself. And John told us the Israelis fled into the wilderness. Jesus promised that this would happen (See Matthew 24:16–20.)

It is my belief that the place in the wilderness where they will flee is Petra in southwest Jordan, beneath the Dead Sea. This ancient land will be one of the few places on earth not controlled by Antichrist. For three and one half years, this fleeing remnant of Jews will live there, nourished by divine providence (the reference to the two wings of the great eagle in verse 14).

The fifth and sixth visions (13:1–10) vividly describe this Satan-energized man known as Antichrist. We have other names given him in the Bible as well: King of Babylon, Little Horn, the Prince that Shall Come, the Man of Sin, and a Beast.

The sea in verse 1 refers to the topsy-turvy world of the Gentiles in these last days. Antichrist will come out of the Gentile world, and what a horrible picture he makes.

In verse 3 we learn more of Satan's masterpiece of deception, and the world again will marvel and follow the beast.

Verses 5 and 6 teach plainly that Antichrist will be the epitome of blasphemy. Many believe that this Antichrist is already living and is being groomed for his takeover the moment Jesus opens the first seal in heaven. But the Book of Revelation presents a somewhat allegorical description of the Antichrist, one that is more symbolic of the havoc he will wreak rather than his actual appearance. Therefore, he will be difficult to recognize unless we understand our faith thoroughly.

1. How did the woman escape the dragon? (12:14)
2. Describe the beast from the sea. (13:1–3)
3. How much do you know about God and His eternal plan? Will that knowledge hold you steady in the face of temptation from the Antichrist?

The Beast from the Land (13:11–18)

This is the last vision in this set of seven visions. There will be other sets of seven visions.

Now another character energized by hell comes into world prominence. We already have Antichrist, Satan's false Messiah. Now we have the False Prophet coming out of the earth. As the sea represents the Gentile nations, so the land represents the Jewish people. This false prophet apparently will be an apostate Jew, who, during the first half of the Tribulation, will have such authority in Israel that he will get the Israeli government to form an alliance with Antichrist.

Notice how Satan propagates falsehood: John said the False Prophet will be presented as a lamb—just as Jesus was. Remember how John the Baptist introduced him, "Behold! The Lamb of God who takes away the sin of the world!" (John 1:29). This false prophet only says those things Satan tells him to say. He will have supernatural powers; therefore, many will be misled by miracles. Try or test the spirits to see if they are of God, if they lift up Jesus Christ. During the Tribulation, the False Prophet will produce miracles in unprecedented manifestations.

In verse 15 there is an interesting development as the False Prophet has a great image or statue made of the beast and he gives power to the image that it should speak. Remember that in 7:3 the faithful had been sealed with a mark on their foreheads. The mark in verses 16–17 is probably a counterpart—only this is the mark of the beast.

We need to understand that the Greeks and Romans did not have a numbering system as such. Rather, certain letters indicated certain numbers. Therefore, by adding the numerical equivalent of the letters in a person's name, scholars have tried to discover the identity of 666, or at least the symbolic identity. The closest they have come is Neron Caesar, of course, come back to life. The numerical equivalents of that name (*Neron* is the Greek form) are 666. The Latin form is *Nero* and is the equivalent of 616, a number found in one of the very early translations of the Book of Revelation. However, to waste too much time trying to determine just who this person is, is useless.

1. Describe the beast from the land. (13:11)
2. What was the significance of the mark? (13:17)
3. What is the number of the beast? (13:18)
4. What are some ways we can measure whether miracles uplift Christ?

DECEMBER 23

Revelation 14:1–20

The Second Set of Seven Visions (14:1–20)

Chapter 14 is a sudden change from the last chapter! In chapter 13 we were on earth, where all the hellish filth Satan can muster is thrown at the nations. In chapter 14 we are at the great throne in heaven where Christ is not blasphemed as He is on earth, but rather adored and worshiped. We are at the heavenly Mount Zion. The writer to the Hebrews clearly pinpointed this place: "But you have come to Mount Zion and to the city of the living God, the heavenly Jerusalem, to an innumerable company of angels, to the general assembly and church of the firstborn who are registered in heaven" (Heb. 12:22–23).

Verses 1–5 make it clear that not all Christians are going to receive the same treatment in heaven. I do not personally believe that all Christians will be at the marriage supper of the Lamb. And I would cite the parable of the five wise and five foolish virgins here. Yes, eternal life will belong to all believers, but not the same eternal rewards.

The remainder of chapter 14 deals with the proclamations of three angels. God gives earth's remaining battered citizens one last altar call!

In verse 8 is another reference to Babylon, that great city of the East. Outside of Berlin, probably no other city has caused more suffering on this earth than Babylon. During Antichrist's days of rule, Babylon will again be a place of commerce and false religion. Dr. Dwight Pentecost has written a marvelous book called *Prophecy for Today,* in which an entire chapter has been dedicated to Babylon and the harlot church. Babylon represents false religion and idolatry and a materialistic society, two factors which will play havoc in our world and, truly, already are.

This segment closes with God's accolade to the Tribulation saints, those who accept Christ during the seven years and die for their new-found faith. Our works follow us; our possessions don't. The principle in verse 13 is vital. As Judge, God will declare what manner of works we did. For many it will be a happy day; for others there will be tears as they suffer loss, even though they are saved.

1. What did John hear from heaven? (14:2)
2. What did the first angel proclaim? (14:7)
3. The second angel? (14:8)
4. The third angel? (14:9–10)
5. What did John see on a white cloud? (14:14)
6. What kind of works are we accomplishing? What motivates us?

Prelude to the Bowl Judgments (15:1–8)

Chapter 15 is the shortest one in the Book of Revelation, but it is most important because it opens up the final three and one-half years of God's wrath, known as the Great Tribulation. This chapter should be preached far more often than it is, for it clearly reveals an important part of God's nature—His wrath.

In verse 2 we are again shown that great sea of glass that John mentioned in chapter 4. We don't know exactly what that is—some magnificent ethereal base upon which the throne rests, perhaps. Now it is mingled with fire, symbolizing the fiery trials of the Tribulation saints on earth. At this time on the planet, Antichrist and the False Prophet are working furiously to destroy every vestige of God that remains. Oppression and tyranny are rampant. And most of the people who accept Christ and refuse to accept the Antichrist will be executed for their faith. Yet verse 2 says that these saints have victory over the beast. What kind of victory is martyrdom? Church history does not record any martyrs who did not anticipate immediate glory.

They sing the victory song of Moses, which is recorded in Exodus 15. Remember that the Israelites had just been supernaturally delivered from the hands of the Egyptians, for they had crossed through the Red Sea on dry land. Their enemies had perished in the water.

Now, in Revelation 15, the Tribulation saints have been delivered from the holocaust on earth, although they have given their lives. (Remember, the day of grace as we know it ends with the Rapture.) The saints are in the presence of God. And they break out in a glorious song of victory.

At this point, seven angels emerge from heaven's temple, clothed in beautiful linen, drawn at the waist with golden belts. From over the throne, one of the huge living creatures (or seraphim) gives the angels seven golden bowls full of the revealed wrath of God. The plagues from each of those bowls will be emptied upon the earth, completing the judgment. Remember; first there were the seal judgments, then the trumpet judgments, now the bowls.

1. Who was on the sea of glass? (15:2)
2. What was opened to John? (15:5)
3. Why could no one enter the temple? (15:8)
4. Little is said nowadays about God's wrath. What other attributes of God are overlooked in current teaching?

DECEMBER 25

Revelation 16:1–21

The Seven Bowls (16:1–21)

Here is a summary of the seven bowls:

1. *The first bowl:* Every person who has taken the mark of the beast will be afflicted with a "foul and loathsome" sore.

2. *The second bowl:* The seas will turn to blood. Earlier we saw a third of the sea thus affected. Now the entirety of the seas is so corrupted that all sea life will perish.

3. *The third bowl:* The rest of the water supply also becomes corrupted by blood.

4. *The fourth bowl:* There is scorching heat from the sun. How much we take the sun for granted! But if the sun were closer to the earth—not much, just a bit closer—the results would be horrendous. And that's apparently what happens with this fourth bowl judgment.

5. *The fifth bowl:* Terrible darkness descends. Jesus himself prophesied this: "But in those days, after that tribulation, the sun will be darkened, and the moon will not give its light" (Mark 13:24).

6. *The sixth bowl:* The Euphrates River will dry up and military forces will come to fight to the death at Armageddon. The kings of the East will march against the king of the West, who is Antichrist.

7. *The seventh bowl:* The earth will be shaken severely. Massive earthquakes will mark the beginning of the collapse of the world system that God has promised He will destroy.

A talent (see v. 21) weighs approximately one hundred pounds.

1. Why is the third plague justified? (16:6)
2. What was people's reaction to the scorching sun? (16:9)
3. What came out of the mouths of the dragon, the beast, and the False Prophet? (16:13)
4. What did the voice from the throne cry? (16:17)
5. What fell on men and how heavy was it? (16:21)
6. With these events in mind, what value do you see in striving for earthly success?

DECEMBER 26
Revelation 17:1–18:8

The Scarlet Woman and the Scarlet Beast (17:1–18)

We are now in a series of seven visions concerning Babylon.

One of the greatest horrors of the Tribulation will be the false religious system (or harlot church), which will be controlled by Satan. John calls this church, "Babylon the Harlot." She is called that because she prostitutes the true gospel for pleasure and profit. Verse 2 informs us that the kings of the earth have committed fornication with her, which means that the religious system has gone to bed with the political system. Verse 6 makes it clear what this church thinks of true Christianity.

In these verses, John has explained the principles of this heinous religious system. I don't accept the belief that the reference in verse 9 is to the seven hills of Rome, but rather to seven kings. Before John went to Ephesus, Rome had been ruled by a succession of five incredibly powerful emperors. During his ministry in Ephesus, the sixth ruler was Domitian, the one who sent him to Patmos in exile. The seventh mighty ruler will be Antichrist.

In verses 16 and 17 we learn that finally Antichrist has so consolidated his worldwide power that he no longer needs the religious system to back him. So, he throws out this power and makes it subject to annihilation—and the kings destroy the very religious system they established.

1. What did the angel say to John? (17:1–2)
2. What did the beast and woman look like? (17:3–4)
3. What was written on the woman's head? (17:5)
4. What were the seven heads? (17:9–11)
5. What should be the relationship between religion and politics?

The Fall of Babylon the Great (18:1–8)

In this passage—the third vision—God destroys the economic system. You see, Babylon really represents two horrible evils—the false religious system and the economic system dominated by Antichrist. God will sovereignly destroy the latter system as we see in chapter 18.

1. How has Babylon affected the other nations? (18:3)
2. What plea comes from heaven? (18:4–5)
3. What is the proportion of Babylon's luxury and her sorrow? (18:7)
4. What will the proportion of our luxury to our sorrow be?

Finality of Babylon's Fall (18:9–24)

This is the fourth vision. In it God invokes the *lex taliones*, or law of revenge. Compare Jeremiah 50:29. But note in verse 6 how Babylon is to be repaid.

Verses 9–10 tell us kings and merchants will mourn the fall of the harlot. Note in verses 12–13 the description of the material wealth of the great city. Compare the mourners in verses 17–18 with the mourners of Tyre (Ezek. 27:32).

Verses 21–24 represent the fifth vision. The scene reflects the one in Jeremiah 50–51 which John used in the previous vision. Note that here again we encounter another mighty angel. Neither Christ nor God takes a direct part in these actions.

1. Who wept for Babylon? (18:9, 11, 15)
2. What merchandise could no one sell? (18:11–13)
3. In what had the great city been clothed? (18:16)
4. How long did it take the city to fall? (18:17)
5. What did the angel throw into the sea? (18:21)
6. What were the signs of the dead city? (18:22–23)
7. Does our nation put value in material wealth, as did Rome?

Heaven Exults over Babylon (19:1–10)

Now the Spirit takes John from the awful destruction on earth to the very hallowed halls of heaven. All the raptured saints have had ringside seats for this whole panorama below. And every time an angel strikes a blow against Satan, the whole heavenly stadium rocks with cheers. This is the sixth vision.

Verses 7 through 10 are the seventh vision, the call to the wedding feast or marriage supper of the Lamb. Verse 9 is chilling. That angel didn't say, "John, tell all the Christians here now that it's time for the marriage supper." No, sir. He said, "Blessed are those who are called to the marriage supper of the Lamb!" This is further evidence that not all the believers will attend the feast. Yes, all believers will be saved and receive eternal life, missing the Tribulation below. But that doesn't mean all believers are going to take part in the rewards and blessings.

1. Who fell before God and worshiped? (19:4)
2. How was the bride of the Lamb arrayed? (19:8)
3. What did the angel say to John? (19:10)
4. What kind of eternal reward do you think you will have?

Armageddon (19:11–21)

With this passage begins a final series of seven visions, these dealing with the end of Satan's evil reign and the beginning of God's righteous age. These visions are previews or prophecies concerning the final gigantic battle between good and evil—Armageddon. The first vision is Christ on a white horse.

You will remember the sixth bowl in 16:12. The River Euphrates dried up, erasing a centuries-old, eighteen-hundred-mile barrier between the eastern and western worlds. Antichrist rules the western nations with a rod of iron. He thinks he is in total command of the world situation. Daniel 11:44 sets the stage for Armageddon: "But news from the east and the north shall trouble him; therefore he shall go out with great fury to destroy and annihilate many." The remaining kings of the East march out to subdue Antichrist and defeat the West. And they meet in the Valley of Jezreel—the Valley of Armageddon. Israel today already has more tanks poised in that valley than were used by all sides in World War 2 combined!

Please remember that the Rapture and the Second Coming are not the same thing. The Rapture is the event that lifts the redeemed church, the body of Christ, out of this world prior to the Tribulation. The Second Coming ends the Tribulation. At the Rapture Christ does not return to this earth; rather, we meet the Lord in the air. At the Second Coming, Christ does come back, His feet once again touching Mount Olivet and, as Zechariah tells us plainly, the great mountain will split in half, east to west. When Christ comes at this time, it will be to institute His world reign for a thousand-year period.

The scene described in verse 13 is a retelling of Isaiah 63:1–6. The armies in verse 14 are probably not angels, but the martyred saints, thus fulfilling the promise that they would have power (see 2:26–27).

Verses 17–21 describe the second vision—Christ's victory over the Antichrist. The "lake of fire" in verse 20 is not the temporary Hades, or Sheol. Rather, it is equivalent to the Greek Hades or the Jewish Gehenna, places of eternal damnation.

Contrast the "feast" (v. 21) with the marriage feast of the Lamb.

1. What was the rider of the white horse called? (19:11, 13)
2. How was He clothed? (19:13)
3. What name was on His robe and thigh? (19:16)
4. Jesus Christ is King of Kings. How are you demonstrating this fact in your life?

The Great White Throne Judgment (20:1–15)

In the third vision (20:1–3) Satan is dealt with personally by an angel who descends from heaven with the key to the bottomless pit. Satan will be bound and imprisoned for a thousand years. Following the Millennium, he will be loosed for a short time—a time which we will study in a moment.

These few verses (4–6) describe the Millennium. What blessed verses they are. This is the fourth vision. The saints of God who were raptured and the Tribulation saints who never took the mark of the beast live and reign with Christ for a thousand years.

Verses 7–10 constitute the fifth vision. Verses 8–9 are based upon a popular story that is first seen in Ezekiel 38–39.

During this thousand-year period there will be millions upon millions of people who never have the opportunity to decide for Christ on their own volition or will. So God will give them that chance just before time ends and eternity begins. Finally, in this short section, we get a summary view of the destruction of Satan himself.

Now it is time for the greatest drama of all history—the Great White Throne Judgment, the sixth vision (see vv. 11–15). Believers in Christ will not be judged; they are completely secure in Christ. This is the judgment for every unredeemed sinner of the ages. The books of works are God's record of our lives in their entirety—and the Book of Life (see v. 12) contains particular names entered at salvation. It is sort of a cross-checking system. There will be no appeals, no drawn-out hearings. It will all be over very quickly. The day of amazing grace will be over, and those who are not saved will be lost for all time.

1. What happened to those who had been beheaded for their witness? (20:4)
2. What are the nations of the earth called? (20:8)
3. What happened to those not found in the Book of Life? (20:15)
4. Will you be present at this judgment?

DECEMBER 30
Revelation 21:1–27

All Things Made New (21:1–8)

God is not only going to destroy this planet as we know it, but the stars and planets as we know them. There will be a new creation for God's redeemed people for all eternity.

Now somewhere in the atmosphere there will be a New Jerusalem, the holy city, the capital of eternity's realm. It will be a perfect place. God will dwell with us just as surely as He dwelt with Adam and Eve.

But not everyone will be able to enjoy this paradise. They will have been judged at the Great White Throne and sent into everlasting torment of hell.

1. What was no more? (21:1)
2. What is the relationship between God and His people? (21:3–4)
3. What did God call Himself? (21:6)
4. Which people were condemned to the second death? (21:8)
5. What is your idea of the new heaven and the new earth?

The New Jerusalem (21:9–27)

The rest of chapter 21 is the best description of the heavenly holy city that we have. We don't know much about heaven. I think there is a reason for that. In fact, we know more about hell than we know about heaven.

Twelve thousand furlongs is about fifteen hundred miles. So this holy city will be fifteen hundred miles long, fifteen hundred miles across and fifteen hundred miles high. Note the magnificence of this holy city as compared to Babylon, the harlot (see 17:3–6, 18). The twelve precious stones roughly resemble those that adorned the breastplate of the high priest (see Ex. 28:17–21; 39:10–14). However, rather than being engraved with the names of the twelve tribes of Israel, they were engraved with the names of the twelve apostles.

1. How does John describe the New Jerusalem's light? (21:11)
2. Describe the gates of the city. (21:12–13)
3. Of what was the wall constructed? (21:18–20)
4. Of what were the gates made? (21:21)
5. What was the temple in the New Jerusalem? (21:22)
6. How did the city receive light? (21:23)
7. When were the gates closed? (21:25)
8. What point do you think the description of the New Jerusalem is making?

DECEMBER 31
Revelation 22:1–21

The River of Life (22:1–5)

It is fascinating to note the similarities between Genesis 1 and 2 and Revelation 22. Both are set in paradise, a perfect, sinless, theocratic (or God-ruled), environment.

Note verse 4. In the Old Testament, no one could see God's face (see Ex. 33:20).

1. Describe the river. (22:1)
2. Where was the tree of life? (22:2)
3. What will happen to the night? (22:5)
4. Life is short and filled with sorrow. Explain your feelings about eternal life in a setting free of the curse.

Epilogue (22:6–21)

Once more God gives a warning to those of us who are still struggling through this life. He has opened the door to the future so that we may have a brief glimpse of the glories that await us. Verse 7 is a solemn reminder to us that we must always anticipate the Rapture.

Jesus gives us a marvelous promise in verse 12. There is a lot of injustice in this world. People who have worked hard and faithfully sometimes end up with nothing materially. On the other hand, those who have not adhered to the faith seem to gain everything. But the real rewards and trophies are not passed out now. We are not laboring for a pat on the back from committees and boards. We are working to please the Lord. And He said that, when He returned, *then* the rewards would be meted out.

Notice for a moment the admonition in verse 14. It's not just knowing what God's commandments are; it is doing them!

Verse 17 is beautiful. There is not a person in the world who cannot come to Christ *if he or she wants to.*

The Book of Revelation is a godsend to us to remind us of the urgency of the times and the imminence of the coming of Christ.

1. What did Jesus say about His coming? (22:7, 12)
2. What did John do that disturbed the angel? (22:8–9)
3. What does Jesus call Himself? (22:16)
4. What was the warning? (22:18–19)
5. What was the promise? (22:20)
6. Are you looking for Jesus' return or are you so comfortable in this world system that you would feel inconvenienced by the Lord's coming?